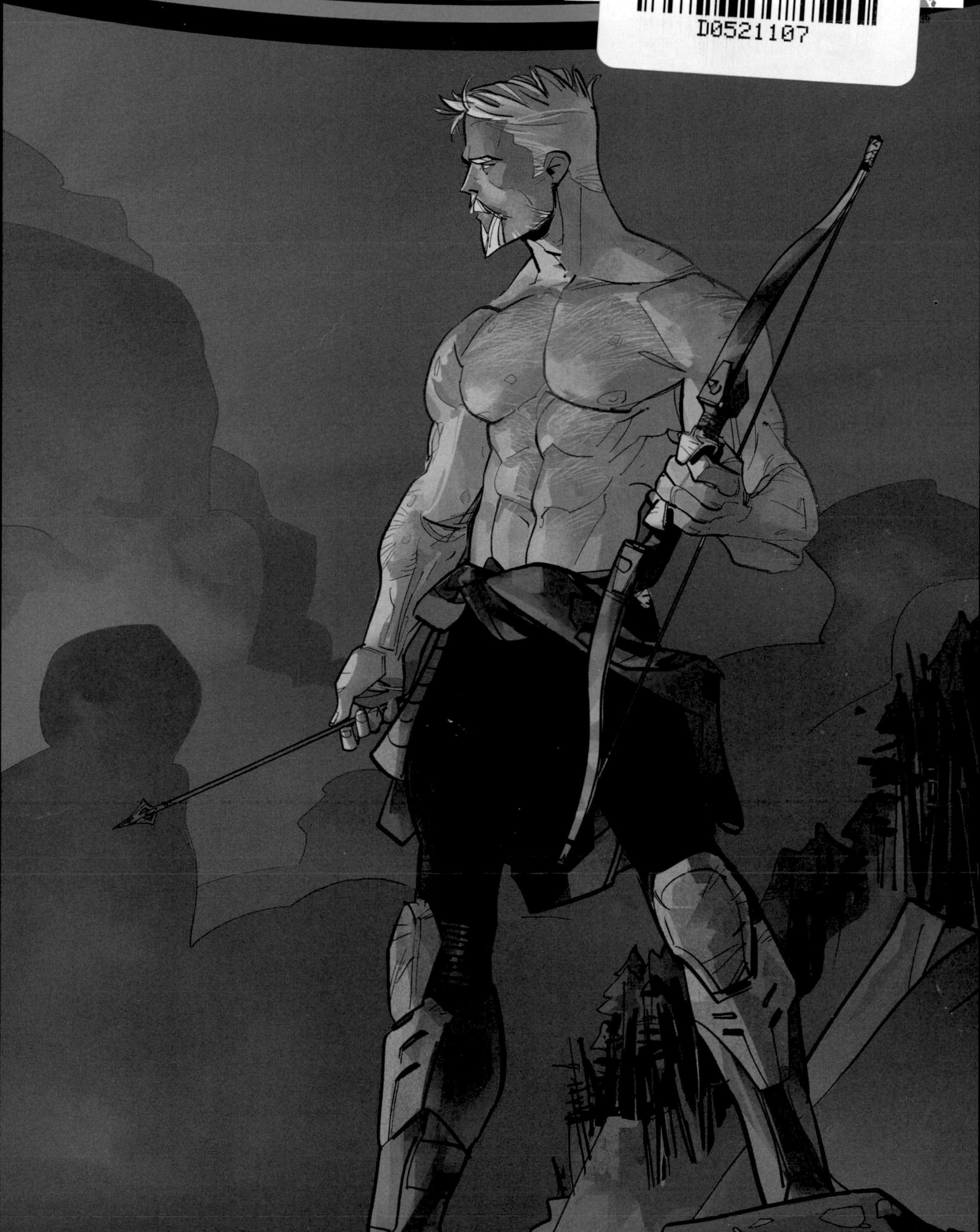

GREEN ARROW

VOL.3 EMERALD OUTLAW

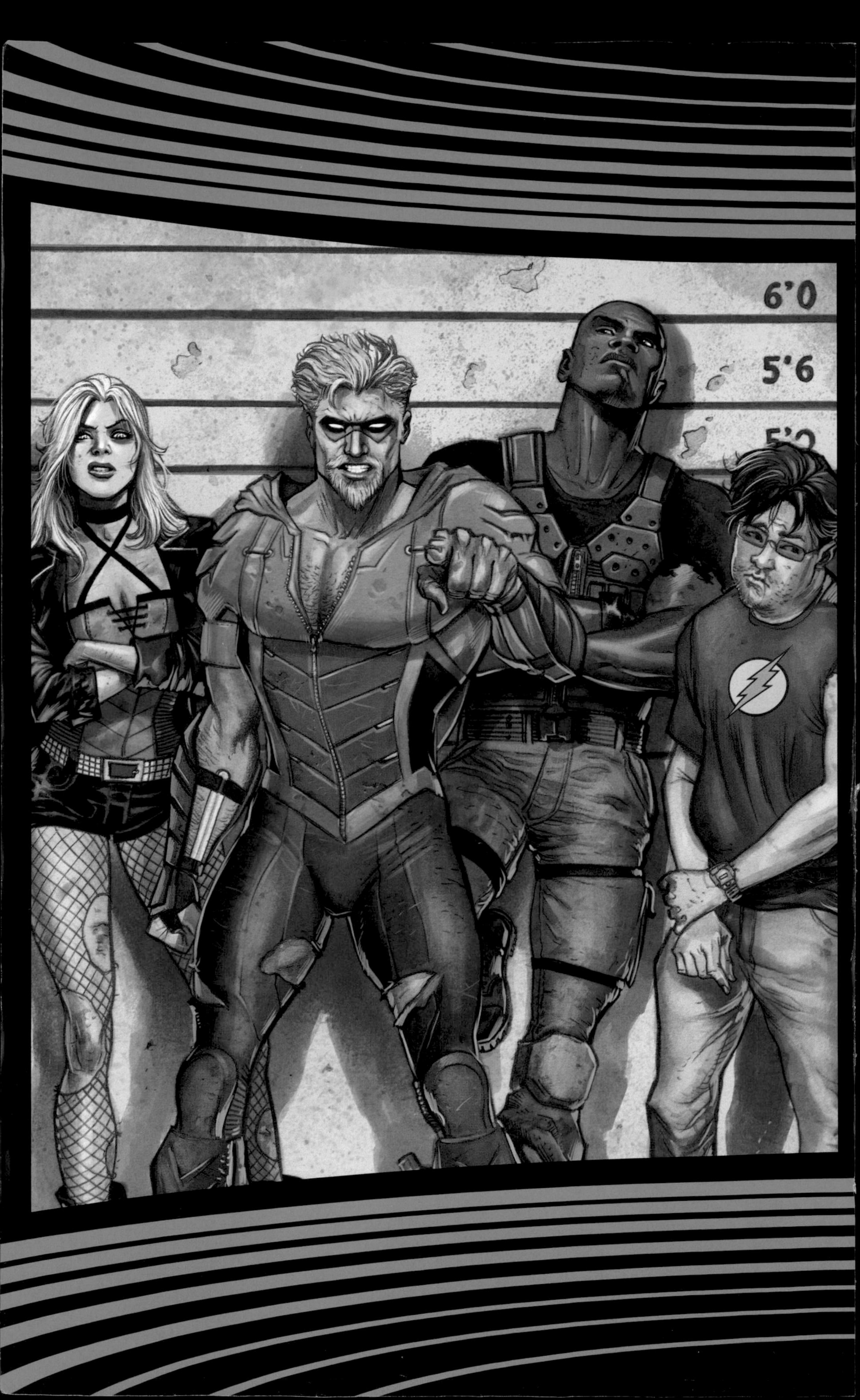
6'0
5'6

GREEN ARROW
VOL.3 EMERALD OUTLAW

BENJAMIN PERCY
writer

OTTO SCHMIDT
JUAN FERREYRA * ELEONORA CARLINI
CARLOS RODRIGUEZ * GUS VAZQUEZ
artists

OTTO SCHMIDT
JUAN FERREYRA * HI-FI
colorists

NATE PIEKOS OF BLAMBOT®
letterer

JUAN FERREYRA
collection cover artist

ANDY KHOURI Editor – Original Series ✳ HARVEY RICHARDS Associate Editor – Original Series
JEB WOODARD Group Editor – Collected Editions ✳ STEVE COOK Design Director – Books ✳ MONIQUE GRUSPE Publication Design

BOB HARRAS Senior VP – Editor-in-Chief, DC Comics

DIANE NELSON President ✳ DAN DiDIO Publisher ✳ JIM LEE Publisher ✳ GEOFF JOHNS President & Chief Creative Officer
AMIT DESAI Executive VP – Business & Marketing Strategy, Direct to Consumer & Global Franchise Management ✳ SAM ADES Senior VP – Direct to Consumer
BOBBIE CHASE VP – Talent Development ✳ MARK CHIARELLO Senior VP – Art, Design & Collected Editions
JOHN CUNNINGHAM Senior VP – Sales & Trade Marketing ✳ ANNE DePIES Senior VP – Business Strategy, Finance & Administration
DON FALLETTI VP – Manufacturing Operations ✳ LAWRENCE GANEM VP – Editorial Administration & Talent Relations
ALISON GILL Senior VP – Manufacturing & Operations ✳ HANK KANALZ Senior VP – Editorial Strategy & Administration
JAY KOGAN VP – Legal Affairs ✳ THOMAS LOFTUS VP – Business Affairs
JACK MAHAN VP – Business Affairs ✳ NICK J. NAPOLITANO VP – Manufacturing Administration
EDDIE SCANNELL VP – Consumer Marketing ✳ COURTNEY SIMMONS Senior VP – Publicity & Communications
JIM (SKI) SOKOLOWSKI VP – Comic Book Specialty Sales & Trade Marketing ✳ NANCY SPEARS VP – Mass, Book, Digital Sales & Trade Marketing

GREEN ARROW VOLUME 3: EMERALD OUTLAW

Published by DC Comics. Compilation and all new material Copyright © 2017 DC Comics. All Rights Reserved.
Originally published in single magazine form in GREEN ARROW 12-17. Copyright © 2016, 2017 DC Comics.
All Rights Reserved. All characters, their distinctive likenesses and related elements featured in this publication are trademarks of DC Comics.
The stories, characters and incidents featured in this publication are entirely fictional.
DC Comics does not read or accept unsolicited submissions of ideas, stories or artwork.

DC Comics, 2900 West Alameda Ave., Burbank, CA 91505.
Printed by LSC Communications, Owensville, MO, USA. 6/30/17. First Printing.
ISBN: 978-1-4012-7133-6

Library of Congress Cataloging-in-Publication Data is available.

PEFC Certified

Printed on paper from
sustainably managed
forests, controlled
sources

PEFC/29-31-337   www.pefc.org

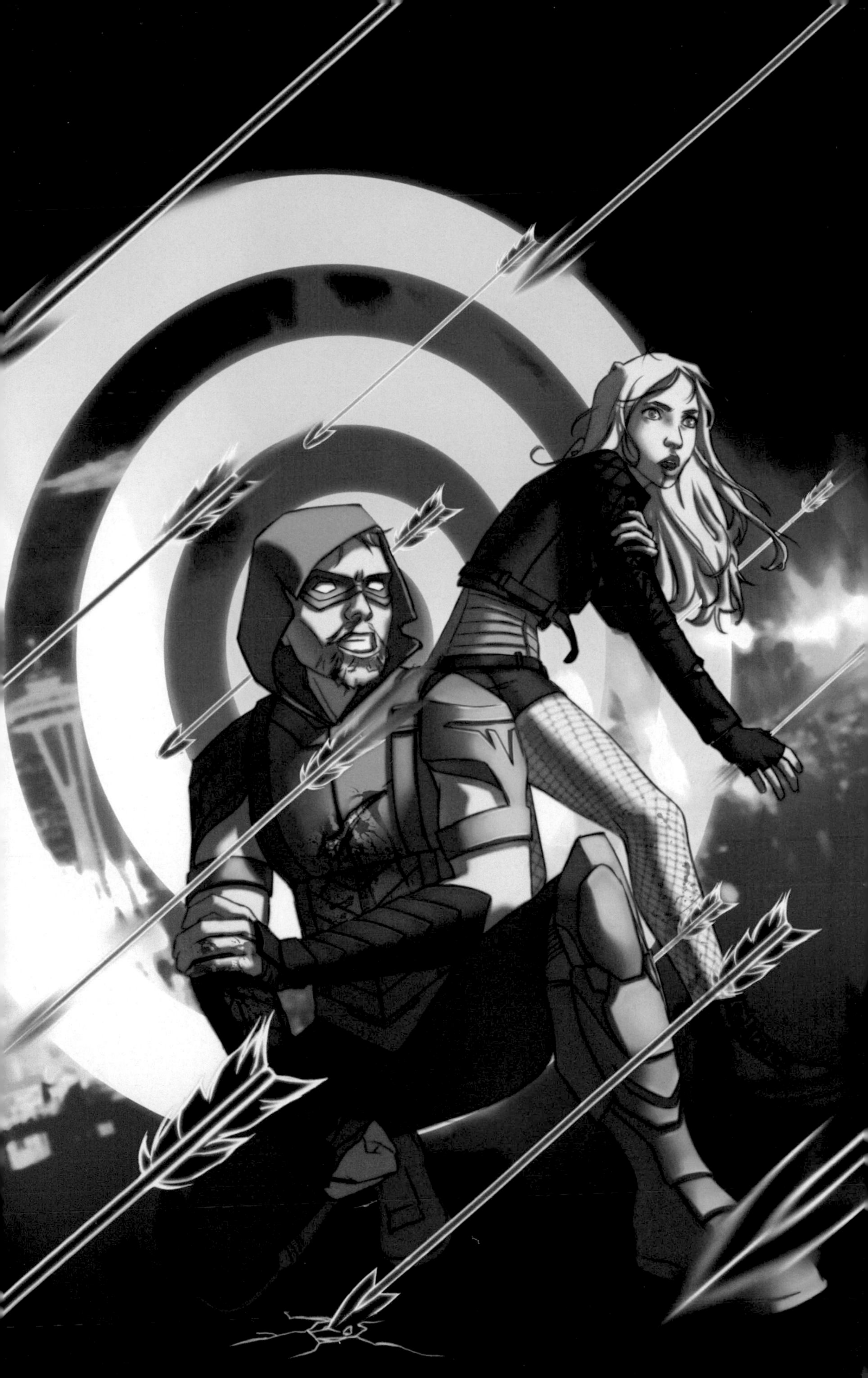

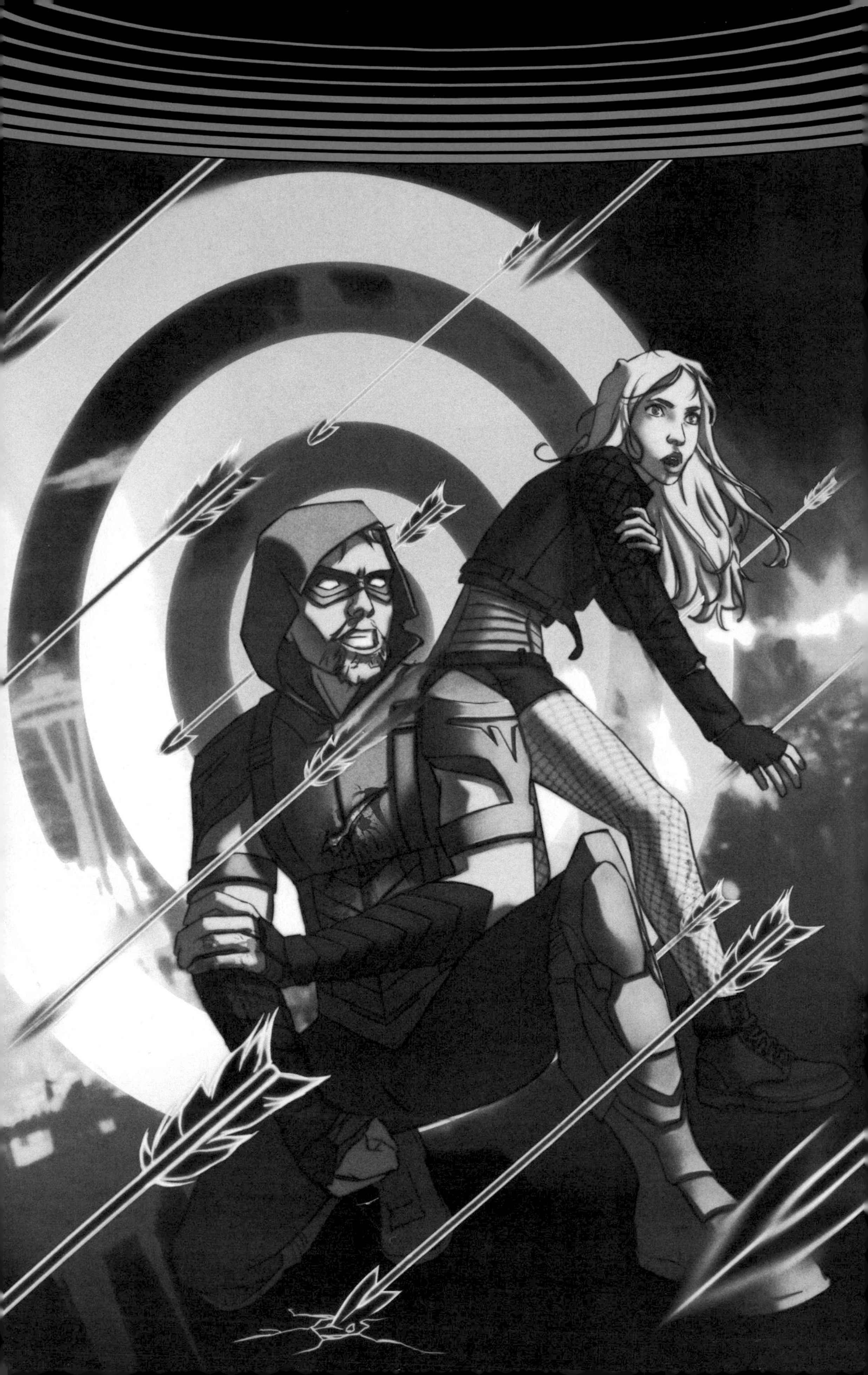

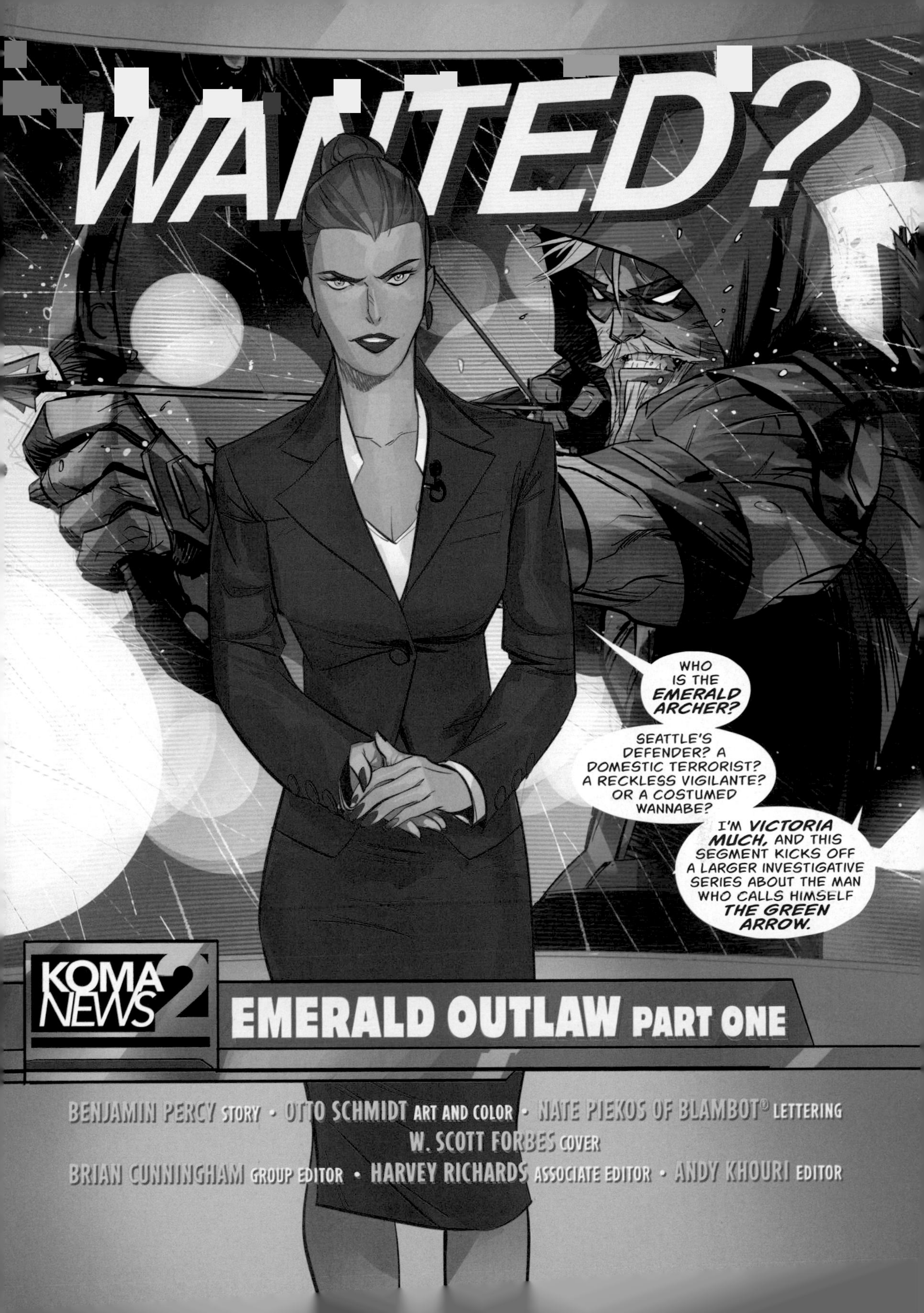
WANTED?
WHO IS THE EMERALD ARCHER?
SEATTLE'S DEFENDER? A DOMESTIC TERRORIST? A RECKLESS VIGILANTE? OR A COSTUMED WANNABE?
I'M VICTORIA MUCH, AND THIS SEGMENT KICKS OFF A LARGER INVESTIGATIVE SERIES ABOUT THE MAN WHO CALLS HIMSELF THE GREEN ARROW.
KOMA NEWS 2
EMERALD OUTLAW PART ONE
BENJAMIN PERCY STORY • OTTO SCHMIDT ART AND COLOR • NATE PIEKOS OF BLAMBOT® LETTERING
W. SCOTT FORBES COVER
BRIAN CUNNINGHAM GROUP EDITOR • HARVEY RICHARDS ASSOCIATE EDITOR • ANDY KHOURI EDITOR

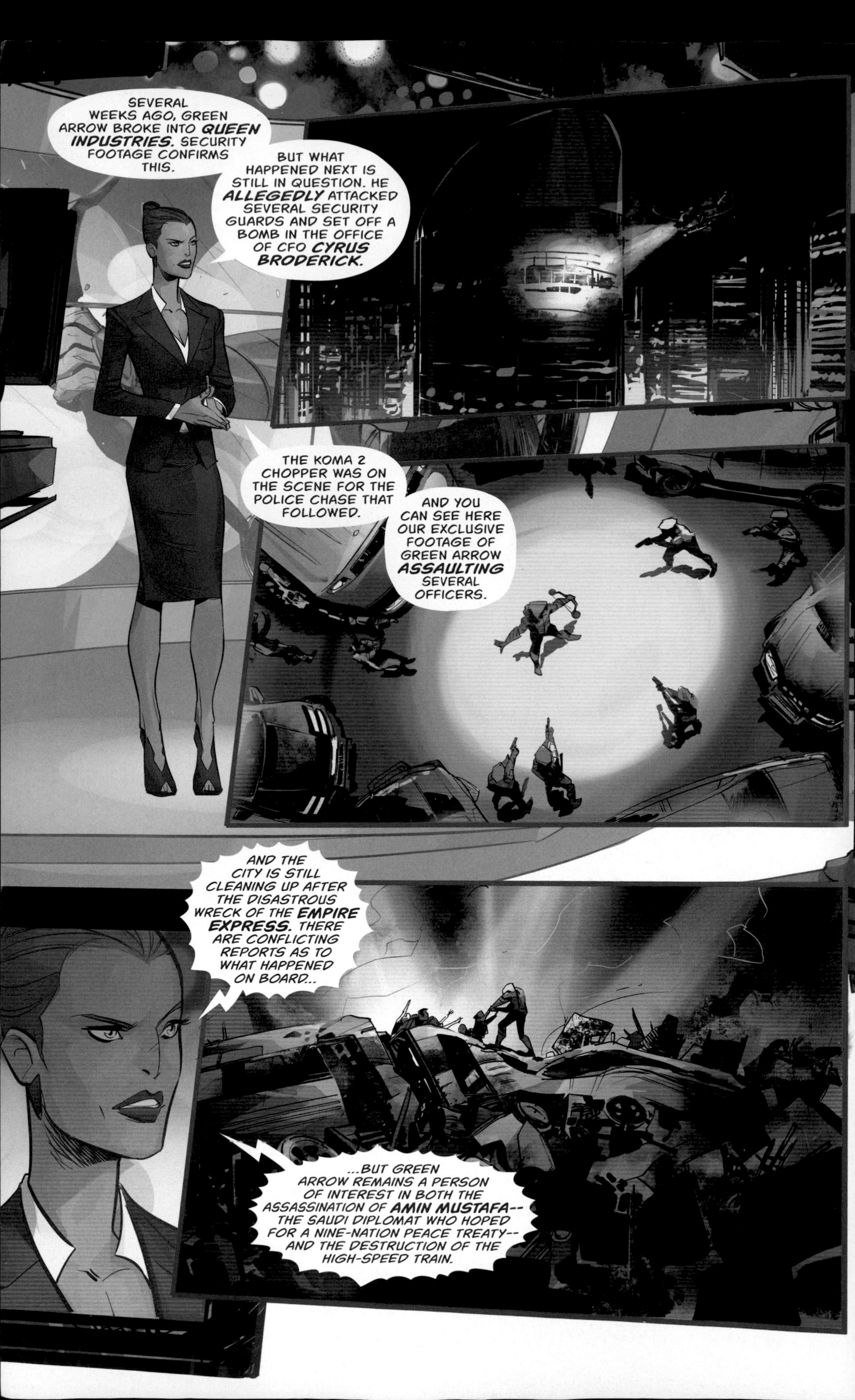
SEVERAL WEEKS AGO, GREEN ARROW BROKE INTO QUEEN INDUSTRIES. SECURITY FOOTAGE CONFIRMS THIS.
BUT WHAT HAPPENED NEXT IS STILL IN QUESTION. HE ALLEGEDLY ATTACKED SEVERAL SECURITY GUARDS AND SET OFF A BOMB IN THE OFFICE OF CFO CYRUS BRODERICK.
THE KOMA 2 CHOPPER WAS ON THE SCENE FOR THE POLICE CHASE THAT FOLLOWED.
AND YOU CAN SEE HERE OUR EXCLUSIVE FOOTAGE OF GREEN ARROW ASSAULTING SEVERAL OFFICERS.
AND THE CITY IS STILL CLEANING UP AFTER THE DISASTROUS WRECK OF THE EMPIRE EXPRESS. THERE ARE CONFLICTING REPORTS AS TO WHAT HAPPENED ON BOARD...
...BUT GREEN ARROW REMAINS A PERSON OF INTEREST IN BOTH THE ASSASSINATION OF AMIN MUSTAFA-- THE SAUDI DIPLOMAT WHO HOPED FOR A NINE-NATION PEACE TREATY-- AND THE DESTRUCTION OF THE HIGH-SPEED TRAIN.

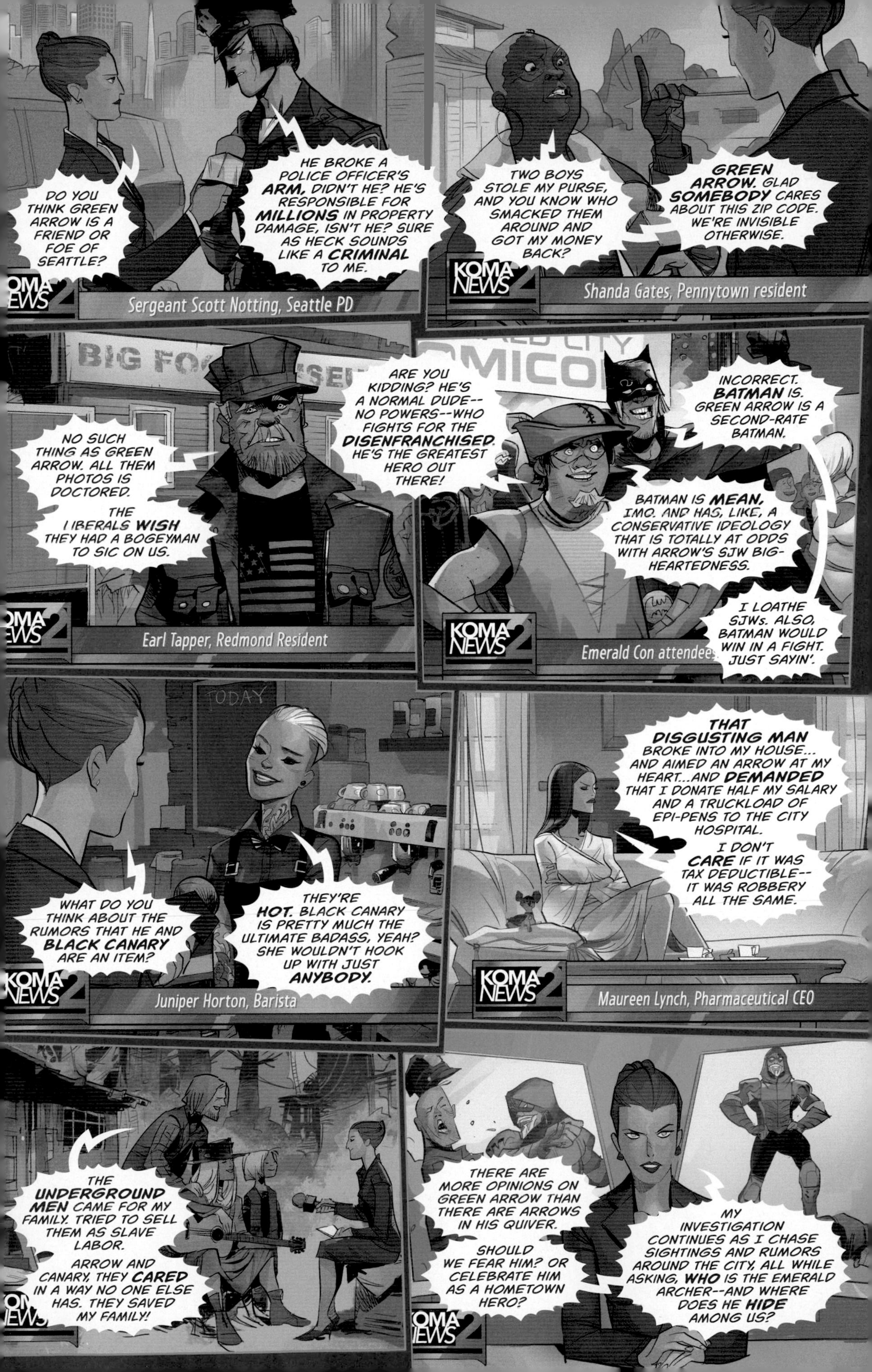
DO YOU THINK GREEN ARROW IS A FRIEND OR FOE OF SEATTLE?
HE BROKE A POLICE OFFICER'S ARM, DIDN'T HE? HE'S RESPONSIBLE FOR MILLIONS IN PROPERTY DAMAGE, ISN'T HE? SURE AS HECK SOUNDS LIKE A CRIMINAL TO ME.
KOMA NEWS 2
Sergeant Scott Notting, Seattle PD
TWO BOYS STOLE MY PURSE, AND YOU KNOW WHO SMACKED THEM AROUND AND GOT MY MONEY BACK?
GREEN ARROW. GLAD SOMEBODY CARES ABOUT THIS ZIP CODE. WE'RE INVISIBLE OTHERWISE.
KOMA NEWS 2
Shanda Gates, Pennytown resident
BIG FO
NO SUCH THING AS GREEN ARROW. ALL THEM PHOTOS IS DOCTORED.
THE LIBERALS WISH THEY HAD A BOGEYMAN TO SIC ON US.
KOMA NEWS 2
Earl Tapper, Redmond Resident
MICO
ARE YOU KIDDING? HE'S A NORMAL DUDE--NO POWERS--WHO FIGHTS FOR THE DISENFRANCHISED. HE'S THE GREATEST HERO OUT THERE!
INCORRECT. BATMAN IS. GREEN ARROW IS A SECOND-RATE BATMAN.
BATMAN IS MEAN, IMO. AND HAS, LIKE, A CONSERVATIVE IDEOLOGY THAT IS TOTALLY AT ODDS WITH ARROW'S SJW BIG-HEARTEDNESS.
I LOATHE SJWs. ALSO, BATMAN WOULD WIN IN A FIGHT. JUST SAYIN'.
KOMA NEWS 2
Emerald Con attendees
TODAY
WHAT DO YOU THINK ABOUT THE RUMORS THAT HE AND BLACK CANARY ARE AN ITEM?
THEY'RE HOT. BLACK CANARY IS PRETTY MUCH THE ULTIMATE BADASS, YEAH? SHE WOULDN'T HOOK UP WITH JUST ANYBODY.
KOMA NEWS 2
Juniper Horton, Barista
THAT DISGUSTING MAN BROKE INTO MY HOUSE... AND AIMED AN ARROW AT MY HEART...AND DEMANDED THAT I DONATE HALF MY SALARY AND A TRUCKLOAD OF EPI-PENS TO THE CITY HOSPITAL.
I DON'T CARE IF IT WAS TAX DEDUCTIBLE--IT WAS ROBBERY ALL THE SAME.
KOMA NEWS 2
Maureen Lynch, Pharmaceutical CEO
THE UNDERGROUND MEN CAME FOR MY FAMILY. TRIED TO SELL THEM AS SLAVE LABOR.
ARROW AND CANARY, THEY CARED IN A WAY NO ONE ELSE HAS. THEY SAVED MY FAMILY!
THERE ARE MORE OPINIONS ON GREEN ARROW THAN THERE ARE ARROWS IN HIS QUIVER.
SHOULD WE FEAR HIM? OR CELEBRATE HIM AS A HOMETOWN HERO?
MY INVESTIGATION CONTINUES AS I CHASE SIGHTINGS AND RUMORS AROUND THE CITY, ALL WHILE ASKING, WHO IS THE EMERALD ARCHER--AND WHERE DOES HE HIDE AMONG US?
KOMA NEWS 2

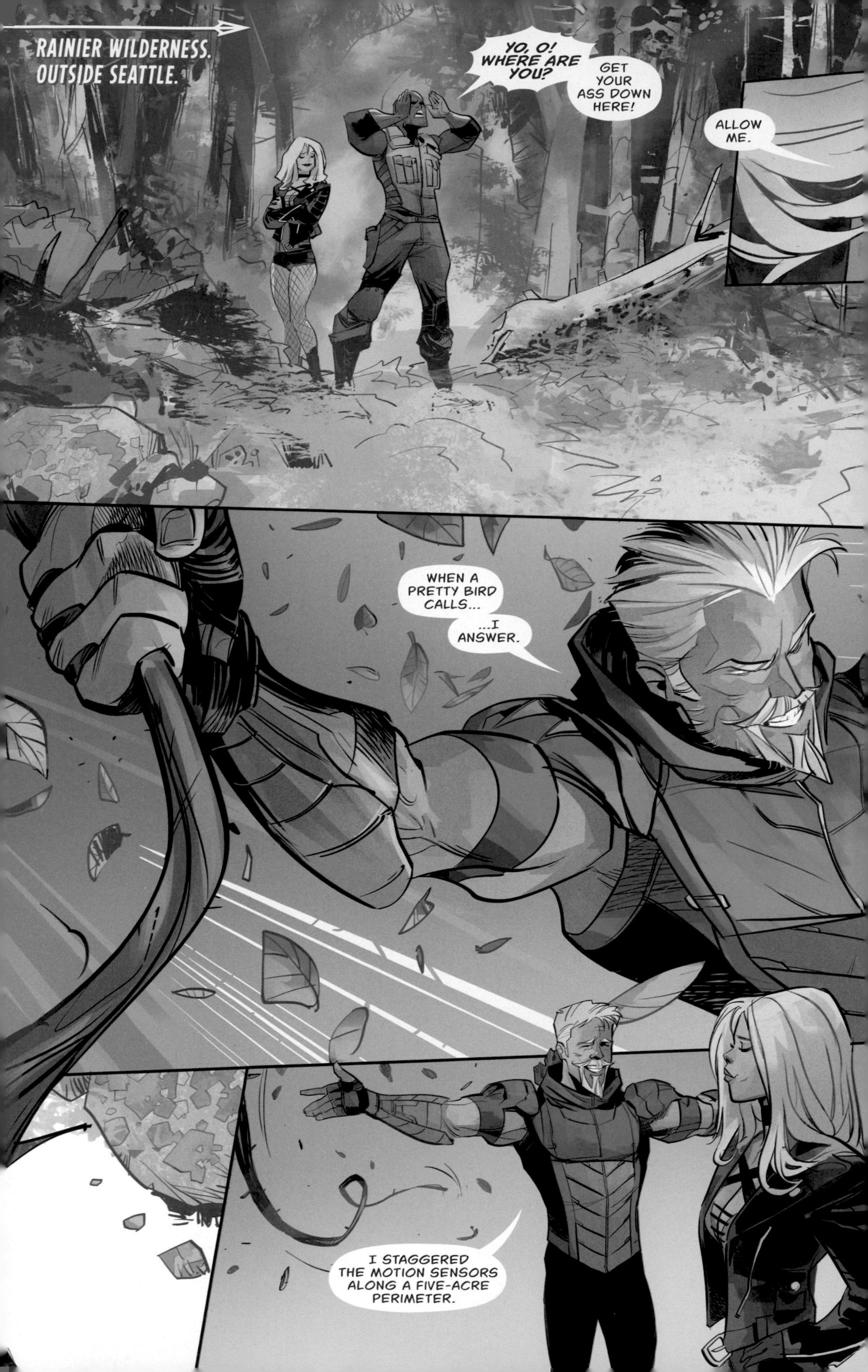
RAINIER WILDERNESS. OUTSIDE SEATTLE.
YO, O! WHERE ARE YOU?
GET YOUR ASS DOWN HERE!
ALLOW ME.
WHEN A PRETTY BIRD CALLS...
...I ANSWER.
I STAGGERED THE MOTION SENSORS ALONG A FIVE-ACRE PERIMETER.

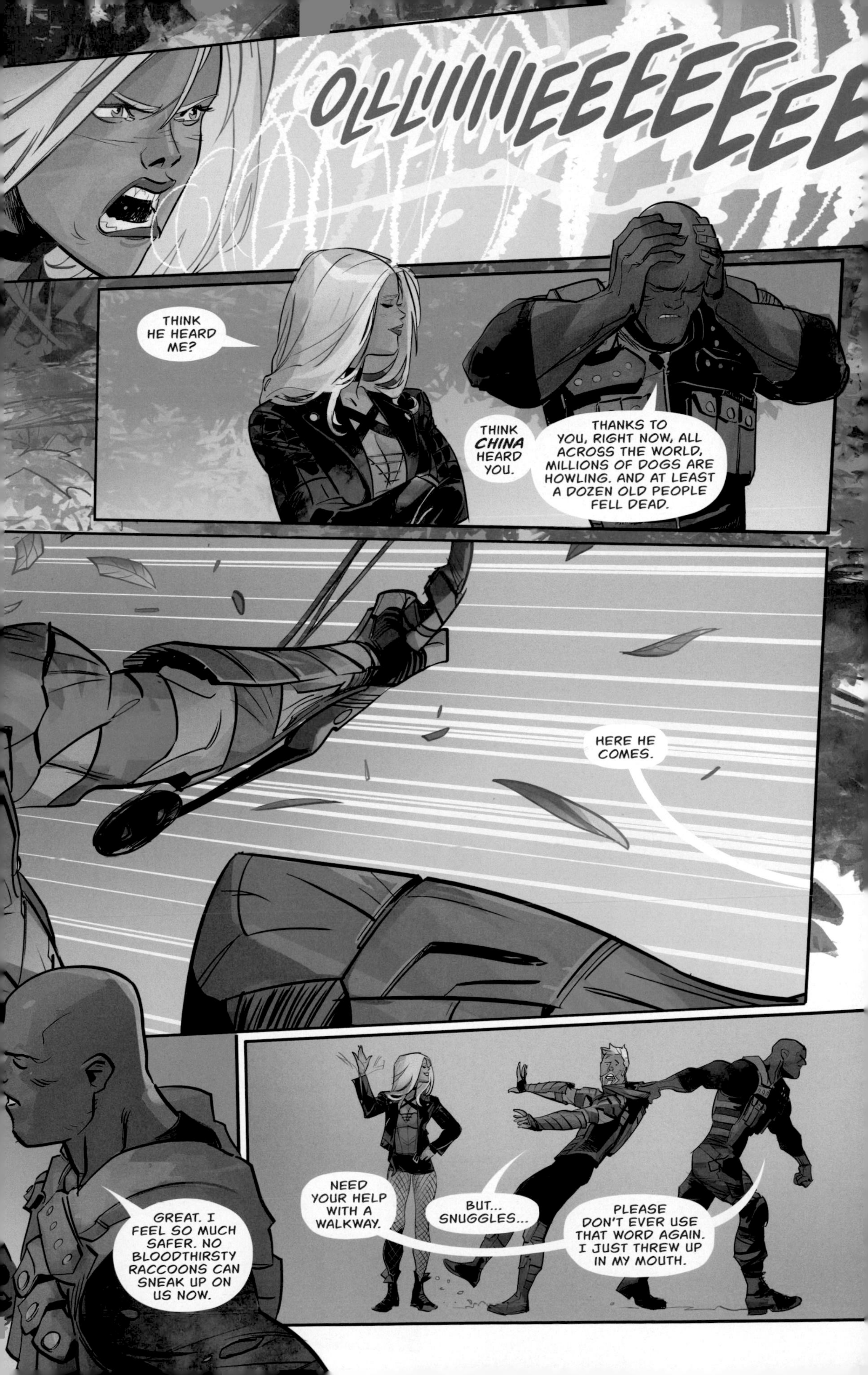
OLLLLLLEEEEEEEE
THINK HE HEARD ME?
THINK *CHINA* HEARD YOU.
THANKS TO YOU, RIGHT NOW, ALL ACROSS THE WORLD, MILLIONS OF DOGS ARE HOWLING. AND AT LEAST A DOZEN OLD PEOPLE FELL DEAD.
HERE HE COMES.
GREAT. I FEEL SO MUCH SAFER. NO BLOODTHIRSTY RACCOONS CAN SNEAK UP ON US NOW.
NEED YOUR HELP WITH A WALKWAY.
BUT... SNUGGLES...
PLEASE DON'T EVER USE THAT WORD AGAIN. I JUST THREW UP IN MY MOUTH.

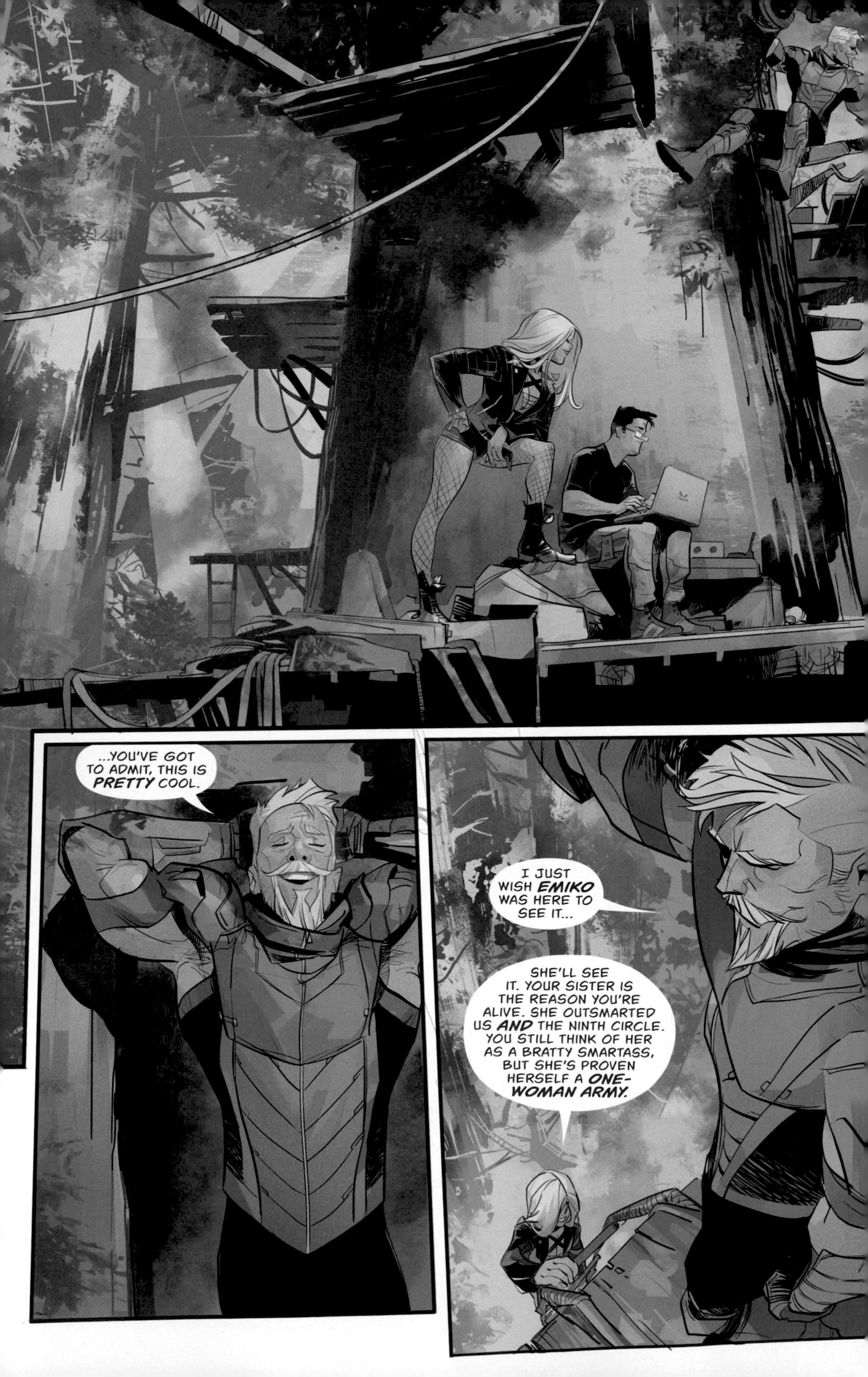
...YOU'VE GOT TO ADMIT, THIS IS PRETTY COOL.
I JUST WISH EMIKO WAS HERE TO SEE IT...
SHE'LL SEE IT. YOUR SISTER IS THE REASON YOU'RE ALIVE. SHE OUTSMARTED US AND THE NINTH CIRCLE. YOU STILL THINK OF HER AS A BRATTY SMARTASS, BUT SHE'S PROVEN HERSELF A ONE-WOMAN ARMY.

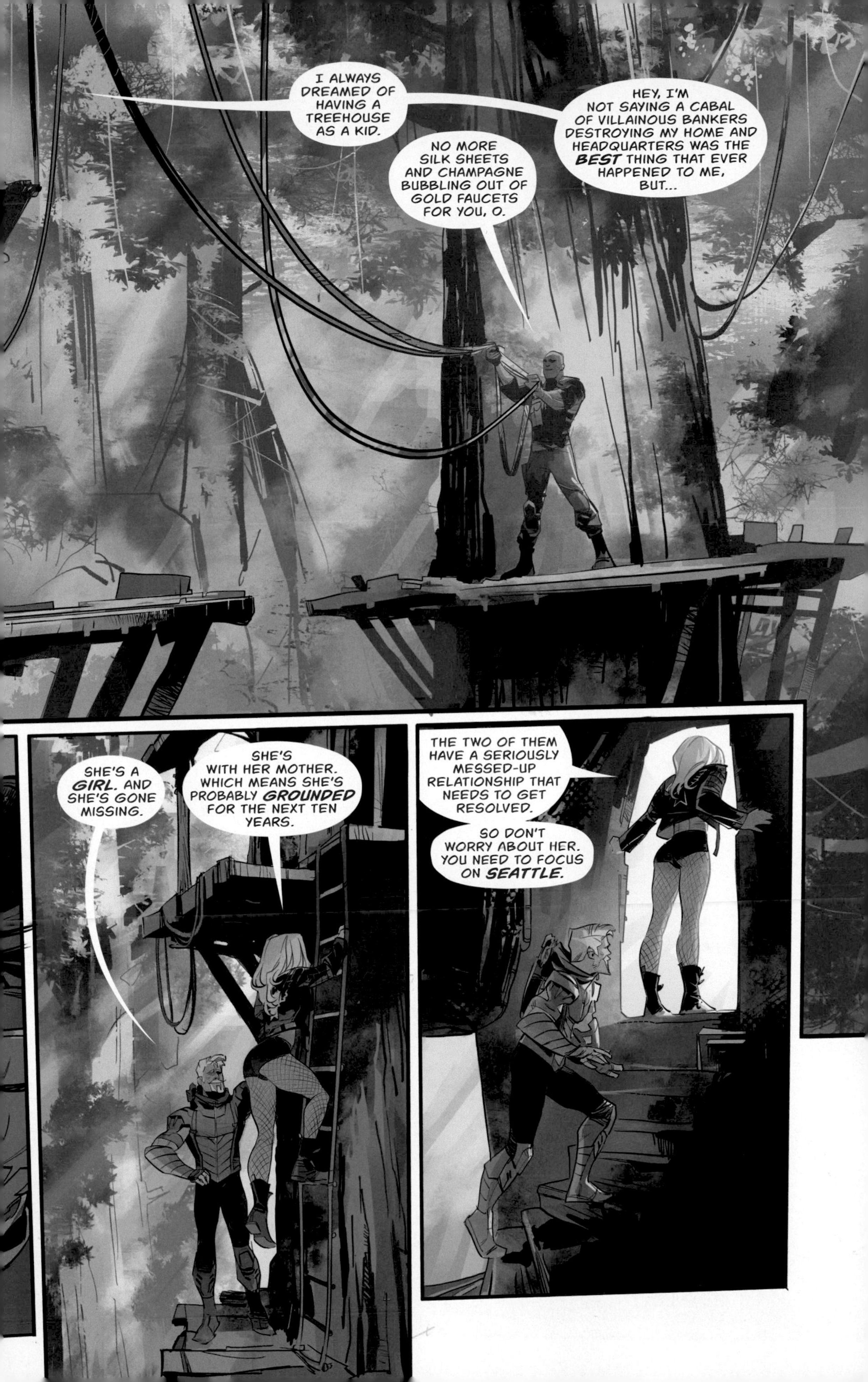
I ALWAYS DREAMED OF HAVING A TREEHOUSE AS A KID.
HEY, I'M NOT SAYING A CABAL OF VILLAINOUS BANKERS DESTROYING MY HOME AND HEADQUARTERS WAS THE ***BEST*** THING THAT EVER HAPPENED TO ME, BUT...
NO MORE SILK SHEETS AND CHAMPAGNE BUBBLING OUT OF GOLD FAUCETS FOR YOU, O.
SHE'S A ***GIRL.*** AND SHE'S GONE MISSING.
SHE'S WITH HER MOTHER. WHICH MEANS SHE'S PROBABLY ***GROUNDED*** FOR THE NEXT TEN YEARS.
THE TWO OF THEM HAVE A SERIOUSLY MESSED-UP RELATIONSHIP THAT NEEDS TO GET RESOLVED.
SO DON'T WORRY ABOUT HER. YOU NEED TO FOCUS ON ***SEATTLE.***

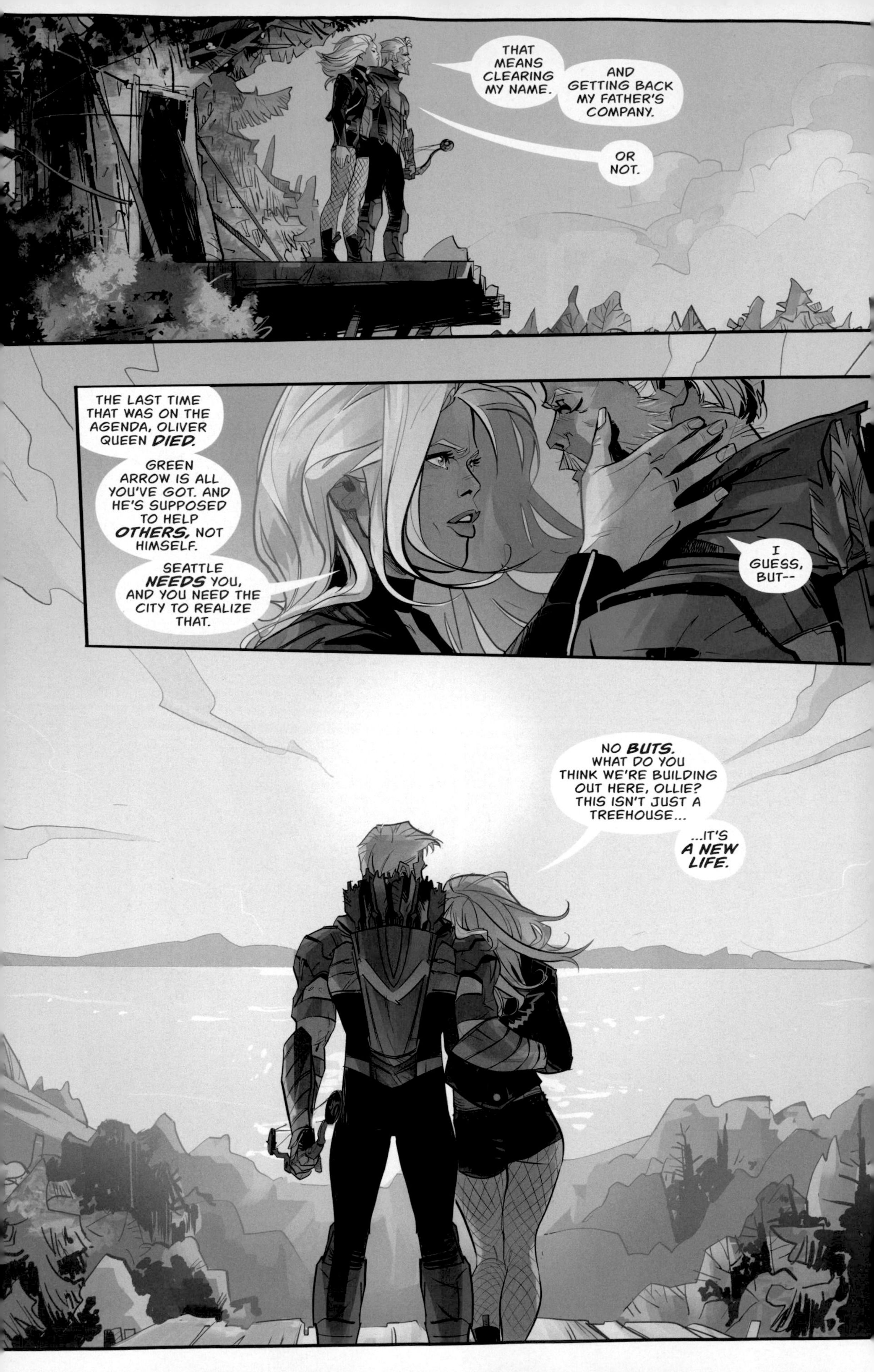
THAT MEANS CLEARING MY NAME.
AND GETTING BACK MY FATHER'S COMPANY.
OR NOT.
THE LAST TIME THAT WAS ON THE AGENDA, OLIVER QUEEN DIED.
GREEN ARROW IS ALL YOU'VE GOT. AND HE'S SUPPOSED TO HELP OTHERS, NOT HIMSELF.
SEATTLE NEEDS YOU, AND YOU NEED THE CITY TO REALIZE THAT.
I GUESS, BUT--
NO BUTS. WHAT DO YOU THINK WE'RE BUILDING OUT HERE, OLLIE? THIS ISN'T JUST A TREEHOUSE...
...IT'S A NEW LIFE.

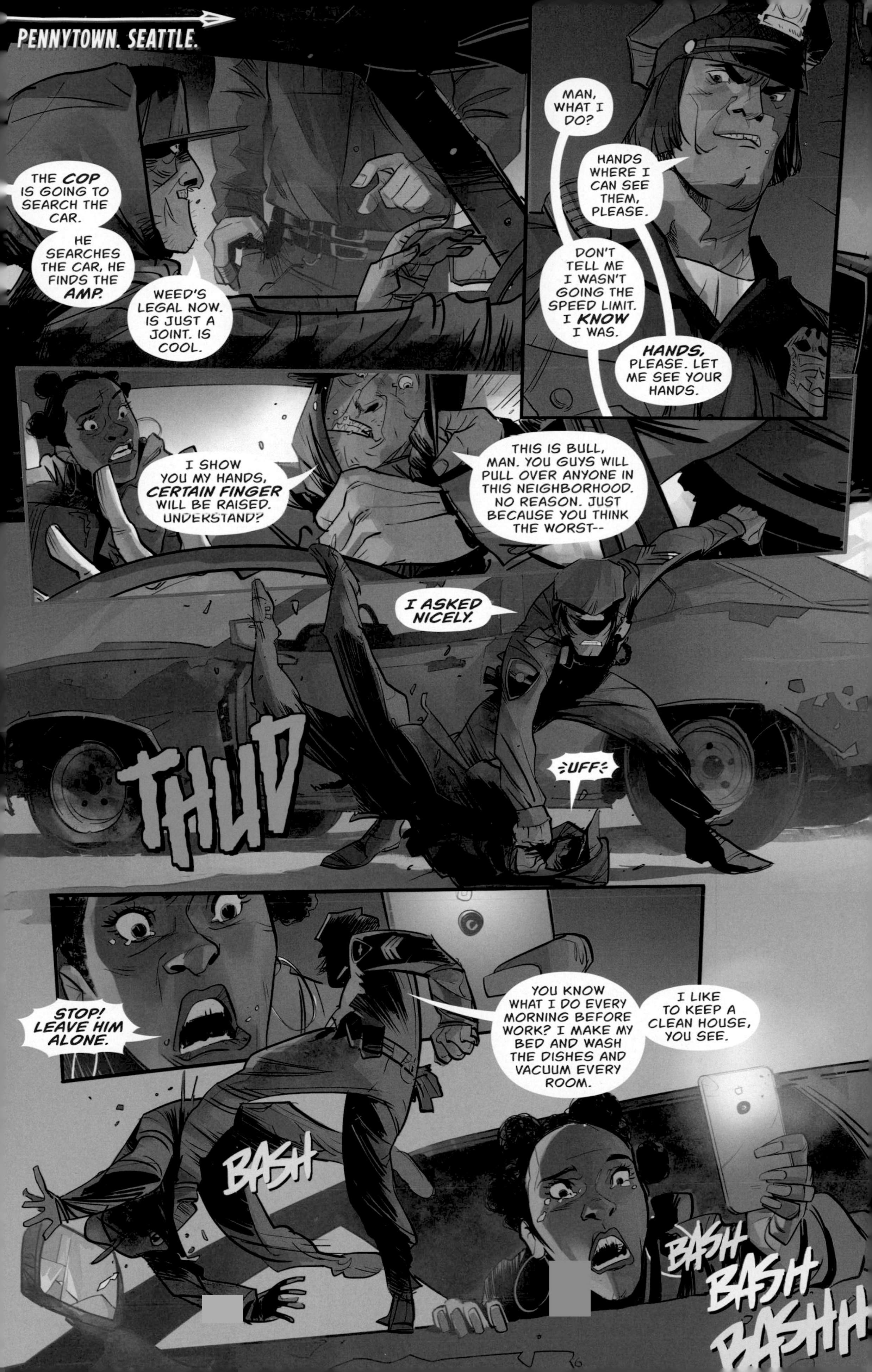
PENNYTOWN. SEATTLE.
THE COP IS GOING TO SEARCH THE CAR.
HE SEARCHES THE CAR, HE FINDS THE AMP.
WEED'S LEGAL NOW. IS JUST A JOINT. IS COOL.
MAN, WHAT I DO?
HANDS WHERE I CAN SEE THEM, PLEASE.
DON'T TELL ME I WASN'T GOING THE SPEED LIMIT. I KNOW I WAS.
HANDS, PLEASE. LET ME SEE YOUR HANDS.
I SHOW YOU MY HANDS, CERTAIN FINGER WILL BE RAISED. UNDERSTAND?
THIS IS BULL, MAN. YOU GUYS WILL PULL OVER ANYONE IN THIS NEIGHBORHOOD. NO REASON. JUST BECAUSE YOU THINK THE WORST--
I ASKED NICELY.
THUD
UFF
STOP! LEAVE HIM ALONE.
YOU KNOW WHAT I DO EVERY MORNING BEFORE WORK? I MAKE MY BED AND WASH THE DISHES AND VACUUM EVERY ROOM.
I LIKE TO KEEP A CLEAN HOUSE, YOU SEE.
BASH
BASH
BASH
BASHH

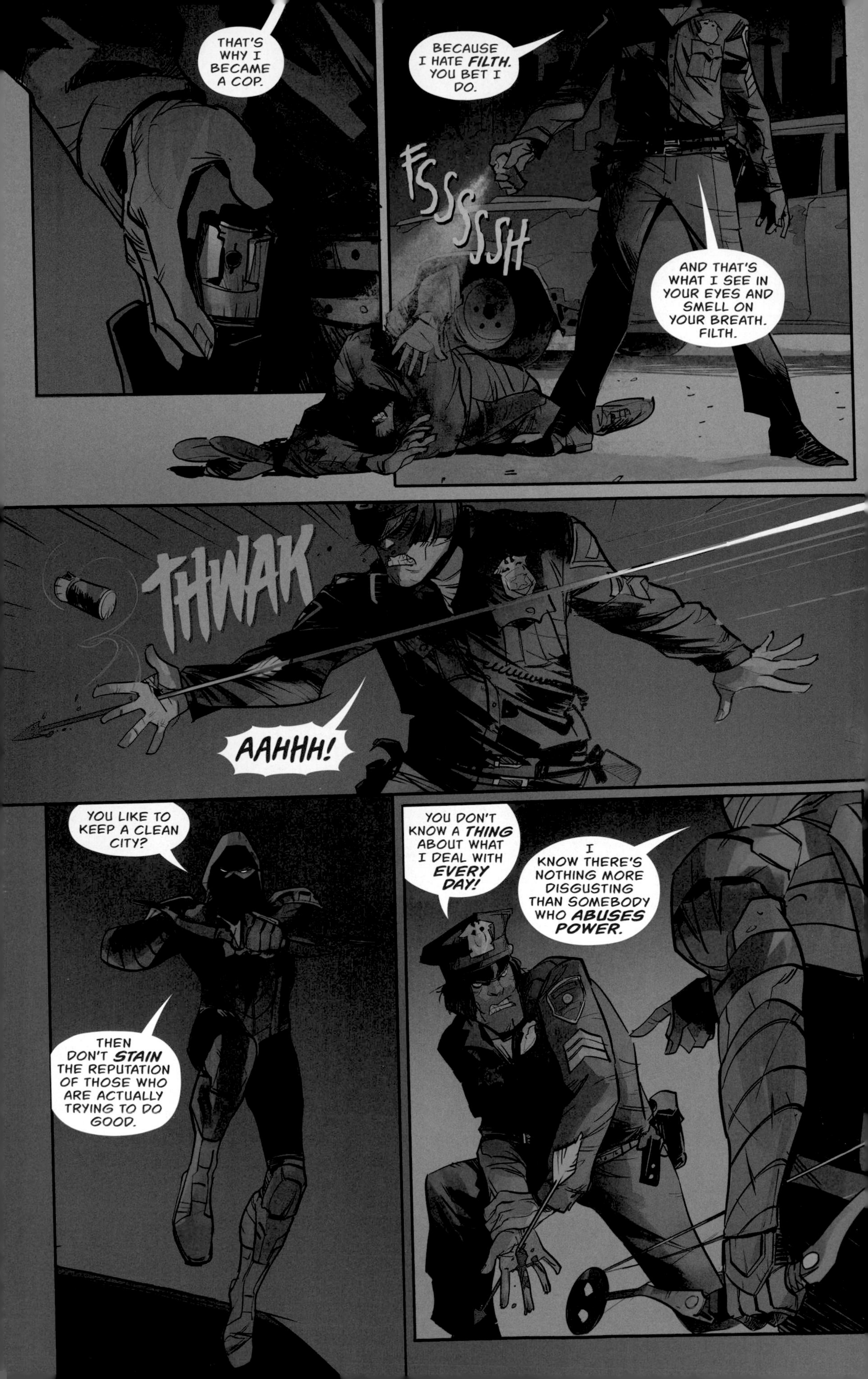
THAT'S WHY I BECAME A COP.
BECAUSE I HATE FILTH. YOU BET I DO.
FSSSSSH
AND THAT'S WHAT I SEE IN YOUR EYES AND SMELL ON YOUR BREATH. FILTH.
THWAK
AAHHH!
YOU LIKE TO KEEP A CLEAN CITY?
THEN DON'T STAIN THE REPUTATION OF THOSE WHO ARE ACTUALLY TRYING TO DO GOOD.
YOU DON'T KNOW A THING ABOUT WHAT I DEAL WITH EVERY DAY!
I KNOW THERE'S NOTHING MORE DISGUSTING THAN SOMEBODY WHO ABUSES POWER.

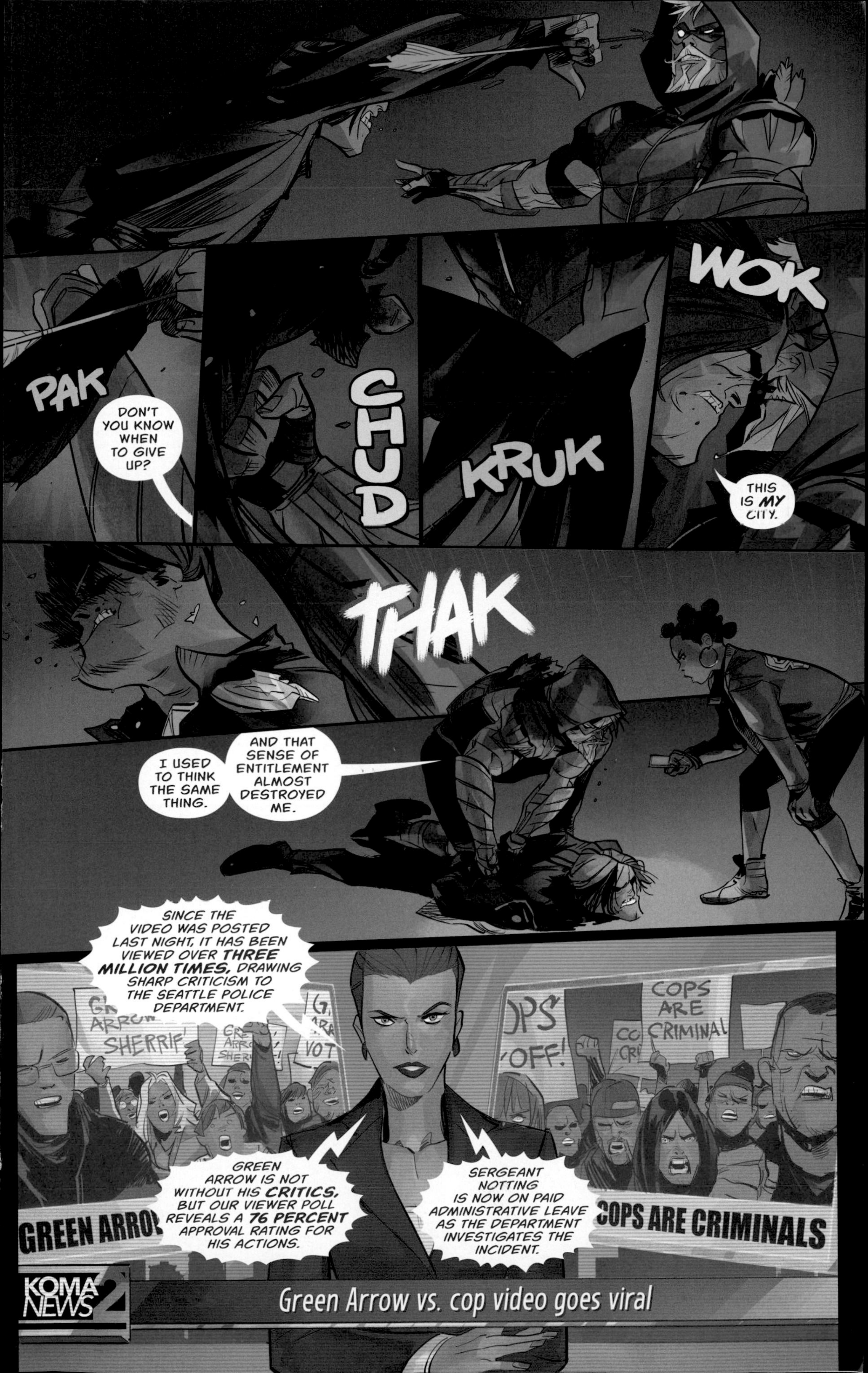
PAK
DON'T YOU KNOW WHEN TO GIVE UP?
CHUD
KRUK
WOK
THIS IS *MY* CITY.
THAK
I USED TO THINK THE SAME THING.
AND THAT SENSE OF ENTITLEMENT ALMOST DESTROYED ME.
SINCE THE VIDEO WAS POSTED LAST NIGHT, IT HAS BEEN VIEWED OVER **THREE MILLION TIMES,** DRAWING SHARP CRITICISM TO THE SEATTLE POLICE DEPARTMENT.
SHERRIF
COPS ARE CRIMINAL
OFF!
GREEN ARROW IS NOT WITHOUT HIS **CRITICS,** BUT OUR VIEWER POLL REVEALS A **76 PERCENT** APPROVAL RATING FOR HIS ACTIONS.
SERGEANT NOTTING IS NOW ON PAID ADMINISTRATIVE LEAVE AS THE DEPARTMENT INVESTIGATES THE INCIDENT.
GREEN ARRO
COPS ARE CRIMINALS
KOMA NEWS 2
Green Arrow vs. cop video goes viral

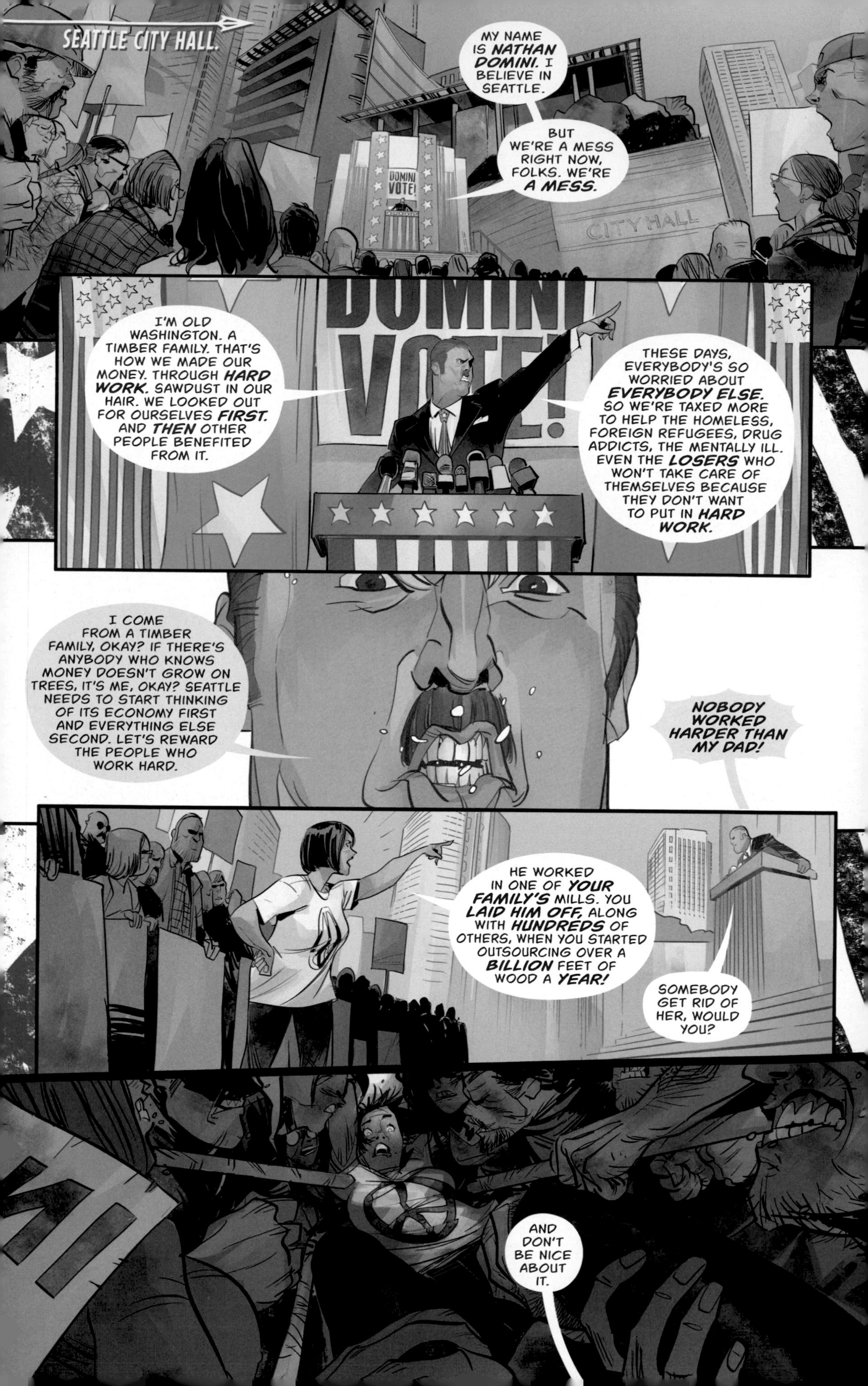
SEATTLE CITY HALL.
MY NAME IS NATHAN DOMINI. I BELIEVE IN SEATTLE.
BUT WE'RE A MESS RIGHT NOW, FOLKS. WE'RE A MESS.
DOMINI VOTE!
CITY HALL
I'M OLD WASHINGTON. A TIMBER FAMILY. THAT'S HOW WE MADE OUR MONEY. THROUGH HARD WORK. SAWDUST IN OUR HAIR. WE LOOKED OUT FOR OURSELVES FIRST. AND THEN OTHER PEOPLE BENEFITED FROM IT.
THESE DAYS, EVERYBODY'S SO WORRIED ABOUT EVERYBODY ELSE. SO WE'RE TAXED MORE TO HELP THE HOMELESS, FOREIGN REFUGEES, DRUG ADDICTS, THE MENTALLY ILL. EVEN THE LOSERS WHO WON'T TAKE CARE OF THEMSELVES BECAUSE THEY DON'T WANT TO PUT IN HARD WORK.
I COME FROM A TIMBER FAMILY, OKAY? IF THERE'S ANYBODY WHO KNOWS MONEY DOESN'T GROW ON TREES, IT'S ME, OKAY? SEATTLE NEEDS TO START THINKING OF ITS ECONOMY FIRST AND EVERYTHING ELSE SECOND. LET'S REWARD THE PEOPLE WHO WORK HARD.
NOBODY WORKED HARDER THAN MY DAD!
HE WORKED IN ONE OF YOUR FAMILY'S MILLS. YOU LAID HIM OFF, ALONG WITH HUNDREDS OF OTHERS, WHEN YOU STARTED OUTSOURCING OVER A BILLION FEET OF WOOD A YEAR!
SOMEBODY GET RID OF HER, WOULD YOU?
AND DON'T BE NICE ABOUT IT.

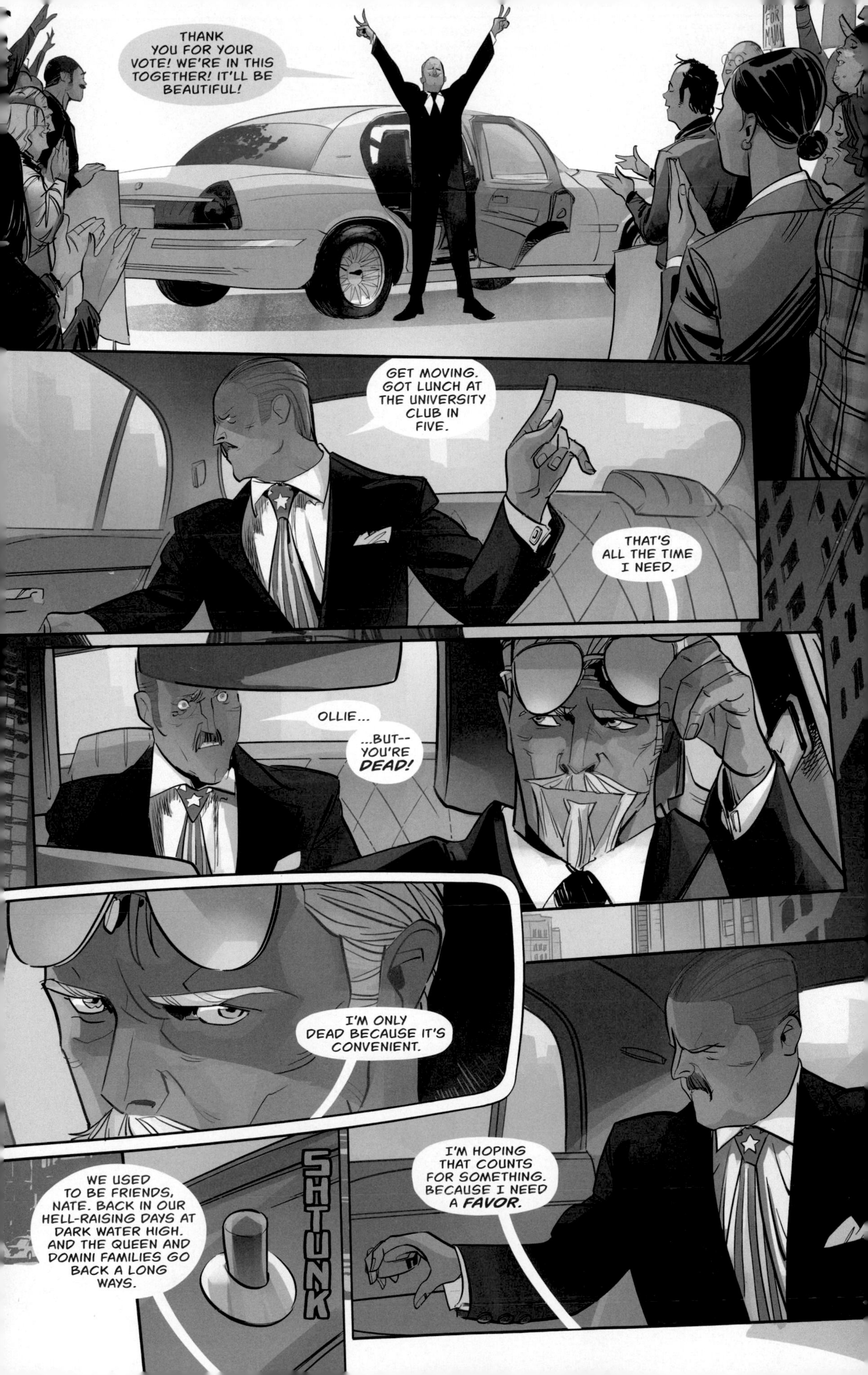
THANK YOU FOR YOUR VOTE! WE'RE IN THIS TOGETHER! IT'LL BE BEAUTIFUL!
GET MOVING. GOT LUNCH AT THE UNIVERSITY CLUB IN FIVE.
THAT'S ALL THE TIME I NEED.
OLLIE...
...BUT-- YOU'RE DEAD!
I'M ONLY DEAD BECAUSE IT'S CONVENIENT.
WE USED TO BE FRIENDS, NATE. BACK IN OUR HELL-RAISING DAYS AT DARK WATER HIGH. AND THE QUEEN AND DOMINI FAMILIES GO BACK A LONG WAYS.
SHTUNK
I'M HOPING THAT COUNTS FOR SOMETHING. BECAUSE I NEED A FAVOR.

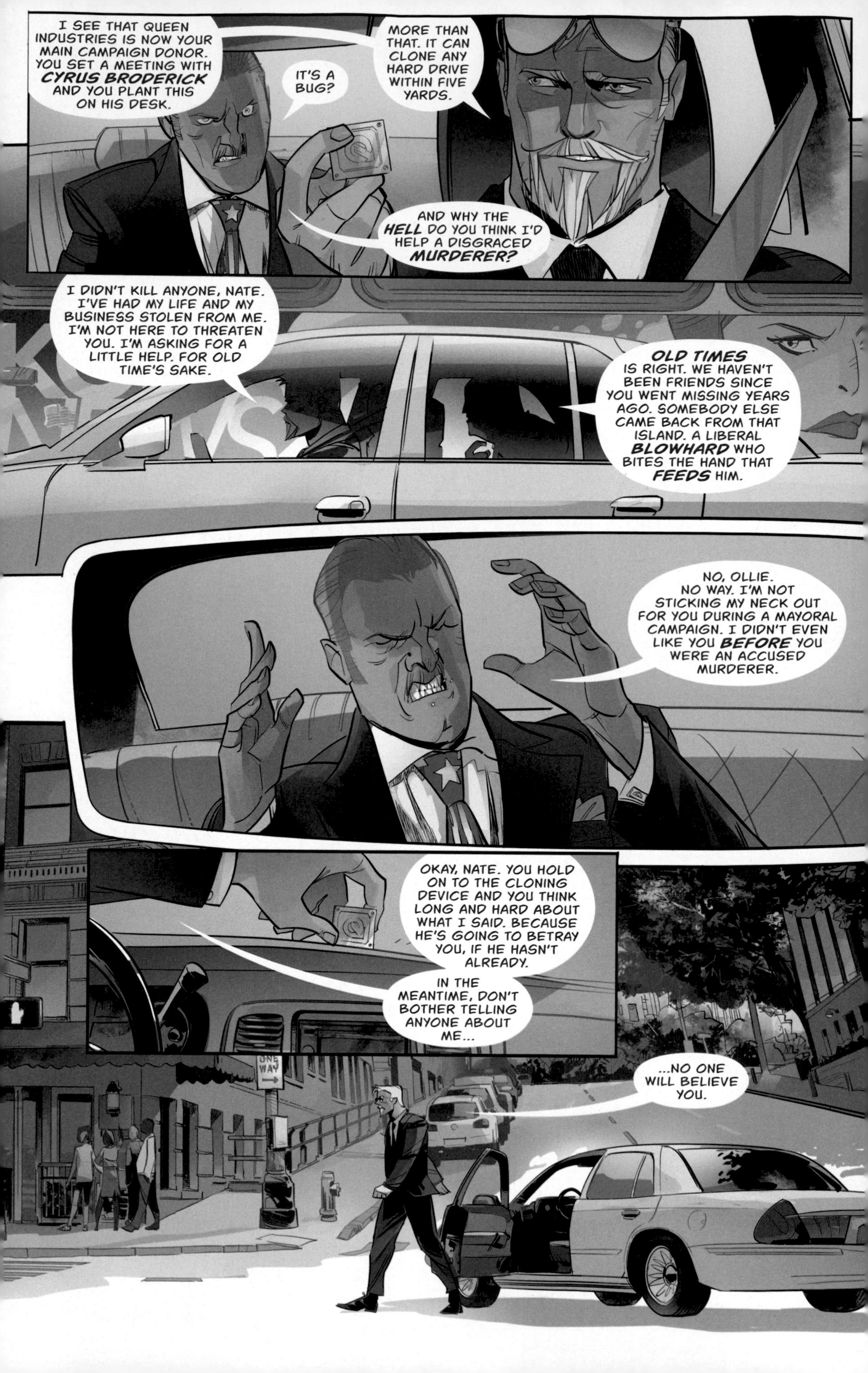
I SEE THAT QUEEN INDUSTRIES IS NOW YOUR MAIN CAMPAIGN DONOR. YOU SET A MEETING WITH CYRUS BRODERICK AND YOU PLANT THIS ON HIS DESK.
IT'S A BUG?
MORE THAN THAT. IT CAN CLONE ANY HARD DRIVE WITHIN FIVE YARDS.
AND WHY THE HELL DO YOU THINK I'D HELP A DISGRACED MURDERER?
I DIDN'T KILL ANYONE, NATE. I'VE HAD MY LIFE AND MY BUSINESS STOLEN FROM ME. I'M NOT HERE TO THREATEN YOU. I'M ASKING FOR A LITTLE HELP. FOR OLD TIME'S SAKE.
OLD TIMES IS RIGHT. WE HAVEN'T BEEN FRIENDS SINCE YOU WENT MISSING YEARS AGO. SOMEBODY ELSE CAME BACK FROM THAT ISLAND. A LIBERAL BLOWHARD WHO BITES THE HAND THAT FEEDS HIM.
NO, OLLIE. NO WAY. I'M NOT STICKING MY NECK OUT FOR YOU DURING A MAYORAL CAMPAIGN. I DIDN'T EVEN LIKE YOU BEFORE YOU WERE AN ACCUSED MURDERER.
OKAY, NATE. YOU HOLD ON TO THE CLONING DEVICE AND YOU THINK LONG AND HARD ABOUT WHAT I SAID. BECAUSE HE'S GOING TO BETRAY YOU, IF HE HASN'T ALREADY.
IN THE MEANTIME, DON'T BOTHER TELLING ANYONE ABOUT ME...
ONE WAY
...NO ONE WILL BELIEVE YOU.

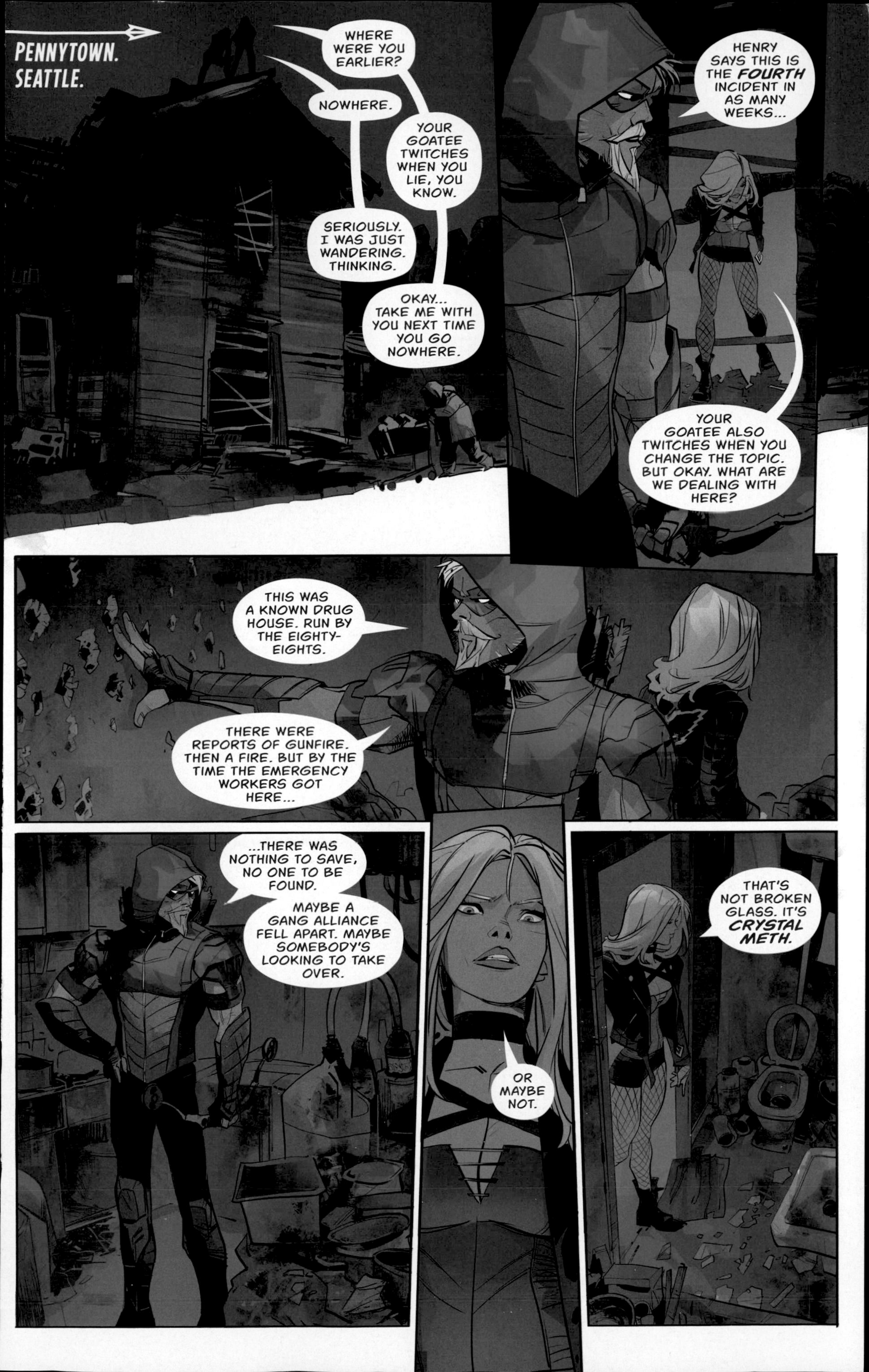
PENNYTOWN. SEATTLE.
WHERE WERE YOU EARLIER?
NOWHERE.
YOUR GOATEE TWITCHES WHEN YOU LIE, YOU KNOW.
SERIOUSLY. I WAS JUST WANDERING. THINKING.
OKAY... TAKE ME WITH YOU NEXT TIME YOU GO NOWHERE.
HENRY SAYS THIS IS THE FOURTH INCIDENT IN AS MANY WEEKS...
YOUR GOATEE ALSO TWITCHES WHEN YOU CHANGE THE TOPIC. BUT OKAY. WHAT ARE WE DEALING WITH HERE?
THIS WAS A KNOWN DRUG HOUSE. RUN BY THE EIGHTY-EIGHTS.
THERE WERE REPORTS OF GUNFIRE. THEN A FIRE. BUT BY THE TIME THE EMERGENCY WORKERS GOT HERE...
...THERE WAS NOTHING TO SAVE, NO ONE TO BE FOUND.
MAYBE A GANG ALLIANCE FELL APART. MAYBE SOMEBODY'S LOOKING TO TAKE OVER.
OR MAYBE NOT.
THAT'S NOT BROKEN GLASS. IT'S CRYSTAL METH.

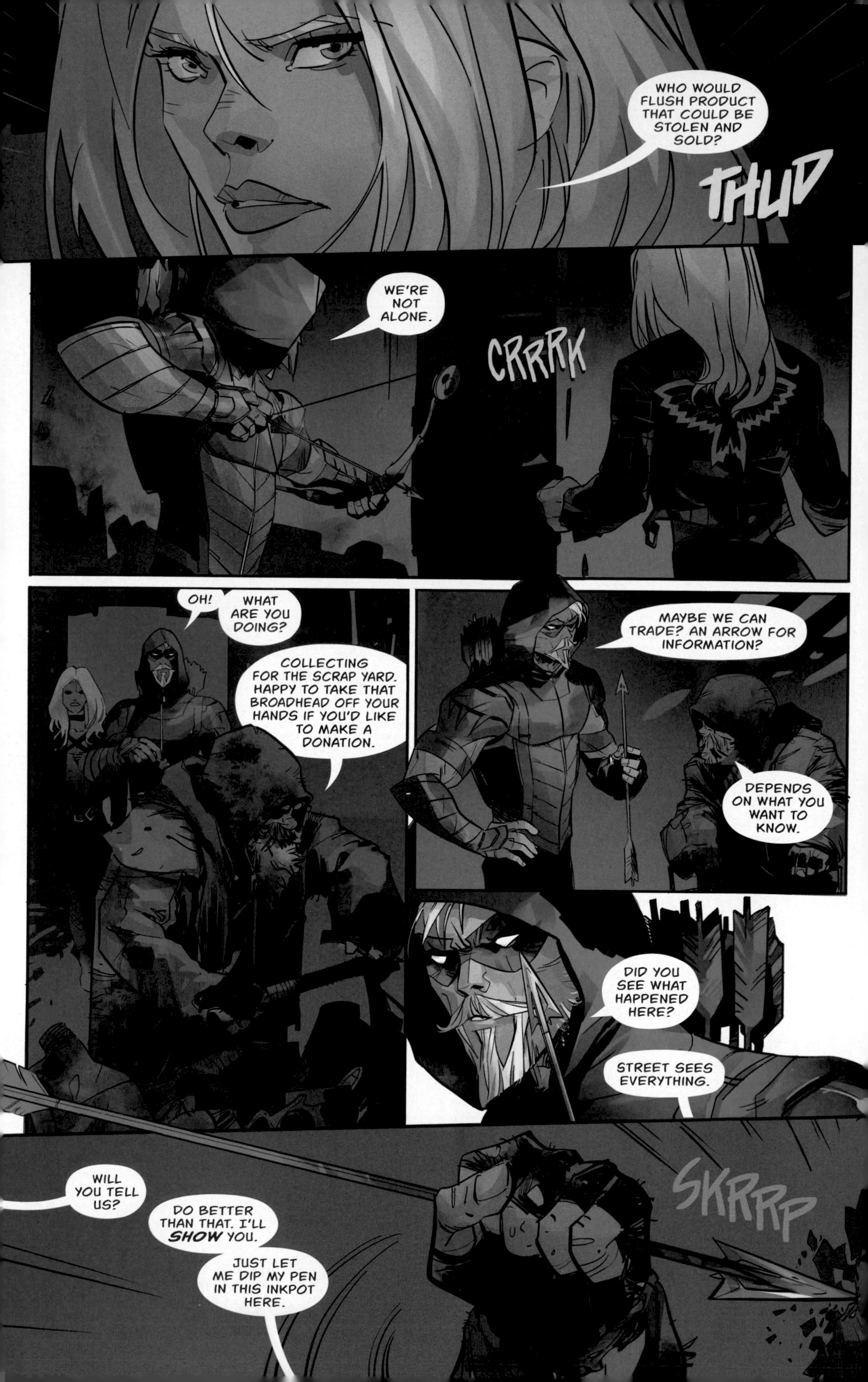
WHO WOULD FLUSH PRODUCT THAT COULD BE STOLEN AND SOLD?
THUD
WE'RE NOT ALONE.
CRRRK
OH!
WHAT ARE YOU DOING?
COLLECTING FOR THE SCRAP YARD. HAPPY TO TAKE THAT BROADHEAD OFF YOUR HANDS IF YOU'D LIKE TO MAKE A DONATION.
MAYBE WE CAN TRADE? AN ARROW FOR INFORMATION?
DEPENDS ON WHAT YOU WANT TO KNOW.
DID YOU SEE WHAT HAPPENED HERE?
STREET SEES EVERYTHING.
WILL YOU TELL US?
DO BETTER THAN THAT. I'LL SHOW YOU.
JUST LET ME DIP MY PEN IN THIS INKPOT HERE.
SKRRP

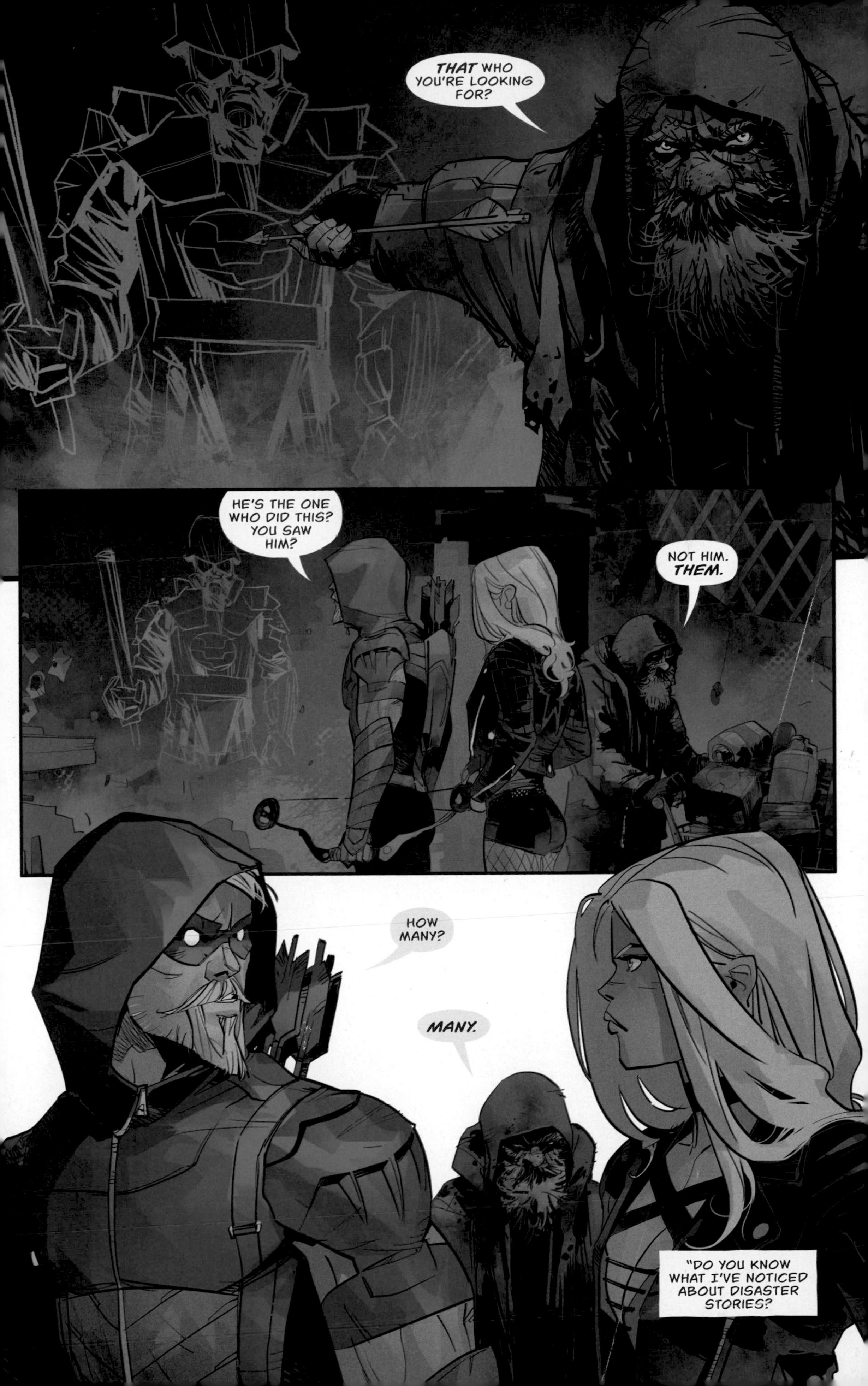
THAT WHO YOU'RE LOOKING FOR?
HE'S THE ONE WHO DID THIS? YOU SAW HIM?
NOT HIM. THEM.
HOW MANY?
MANY.
"DO YOU KNOW WHAT I'VE NOTICED ABOUT DISASTER STORIES?

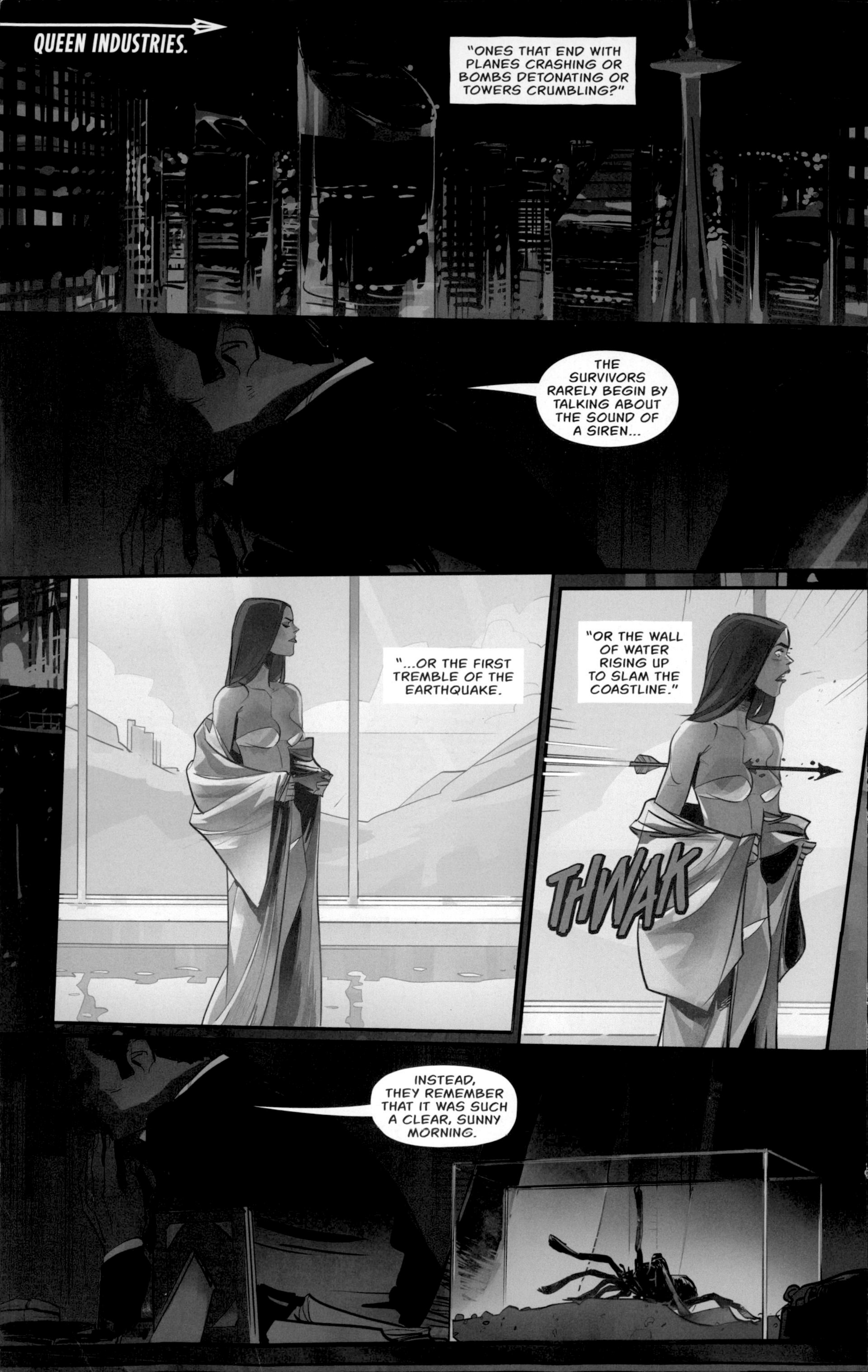
QUEEN INDUSTRIES.
"ONES THAT END WITH PLANES CRASHING OR BOMBS DETONATING OR TOWERS CRUMBLING?"
THE SURVIVORS RARELY BEGIN BY TALKING ABOUT THE SOUND OF A SIREN...
"...OR THE FIRST TREMBLE OF THE EARTHQUAKE.
"OR THE WALL OF WATER RISING UP TO SLAM THE COASTLINE."
THWAK
INSTEAD, THEY REMEMBER THAT IT WAS SUCH A CLEAR, SUNNY MORNING.

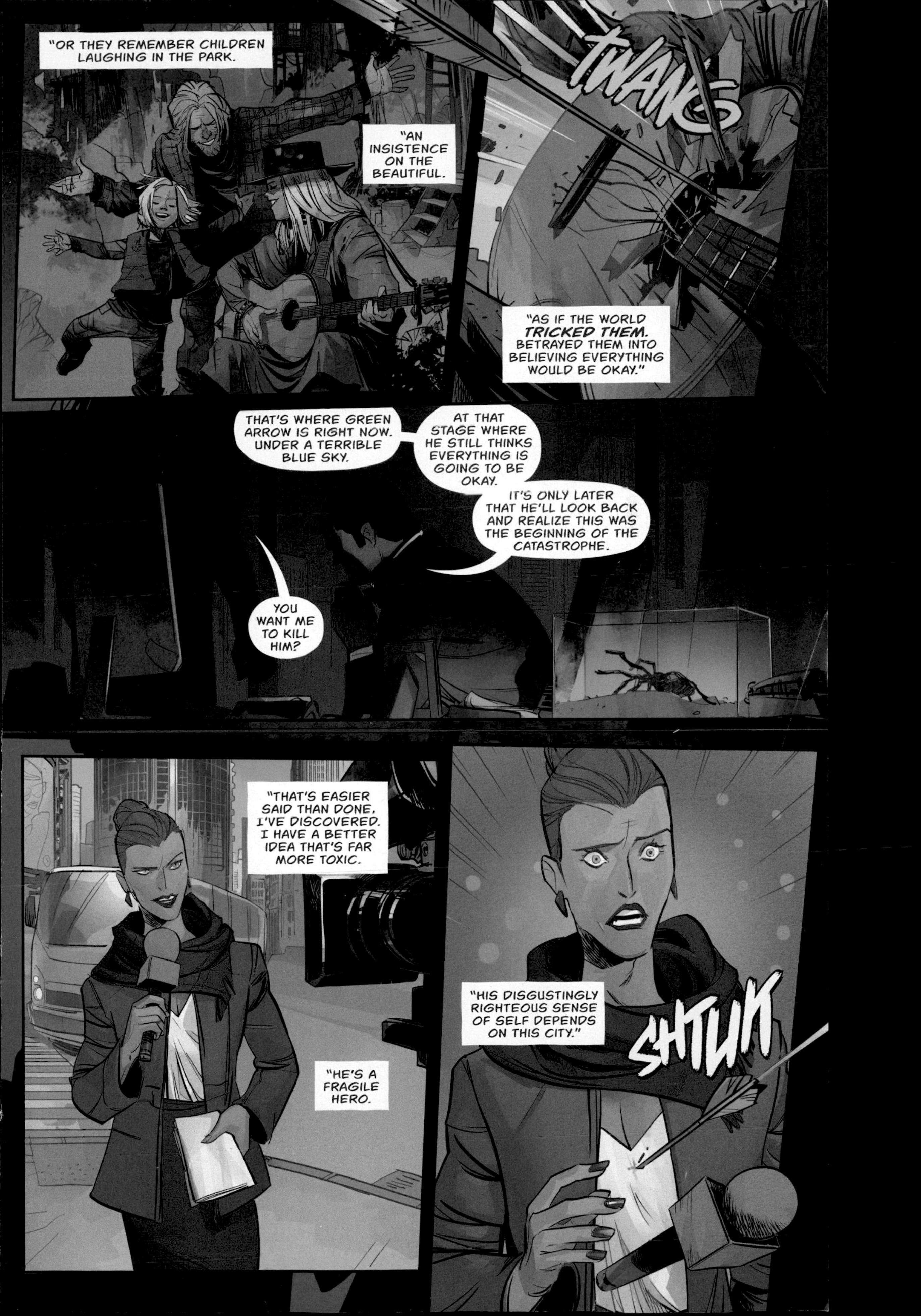
"OR THEY REMEMBER CHILDREN LAUGHING IN THE PARK.
"AN INSISTENCE ON THE BEAUTIFUL.
TWANG
"AS IF THE WORLD TRICKED THEM. BETRAYED THEM INTO BELIEVING EVERYTHING WOULD BE OKAY."
THAT'S WHERE GREEN ARROW IS RIGHT NOW. UNDER A TERRIBLE BLUE SKY.
AT THAT STAGE WHERE HE STILL THINKS EVERYTHING IS GOING TO BE OKAY.
IT'S ONLY LATER THAT HE'LL LOOK BACK AND REALIZE THIS WAS THE BEGINNING OF THE CATASTROPHE.
YOU WANT ME TO KILL HIM?
"THAT'S EASIER SAID THAN DONE, I'VE DISCOVERED. I HAVE A BETTER IDEA THAT'S FAR MORE TOXIC.
"HE'S A FRAGILE HERO.
"HIS DISGUSTINGLY RIGHTEOUS SENSE OF SELF DEPENDS ON THIS CITY."
SHTUK

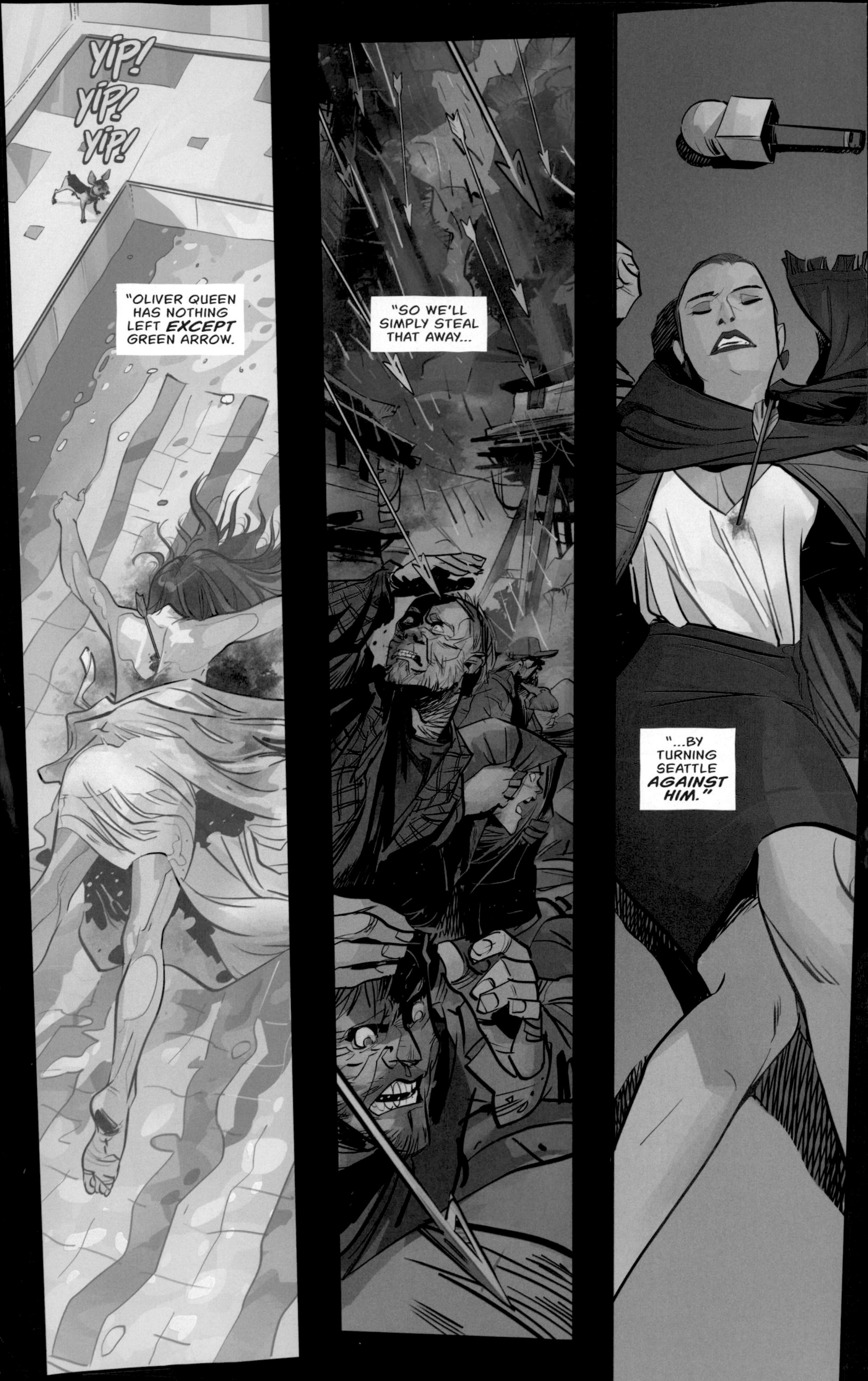
YIP! YIP! YIP!
"OLIVER QUEEN HAS NOTHING LEFT EXCEPT GREEN ARROW.
"SO WE'LL SIMPLY STEAL THAT AWAY...
"...BY TURNING SEATTLE AGAINST HIM."

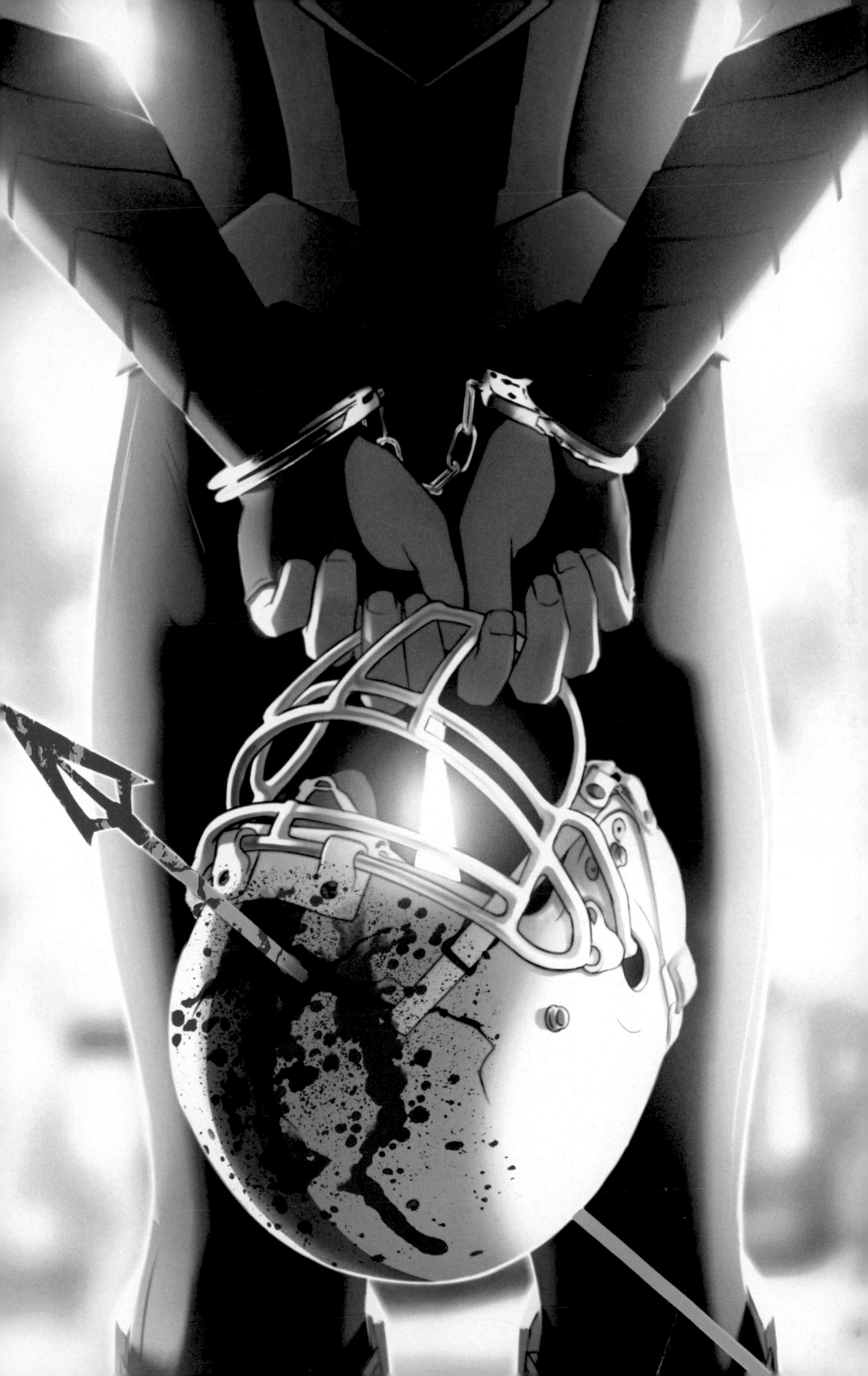

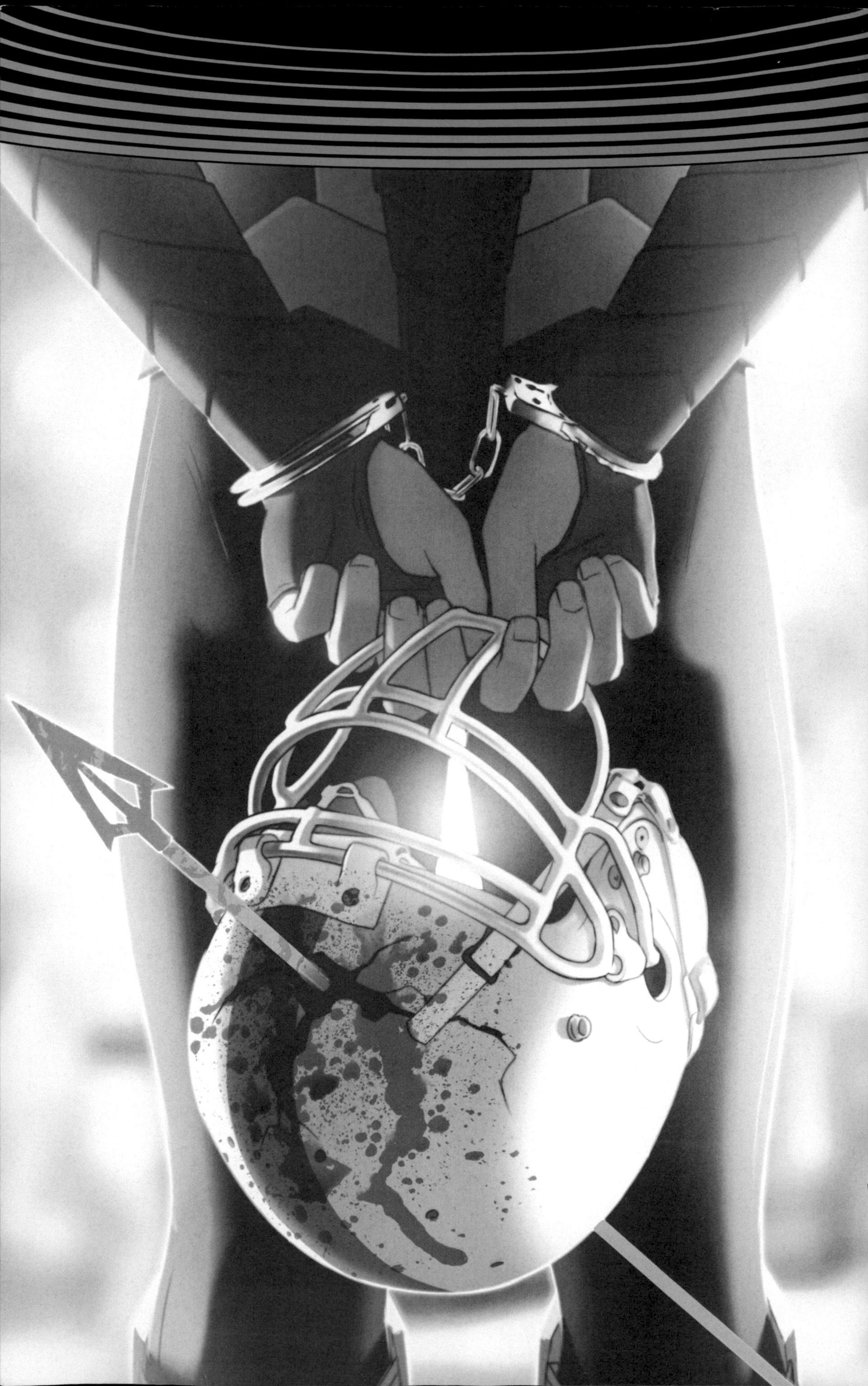

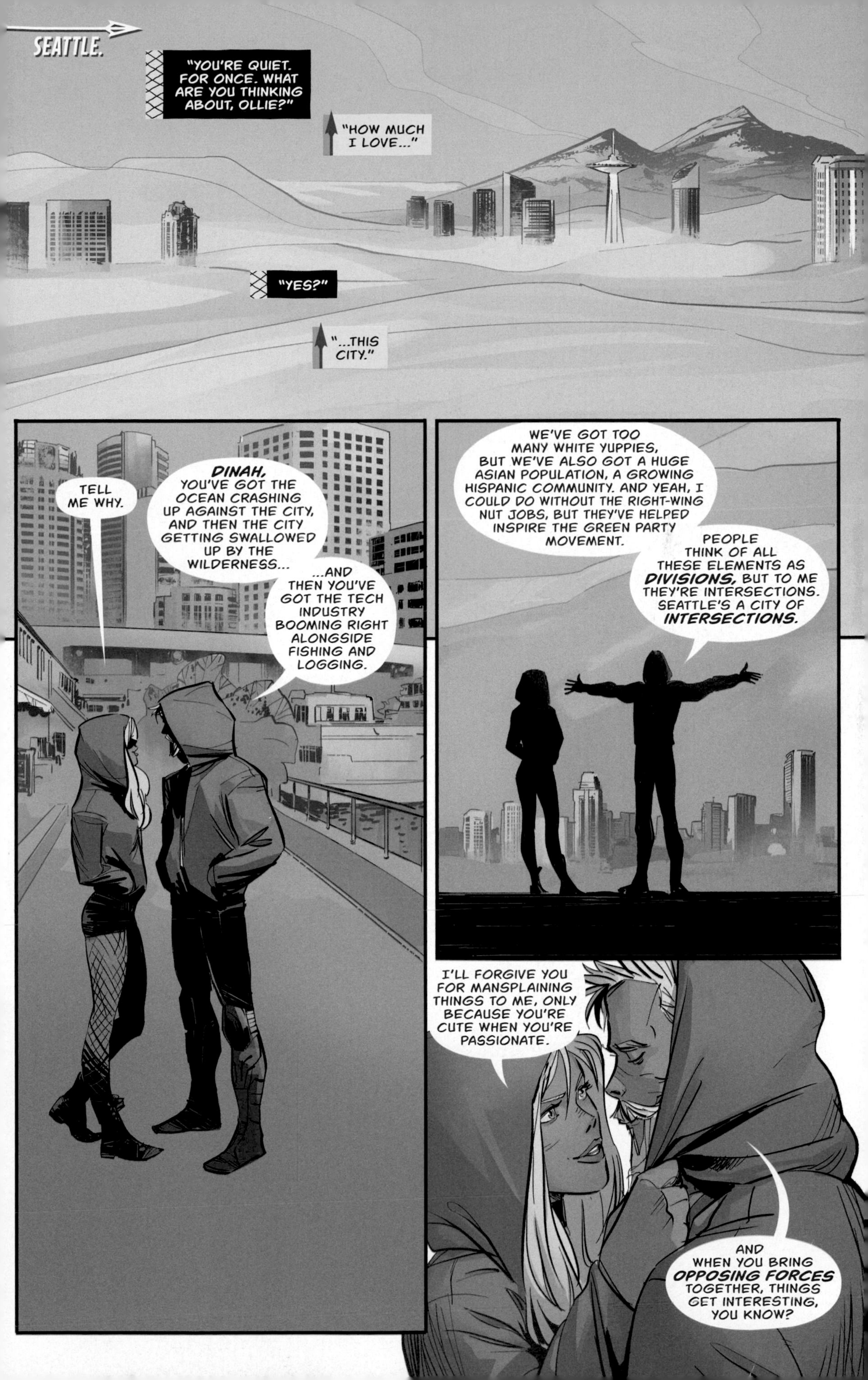
SEATTLE.
"YOU'RE QUIET. FOR ONCE. WHAT ARE YOU THINKING ABOUT, OLLIE?"
"HOW MUCH I LOVE..."
"YES?"
"...THIS CITY."
TELL ME WHY.
DINAH, YOU'VE GOT THE OCEAN CRASHING UP AGAINST THE CITY, AND THEN THE CITY GETTING SWALLOWED UP BY THE WILDERNESS...
...AND THEN YOU'VE GOT THE TECH INDUSTRY BOOMING RIGHT ALONGSIDE FISHING AND LOGGING.
WE'VE GOT TOO MANY WHITE YUPPIES, BUT WE'VE ALSO GOT A HUGE ASIAN POPULATION, A GROWING HISPANIC COMMUNITY. AND YEAH, I COULD DO WITHOUT THE RIGHT-WING NUT JOBS, BUT THEY'VE HELPED INSPIRE THE GREEN PARTY MOVEMENT.
PEOPLE THINK OF ALL THESE ELEMENTS AS DIVISIONS, BUT TO ME THEY'RE INTERSECTIONS. SEATTLE'S A CITY OF INTERSECTIONS.
I'LL FORGIVE YOU FOR MANSPLAINING THINGS TO ME, ONLY BECAUSE YOU'RE CUTE WHEN YOU'RE PASSIONATE.
AND WHEN YOU BRING OPPOSING FORCES TOGETHER, THINGS GET INTERESTING, YOU KNOW?

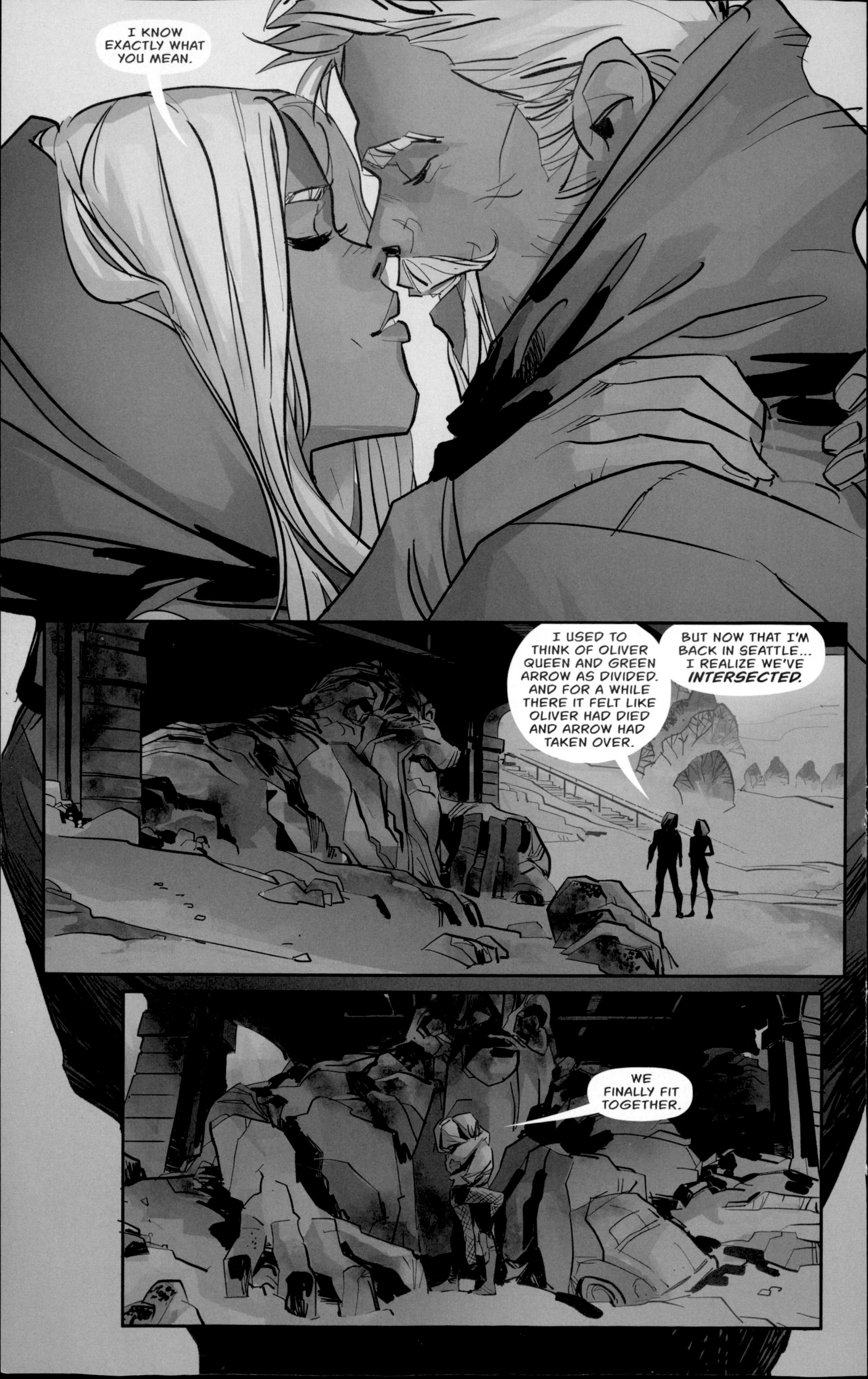
I KNOW EXACTLY WHAT YOU MEAN.
I USED TO THINK OF OLIVER QUEEN AND GREEN ARROW AS DIVIDED. AND FOR A WHILE THERE IT FELT LIKE OLIVER HAD DIED AND ARROW HAD TAKEN OVER.
BUT NOW THAT I'M BACK IN SEATTLE... I REALIZE WE'VE *INTERSECTED.*
WE FINALLY FIT TOGETHER.

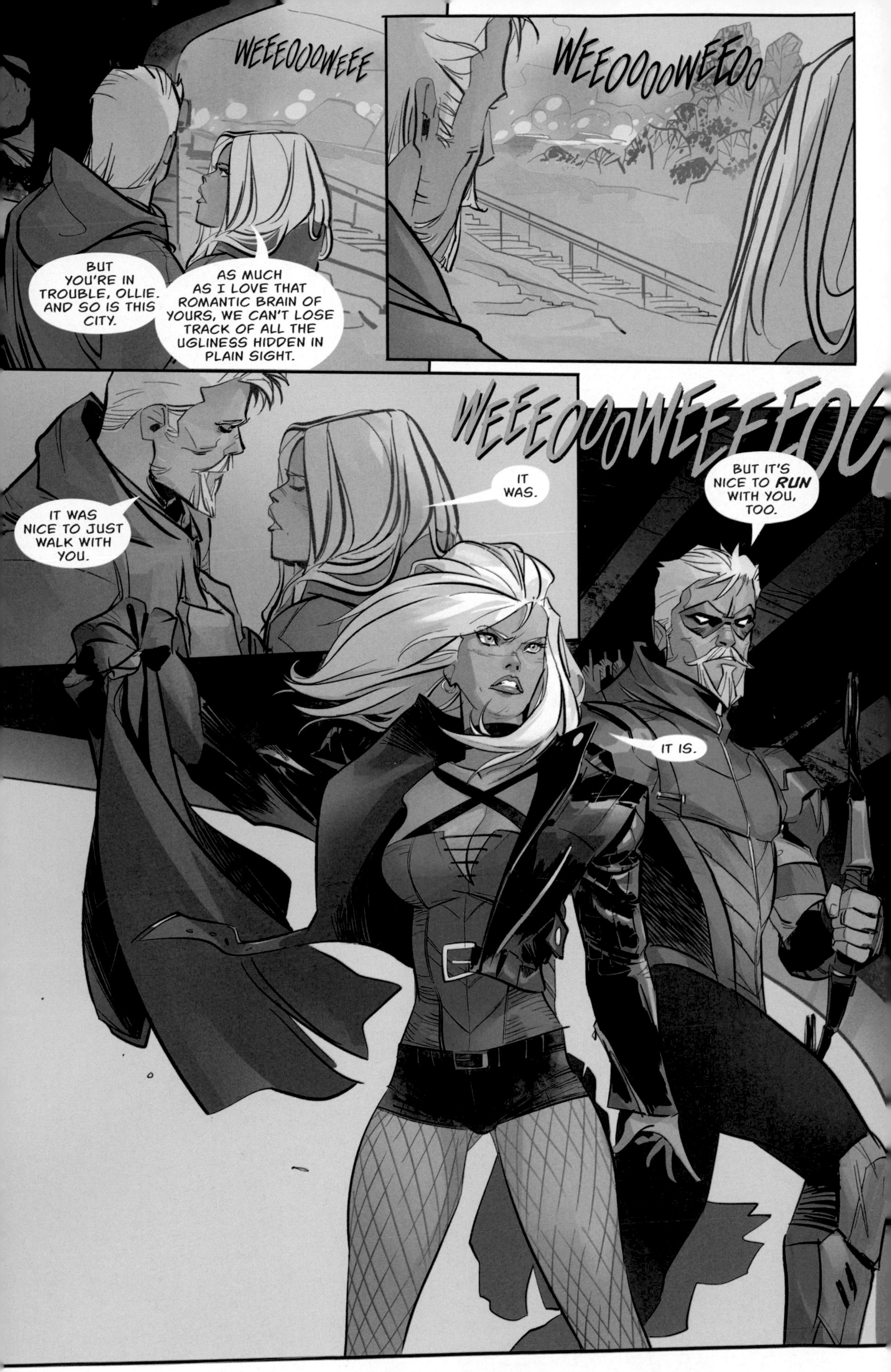
WEEEOOOWEEE
BUT YOU'RE IN TROUBLE, OLLIE. AND SO IS THIS CITY.
AS MUCH AS I LOVE THAT ROMANTIC BRAIN OF YOURS, WE CAN'T LOSE TRACK OF ALL THE UGLINESS HIDDEN IN PLAIN SIGHT.
WEEOOOOWEEOo
WEEEOOOWEEEOO
IT WAS NICE TO JUST WALK WITH YOU.
IT WAS.
BUT IT'S NICE TO **RUN** WITH YOU, TOO.
IT IS.

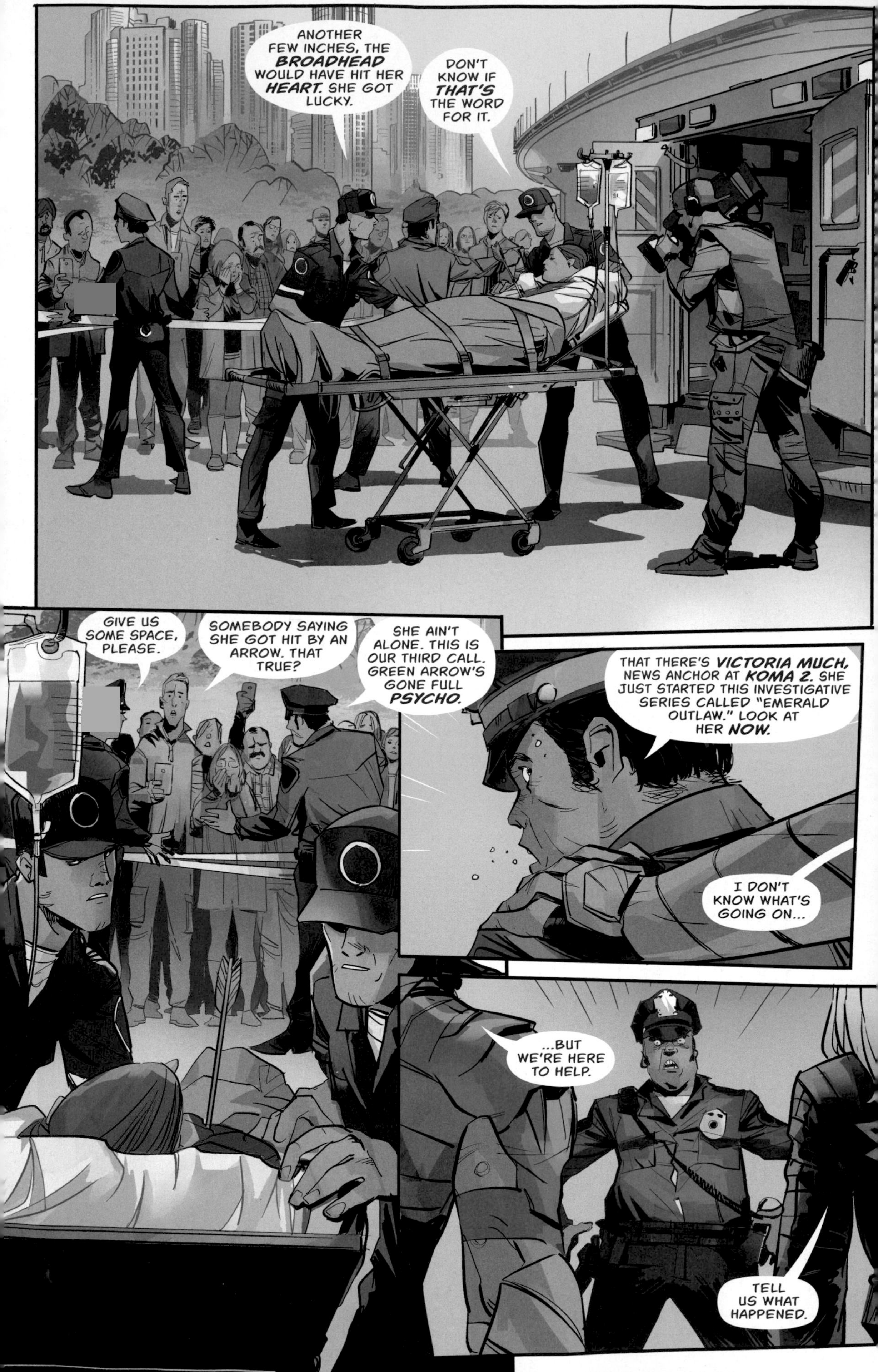

ANOTHER FEW INCHES, THE BROADHEAD WOULD HAVE HIT HER HEART. SHE GOT LUCKY.
DON'T KNOW IF THAT'S THE WORD FOR IT.
GIVE US SOME SPACE, PLEASE.
SOMEBODY SAYING SHE GOT HIT BY AN ARROW. THAT TRUE?
SHE AIN'T ALONE. THIS IS OUR THIRD CALL. GREEN ARROW'S GONE FULL PSYCHO.
THAT THERE'S VICTORIA MUCH, NEWS ANCHOR AT KOMA 2. SHE JUST STARTED THIS INVESTIGATIVE SERIES CALLED "EMERALD OUTLAW." LOOK AT HER NOW.
I DON'T KNOW WHAT'S GOING ON...
...BUT WE'RE HERE TO HELP.
TELL US WHAT HAPPENED.

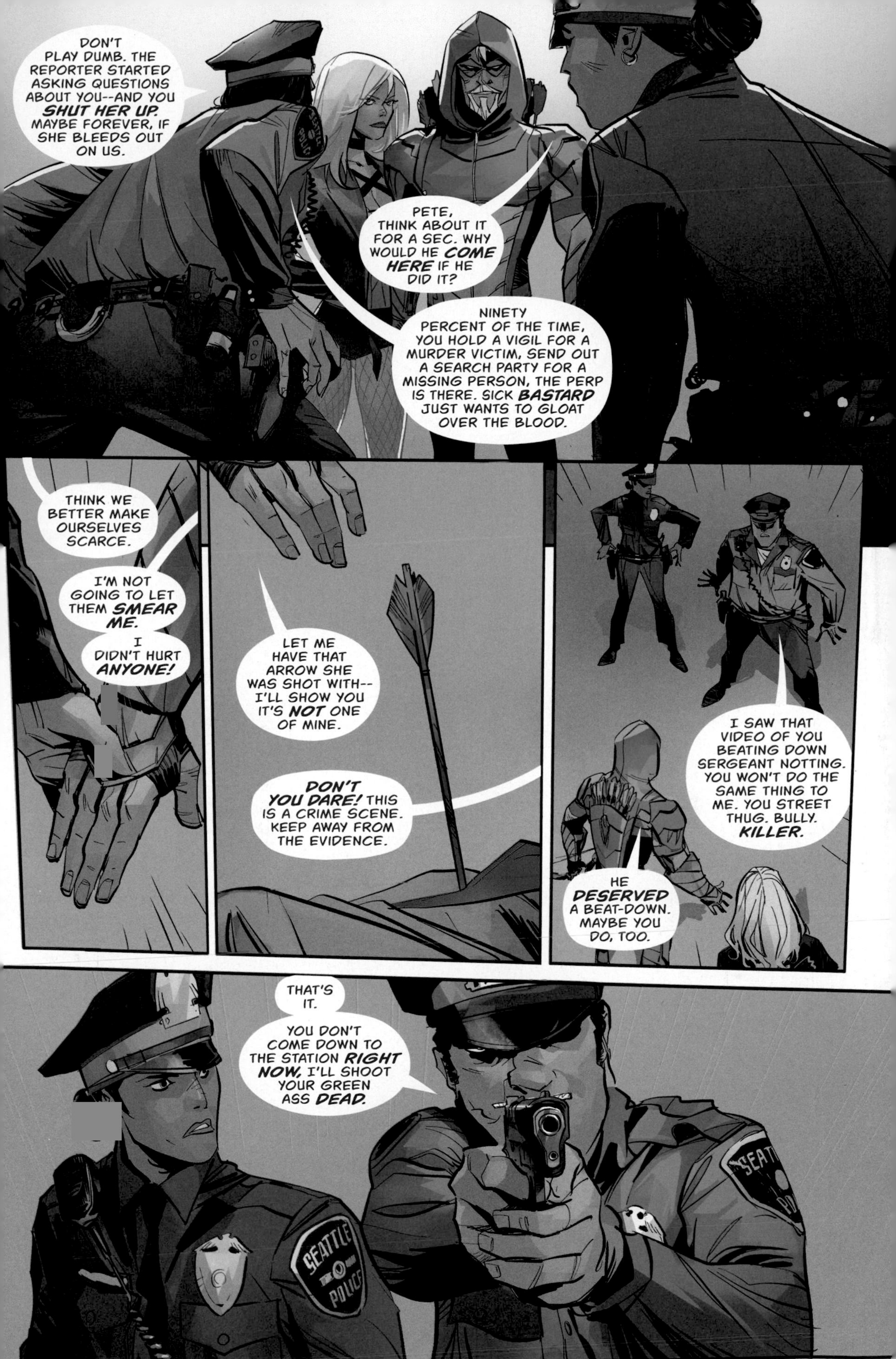
DON'T PLAY DUMB. THE REPORTER STARTED ASKING QUESTIONS ABOUT YOU--AND YOU SHUT HER UP. MAYBE FOREVER, IF SHE BLEEDS OUT ON US.
PETE, THINK ABOUT IT FOR A SEC. WHY WOULD HE COME HERE IF HE DID IT?
NINETY PERCENT OF THE TIME, YOU HOLD A VIGIL FOR A MURDER VICTIM, SEND OUT A SEARCH PARTY FOR A MISSING PERSON, THE PERP IS THERE. SICK BASTARD JUST WANTS TO GLOAT OVER THE BLOOD.
THINK WE BETTER MAKE OURSELVES SCARCE.
I'M NOT GOING TO LET THEM SMEAR ME.
I DIDN'T HURT ANYONE!
LET ME HAVE THAT ARROW SHE WAS SHOT WITH-- I'LL SHOW YOU IT'S NOT ONE OF MINE.
DON'T YOU DARE! THIS IS A CRIME SCENE. KEEP AWAY FROM THE EVIDENCE.
I SAW THAT VIDEO OF YOU BEATING DOWN SERGEANT NOTTING. YOU WON'T DO THE SAME THING TO ME. YOU STREET THUG. BULLY. KILLER.
HE DESERVED A BEAT-DOWN. MAYBE YOU DO, TOO.
THAT'S IT.
YOU DON'T COME DOWN TO THE STATION RIGHT NOW, I'LL SHOOT YOUR GREEN ASS DEAD.

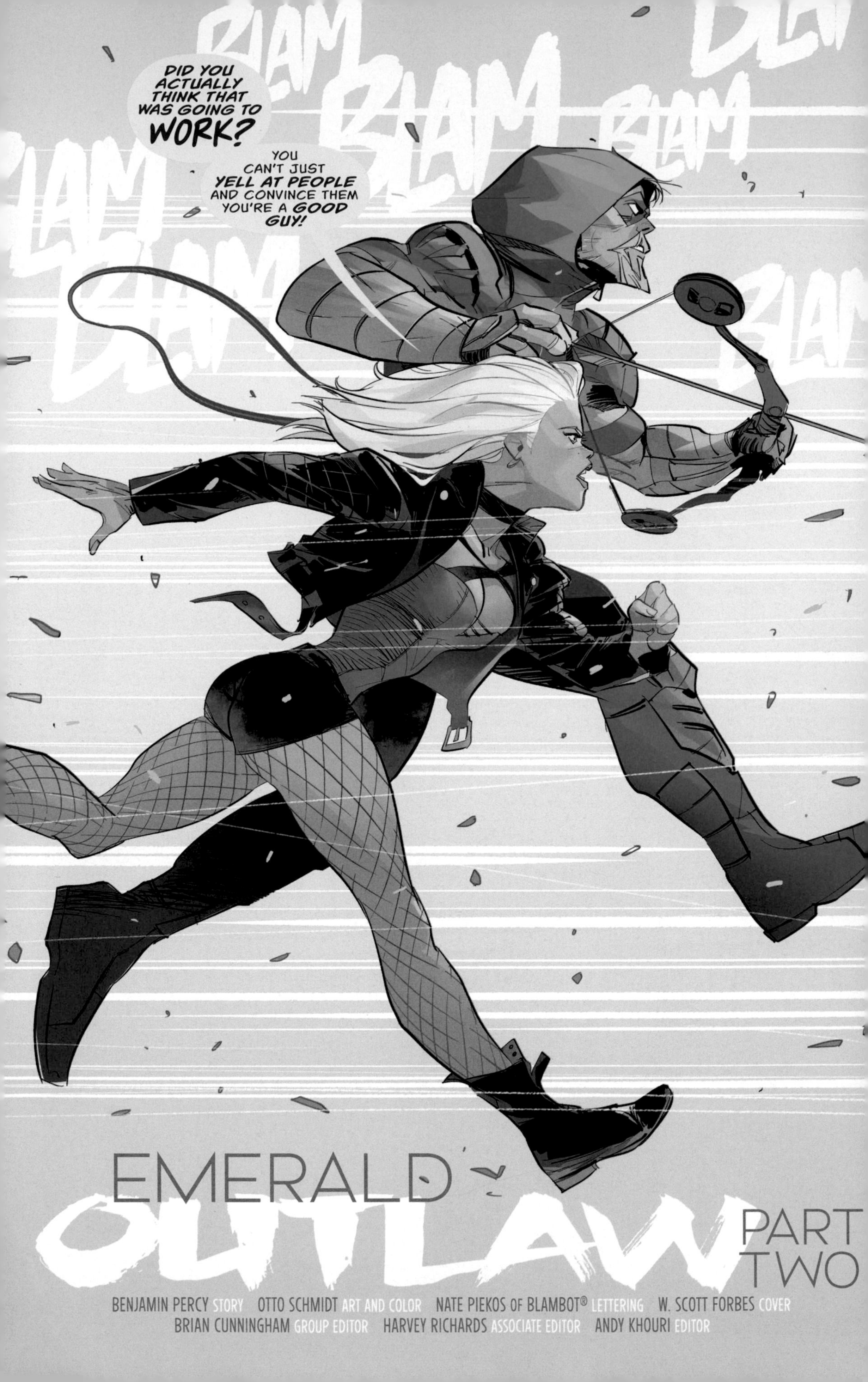
BLAM BLAM BLAM BLAM BLAM BLAM BLAM
DID YOU ACTUALLY THINK THAT WAS GOING TO WORK?
YOU CAN'T JUST YELL AT PEOPLE AND CONVINCE THEM YOU'RE A GOOD GUY!
EMERALD OUTLAW PART TWO
BENJAMIN PERCY STORY OTTO SCHMIDT ART AND COLOR NATE PIEKOS OF BLAMBOT® LETTERING W. SCOTT FORBES COVER
BRIAN CUNNINGHAM GROUP EDITOR HARVEY RICHARDS ASSOCIATE EDITOR ANDY KHOURI EDITOR

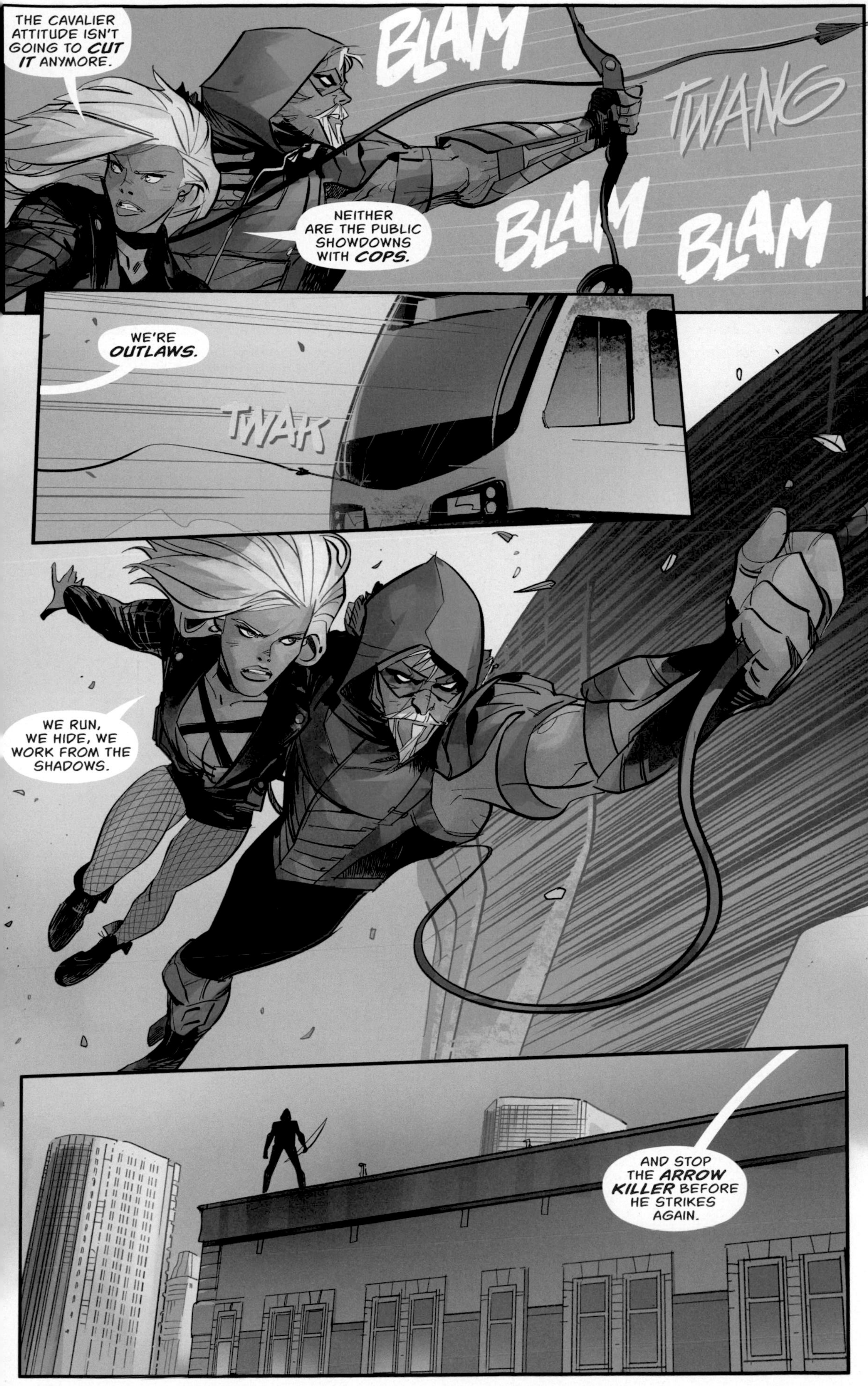
THE CAVALIER ATTITUDE ISN'T GOING TO CUT IT ANYMORE.
BLAM
TWANG
NEITHER ARE THE PUBLIC SHOWDOWNS WITH COPS.
BLAM
BLAM
WE'RE OUTLAWS.
TWAK
WE RUN, WE HIDE, WE WORK FROM THE SHADOWS.
AND STOP THE ARROW KILLER BEFORE HE STRIKES AGAIN.

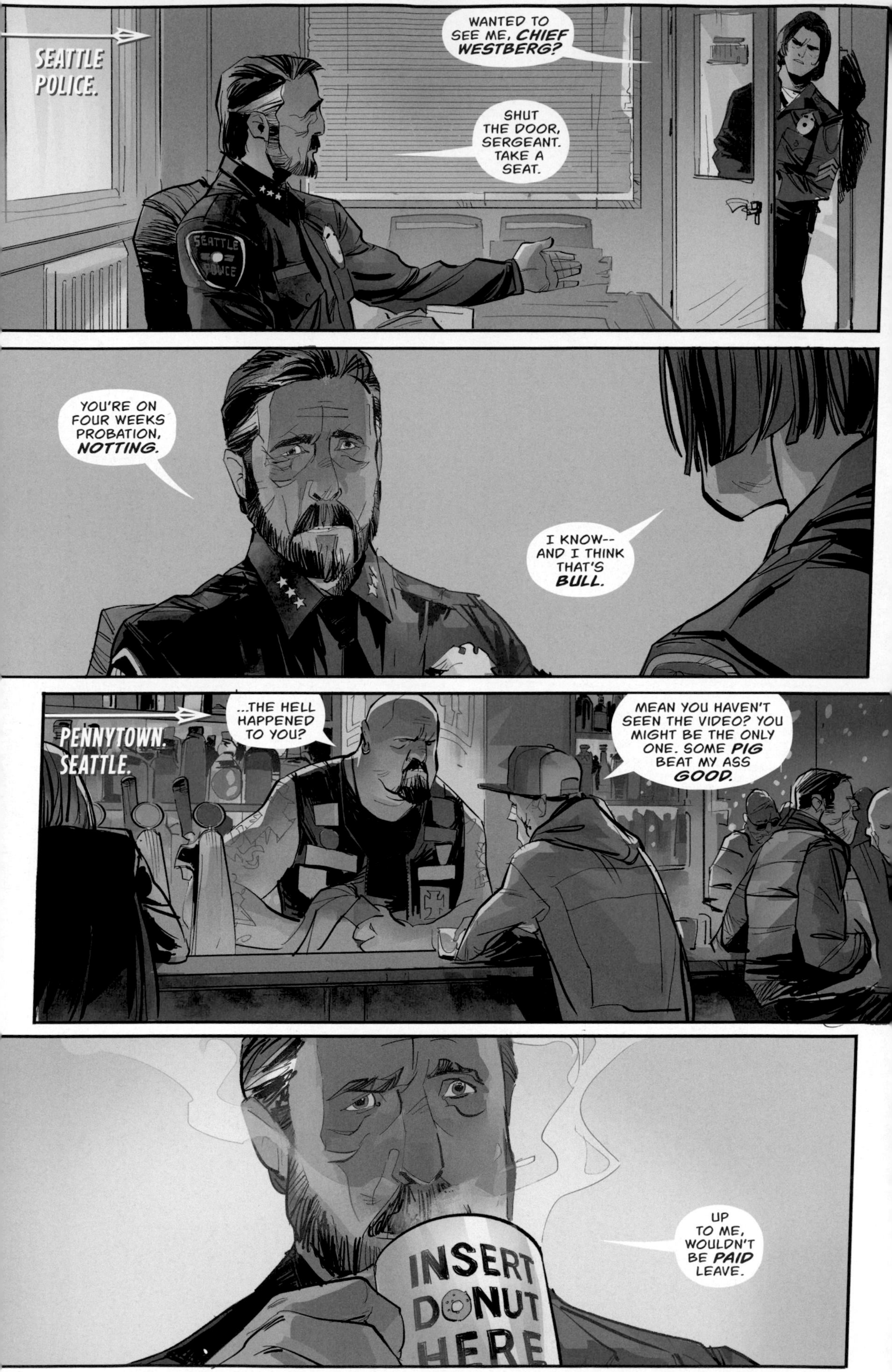
SEATTLE POLICE.
WANTED TO SEE ME, CHIEF WESTBERG?
SHUT THE DOOR, SERGEANT. TAKE A SEAT.
SEATTLE POLICE
YOU'RE ON FOUR WEEKS PROBATION, NOTTING.
I KNOW-- AND I THINK THAT'S BULL.
PENNYTOWN. SEATTLE.
...THE HELL HAPPENED TO YOU?
MEAN YOU HAVEN'T SEEN THE VIDEO? YOU MIGHT BE THE ONLY ONE. SOME PIG BEAT MY ASS GOOD.
UP TO ME, WOULDN'T BE PAID LEAVE.
INSERT DONUT HERE

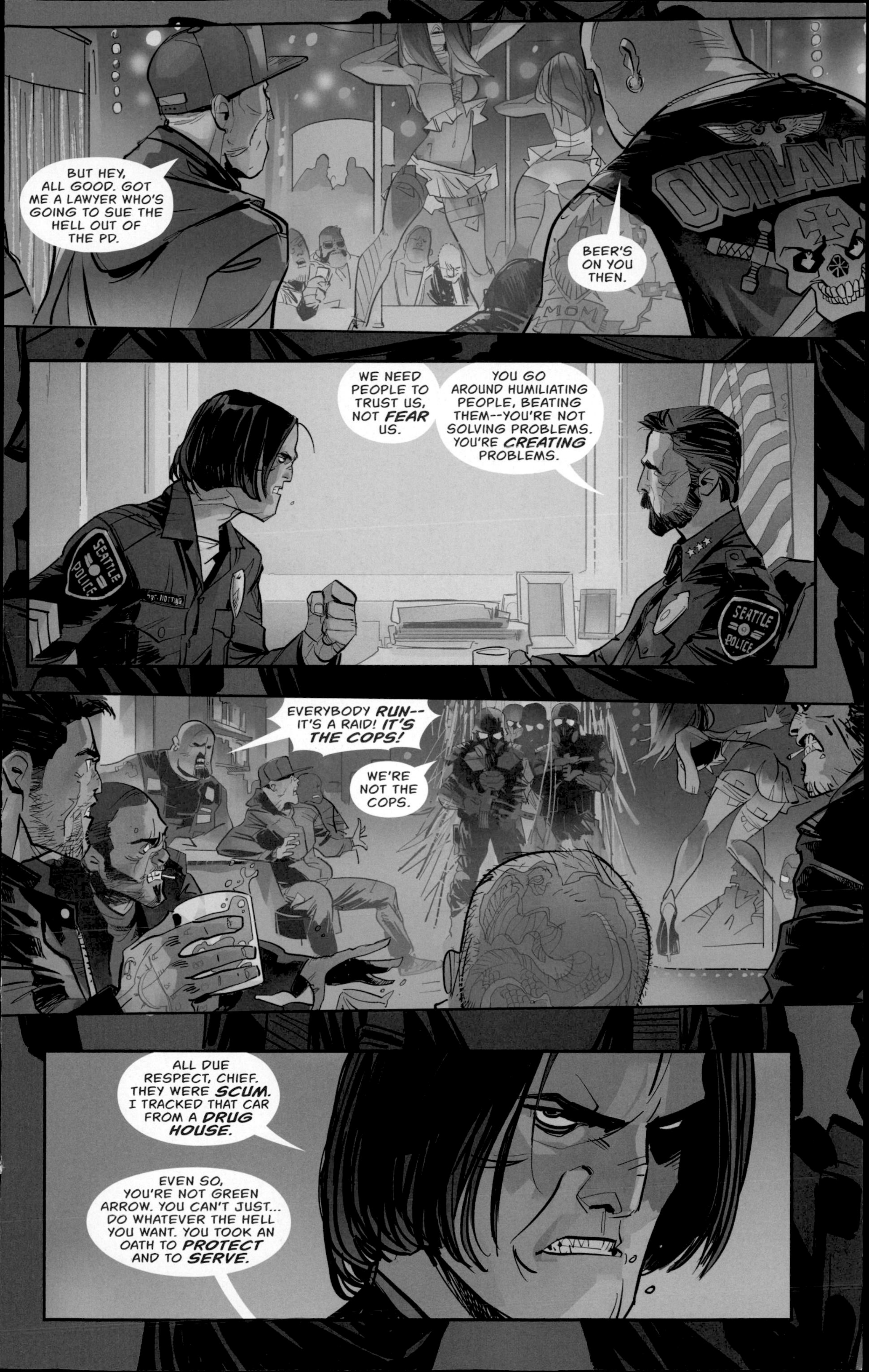

BUT HEY, ALL GOOD. GOT ME A LAWYER WHO'S GOING TO SUE THE HELL OUT OF THE PD.
BEER'S ON YOU THEN.
OUTLAWS
MOM
WE NEED PEOPLE TO TRUST US, NOT FEAR US.
YOU GO AROUND HUMILIATING PEOPLE, BEATING THEM--YOU'RE NOT SOLVING PROBLEMS. YOU'RE CREATING PROBLEMS.
SEATTLE POLICE
SEATTLE POLICE
EVERYBODY RUN-- IT'S A RAID! IT'S THE COPS!
WE'RE NOT THE COPS.
ALL DUE RESPECT, CHIEF. THEY WERE SCUM. I TRACKED THAT CAR FROM A DRUG HOUSE.
EVEN SO, YOU'RE NOT GREEN ARROW. YOU CAN'T JUST... DO WHATEVER THE HELL YOU WANT. YOU TOOK AN OATH TO PROTECT AND TO SERVE.

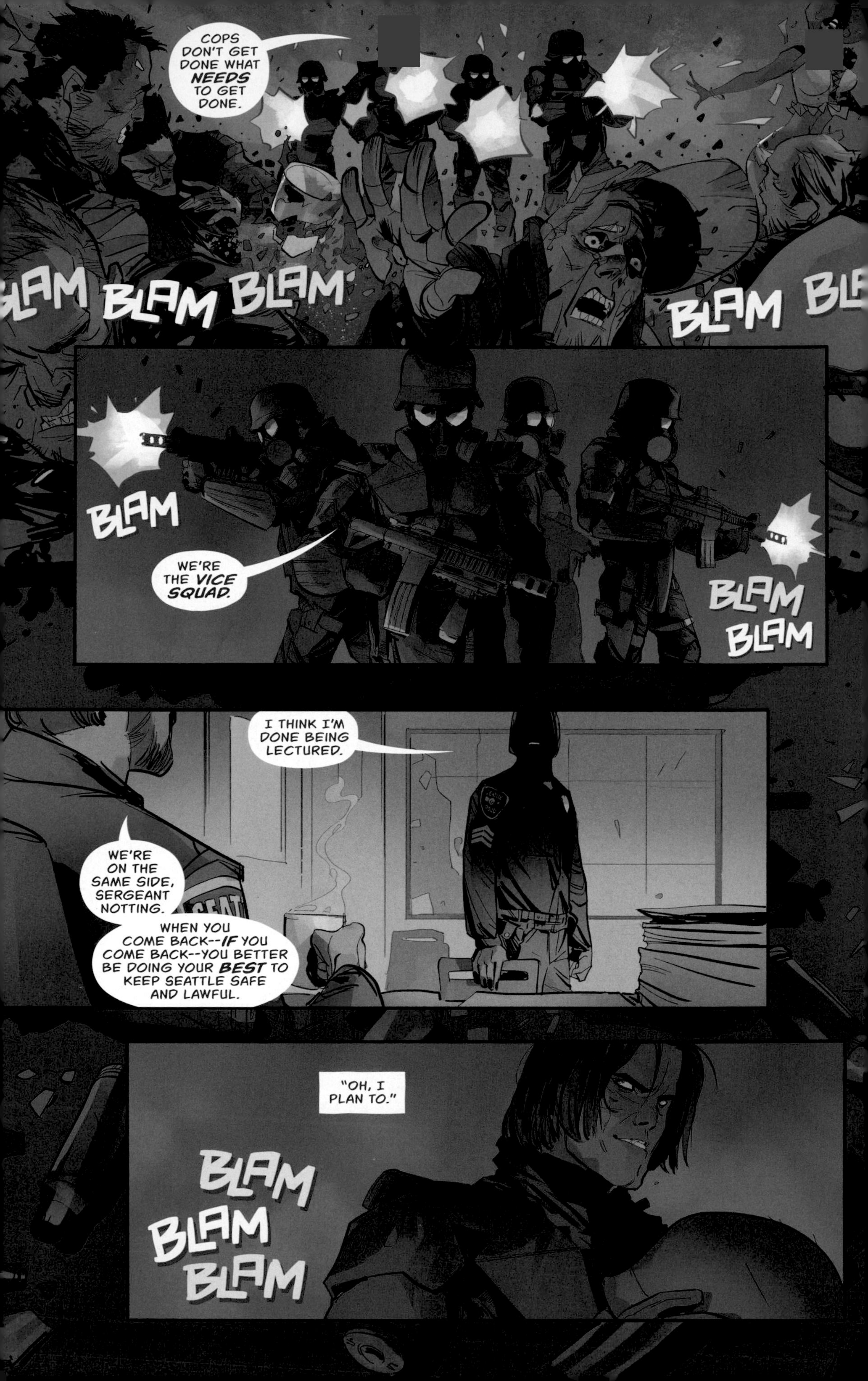
COPS DON'T GET DONE WHAT NEEDS TO GET DONE.
BLAM BLAM BLAM
BLAM
BLAM
WE'RE THE VICE SQUAD.
BLAM BLAM
I THINK I'M DONE BEING LECTURED.
WE'RE ON THE SAME SIDE, SERGEANT NOTTING.
WHEN YOU COME BACK--IF YOU COME BACK--YOU BETTER BE DOING YOUR BEST TO KEEP SEATTLE SAFE AND LAWFUL.
"OH, I PLAN TO."
BLAM BLAM BLAM

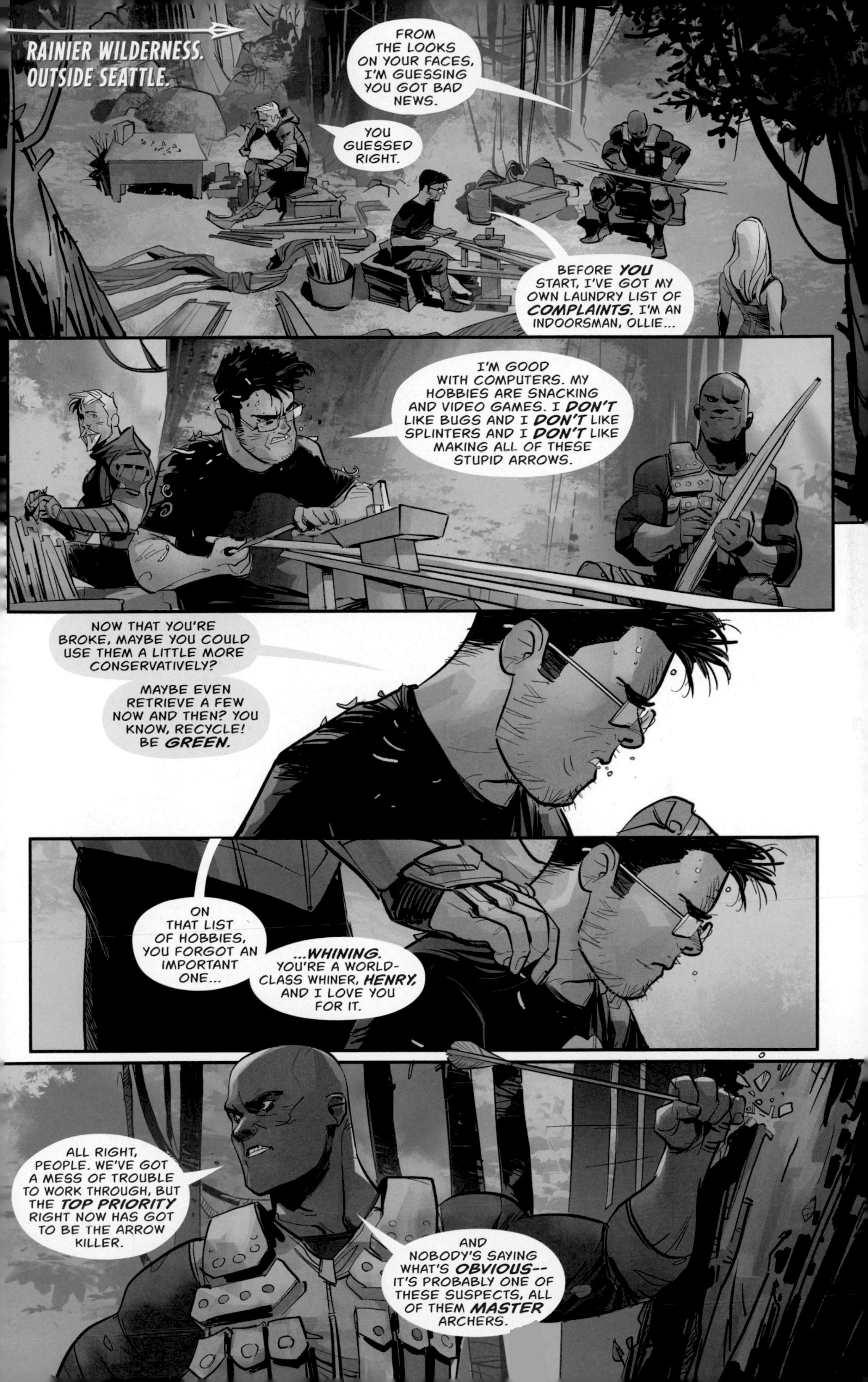
RAINIER WILDERNESS. OUTSIDE SEATTLE.
FROM THE LOOKS ON YOUR FACES, I'M GUESSING YOU GOT BAD NEWS.
YOU GUESSED RIGHT.
BEFORE YOU START, I'VE GOT MY OWN LAUNDRY LIST OF COMPLAINTS. I'M AN INDOORSMAN, OLLIE...
I'M GOOD WITH COMPUTERS. MY HOBBIES ARE SNACKING AND VIDEO GAMES. I DON'T LIKE BUGS AND I DON'T LIKE SPLINTERS AND I DON'T LIKE MAKING ALL OF THESE STUPID ARROWS.
NOW THAT YOU'RE BROKE, MAYBE YOU COULD USE THEM A LITTLE MORE CONSERVATIVELY?
MAYBE EVEN RETRIEVE A FEW NOW AND THEN? YOU KNOW, RECYCLE! BE GREEN.
ON THAT LIST OF HOBBIES, YOU FORGOT AN IMPORTANT ONE...
...WHINING. YOU'RE A WORLD-CLASS WHINER, HENRY, AND I LOVE YOU FOR IT.
ALL RIGHT, PEOPLE. WE'VE GOT A MESS OF TROUBLE TO WORK THROUGH, BUT THE TOP PRIORITY RIGHT NOW HAS GOT TO BE THE ARROW KILLER.
AND NOBODY'S SAYING WHAT'S OBVIOUS-- IT'S PROBABLY ONE OF THESE SUSPECTS, ALL OF THEM MASTER ARCHERS.

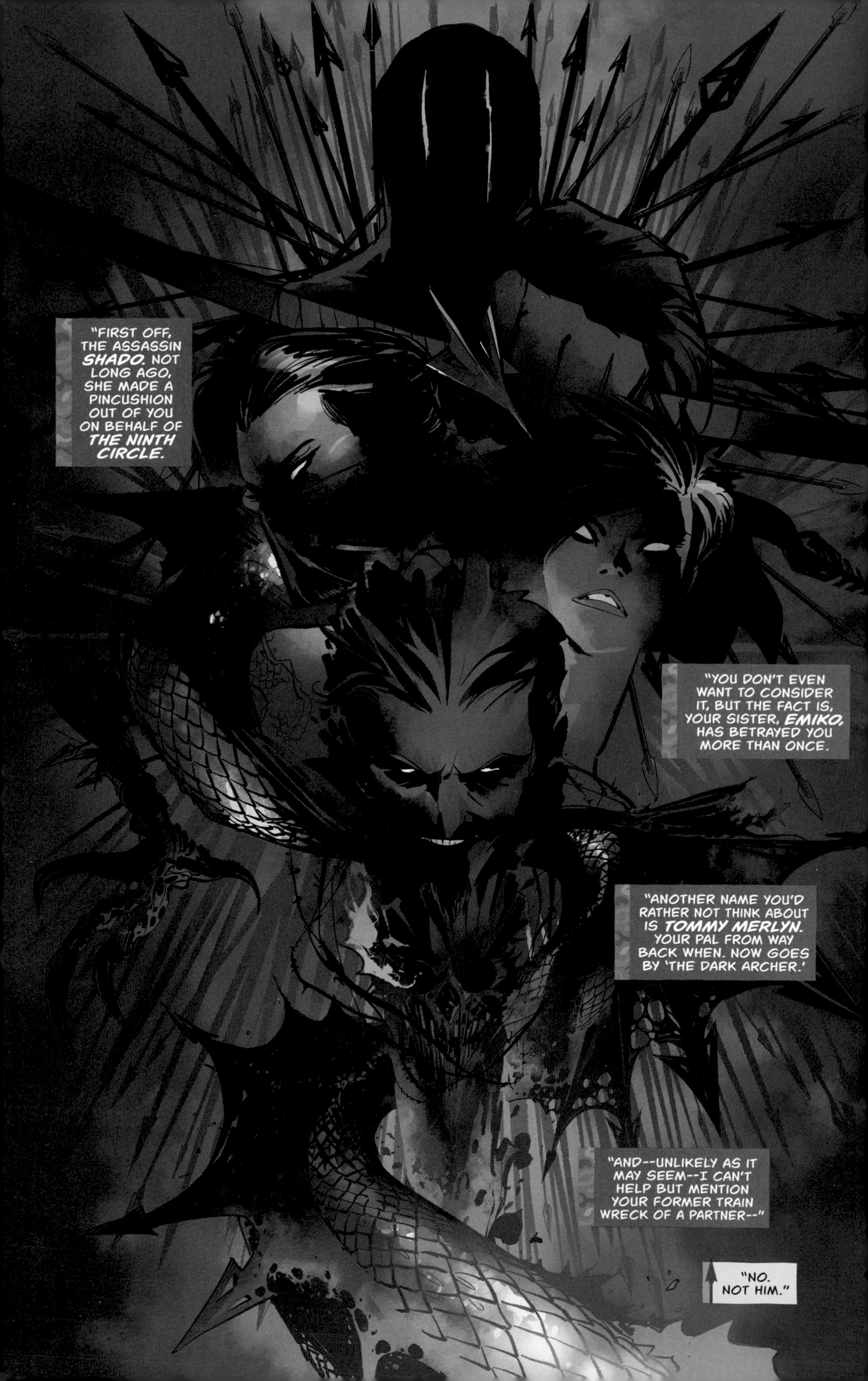
"FIRST OFF, THE ASSASSIN SHADO. NOT LONG AGO, SHE MADE A PINCUSHION OUT OF YOU ON BEHALF OF THE NINTH CIRCLE.
"YOU DON'T EVEN WANT TO CONSIDER IT, BUT THE FACT IS, YOUR SISTER, EMIKO, HAS BETRAYED YOU MORE THAN ONCE.
"ANOTHER NAME YOU'D RATHER NOT THINK ABOUT IS TOMMY MERLYN. YOUR PAL FROM WAY BACK WHEN. NOW GOES BY 'THE DARK ARCHER.'
"AND--UNLIKELY AS IT MAY SEEM--I CAN'T HELP BUT MENTION YOUR FORMER TRAIN WRECK OF A PARTNER--"
"NO. NOT HIM."

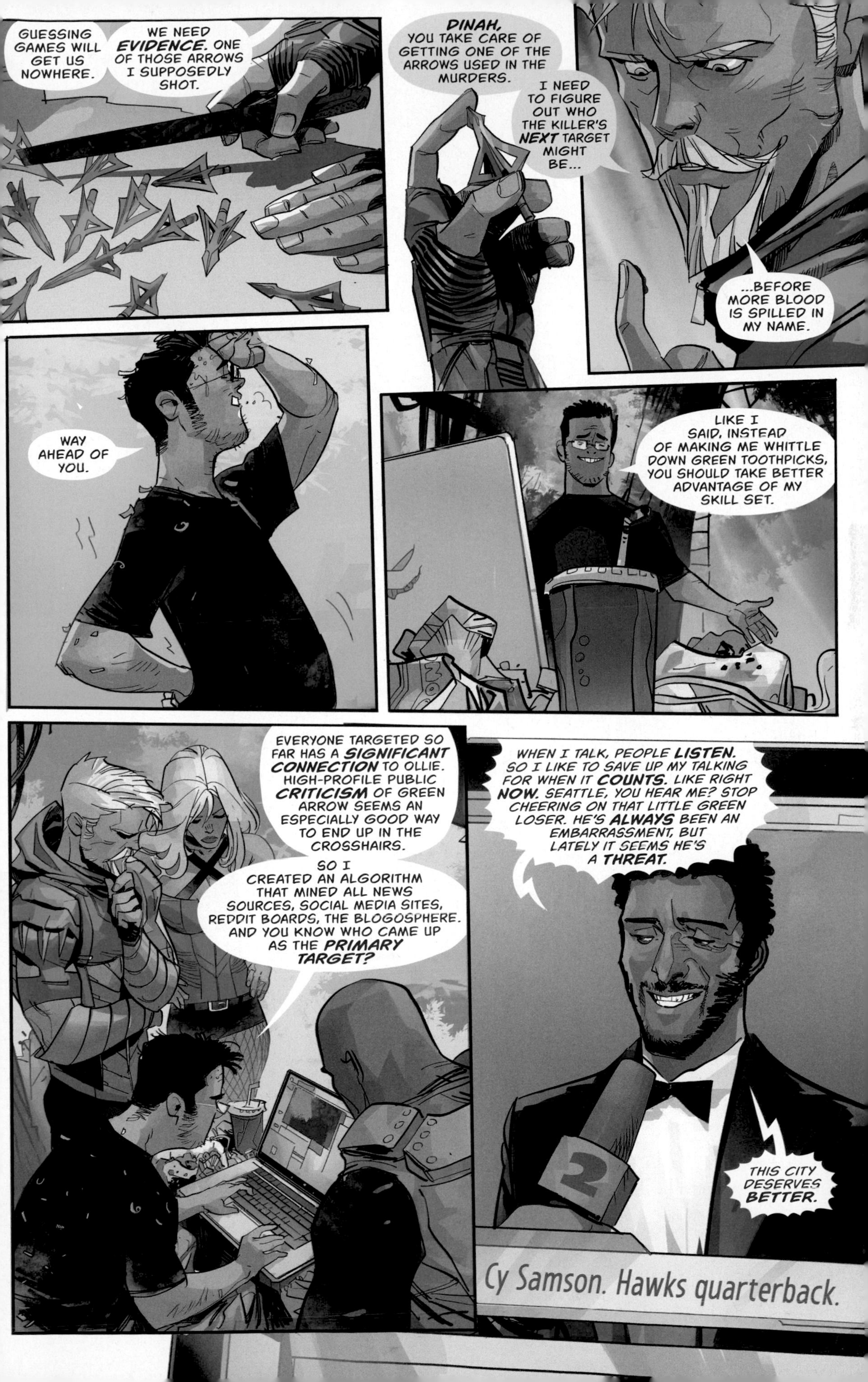
GUESSING GAMES WILL GET US NOWHERE.
WE NEED EVIDENCE. ONE OF THOSE ARROWS I SUPPOSEDLY SHOT.
DINAH, YOU TAKE CARE OF GETTING ONE OF THE ARROWS USED IN THE MURDERS.
I NEED TO FIGURE OUT WHO THE KILLER'S NEXT TARGET MIGHT BE...
...BEFORE MORE BLOOD IS SPILLED IN MY NAME.
WAY AHEAD OF YOU.
LIKE I SAID, INSTEAD OF MAKING ME WHITTLE DOWN GREEN TOOTHPICKS, YOU SHOULD TAKE BETTER ADVANTAGE OF MY SKILL SET.
EVERYONE TARGETED SO FAR HAS A SIGNIFICANT CONNECTION TO OLLIE. HIGH-PROFILE PUBLIC CRITICISM OF GREEN ARROW SEEMS AN ESPECIALLY GOOD WAY TO END UP IN THE CROSSHAIRS.
SO I CREATED AN ALGORITHM THAT MINED ALL NEWS SOURCES, SOCIAL MEDIA SITES, REDDIT BOARDS, THE BLOGOSPHERE. AND YOU KNOW WHO CAME UP AS THE PRIMARY TARGET?
WHEN I TALK, PEOPLE LISTEN. SO I LIKE TO SAVE UP MY TALKING FOR WHEN IT COUNTS. LIKE RIGHT NOW. SEATTLE, YOU HEAR ME? STOP CHEERING ON THAT LITTLE GREEN LOSER. HE'S ALWAYS BEEN AN EMBARRASSMENT, BUT LATELY IT SEEMS HE'S A THREAT.
THIS CITY DESERVES BETTER.
2
Cy Samson. Hawks quarterback.

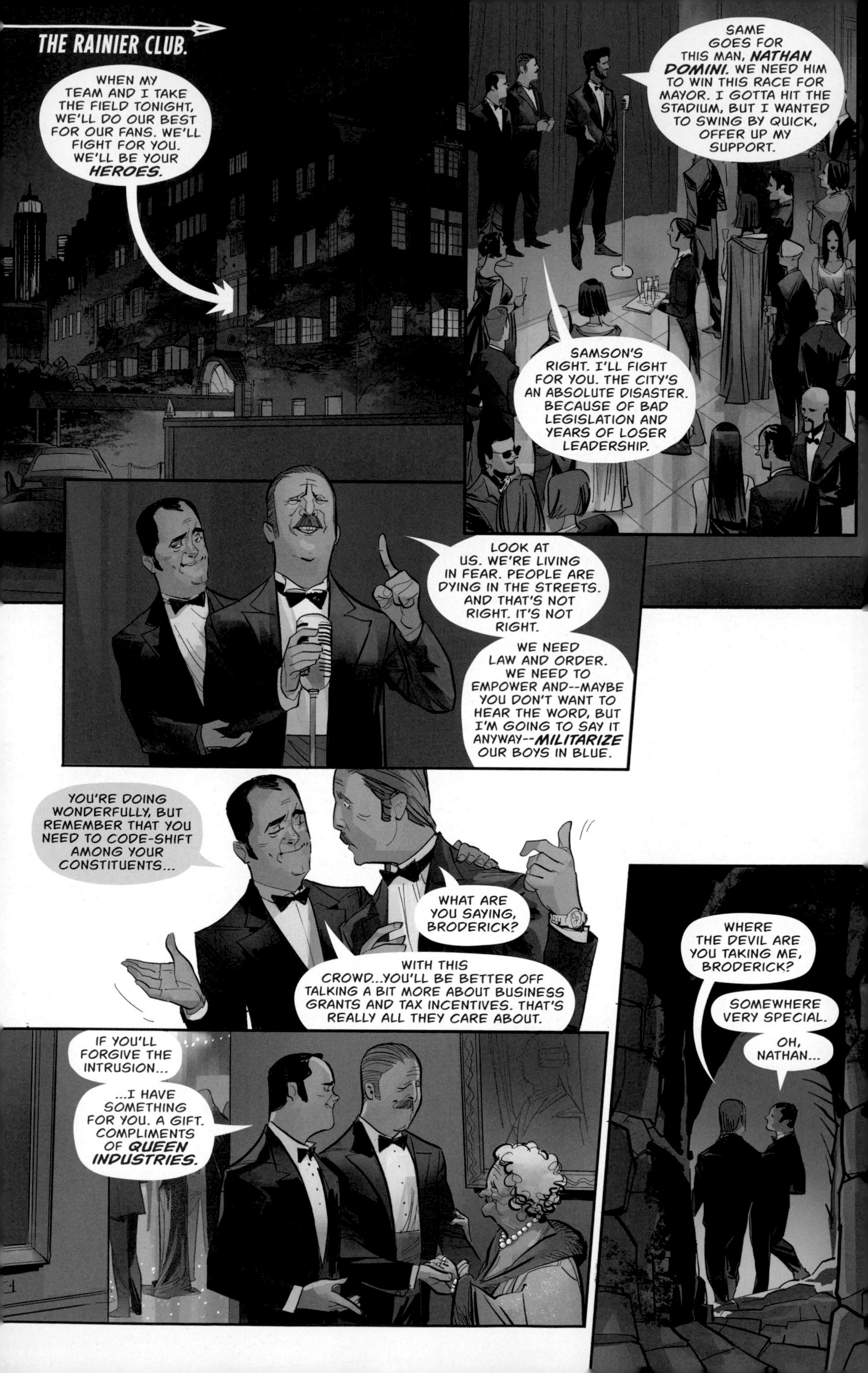
THE RAINIER CLUB.
WHEN MY TEAM AND I TAKE THE FIELD TONIGHT, WE'LL DO OUR BEST FOR OUR FANS. WE'LL FIGHT FOR YOU. WE'LL BE YOUR HEROES.
SAME GOES FOR THIS MAN, NATHAN DOMINI. WE NEED HIM TO WIN THIS RACE FOR MAYOR. I GOTTA HIT THE STADIUM, BUT I WANTED TO SWING BY QUICK, OFFER UP MY SUPPORT.
SAMSON'S RIGHT. I'LL FIGHT FOR YOU. THE CITY'S AN ABSOLUTE DISASTER. BECAUSE OF BAD LEGISLATION AND YEARS OF LOSER LEADERSHIP.
LOOK AT US. WE'RE LIVING IN FEAR. PEOPLE ARE DYING IN THE STREETS. AND THAT'S NOT RIGHT. IT'S NOT RIGHT.
WE NEED LAW AND ORDER. WE NEED TO EMPOWER AND--MAYBE YOU DON'T WANT TO HEAR THE WORD, BUT I'M GOING TO SAY IT ANYWAY--MILITARIZE OUR BOYS IN BLUE.
YOU'RE DOING WONDERFULLY, BUT REMEMBER THAT YOU NEED TO CODE-SHIFT AMONG YOUR CONSTITUENTS...
WHAT ARE YOU SAYING, BRODERICK?
WITH THIS CROWD...YOU'LL BE BETTER OFF TALKING A BIT MORE ABOUT BUSINESS GRANTS AND TAX INCENTIVES. THAT'S REALLY ALL THEY CARE ABOUT.
IF YOU'LL FORGIVE THE INTRUSION...
...I HAVE SOMETHING FOR YOU. A GIFT. COMPLIMENTS OF QUEEN INDUSTRIES.
WHERE THE DEVIL ARE YOU TAKING ME, BRODERICK?
SOMEWHERE VERY SPECIAL.
OH, NATHAN...

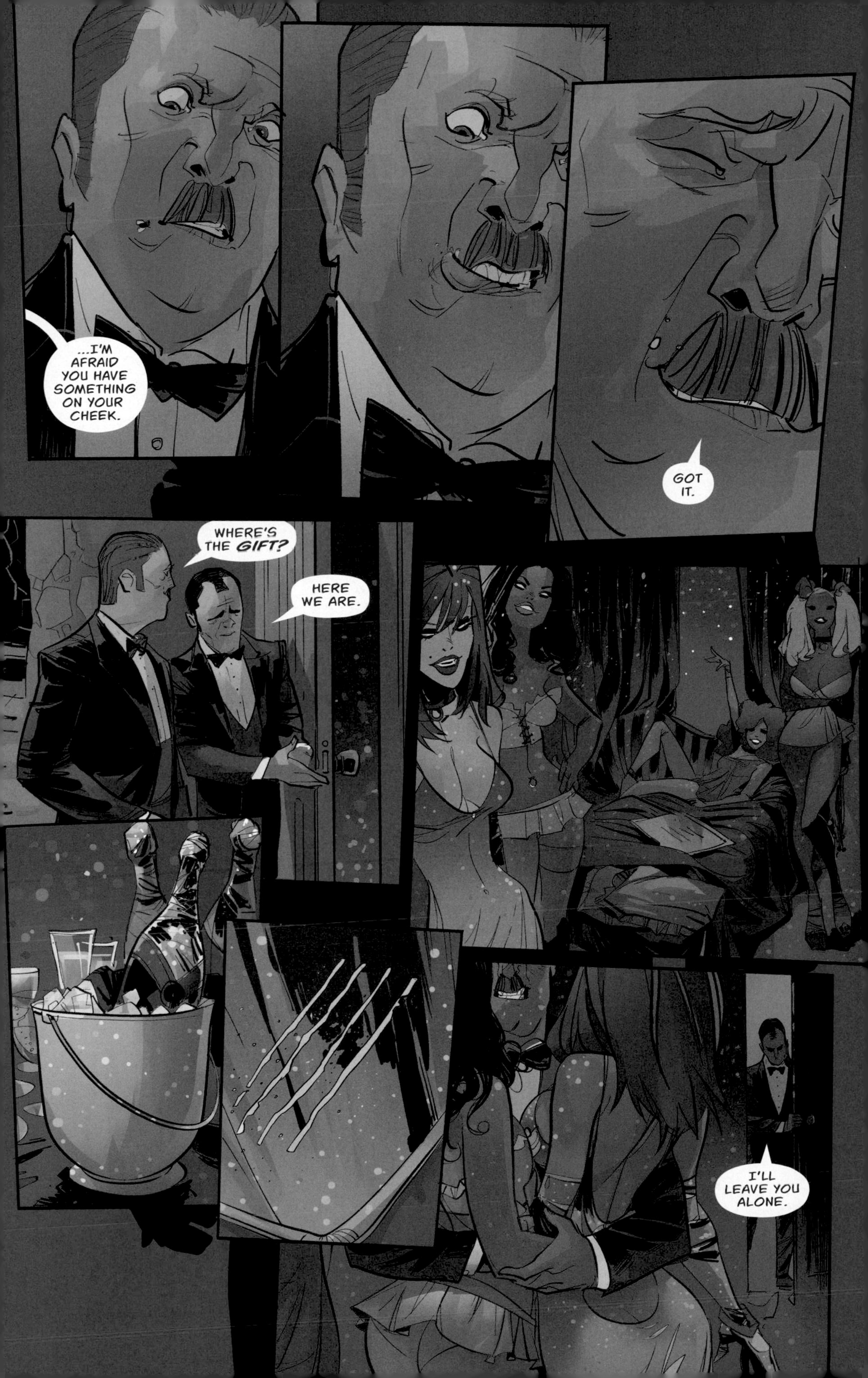
...I'M AFRAID YOU HAVE SOMETHING ON YOUR CHEEK.
GOT IT.
WHERE'S THE GIFT?
HERE WE ARE.
I'LL LEAVE YOU ALONE.

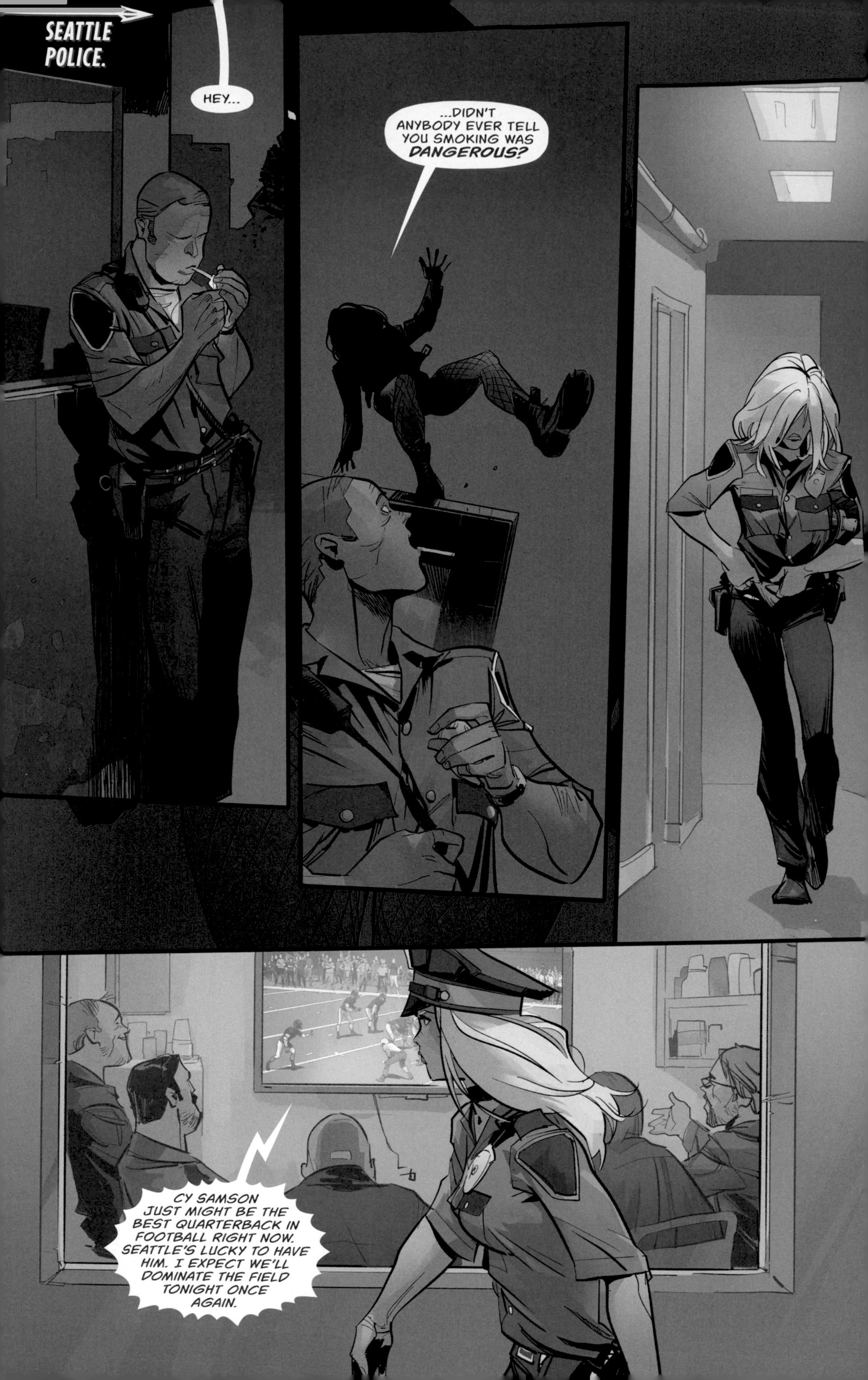
SEATTLE POLICE.
HEY...
...DIDN'T ANYBODY EVER TELL YOU SMOKING WAS DANGEROUS?
CY SAMSON JUST MIGHT BE THE BEST QUARTERBACK IN FOOTBALL RIGHT NOW. SEATTLE'S LUCKY TO HAVE HIM. I EXPECT WE'LL DOMINATE THE FIELD TONIGHT ONCE AGAIN.

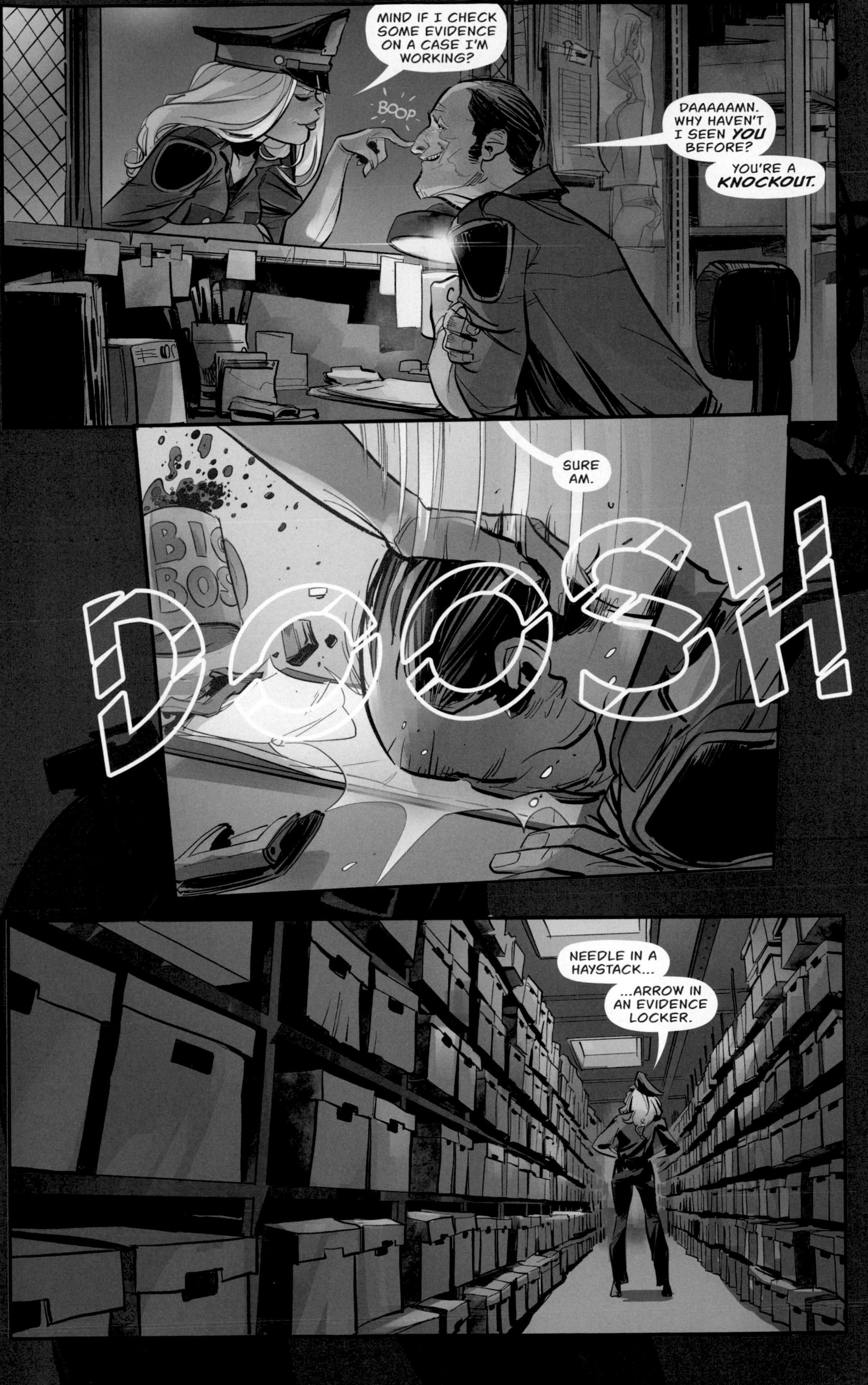
MIND IF I CHECK SOME EVIDENCE ON A CASE I'M WORKING?
BOOP
DAAAAAMN. WHY HAVEN'T I SEEN YOU BEFORE?
YOU'RE A KNOCKOUT.
SURE AM.
DOOSH!
NEEDLE IN A HAYSTACK...
...ARROW IN AN EVIDENCE LOCKER.

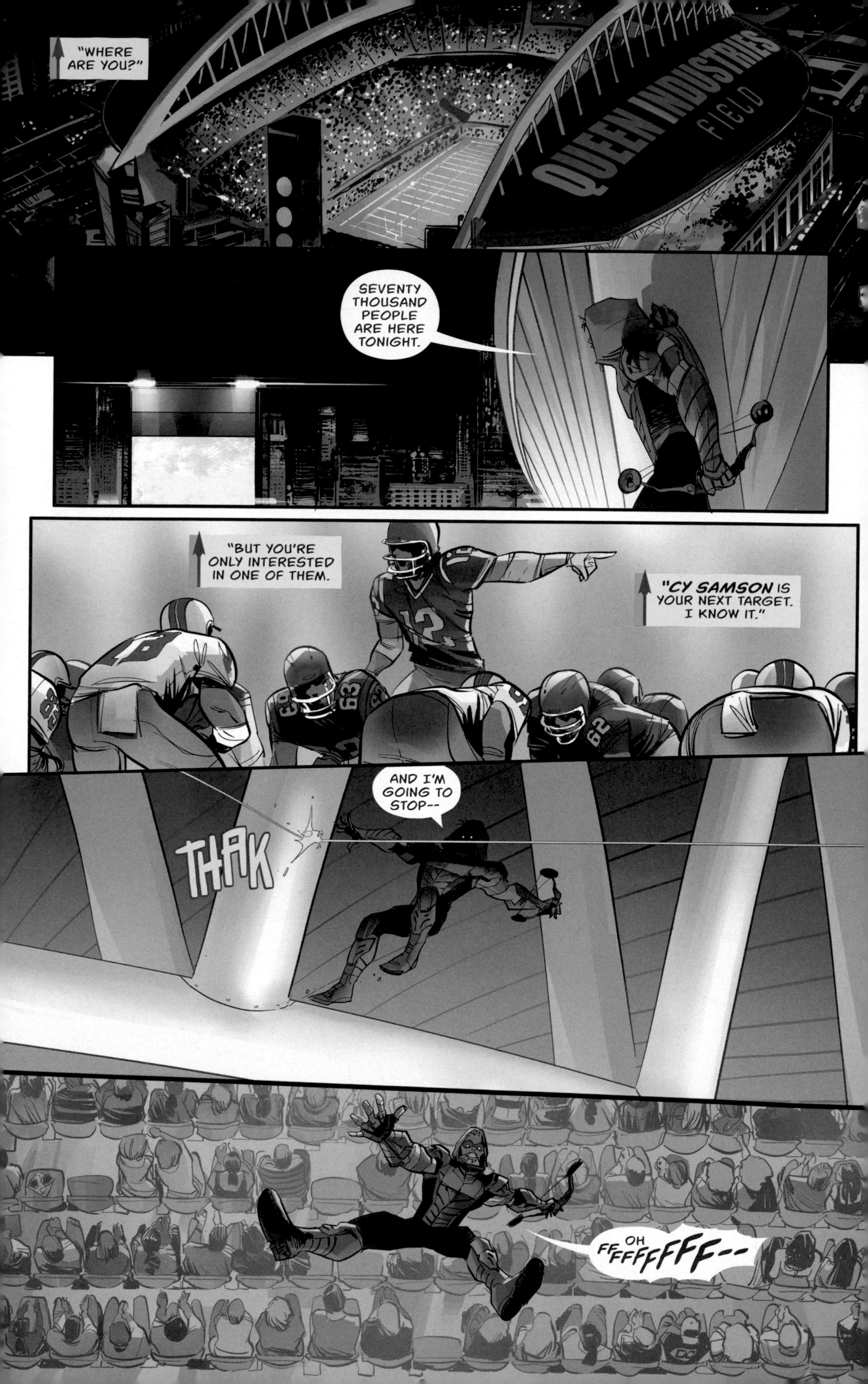
"WHERE ARE YOU?"
QUEEN INDUSTRIES FIELD
SEVENTY THOUSAND PEOPLE ARE HERE TONIGHT.
"BUT YOU'RE ONLY INTERESTED IN ONE OF THEM.
"CY SAMSON IS YOUR NEXT TARGET. I KNOW IT."
AND I'M GOING TO STOP--
THAK
OH FFFFFFFFF--

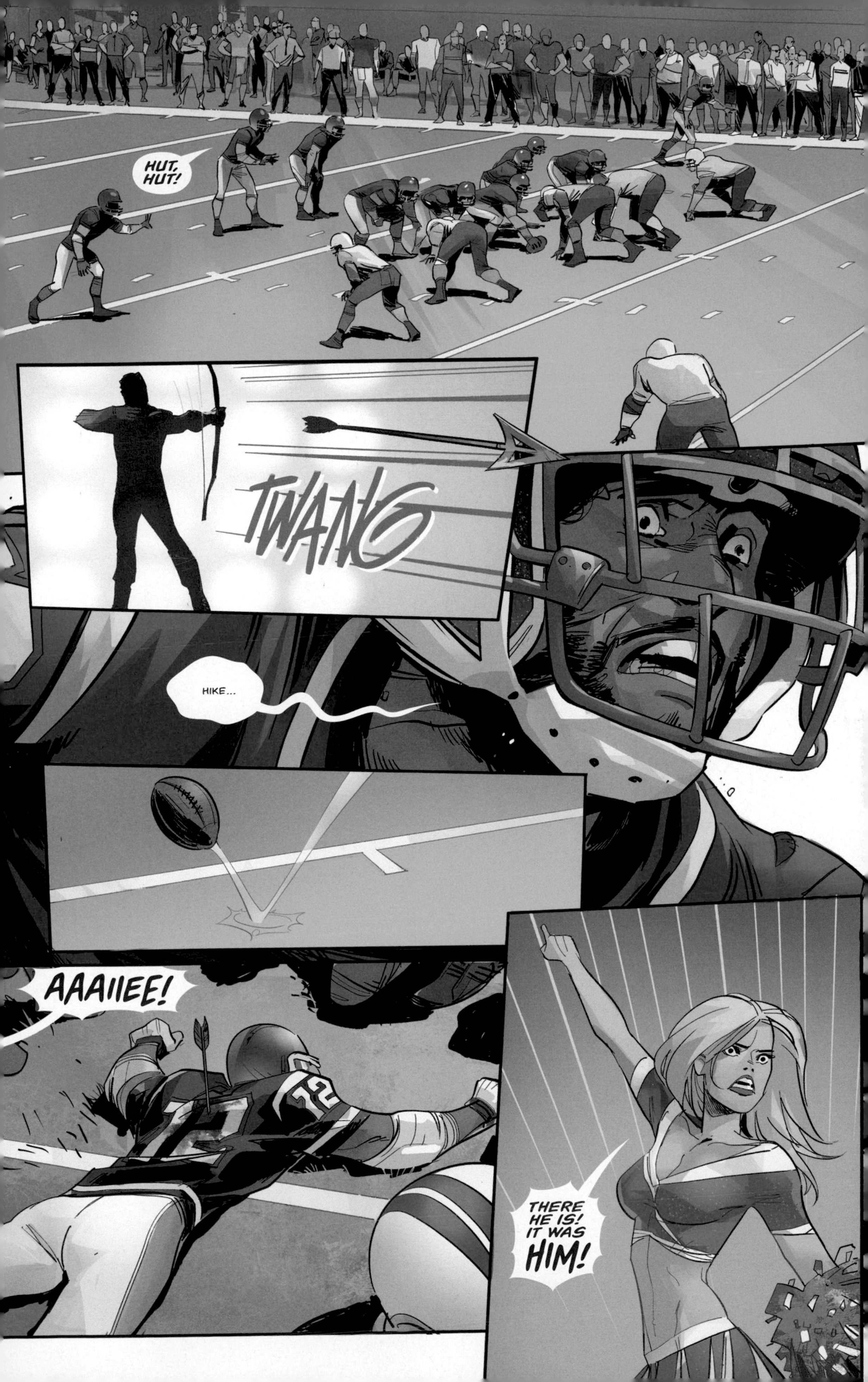
HUT, HUT!
TWANG
HIKE...
AAAIIEE!
THERE HE IS! IT WAS HIM!

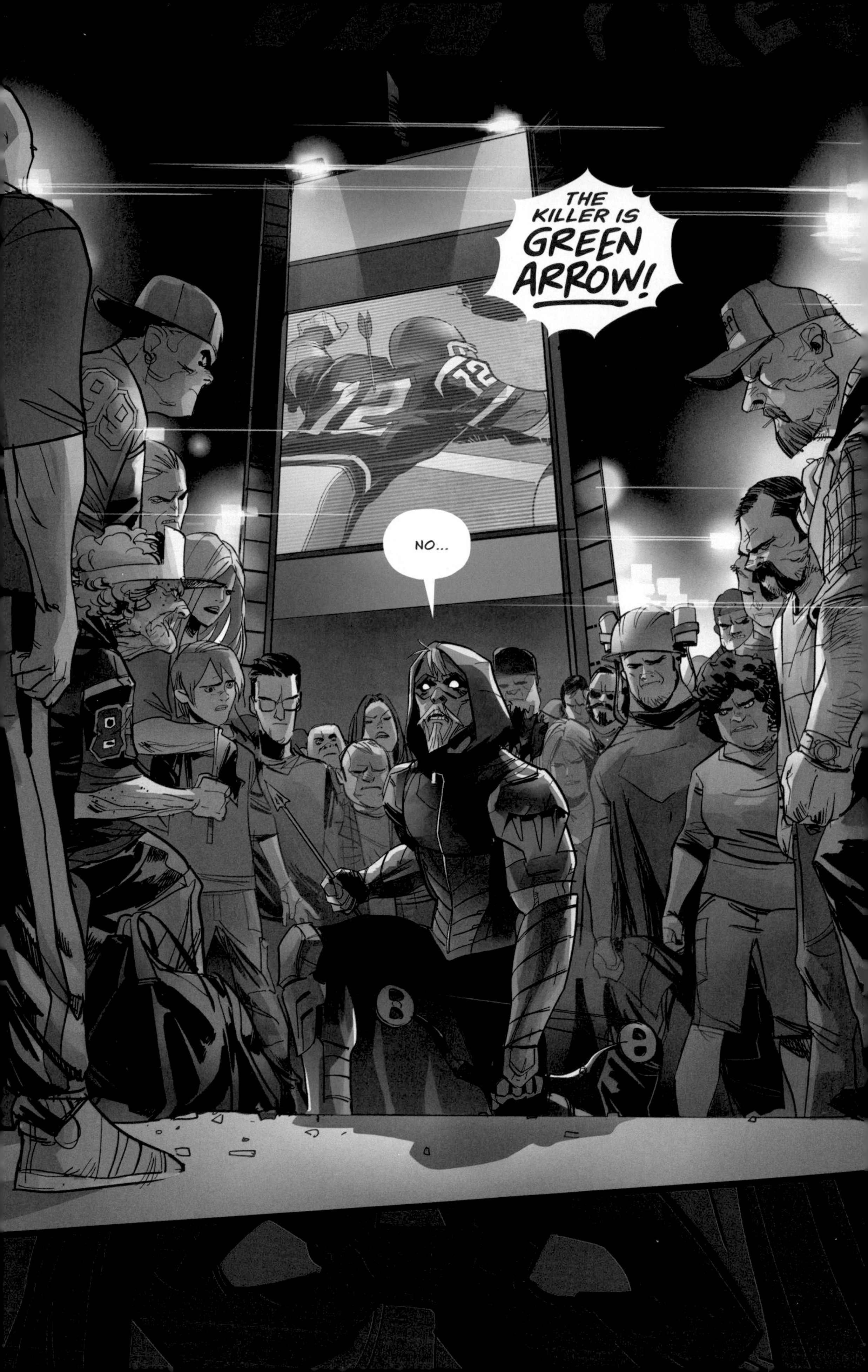
THE KILLER IS GREEN ARROW!
NO...

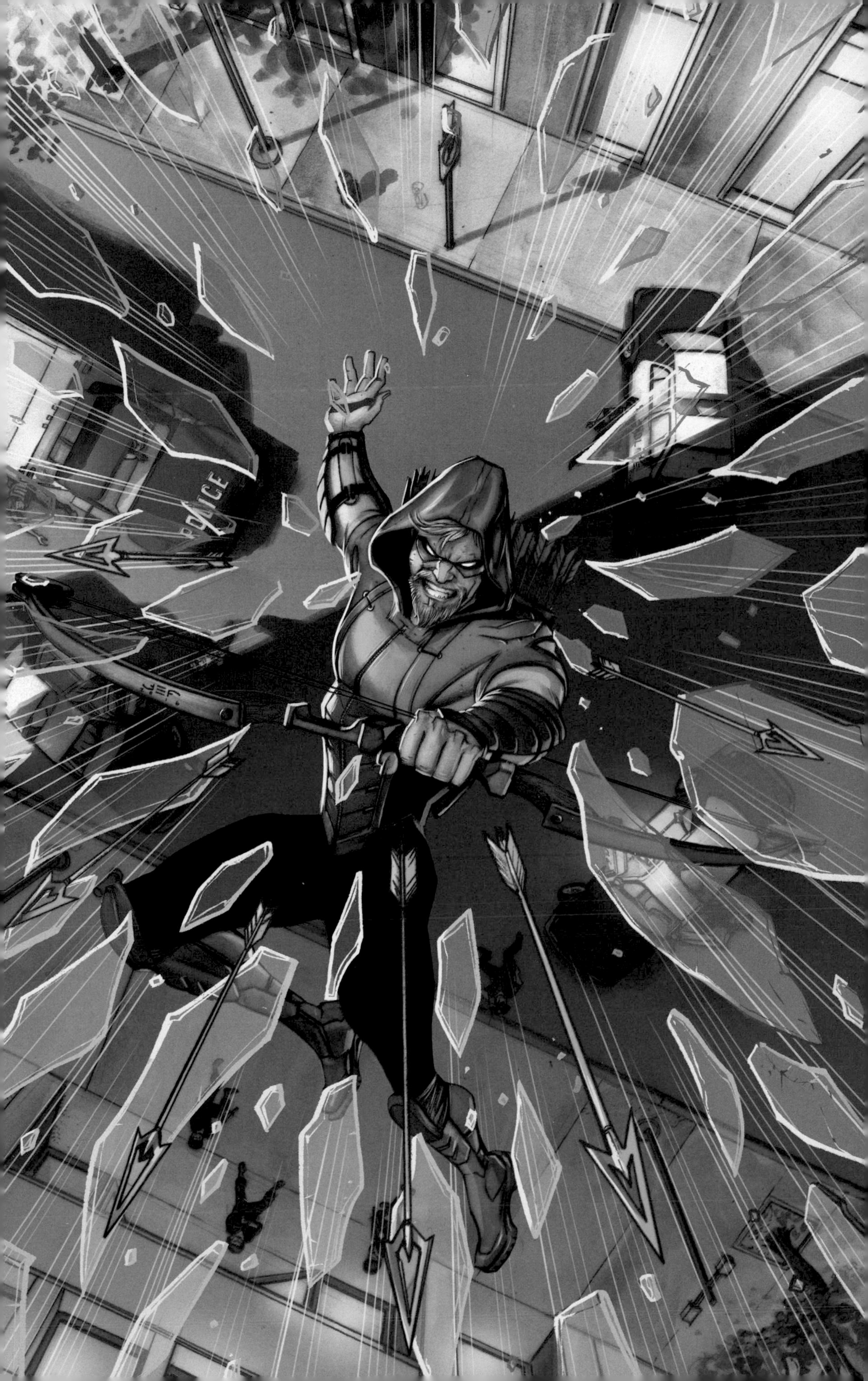
POLICE

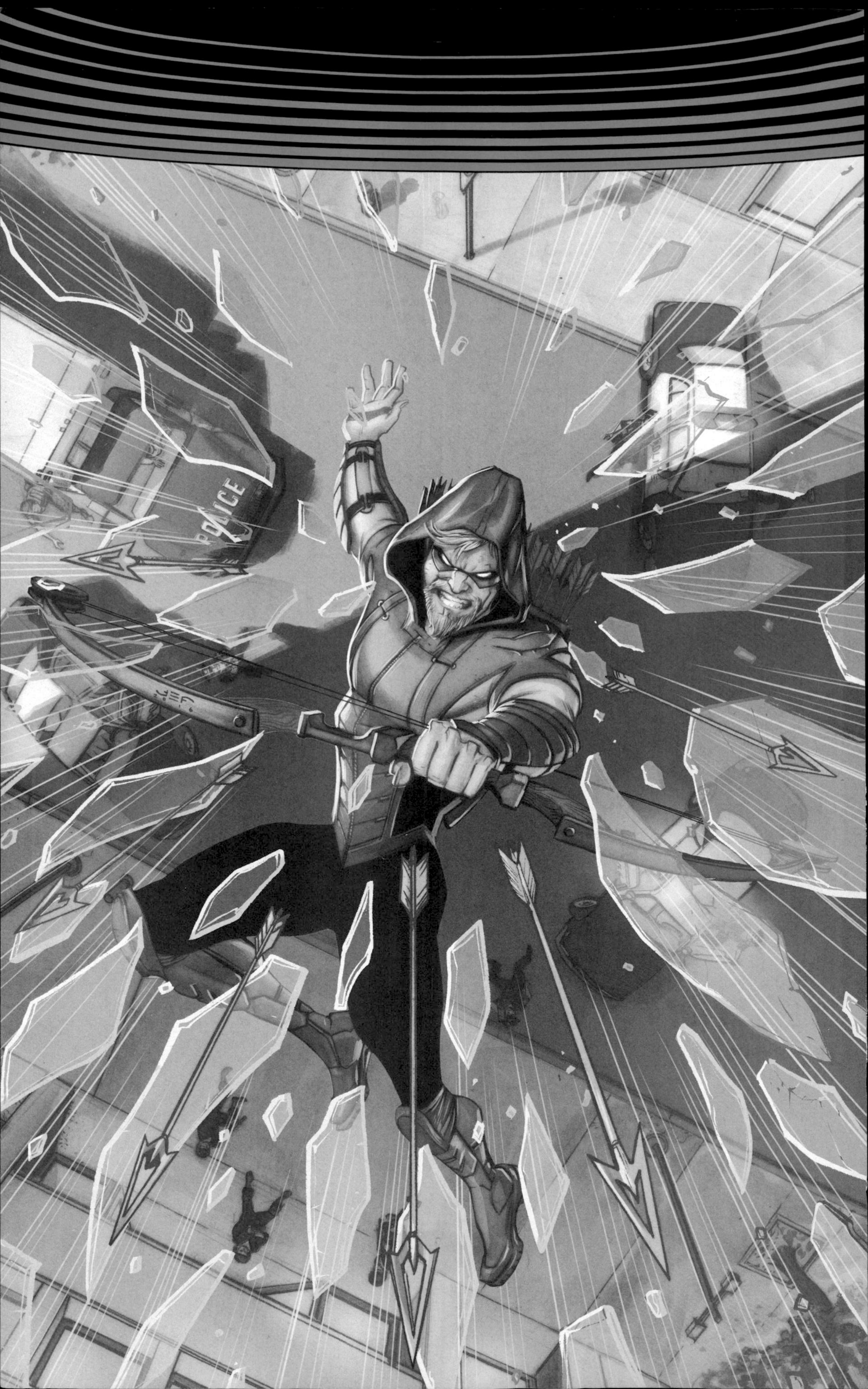
POLICE

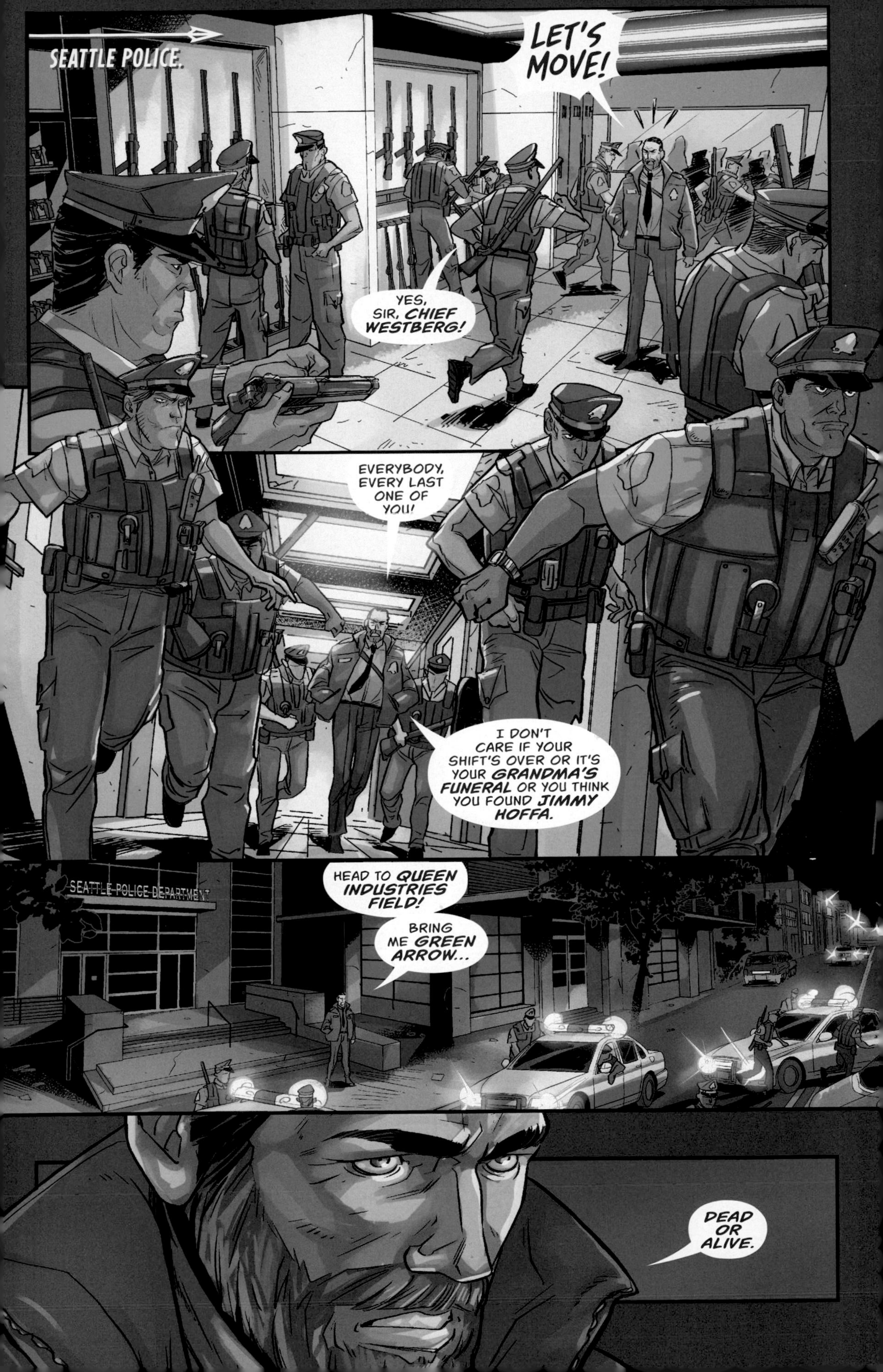
SEATTLE POLICE.
LET'S MOVE!
YES, SIR, CHIEF WESTBERG!
EVERYBODY, EVERY LAST ONE OF YOU!
I DON'T CARE IF YOUR SHIFT'S OVER OR IT'S YOUR GRANDMA'S FUNERAL OR YOU THINK YOU FOUND JIMMY HOFFA.
SEATTLE POLICE DEPARTMENT
HEAD TO QUEEN INDUSTRIES FIELD!
BRING ME GREEN ARROW...
DEAD OR ALIVE.

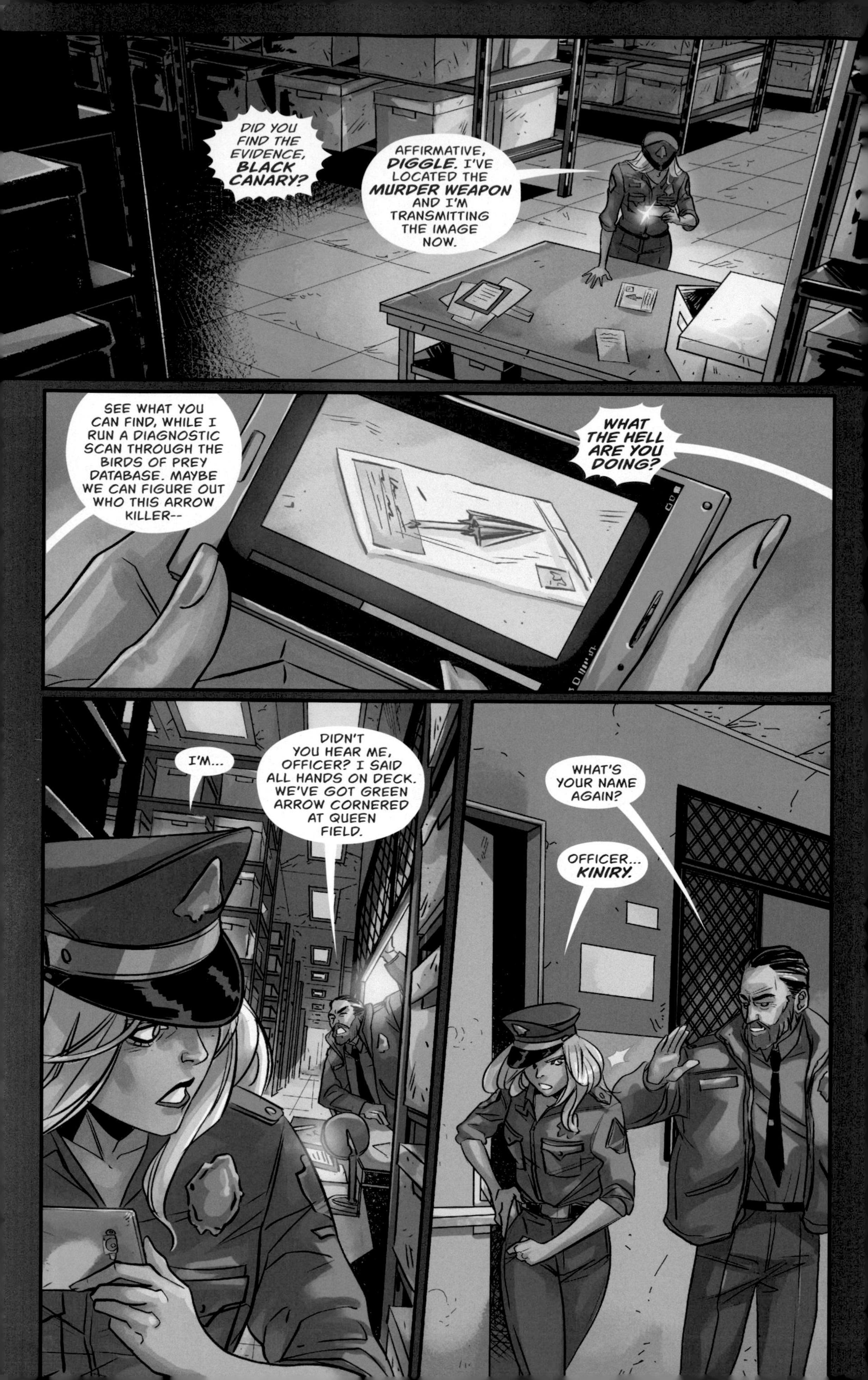
DID YOU FIND THE EVIDENCE, BLACK CANARY?
AFFIRMATIVE, DIGGLE. I'VE LOCATED THE MURDER WEAPON AND I'M TRANSMITTING THE IMAGE NOW.
SEE WHAT YOU CAN FIND, WHILE I RUN A DIAGNOSTIC SCAN THROUGH THE BIRDS OF PREY DATABASE. MAYBE WE CAN FIGURE OUT WHO THIS ARROW KILLER--
WHAT THE HELL ARE YOU DOING?
I'M...
DIDN'T YOU HEAR ME, OFFICER? I SAID ALL HANDS ON DECK. WE'VE GOT GREEN ARROW CORNERED AT QUEEN FIELD.
WHAT'S YOUR NAME AGAIN?
OFFICER... KINIRY.

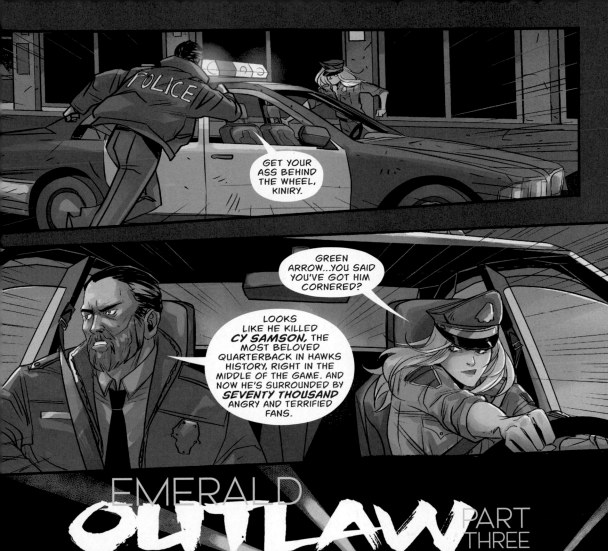

GET YOUR ASS BEHIND THE WHEEL, KINIRY.

GREEN ARROW...YOU SAID YOU'VE GOT HIM CORNERED?

LOOKS LIKE HE KILLED **CY SAMSON,** THE MOST BELOVED QUARTERBACK IN HAWKS HISTORY, RIGHT IN THE MIDDLE OF THE GAME. AND NOW HE'S SURROUNDED BY **SEVENTY THOUSAND** ANGRY AND TERRIFIED FANS.

EMERALD OUTLAW PART THREE

IF THEY DON'T TEAR THAT SON OF A BITCH TO PIECES, **WE WILL.**

HIS ASSAULT ON **SEATTLE** ENDS TONIGHT!

BENJAMIN PERCY STORY   **ELEONORA CARLINI, CARLOS RODRIGUEZ, GUS VAZQUEZ** ART

HI-FI COLOR   **NATE PIEKOS OF BLAMBOT®** LETTERING   **JUAN FERREYRA** COVER

BRIAN CUNNINGHAM GROUP EDITOR   **HARVEY RICHARDS** ASSOCIATE EDITOR   **ANDY KHOURI** EDITOR

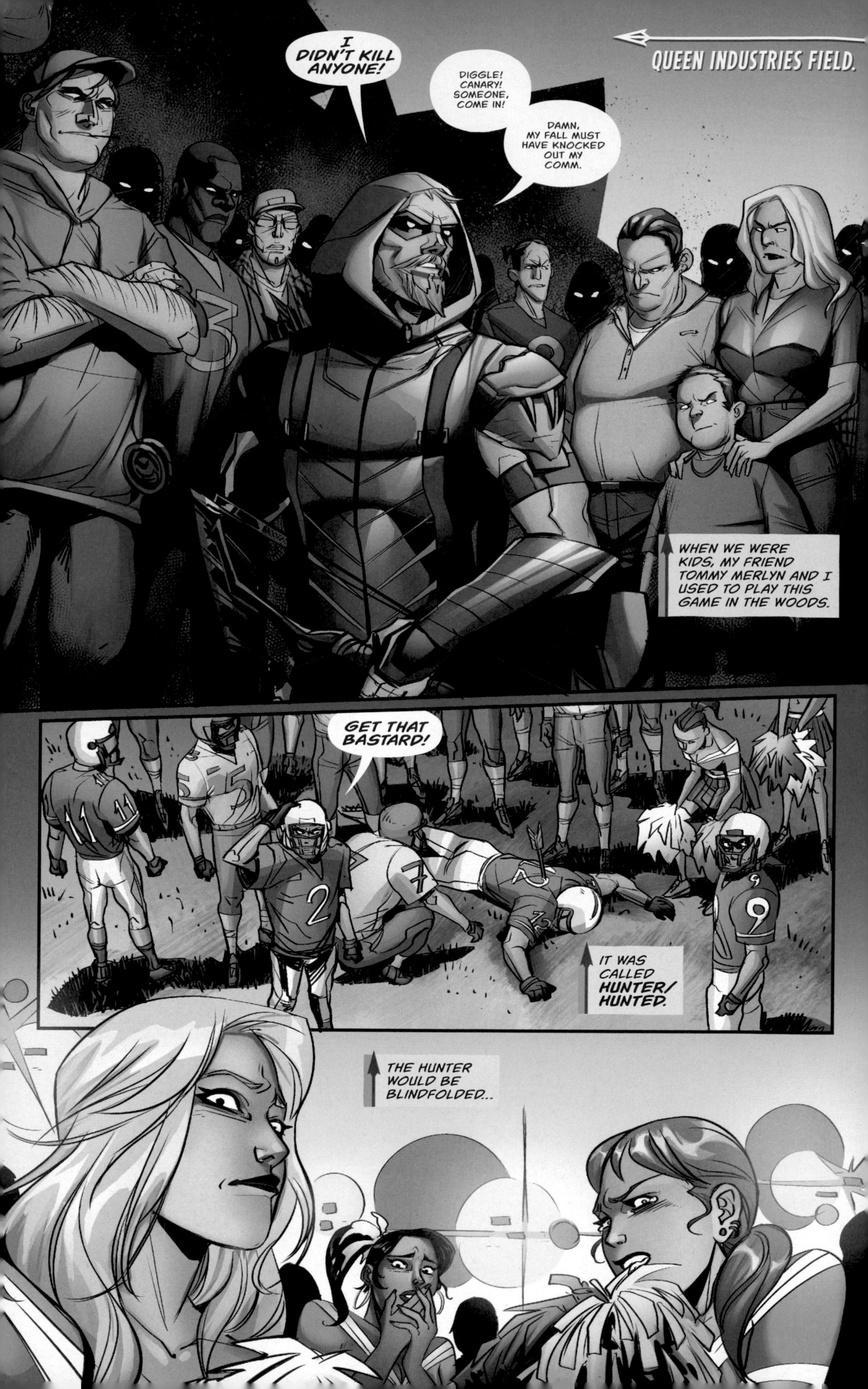
QUEEN INDUSTRIES FIELD.
I DIDN'T KILL ANYONE!
DIGGLE! CANARY! SOMEONE, COME IN!
DAMN, MY FALL MUST HAVE KNOCKED OUT MY COMM.
WHEN WE WERE KIDS, MY FRIEND TOMMY MERLYN AND I USED TO PLAY THIS GAME IN THE WOODS.
GET THAT BASTARD!
IT WAS CALLED HUNTER/ HUNTED.
THE HUNTER WOULD BE BLINDFOLDED...

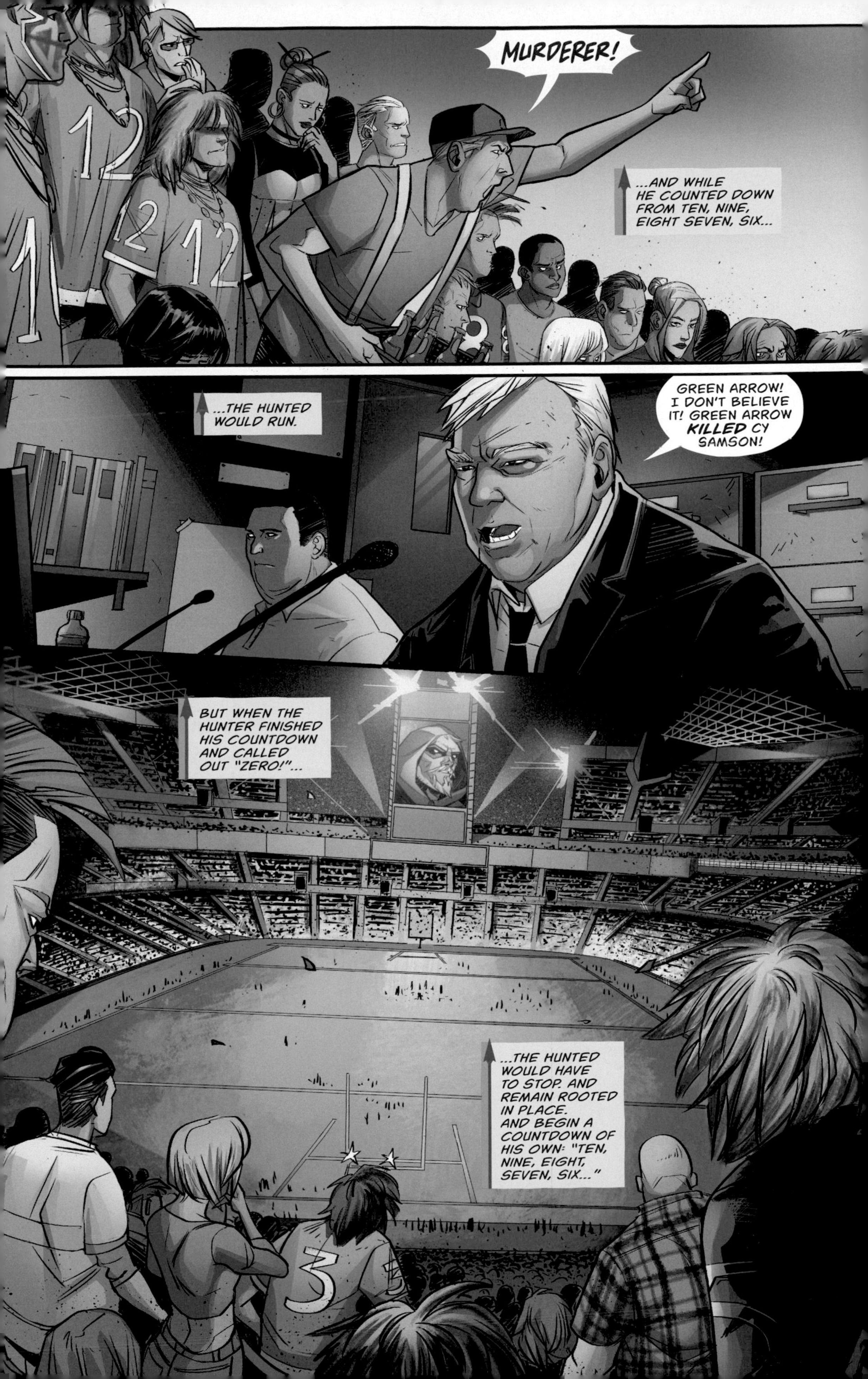
MURDERER!
...AND WHILE HE COUNTED DOWN FROM TEN, NINE, EIGHT SEVEN, SIX...
...THE HUNTED WOULD RUN.
GREEN ARROW! I DON'T BELIEVE IT! GREEN ARROW KILLED CY SAMSON!
BUT WHEN THE HUNTER FINISHED HIS COUNTDOWN AND CALLED OUT "ZERO!"...
...THE HUNTED WOULD HAVE TO STOP. AND REMAIN ROOTED IN PLACE. AND BEGIN A COUNTDOWN OF HIS OWN: "TEN, NINE, EIGHT, SEVEN, SIX..."

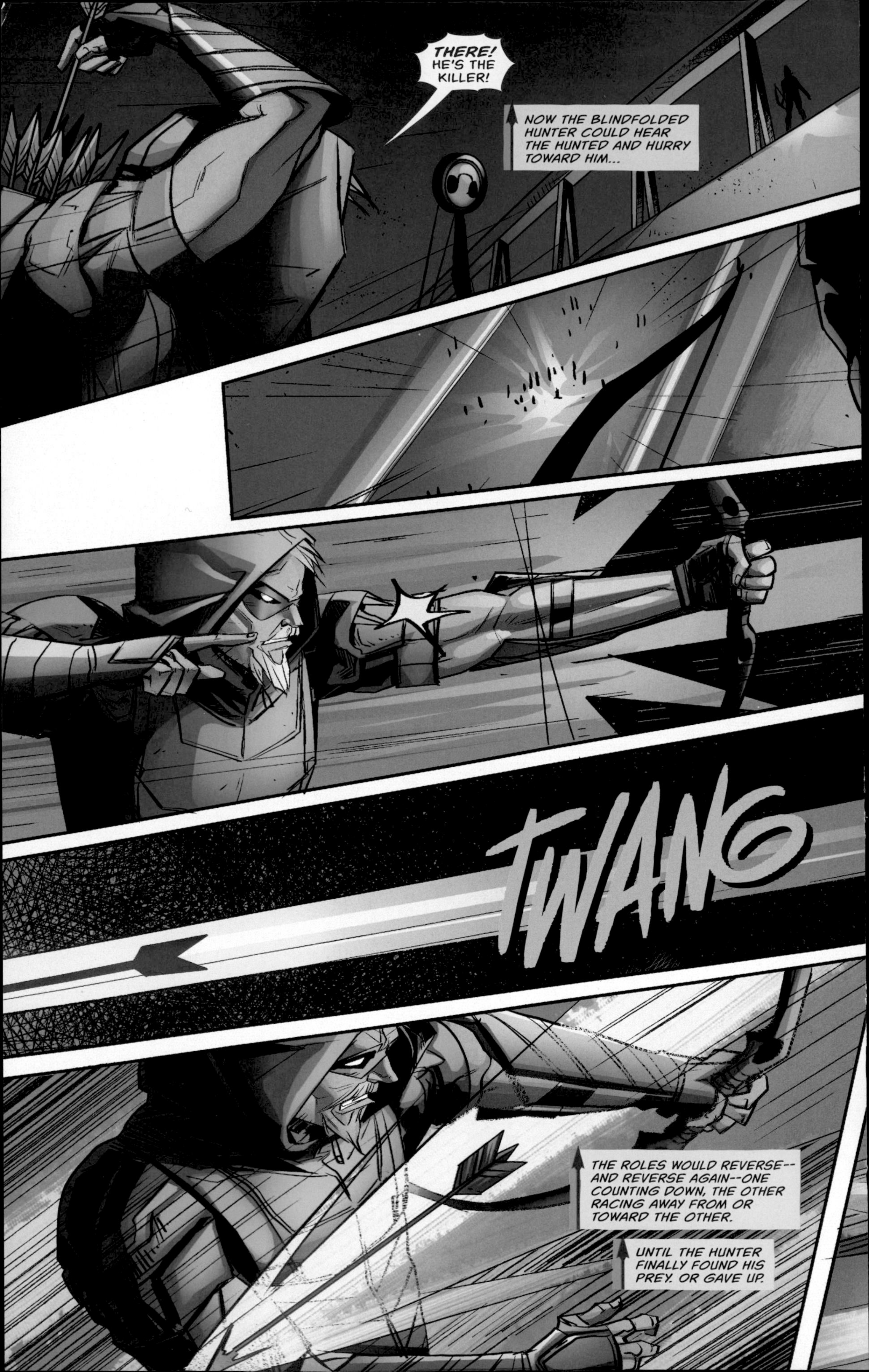
THERE! HE'S THE KILLER!
NOW THE BLINDFOLDED HUNTER COULD HEAR THE HUNTED AND HURRY TOWARD HIM...
TWANG
THE ROLES WOULD REVERSE-- AND REVERSE AGAIN--ONE COUNTING DOWN, THE OTHER RACING AWAY FROM OR TOWARD THE OTHER.
UNTIL THE HUNTER FINALLY FOUND HIS PREY. OR GAVE UP.

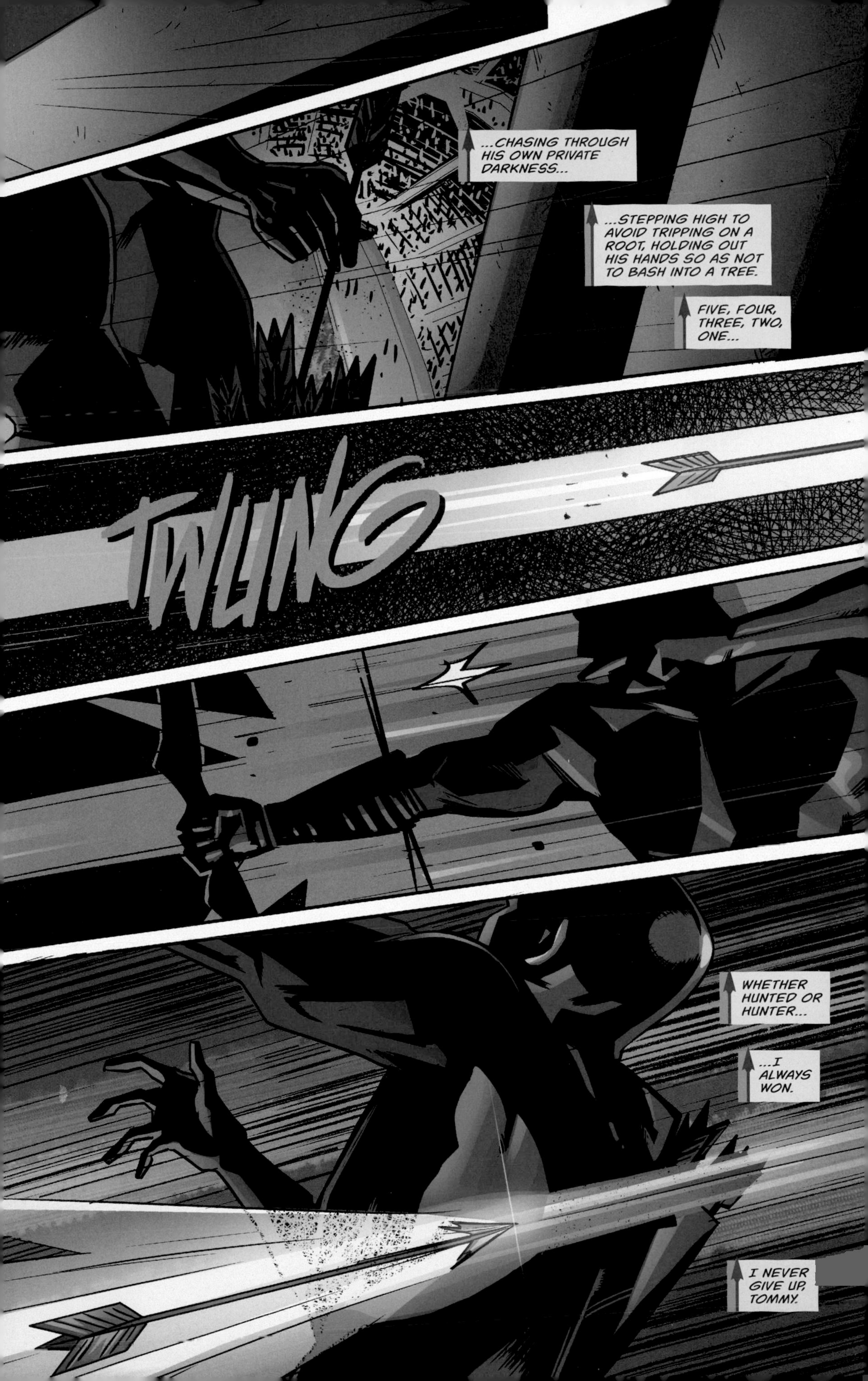
...CHASING THROUGH HIS OWN PRIVATE DARKNESS...
...STEPPING HIGH TO AVOID TRIPPING ON A ROOT, HOLDING OUT HIS HANDS SO AS NOT TO BASH INTO A TREE.
FIVE, FOUR, THREE, TWO, ONE...
TWUNG
WHETHER HUNTED OR HUNTER...
...I ALWAYS WON.
I NEVER GIVE UP, TOMMY.

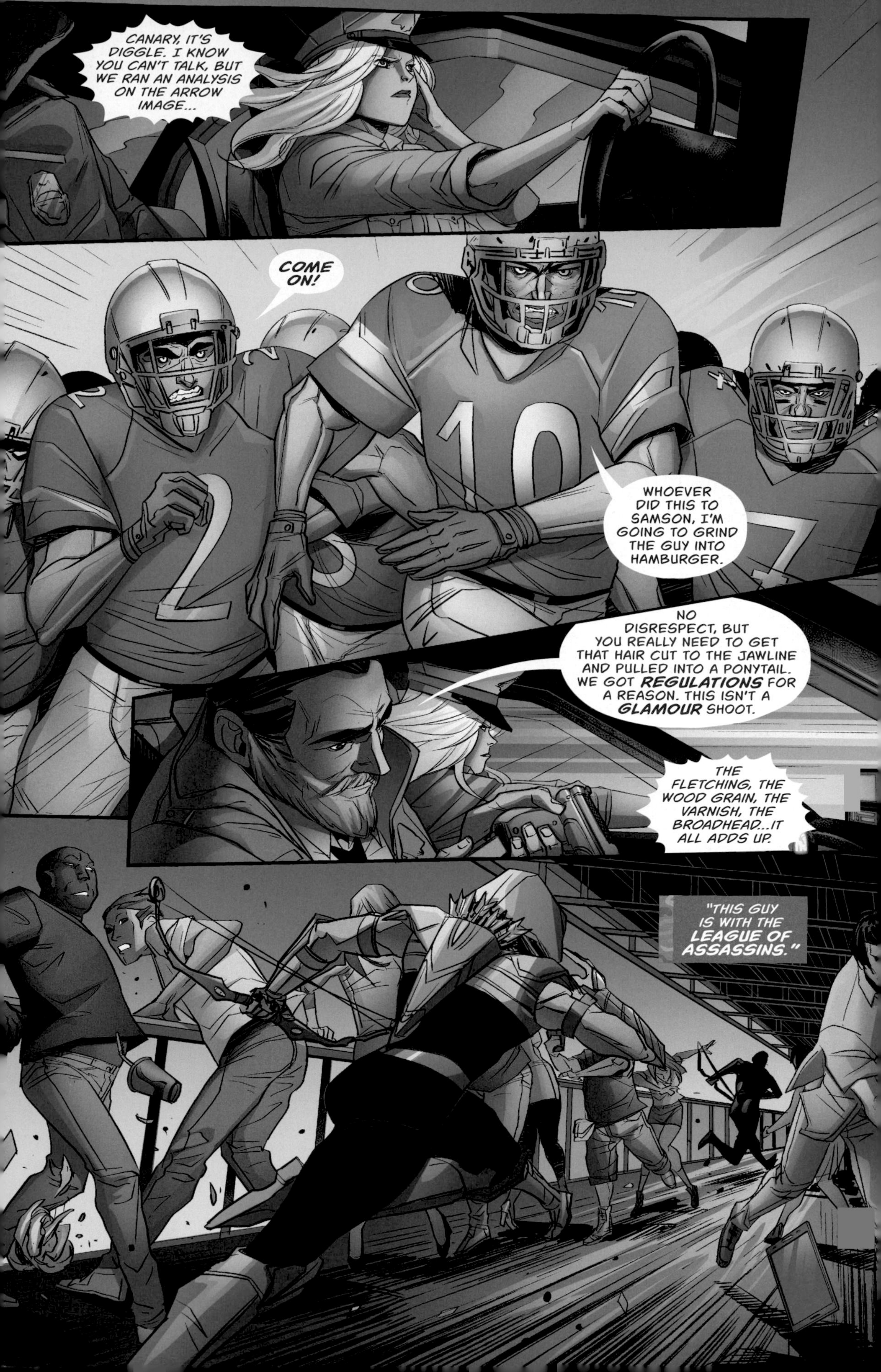
CANARY, IT'S DIGGLE. I KNOW YOU CAN'T TALK, BUT WE RAN AN ANALYSIS ON THE ARROW IMAGE...
COME ON!
WHOEVER DID THIS TO SAMSON, I'M GOING TO GRIND THE GUY INTO HAMBURGER.
NO DISRESPECT, BUT YOU REALLY NEED TO GET THAT HAIR CUT TO THE JAWLINE AND PULLED INTO A PONYTAIL. WE GOT **REGULATIONS** FOR A REASON. THIS ISN'T A **GLAMOUR** SHOOT.
THE FLETCHING, THE WOOD GRAIN, THE VARNISH, THE BROADHEAD...IT ALL ADDS UP.
"THIS GUY IS WITH THE **LEAGUE OF ASSASSINS.**"

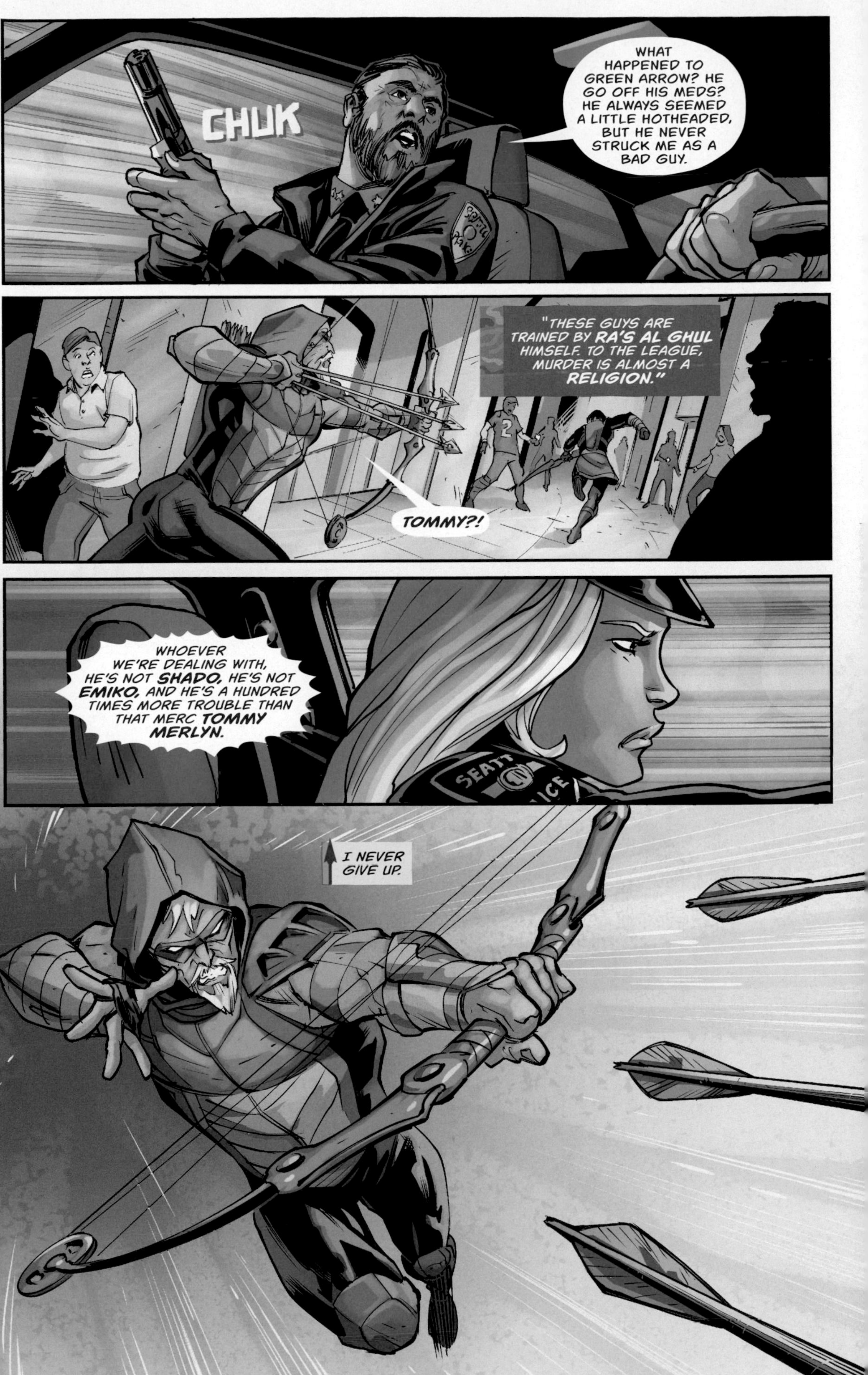

CHUK
WHAT HAPPENED TO GREEN ARROW? HE GO OFF HIS MEDS? HE ALWAYS SEEMED A LITTLE HOTHEADED, BUT HE NEVER STRUCK ME AS A BAD GUY.
"THESE GUYS ARE TRAINED BY RA'S AL GHUL HIMSELF. TO THE LEAGUE, MURDER IS ALMOST A RELIGION."
TOMMY?!
WHOEVER WE'RE DEALING WITH, HE'S NOT SHADO, HE'S NOT EMIKO, AND HE'S A HUNDRED TIMES MORE TROUBLE THAN THAT MERC TOMMY MERLYN.
I NEVER GIVE UP.

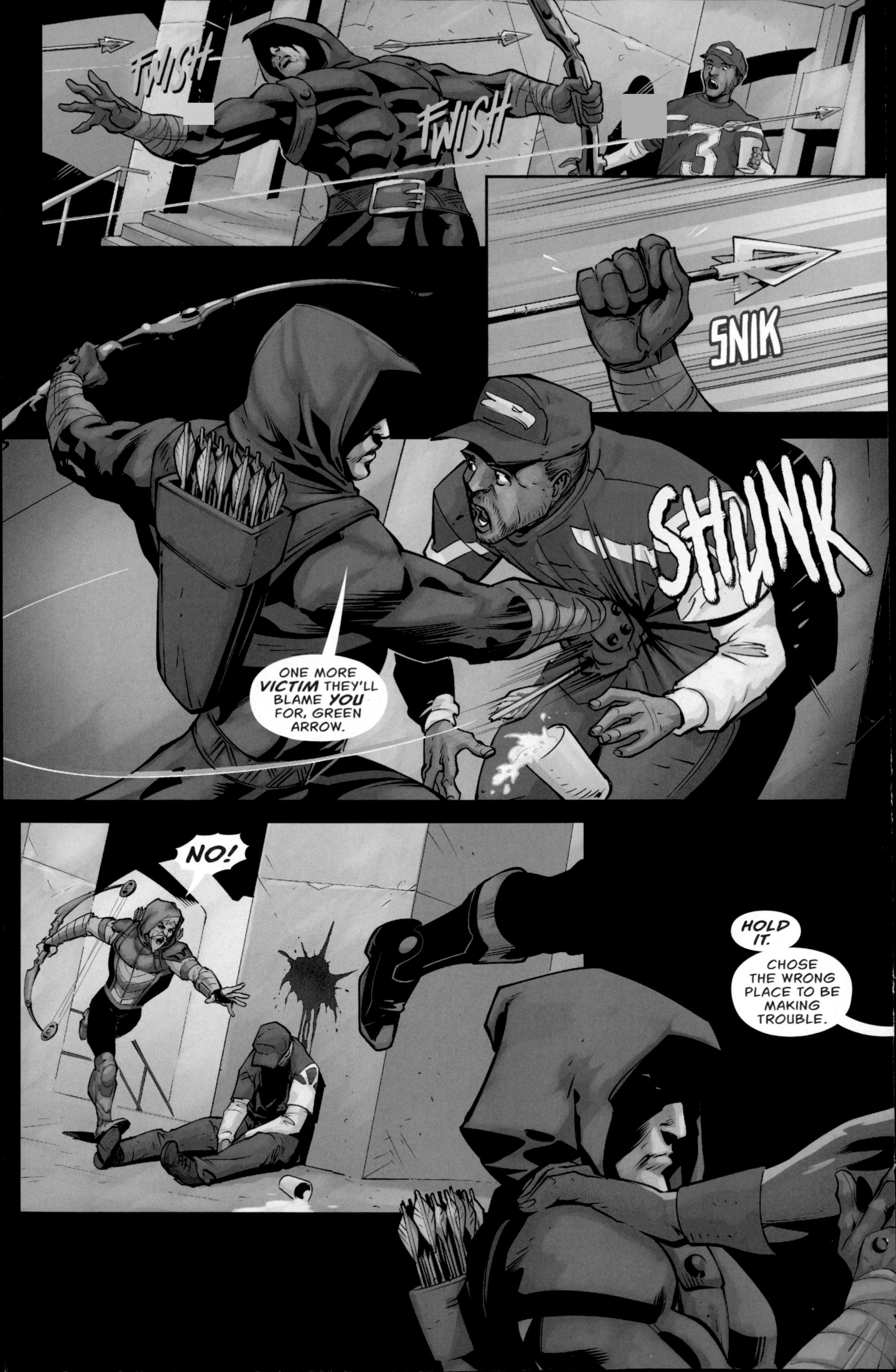
FWISH
FWISH
SNIK
SHUNK
ONE MORE VICTIM THEY'LL BLAME YOU FOR, GREEN ARROW.
NO!
HOLD IT.
CHOSE THE WRONG PLACE TO BE MAKING TROUBLE.

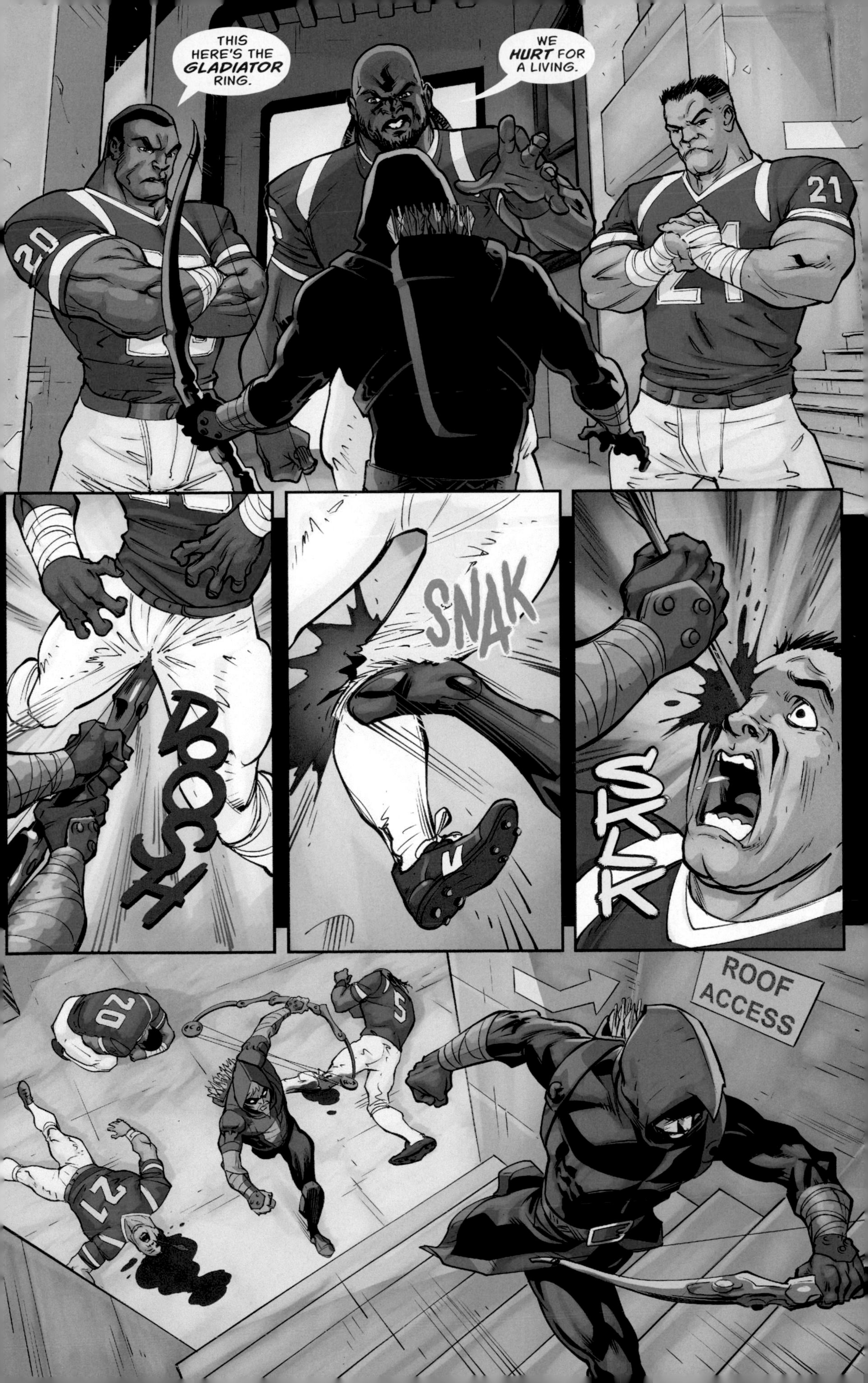
THIS HERE'S THE GLADIATOR RING.
WE HURT FOR A LIVING.
20
21
DOOSH
SNAK
SKLK
20
5
21
ROOF ACCESS

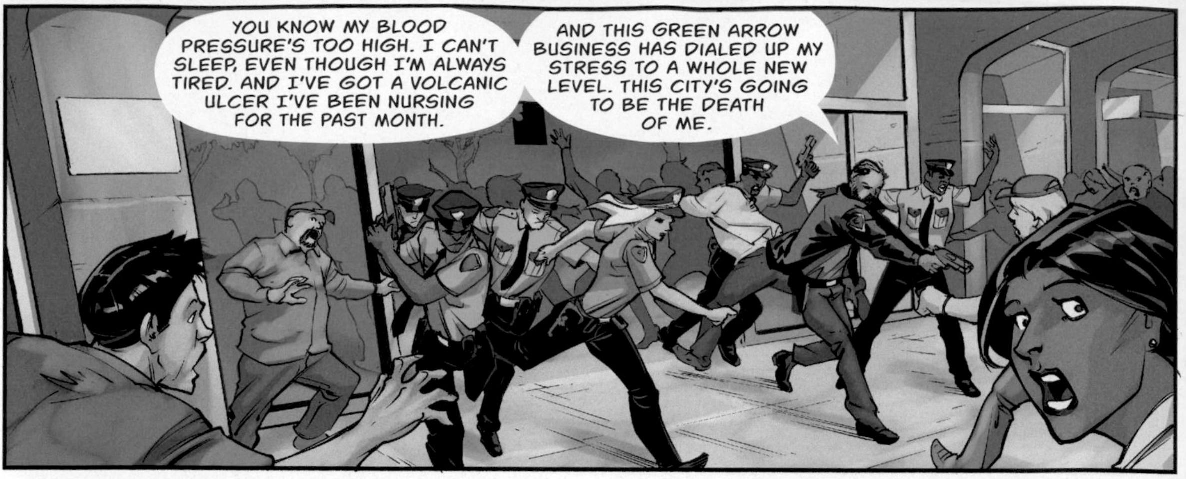
YOU KNOW MY BLOOD PRESSURE'S TOO HIGH. I CAN'T SLEEP, EVEN THOUGH I'M ALWAYS TIRED. AND I'VE GOT A VOLCANIC ULCER I'VE BEEN NURSING FOR THE PAST MONTH.
AND THIS GREEN ARROW BUSINESS HAS DIALED UP MY STRESS TO A WHOLE NEW LEVEL. THIS CITY'S GOING TO BE THE DEATH OF ME.

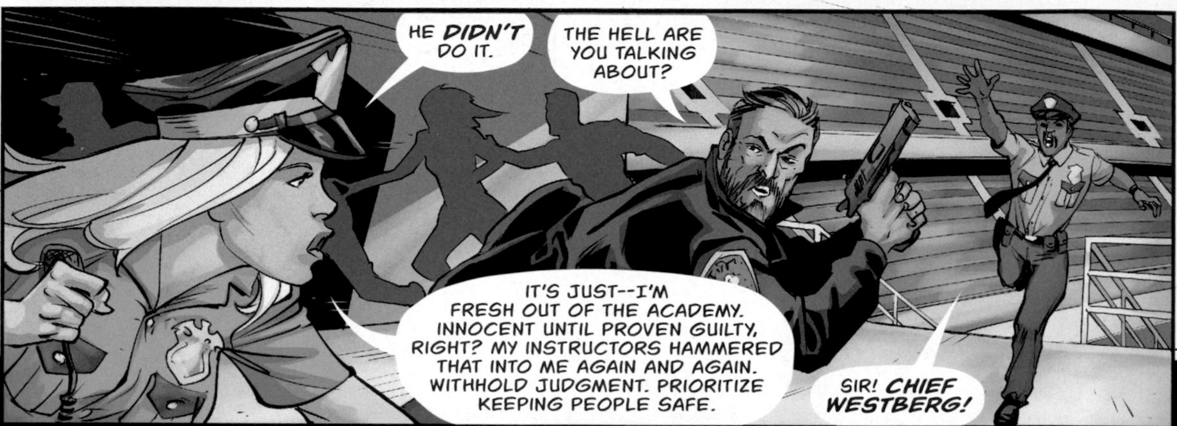
HE ***DIDN'T*** DO IT.
THE HELL ARE YOU TALKING ABOUT?
IT'S JUST--I'M FRESH OUT OF THE ACADEMY. INNOCENT UNTIL PROVEN GUILTY, RIGHT? MY INSTRUCTORS HAMMERED THAT INTO ME AGAIN AND AGAIN. WITHHOLD JUDGMENT. PRIORITIZE KEEPING PEOPLE SAFE.
SIR! ***CHIEF WESTBERG!***

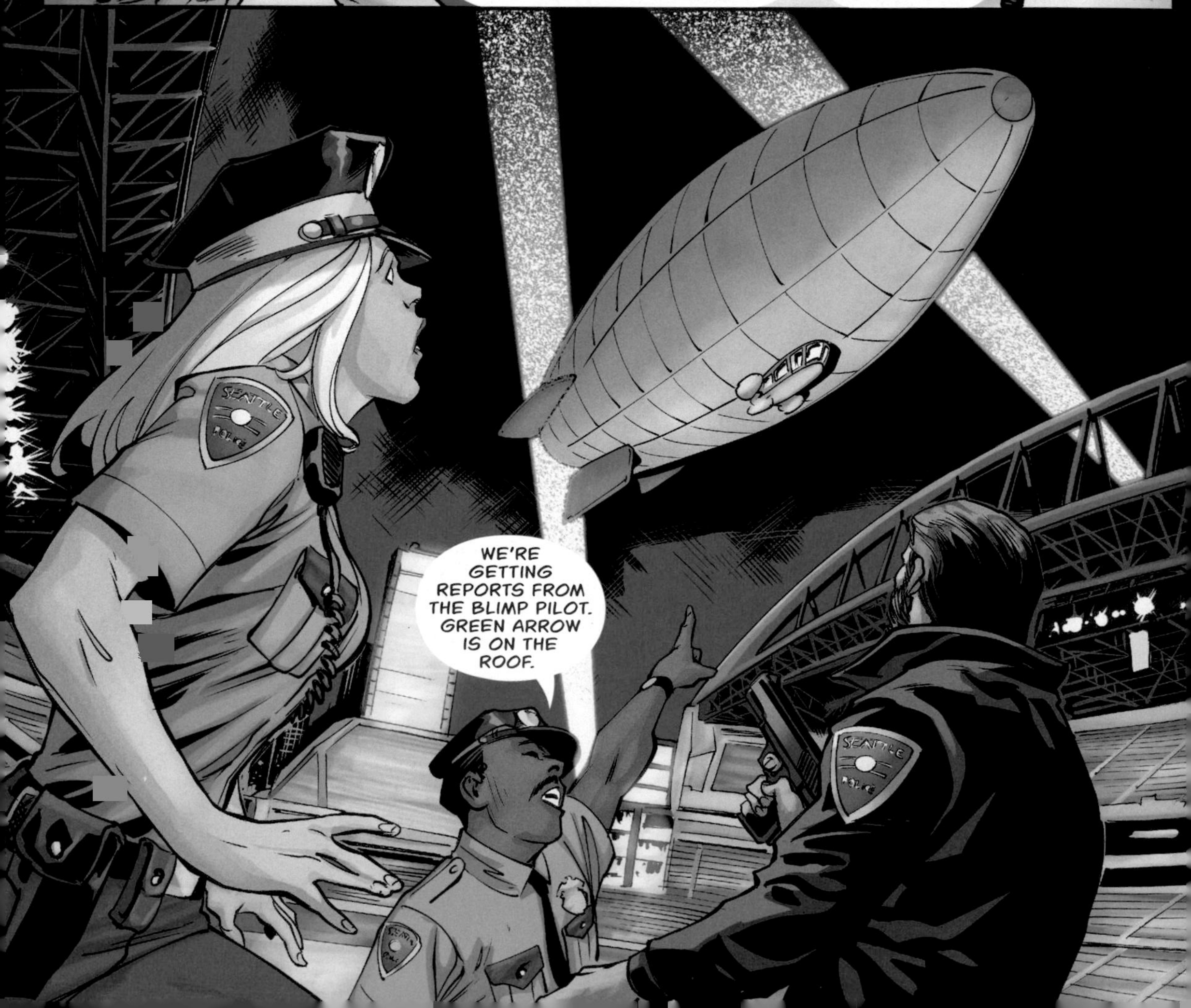
WE'RE GETTING REPORTS FROM THE BLIMP PILOT. GREEN ARROW IS ON THE ROOF.

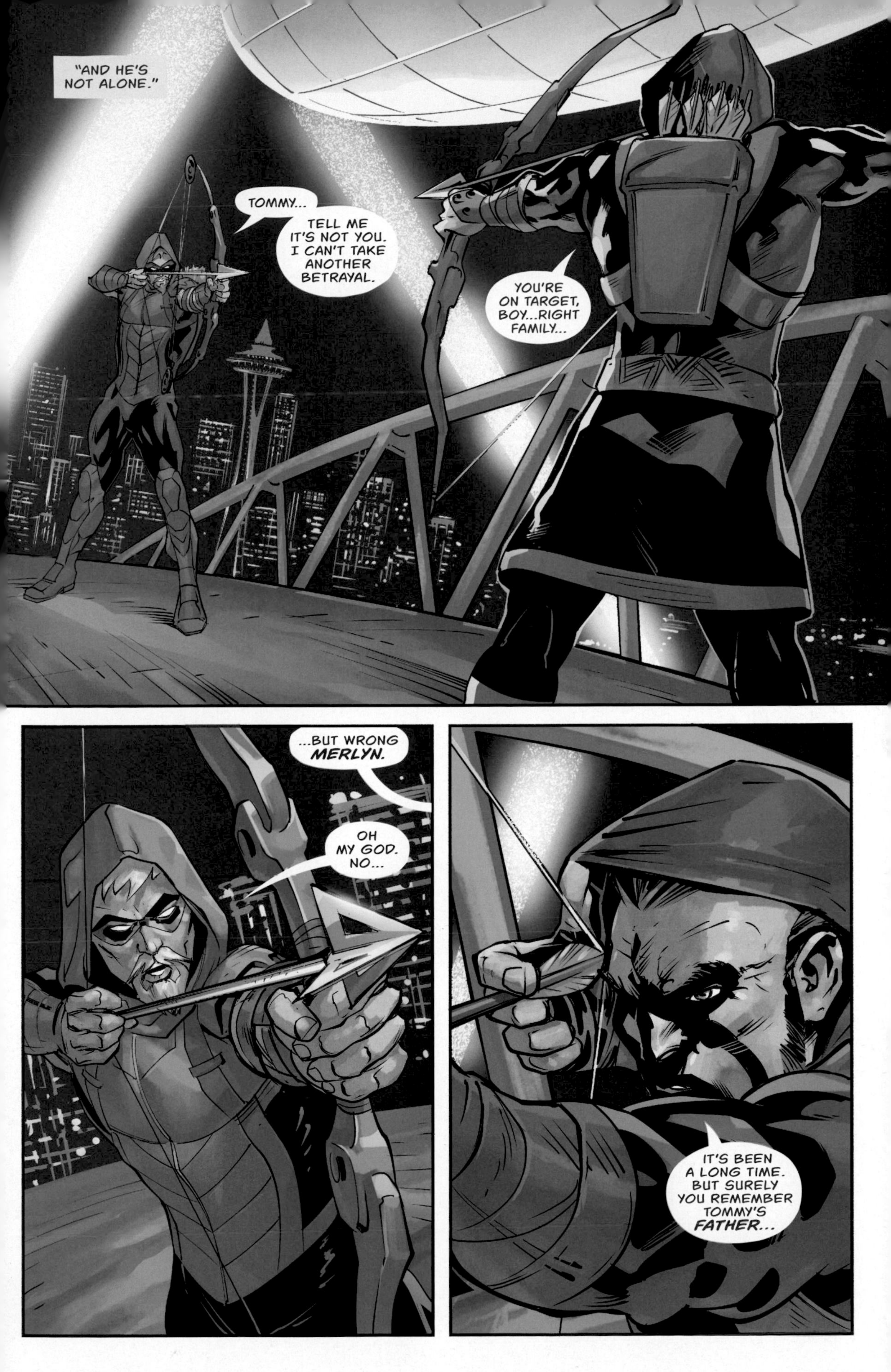
"AND HE'S NOT ALONE."
TOMMY... TELL ME IT'S NOT YOU. I CAN'T TAKE ANOTHER BETRAYAL.
YOU'RE ON TARGET, BOY...RIGHT FAMILY...
...BUT WRONG MERLYN.
OH MY GOD. NO...
IT'S BEEN A LONG TIME. BUT SURELY YOU REMEMBER TOMMY'S FATHER...

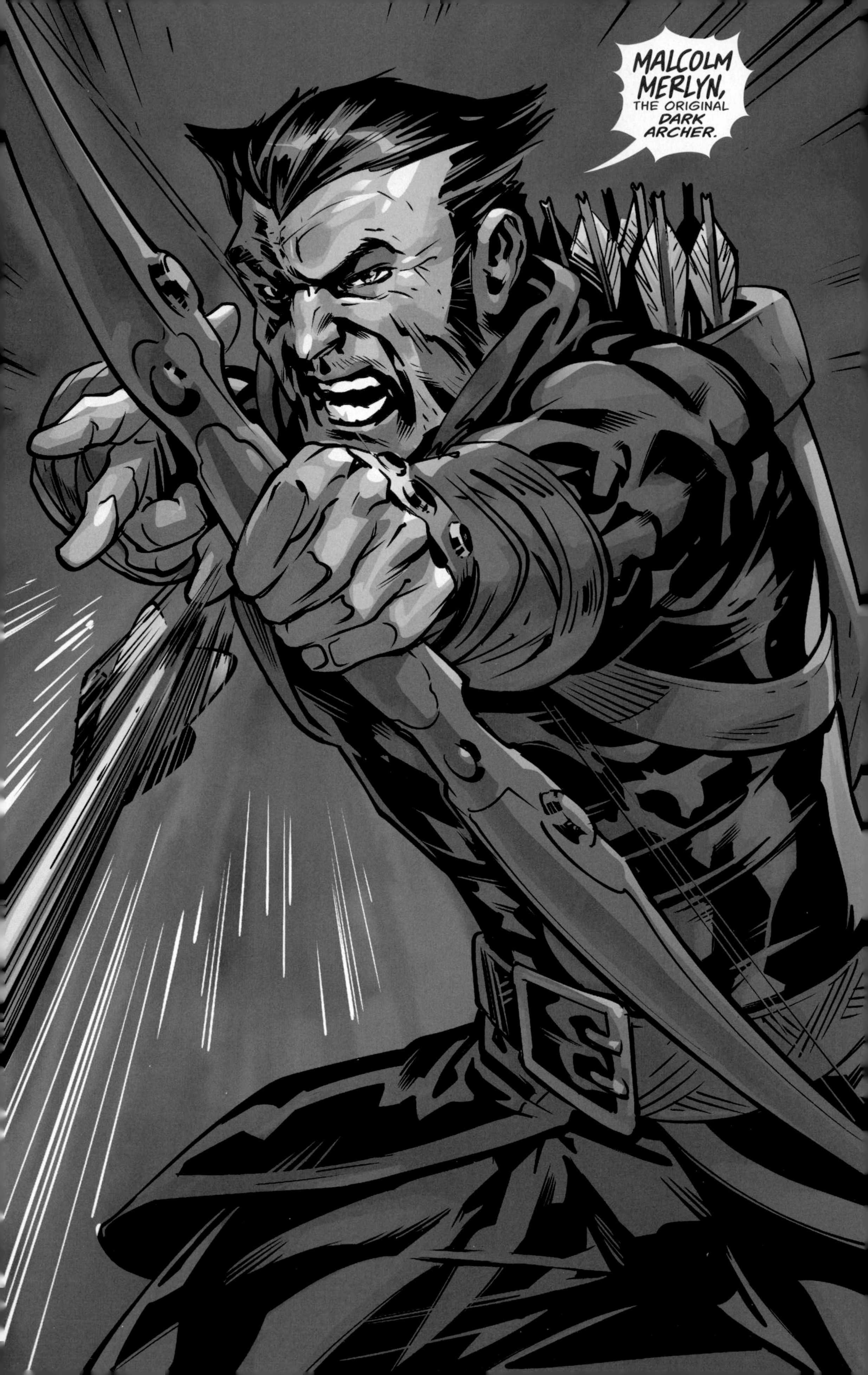
MALCOLM MERLYN, THE ORIGINAL DARK ARCHER.

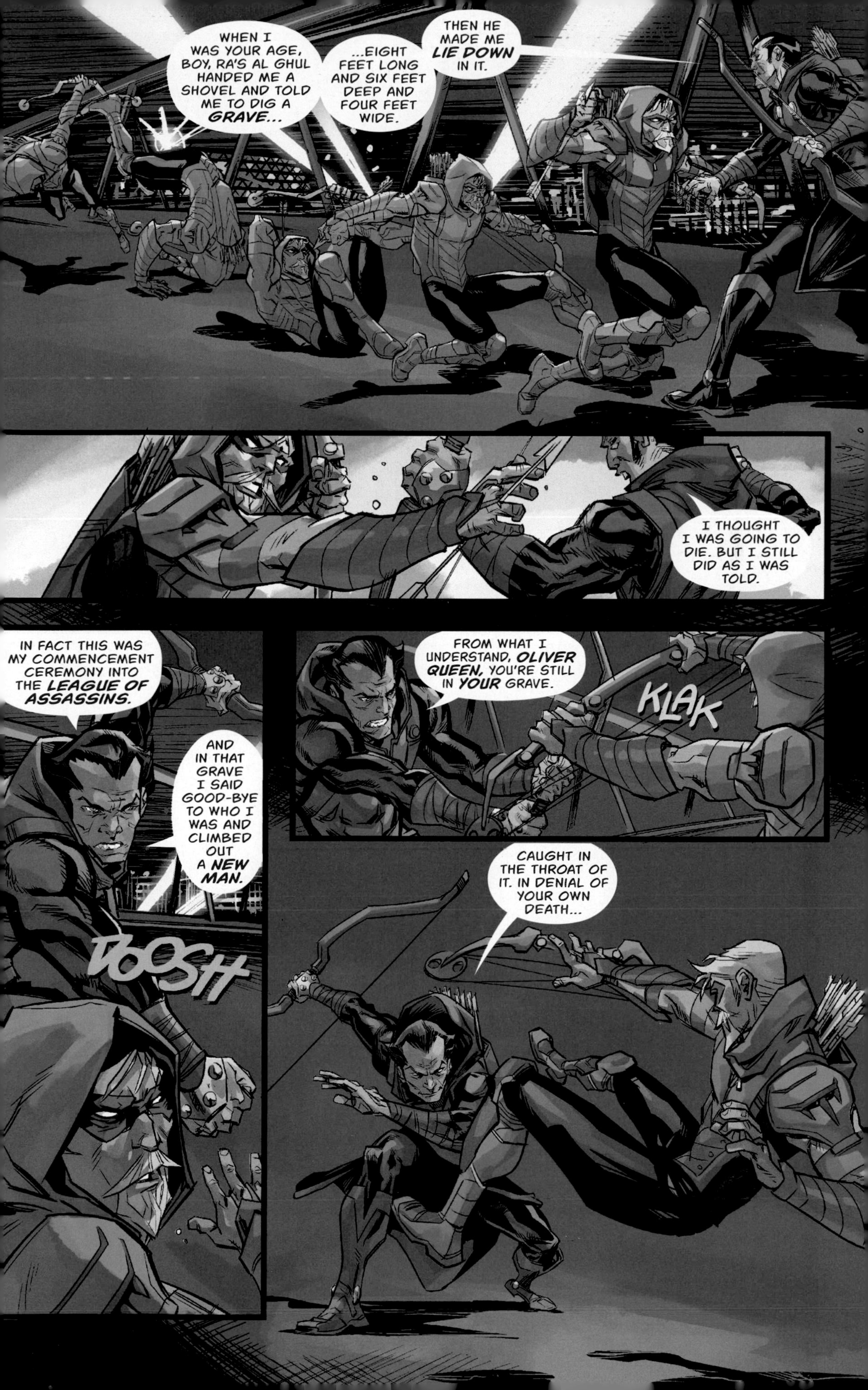

WHEN I WAS YOUR AGE, BOY, RA'S AL GHUL HANDED ME A SHOVEL AND TOLD ME TO DIG A GRAVE...
...EIGHT FEET LONG AND SIX FEET DEEP AND FOUR FEET WIDE.
THEN HE MADE ME LIE DOWN IN IT.
I THOUGHT I WAS GOING TO DIE. BUT I STILL DID AS I WAS TOLD.
IN FACT THIS WAS MY COMMENCEMENT CEREMONY INTO THE LEAGUE OF ASSASSINS.
AND IN THAT GRAVE I SAID GOOD-BYE TO WHO I WAS AND CLIMBED OUT A NEW MAN.
DOOSH
FROM WHAT I UNDERSTAND, OLIVER QUEEN, YOU'RE STILL IN YOUR GRAVE.
KLAK
CAUGHT IN THE THROAT OF IT. IN DENIAL OF YOUR OWN DEATH...

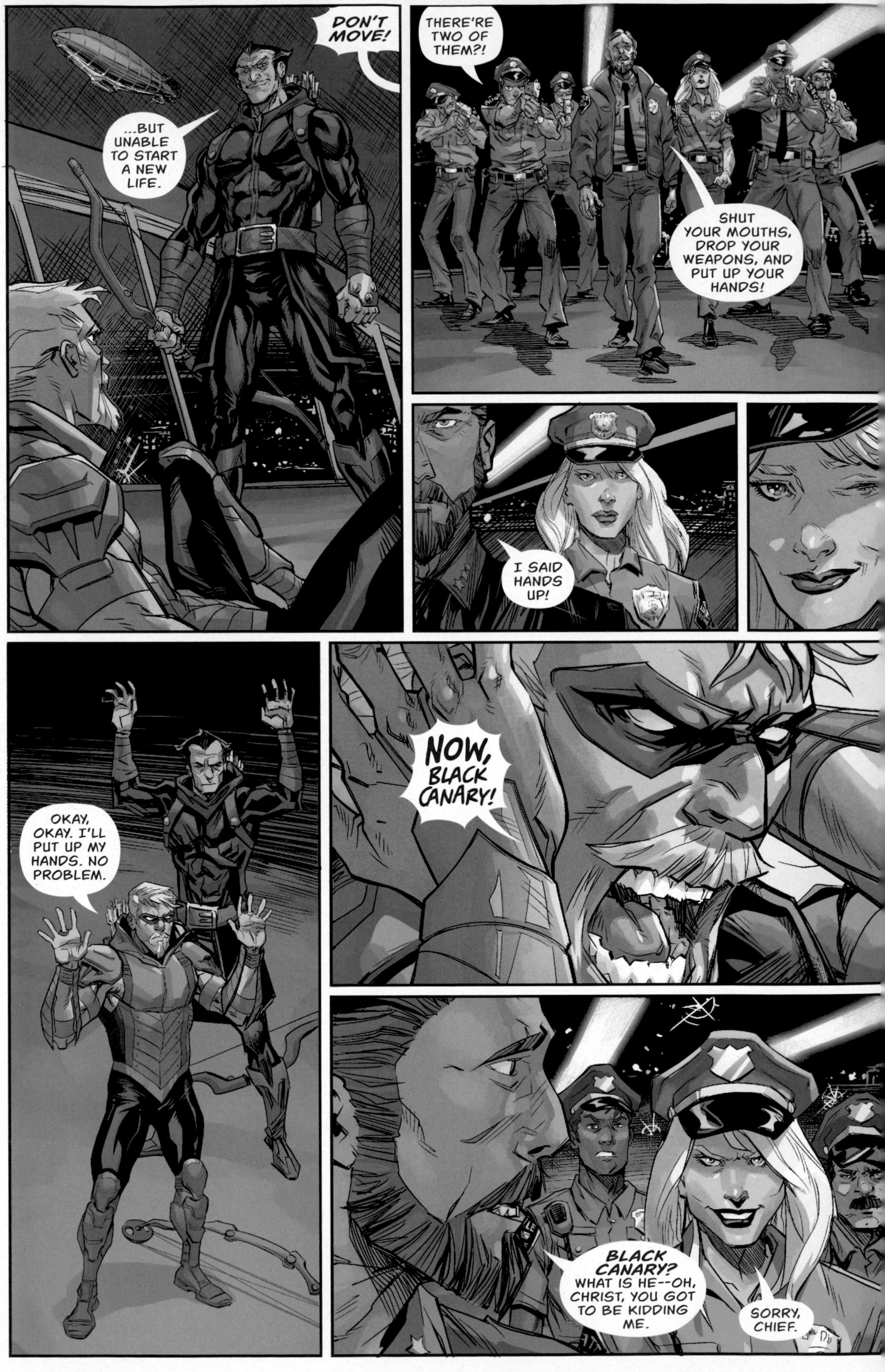
...BUT UNABLE TO START A NEW LIFE.
DON'T MOVE!
THERE'RE TWO OF THEM?!
SHUT YOUR MOUTHS, DROP YOUR WEAPONS, AND PUT UP YOUR HANDS!
I SAID HANDS UP!
OKAY, OKAY. I'LL PUT UP MY HANDS. NO PROBLEM.
NOW, BLACK CANARY!
BLACK CANARY? WHAT IS HE--OH, CHRIST, YOU GOT TO BE KIDDING ME.
SORRY, CHIEF.

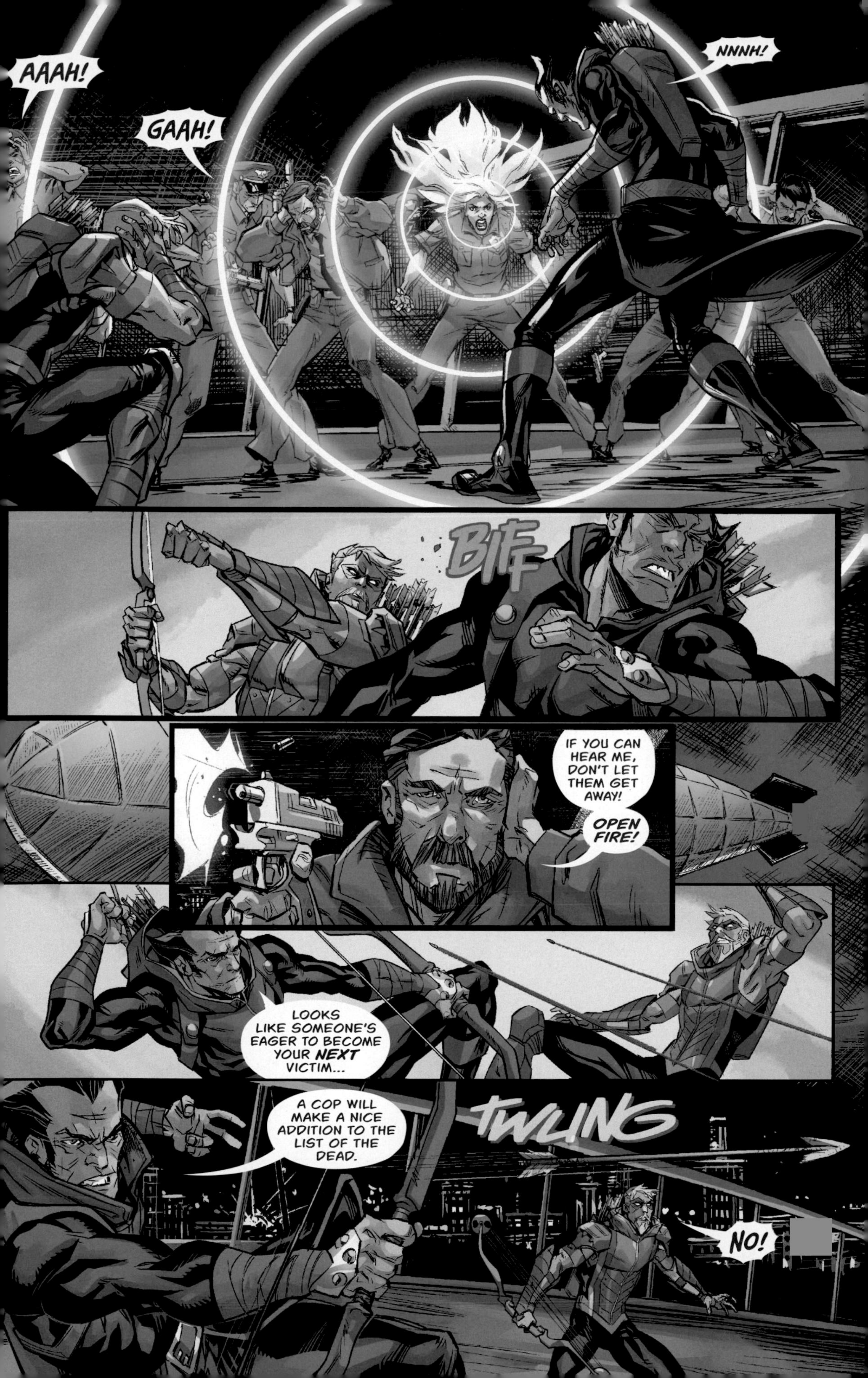
AAAH!
GAAH!
NNNH!
BIFF
IF YOU CAN HEAR ME, DON'T LET THEM GET AWAY!
OPEN FIRE!
LOOKS LIKE SOMEONE'S EAGER TO BECOME YOUR NEXT VICTIM...
A COP WILL MAKE A NICE ADDITION TO THE LIST OF THE DEAD.
TWUNG
NO!

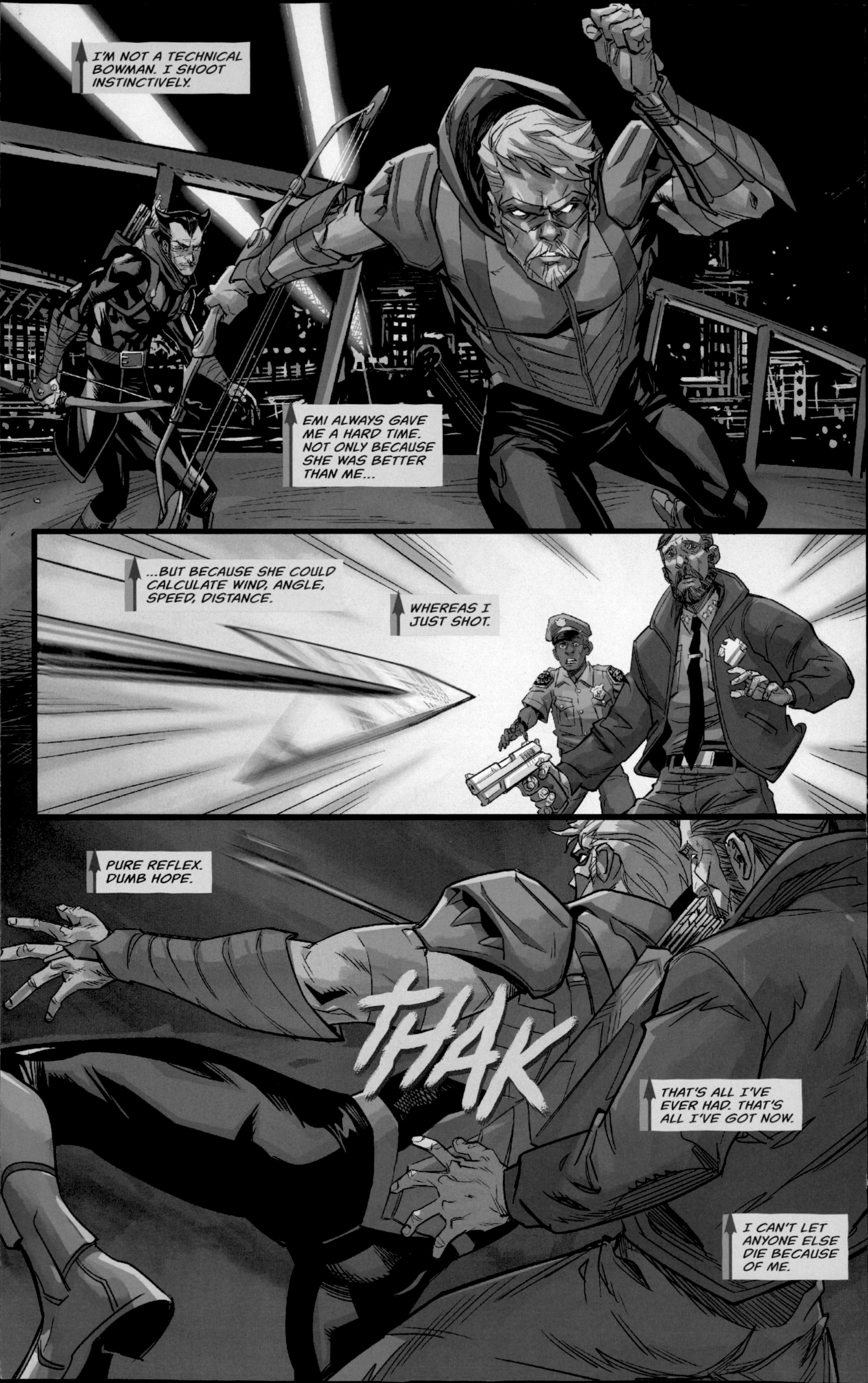
I'M NOT A TECHNICAL BOWMAN. I SHOOT INSTINCTIVELY.
EMI ALWAYS GAVE ME A HARD TIME. NOT ONLY BECAUSE SHE WAS BETTER THAN ME...
...BUT BECAUSE SHE COULD CALCULATE WIND, ANGLE, SPEED, DISTANCE.
WHEREAS I JUST SHOT.
PURE REFLEX. DUMB HOPE.
THAK
THAT'S ALL I'VE EVER HAD. THAT'S ALL I'VE GOT NOW.
I CAN'T LET ANYONE ELSE DIE BECAUSE OF ME.

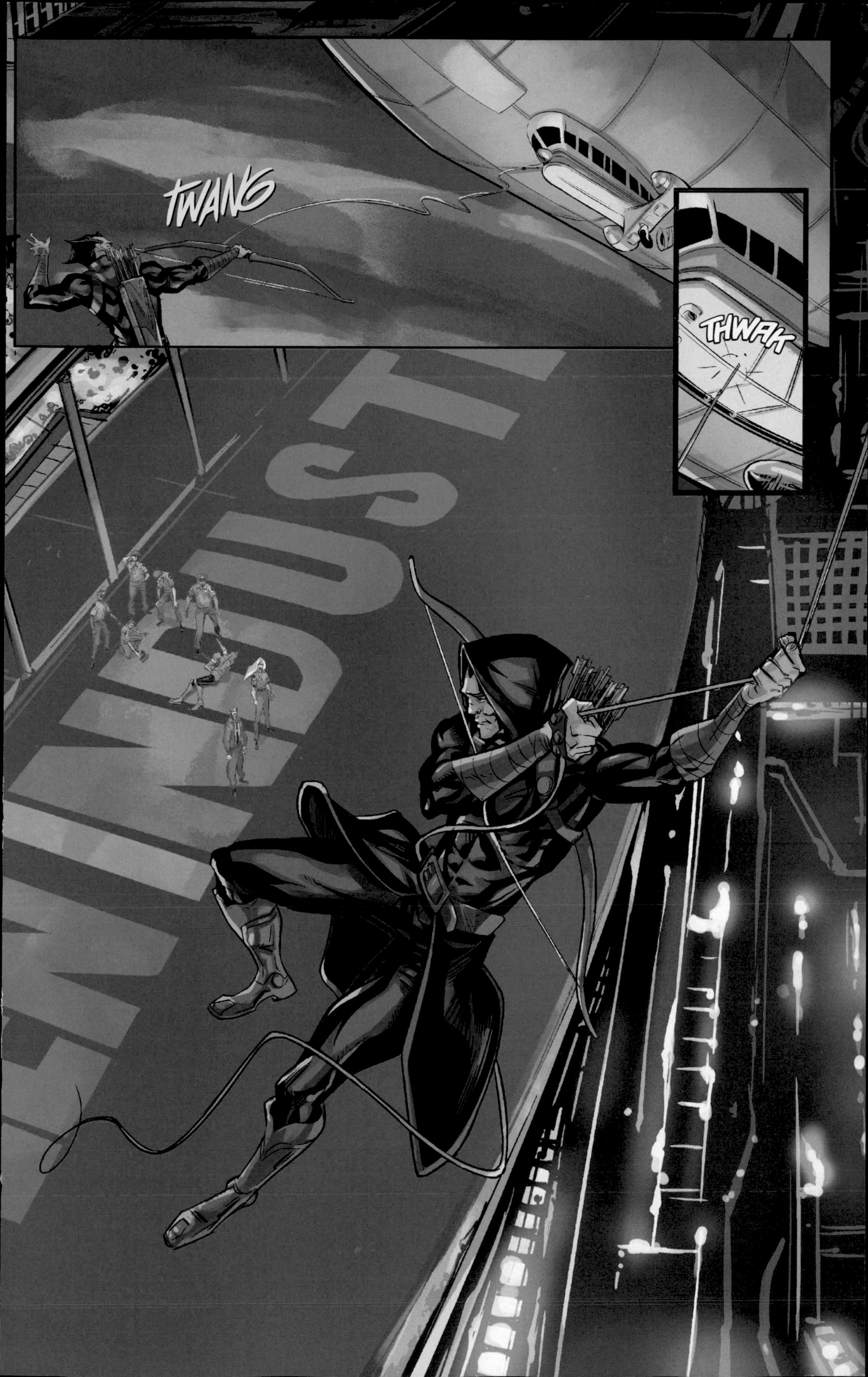
TWANG
THWAK

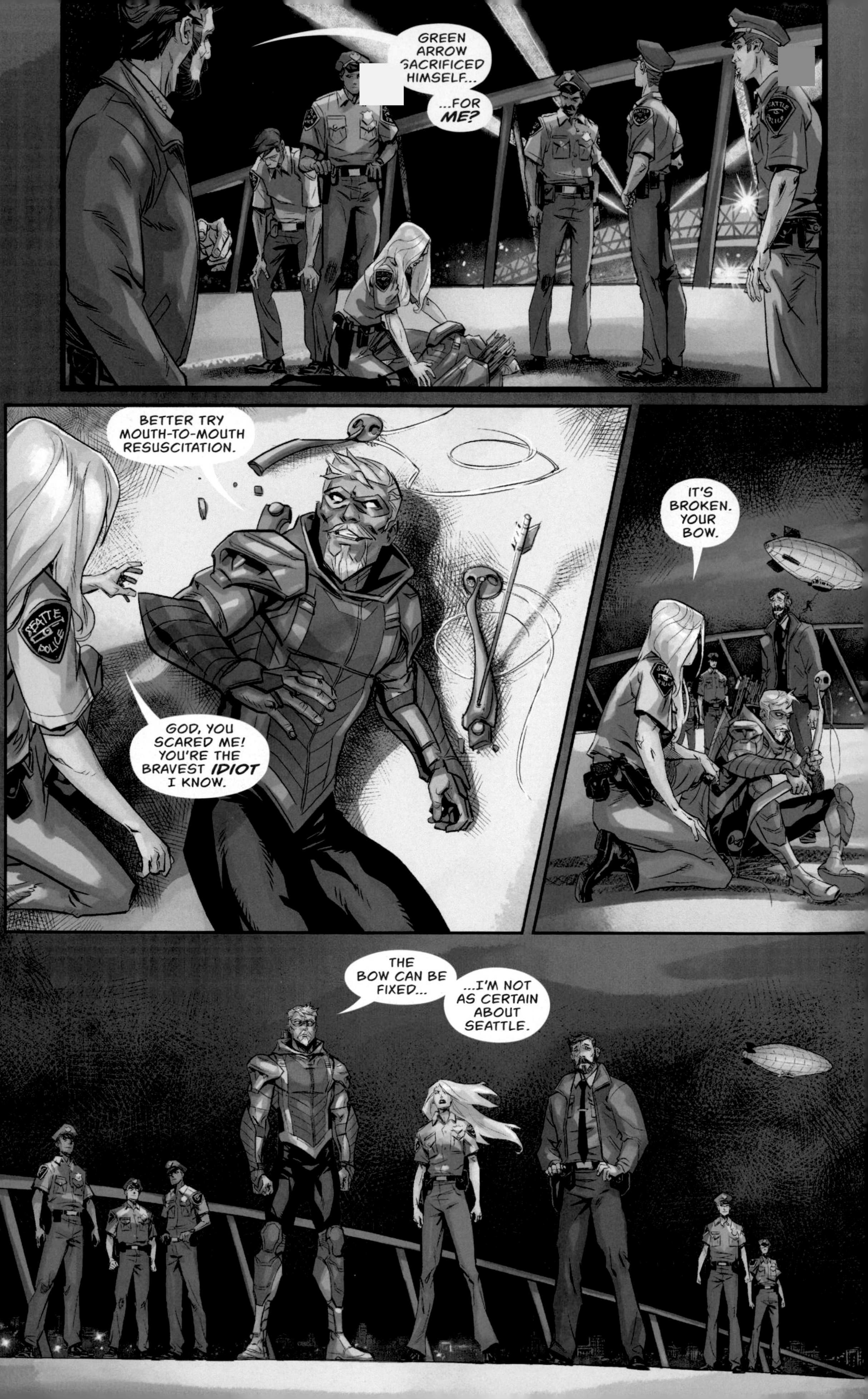
GREEN ARROW SACRIFICED HIMSELF...
...FOR *ME?*
BETTER TRY MOUTH-TO-MOUTH RESUSCITATION.
GOD, YOU SCARED ME! YOU'RE THE BRAVEST *IDIOT* I KNOW.
IT'S BROKEN. YOUR BOW.
THE BOW CAN BE FIXED...
...I'M NOT AS CERTAIN ABOUT SEATTLE.

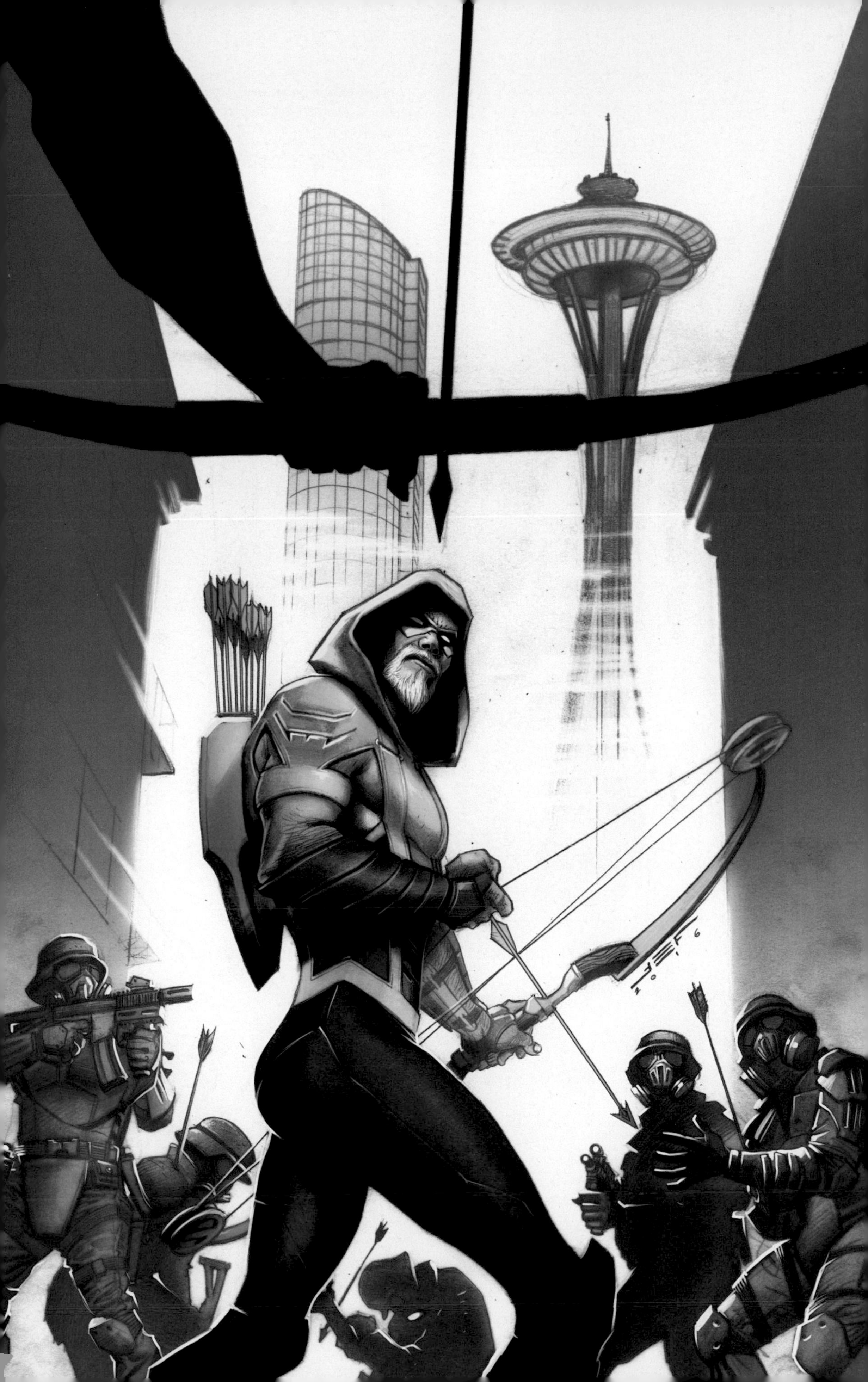

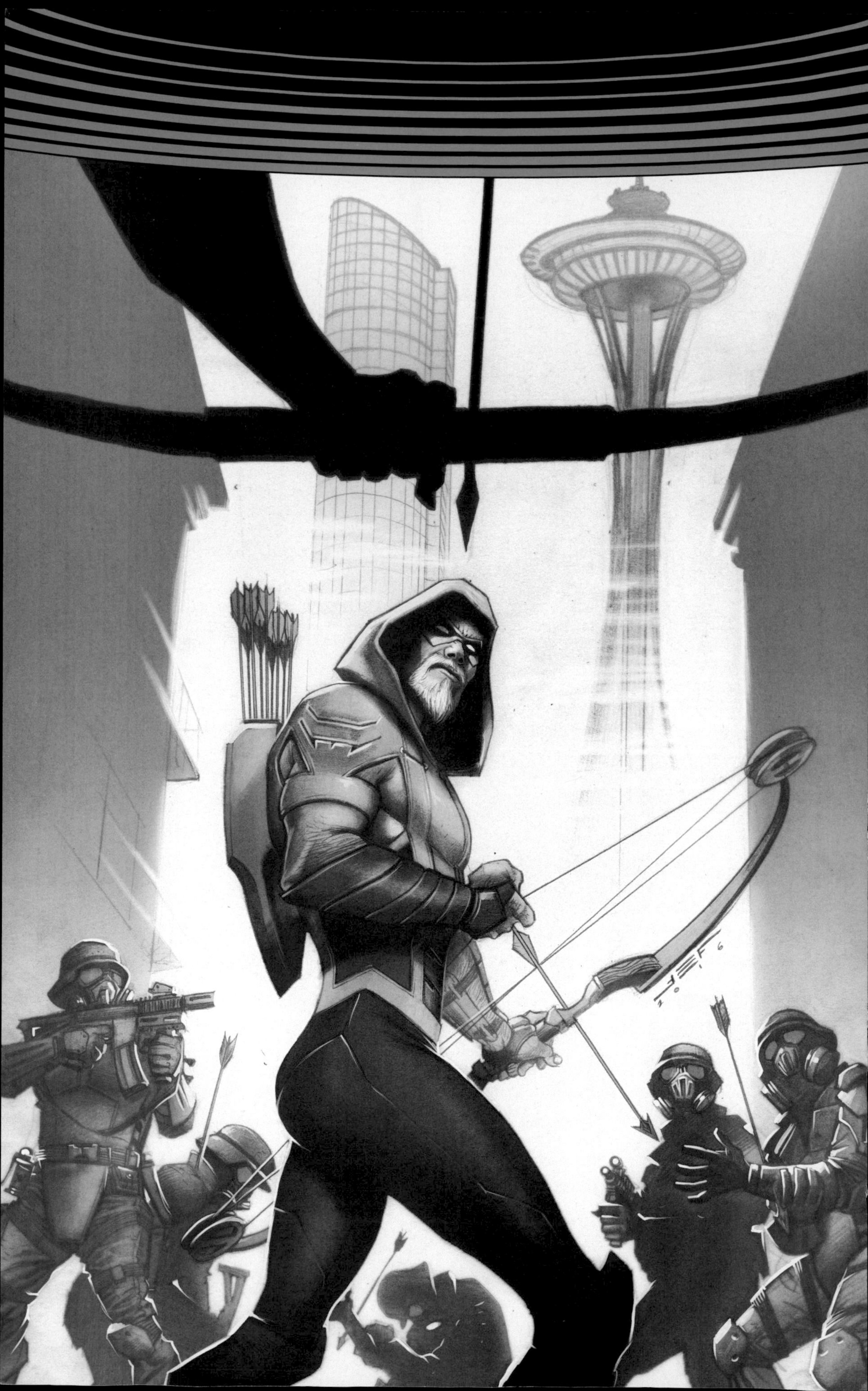

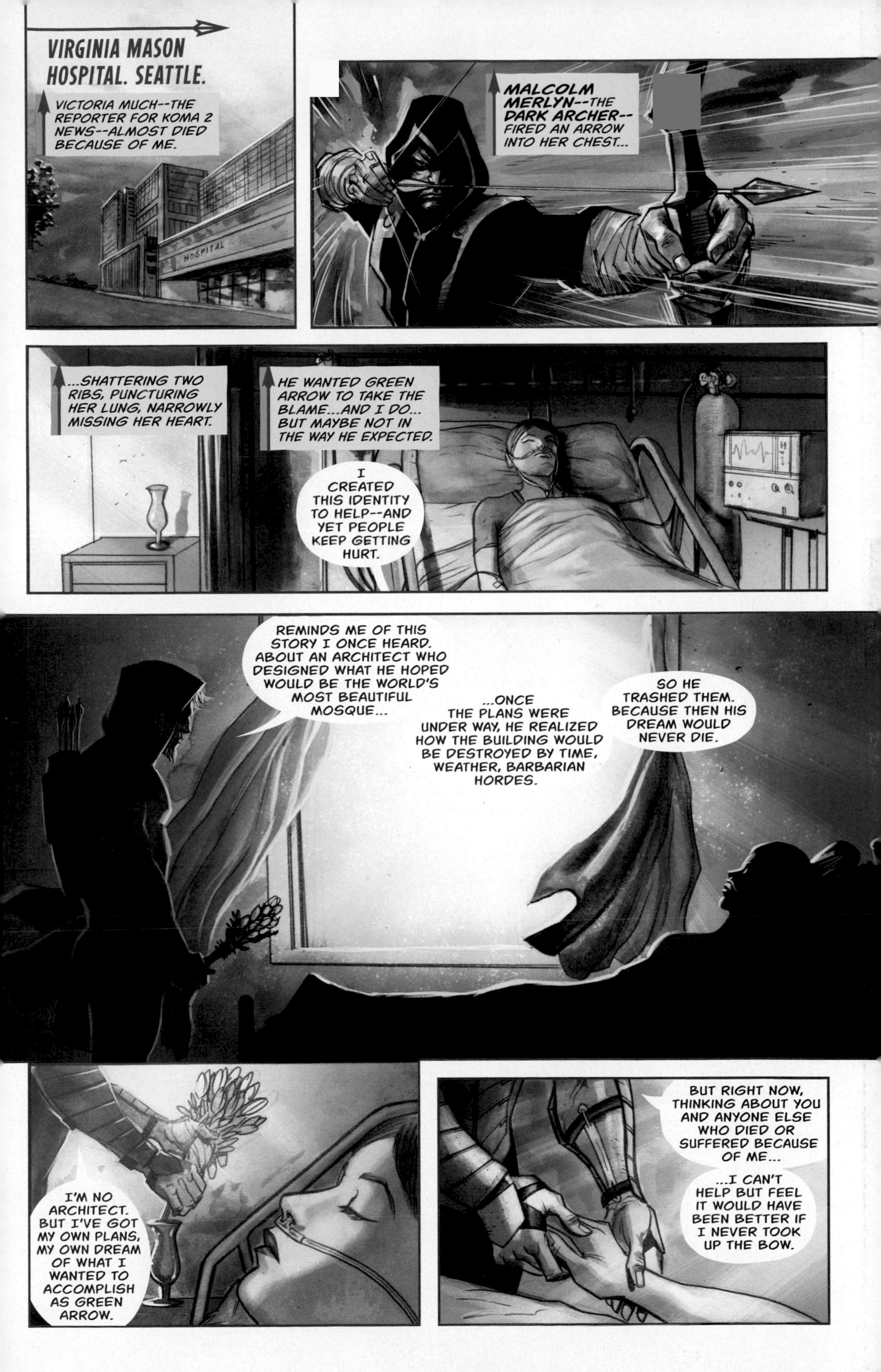
VIRGINIA MASON HOSPITAL. SEATTLE.
VICTORIA MUCH--THE REPORTER FOR KOMA 2 NEWS--ALMOST DIED BECAUSE OF ME.
HOSPITAL
MALCOLM MERLYN--THE DARK ARCHER--FIRED AN ARROW INTO HER CHEST...
...SHATTERING TWO RIBS, PUNCTURING HER LUNG, NARROWLY MISSING HER HEART.
HE WANTED GREEN ARROW TO TAKE THE BLAME...AND I DO... BUT MAYBE NOT IN THE WAY HE EXPECTED.
I CREATED THIS IDENTITY TO HELP--AND YET PEOPLE KEEP GETTING HURT.
REMINDS ME OF THIS STORY I ONCE HEARD. ABOUT AN ARCHITECT WHO DESIGNED WHAT HE HOPED WOULD BE THE WORLD'S MOST BEAUTIFUL MOSQUE...
...ONCE THE PLANS WERE UNDER WAY, HE REALIZED HOW THE BUILDING WOULD BE DESTROYED BY TIME, WEATHER, BARBARIAN HORDES.
SO HE TRASHED THEM. BECAUSE THEN HIS DREAM WOULD NEVER DIE.
I'M NO ARCHITECT. BUT I'VE GOT MY OWN PLANS, MY OWN DREAM OF WHAT I WANTED TO ACCOMPLISH AS GREEN ARROW.
BUT RIGHT NOW, THINKING ABOUT YOU AND ANYONE ELSE WHO DIED OR SUFFERED BECAUSE OF ME...
...I CAN'T HELP BUT FEEL IT WOULD HAVE BEEN BETTER IF I NEVER TOOK UP THE BOW.

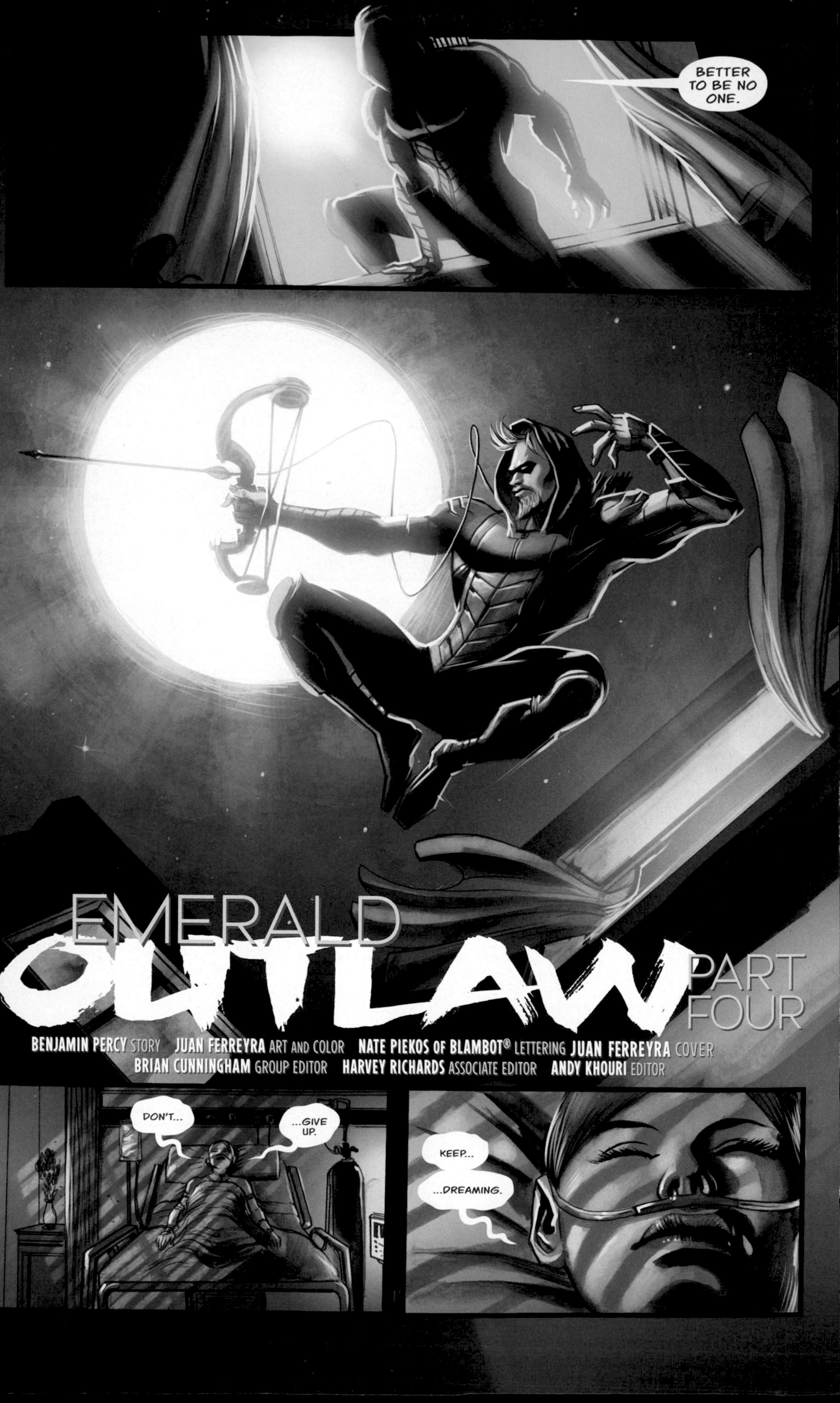

BETTER TO BE NO ONE.
EMERALD
OUTLAW
PART FOUR
BENJAMIN PERCY STORY JUAN FERREYRA ART AND COLOR NATE PIEKOS OF BLAMBOT® LETTERING JUAN FERREYRA COVER
BRIAN CUNNINGHAM GROUP EDITOR HARVEY RICHARDS ASSOCIATE EDITOR ANDY KHOURI EDITOR
DON'T...
...GIVE UP.
KEEP...
...DREAMING.

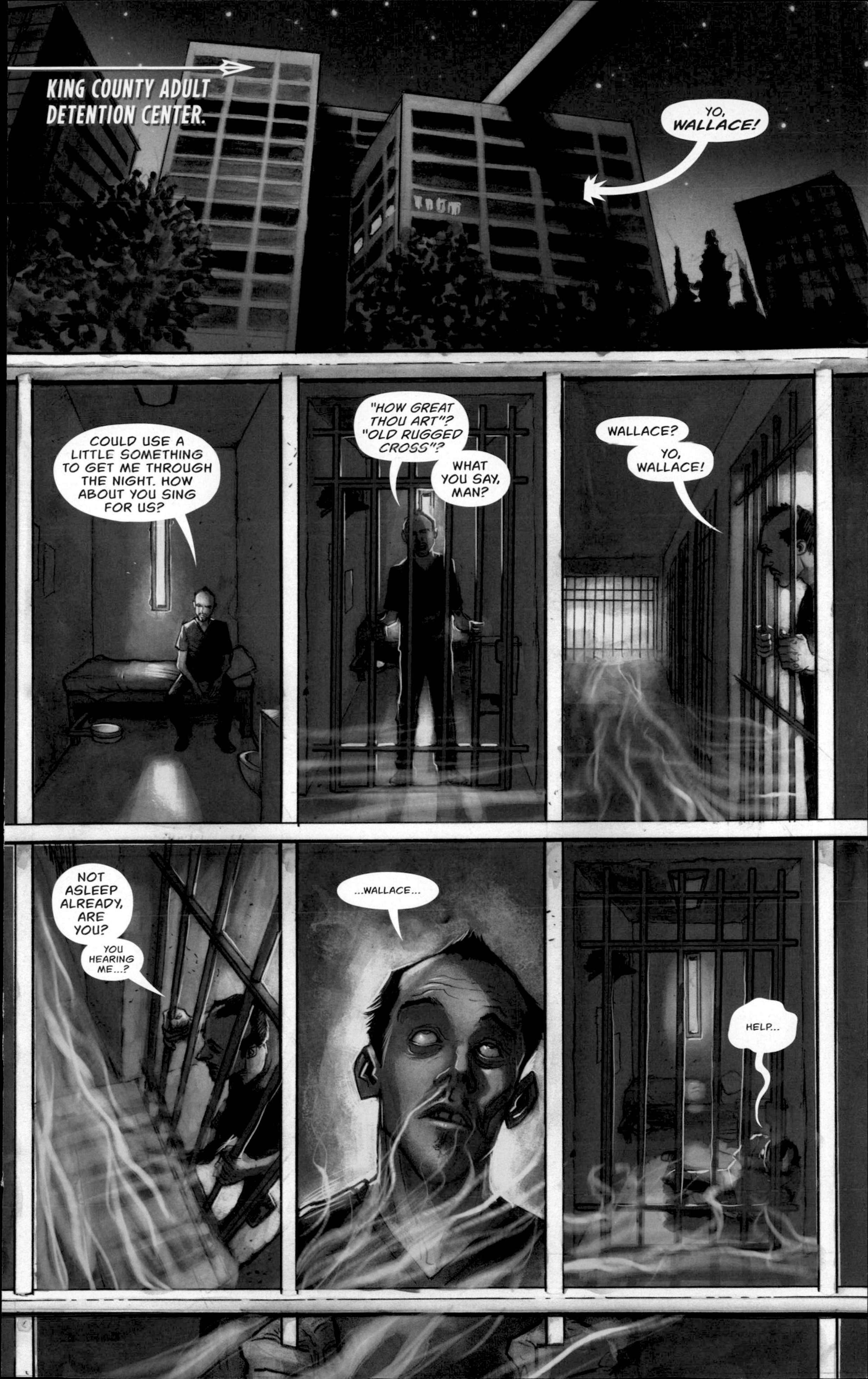

KING COUNTY ADULT DETENTION CENTER.
YO, WALLACE!
COULD USE A LITTLE SOMETHING TO GET ME THROUGH THE NIGHT. HOW ABOUT YOU SING FOR US?
"HOW GREAT THOU ART"? "OLD RUGGED CROSS"?
WHAT YOU SAY, MAN?
WALLACE?
YO, WALLACE!
NOT ASLEEP ALREADY, ARE YOU?
YOU HEARING ME...?
...WALLACE...
HELP...

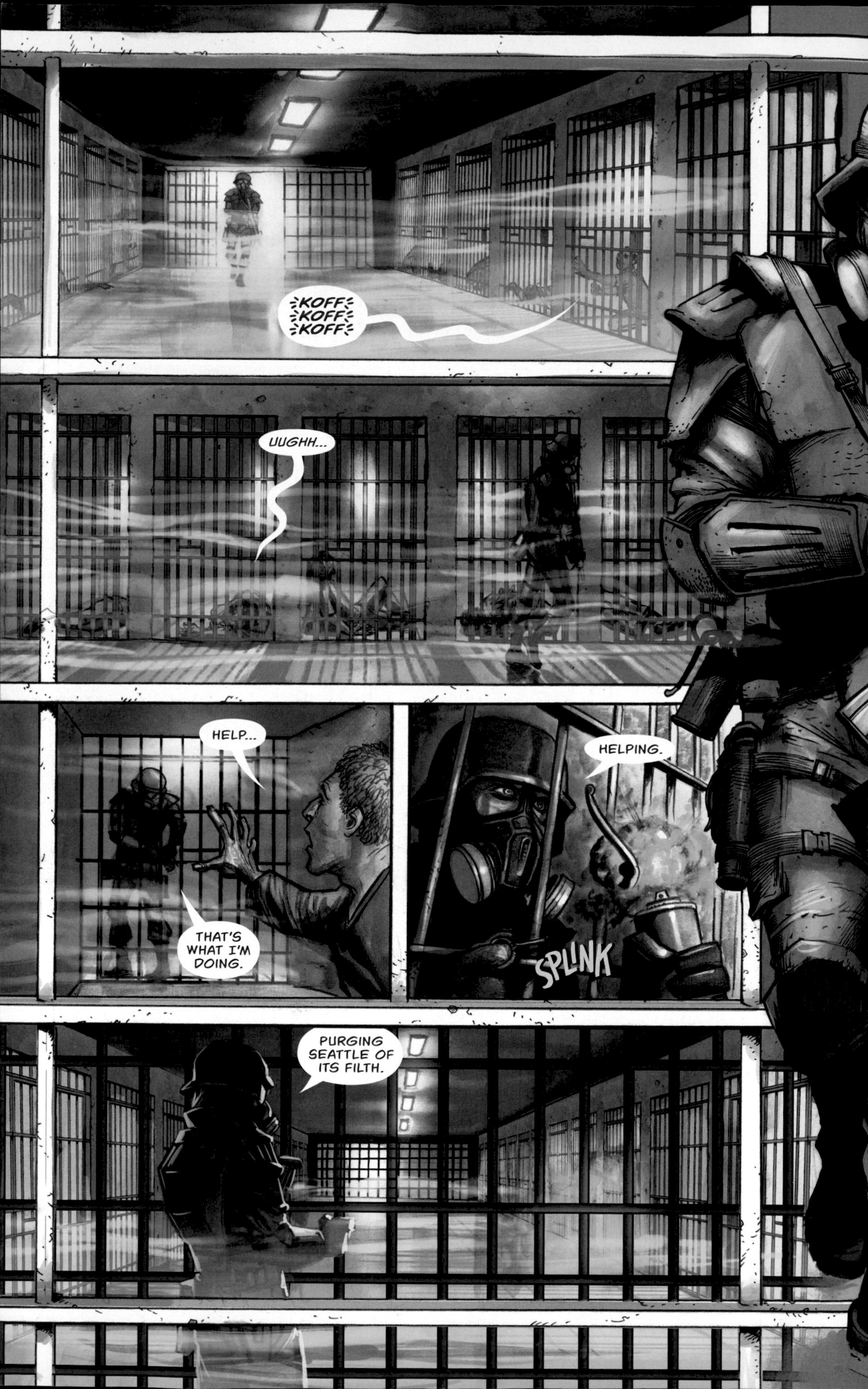
KOFF KOFF KOFF
UUGHH...
HELP...
THAT'S WHAT I'M DOING.
HELPING.
SPLINK
PURGING SEATTLE OF ITS FILTH.

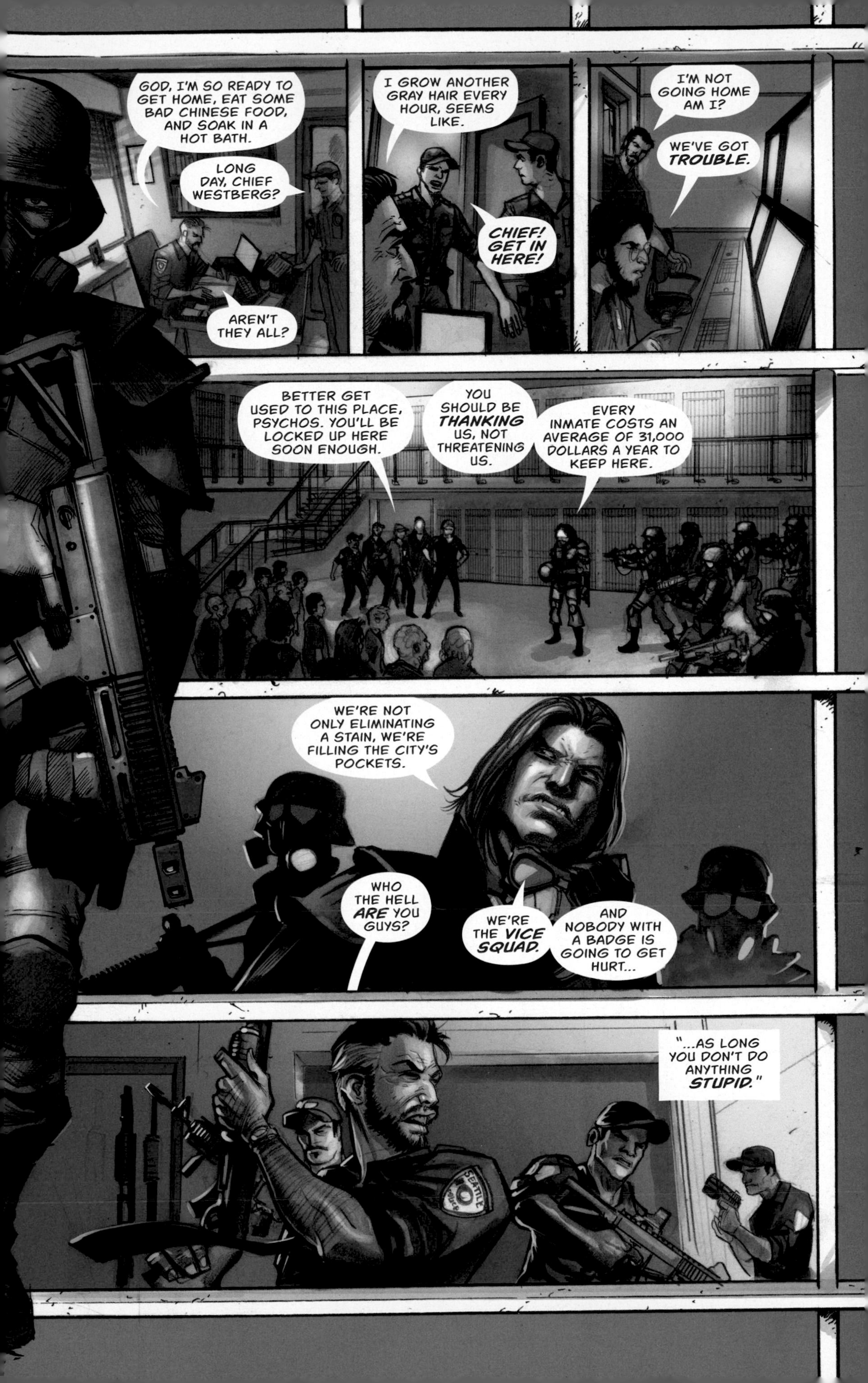
GOD, I'M SO READY TO GET HOME, EAT SOME BAD CHINESE FOOD, AND SOAK IN A HOT BATH.
LONG DAY, CHIEF WESTBERG?
AREN'T THEY ALL?
I GROW ANOTHER GRAY HAIR EVERY HOUR, SEEMS LIKE.
CHIEF! GET IN HERE!
I'M NOT GOING HOME AM I?
WE'VE GOT TROUBLE.
BETTER GET USED TO THIS PLACE, PSYCHOS. YOU'LL BE LOCKED UP HERE SOON ENOUGH.
YOU SHOULD BE THANKING US, NOT THREATENING US.
EVERY INMATE COSTS AN AVERAGE OF 31,000 DOLLARS A YEAR TO KEEP HERE.
WE'RE NOT ONLY ELIMINATING A STAIN, WE'RE FILLING THE CITY'S POCKETS.
WHO THE HELL ARE YOU GUYS?
WE'RE THE VICE SQUAD.
AND NOBODY WITH A BADGE IS GOING TO GET HURT...
"...AS LONG YOU DON'T DO ANYTHING STUPID."

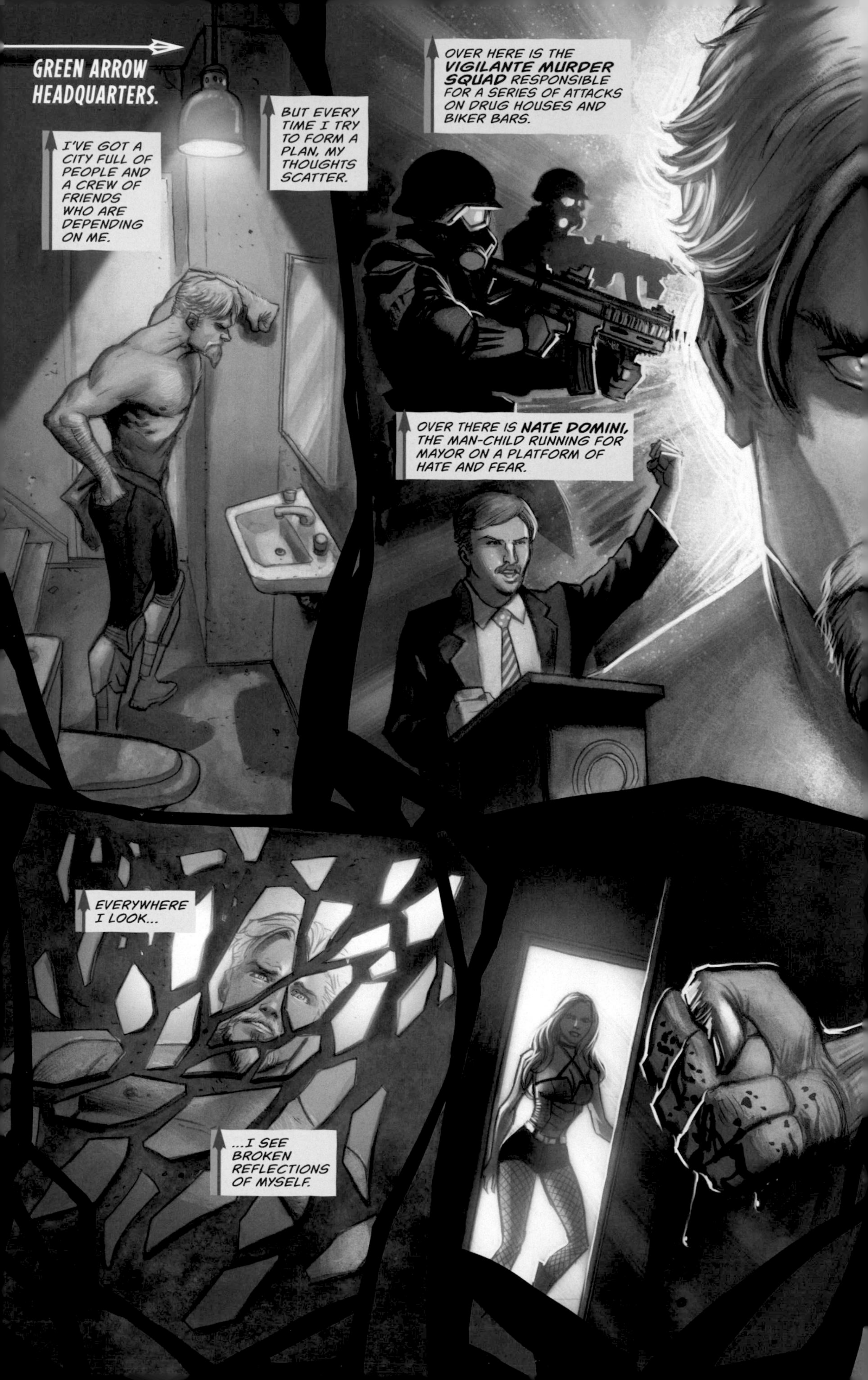
GREEN ARROW HEADQUARTERS.
I'VE GOT A CITY FULL OF PEOPLE AND A CREW OF FRIENDS WHO ARE DEPENDING ON ME.
BUT EVERY TIME I TRY TO FORM A PLAN, MY THOUGHTS SCATTER.
OVER HERE IS THE VIGILANTE MURDER SQUAD RESPONSIBLE FOR A SERIES OF ATTACKS ON DRUG HOUSES AND BIKER BARS.
OVER THERE IS NATE DOMINI, THE MAN-CHILD RUNNING FOR MAYOR ON A PLATFORM OF HATE AND FEAR.
EVERYWHERE I LOOK...
...I SEE BROKEN REFLECTIONS OF MYSELF.

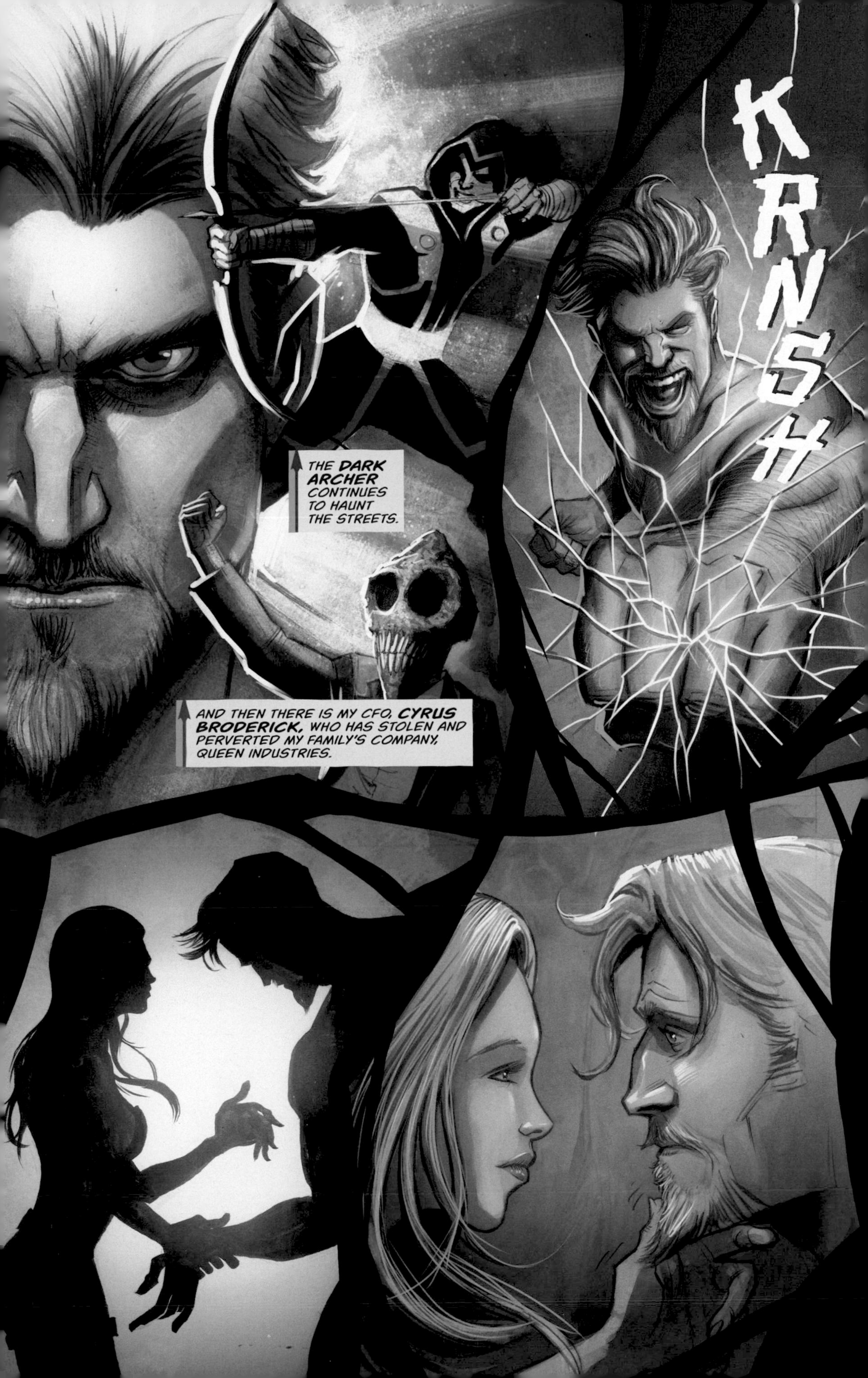
KRNSH
THE DARK ARCHER CONTINUES TO HAUNT THE STREETS.
AND THEN THERE IS MY CFO, CYRUS BRODERICK, WHO HAS STOLEN AND PERVERTED MY FAMILY'S COMPANY, QUEEN INDUSTRIES.

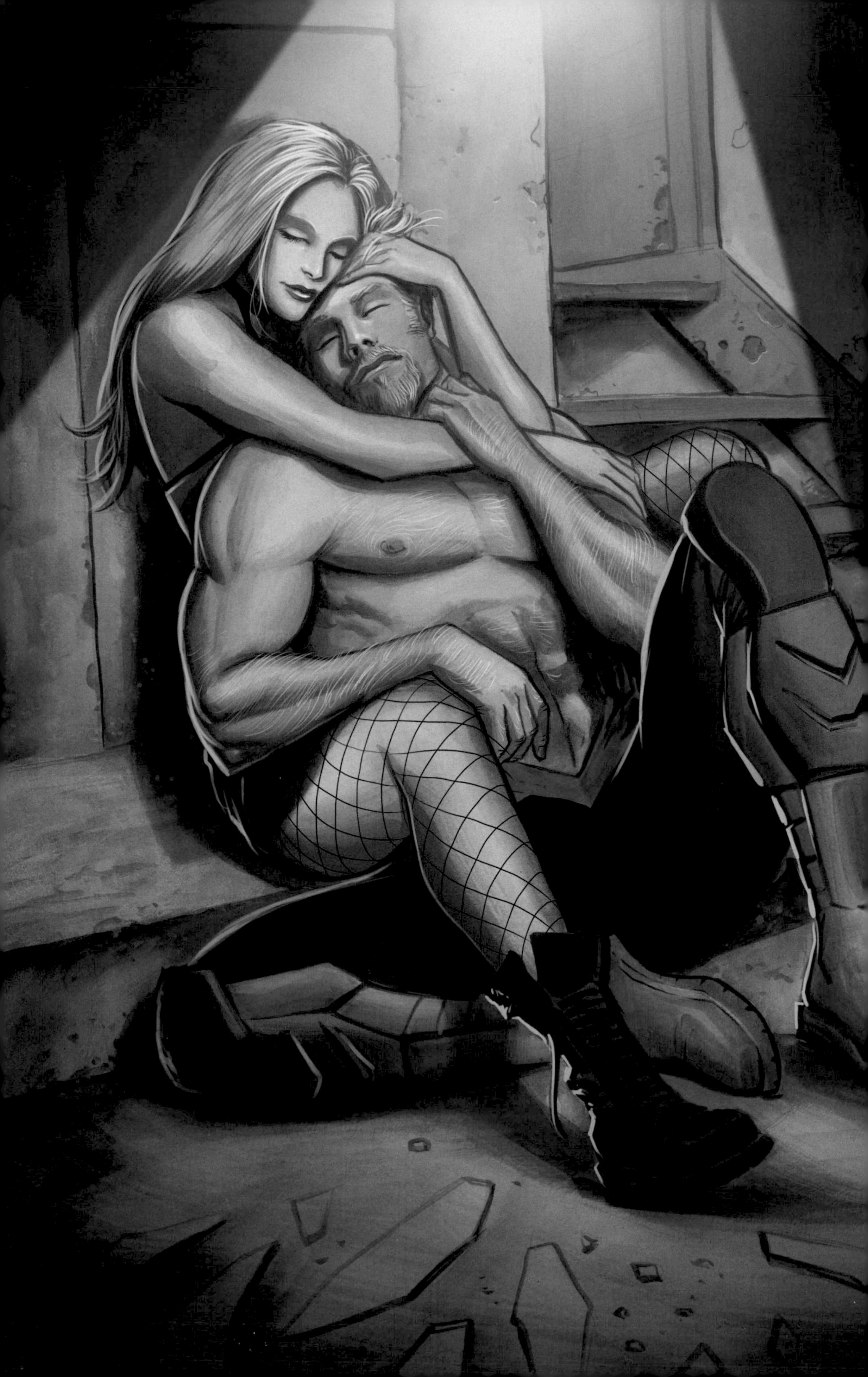

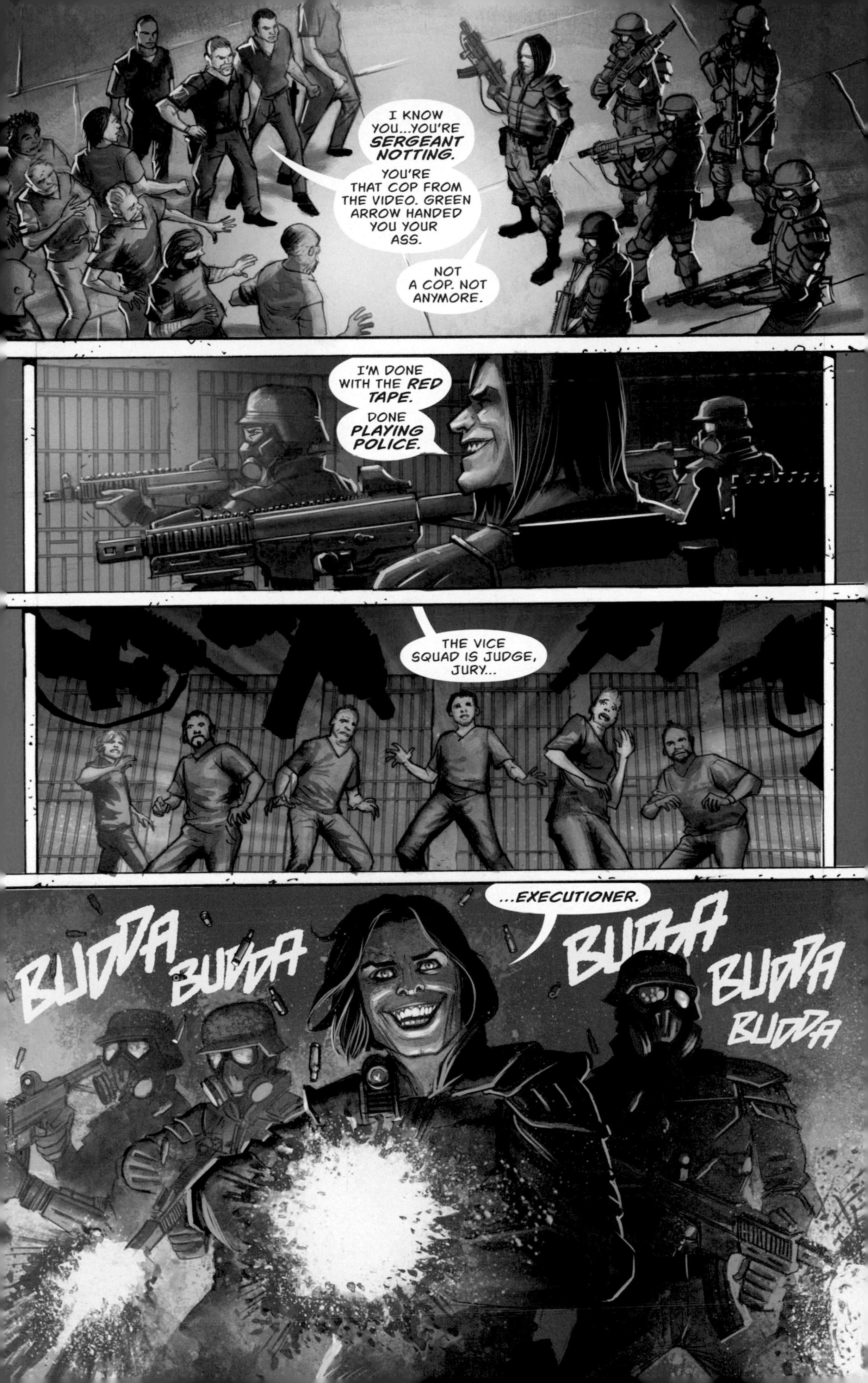
I KNOW YOU...YOU'RE SERGEANT NOTTING.
YOU'RE THAT COP FROM THE VIDEO. GREEN ARROW HANDED YOU YOUR ASS.
NOT A COP. NOT ANYMORE.
I'M DONE WITH THE RED TAPE.
DONE PLAYING POLICE.
THE VICE SQUAD IS JUDGE, JURY...
...EXECUTIONER.
BUDDA BUDDA
BUDDA BUDDA BUDDA

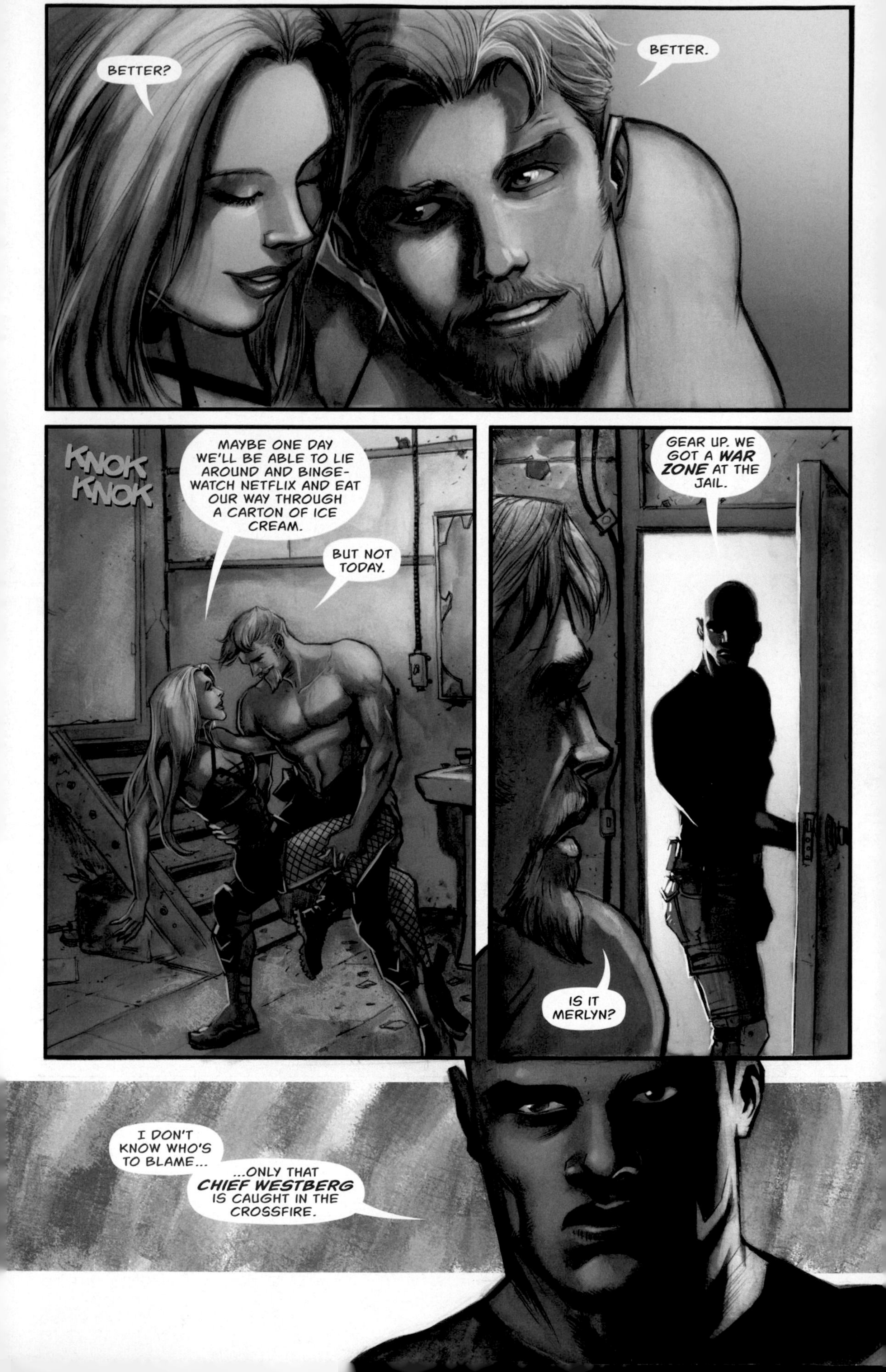
BETTER?
BETTER.
KNOK KNOK
MAYBE ONE DAY WE'LL BE ABLE TO LIE AROUND AND BINGE-WATCH NETFLIX AND EAT OUR WAY THROUGH A CARTON OF ICE CREAM.
BUT NOT TODAY.
GEAR UP. WE GOT A WAR ZONE AT THE JAIL.
IS IT MERLYN?
I DON'T KNOW WHO'S TO BLAME...
...ONLY THAT CHIEF WESTBERG IS CAUGHT IN THE CROSSFIRE.

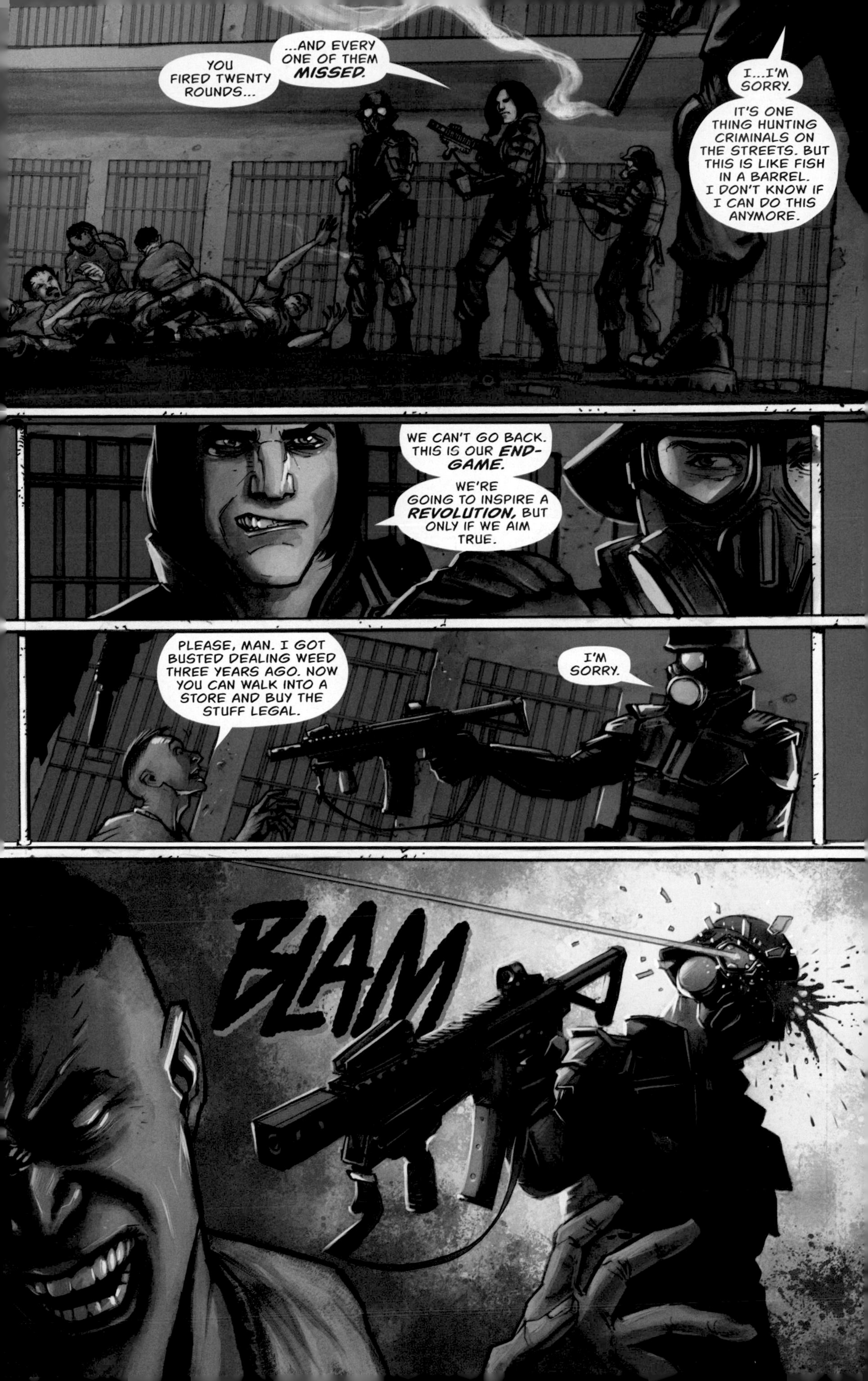
YOU FIRED TWENTY ROUNDS...
...AND EVERY ONE OF THEM MISSED.
I...I'M SORRY.
IT'S ONE THING HUNTING CRIMINALS ON THE STREETS. BUT THIS IS LIKE FISH IN A BARREL. I DON'T KNOW IF I CAN DO THIS ANYMORE.
WE CAN'T GO BACK. THIS IS OUR END-GAME.
WE'RE GOING TO INSPIRE A REVOLUTION, BUT ONLY IF WE AIM TRUE.
PLEASE, MAN. I GOT BUSTED DEALING WEED THREE YEARS AGO. NOW YOU CAN WALK INTO A STORE AND BUY THE STUFF LEGAL.
I'M SORRY.
BLAM

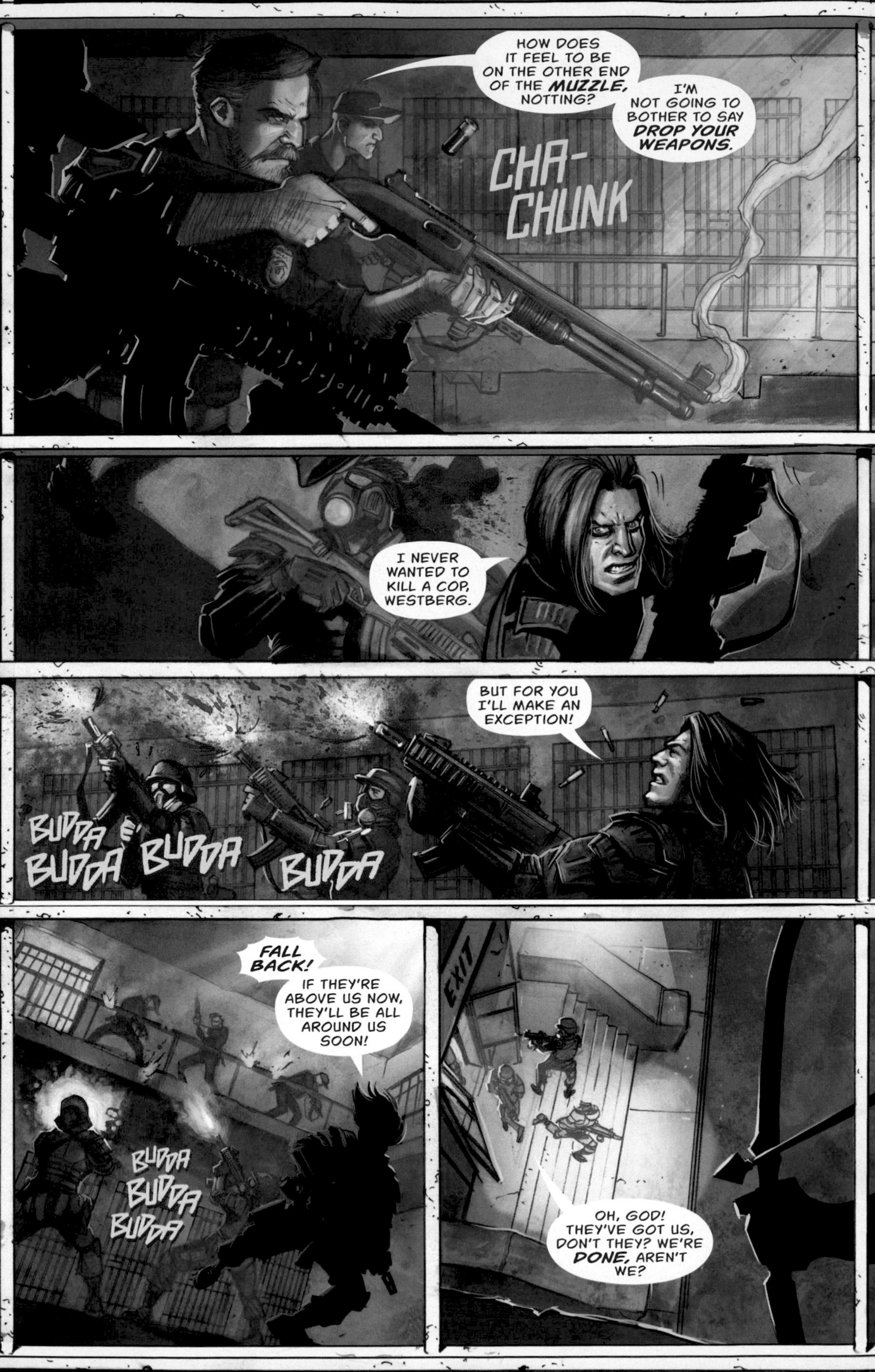
HOW DOES IT FEEL TO BE ON THE OTHER END OF THE MUZZLE, NOTTING?
I'M NOT GOING TO BOTHER TO SAY DROP YOUR WEAPONS.
CHA-CHUNK
I NEVER WANTED TO KILL A COP, WESTBERG.
BUT FOR YOU I'LL MAKE AN EXCEPTION!
BUDDA BUDDA BUDDA
BUDDA
FALL BACK!
IF THEY'RE ABOVE US NOW, THEY'LL BE ALL AROUND US SOON!
BUDDA BUDDA BUDDA
EXIT
OH, GOD! THEY'VE GOT US, DON'T THEY? WE'RE DONE, AREN'T WE?

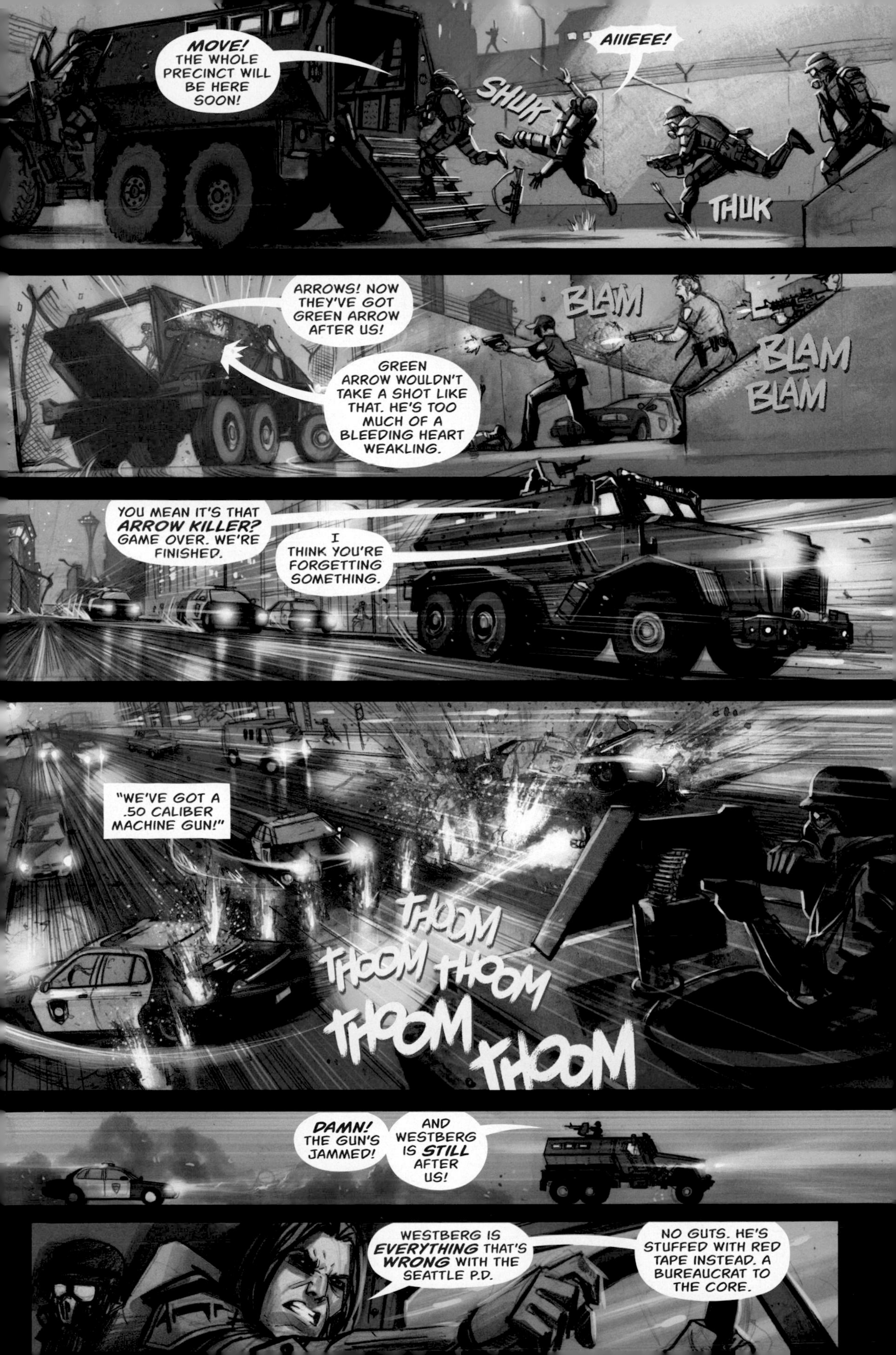
MOVE! THE WHOLE PRECINCT WILL BE HERE SOON!
AIIIEEE!
SHUK
THUK
ARROWS! NOW THEY'VE GOT GREEN ARROW AFTER US!
GREEN ARROW WOULDN'T TAKE A SHOT LIKE THAT. HE'S TOO MUCH OF A BLEEDING HEART WEAKLING.
BLAM
BLAM BLAM
YOU MEAN IT'S THAT ARROW KILLER? GAME OVER. WE'RE FINISHED.
I THINK YOU'RE FORGETTING SOMETHING.
"WE'VE GOT A .50 CALIBER MACHINE GUN!"
THOOM THOOM THOOM THOOM THOOM
DAMN! THE GUN'S JAMMED!
AND WESTBERG IS STILL AFTER US!
WESTBERG IS EVERYTHING THAT'S WRONG WITH THE SEATTLE P.D.
NO GUTS. HE'S STUFFED WITH RED TAPE INSTEAD. A BUREAUCRAT TO THE CORE.

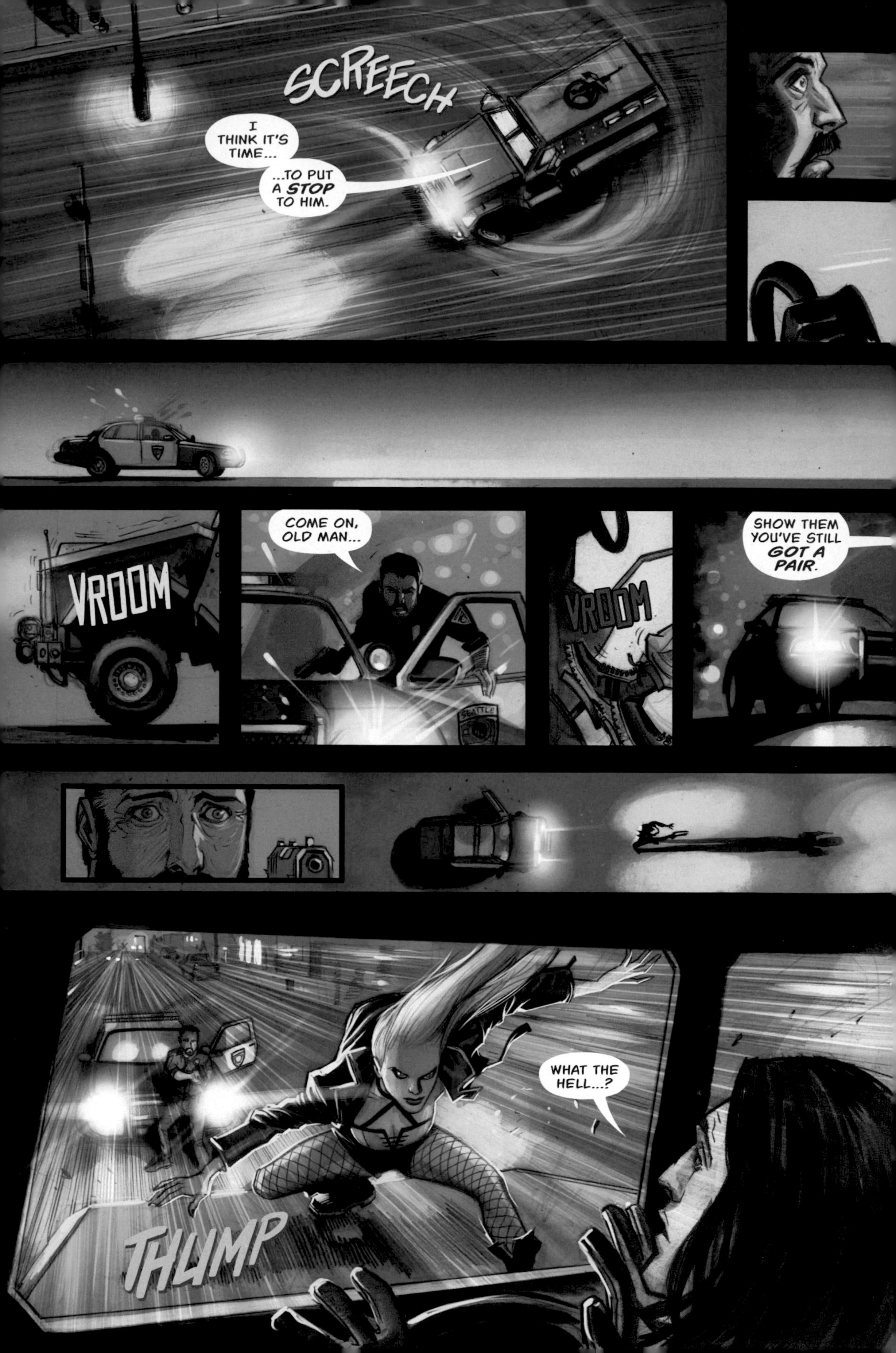
SCREECH
I THINK IT'S TIME...
...TO PUT A STOP TO HIM.
VROOM
COME ON, OLD MAN...
VROOM
SHOW THEM YOU'VE STILL GOT A PAIR.
WHAT THE HELL...?
THUMP

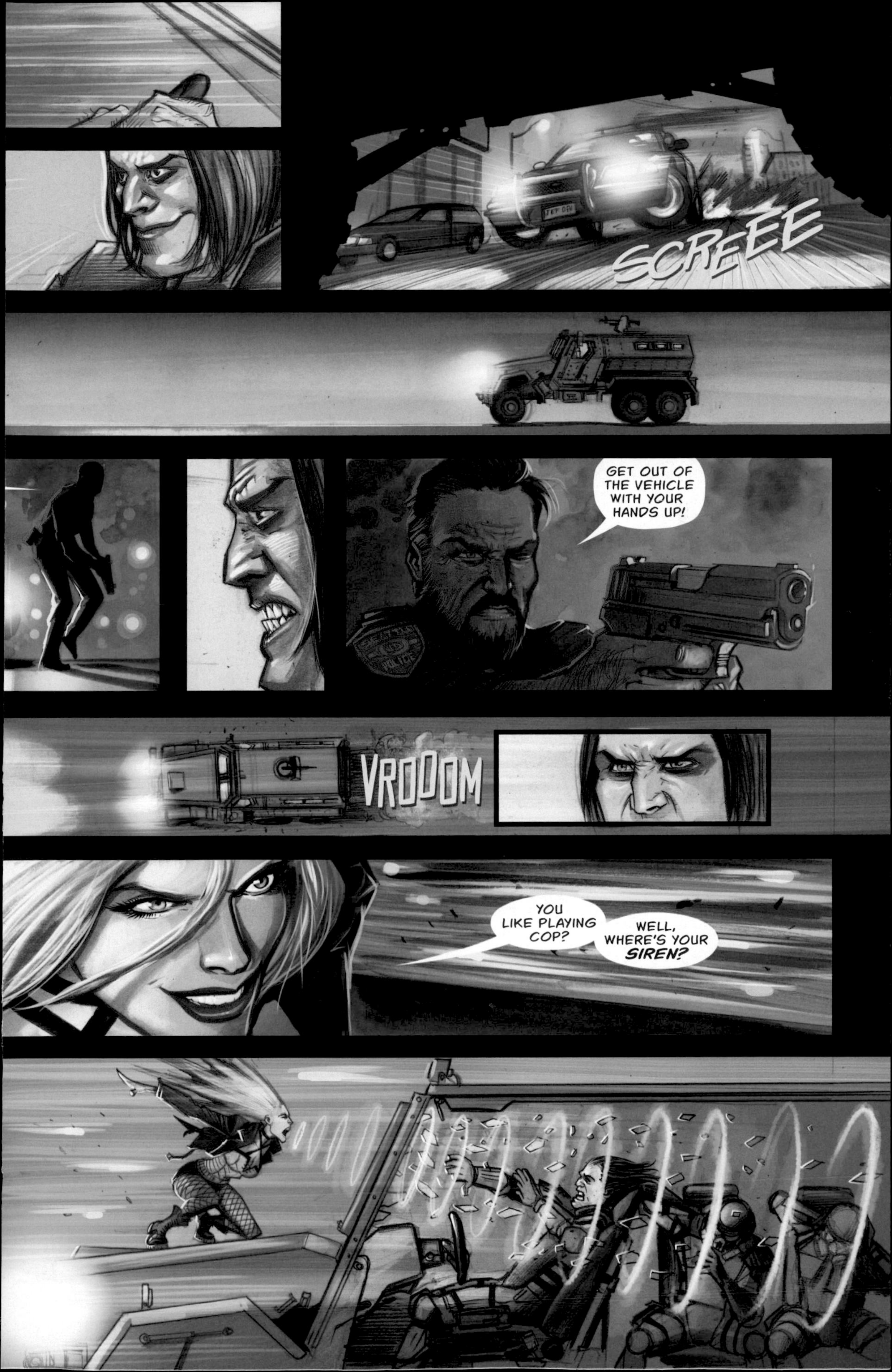
SCREEE
GET OUT OF THE VEHICLE WITH YOUR HANDS UP!
VROOOM
YOU LIKE PLAYING COP?
WELL, WHERE'S YOUR SIREN?

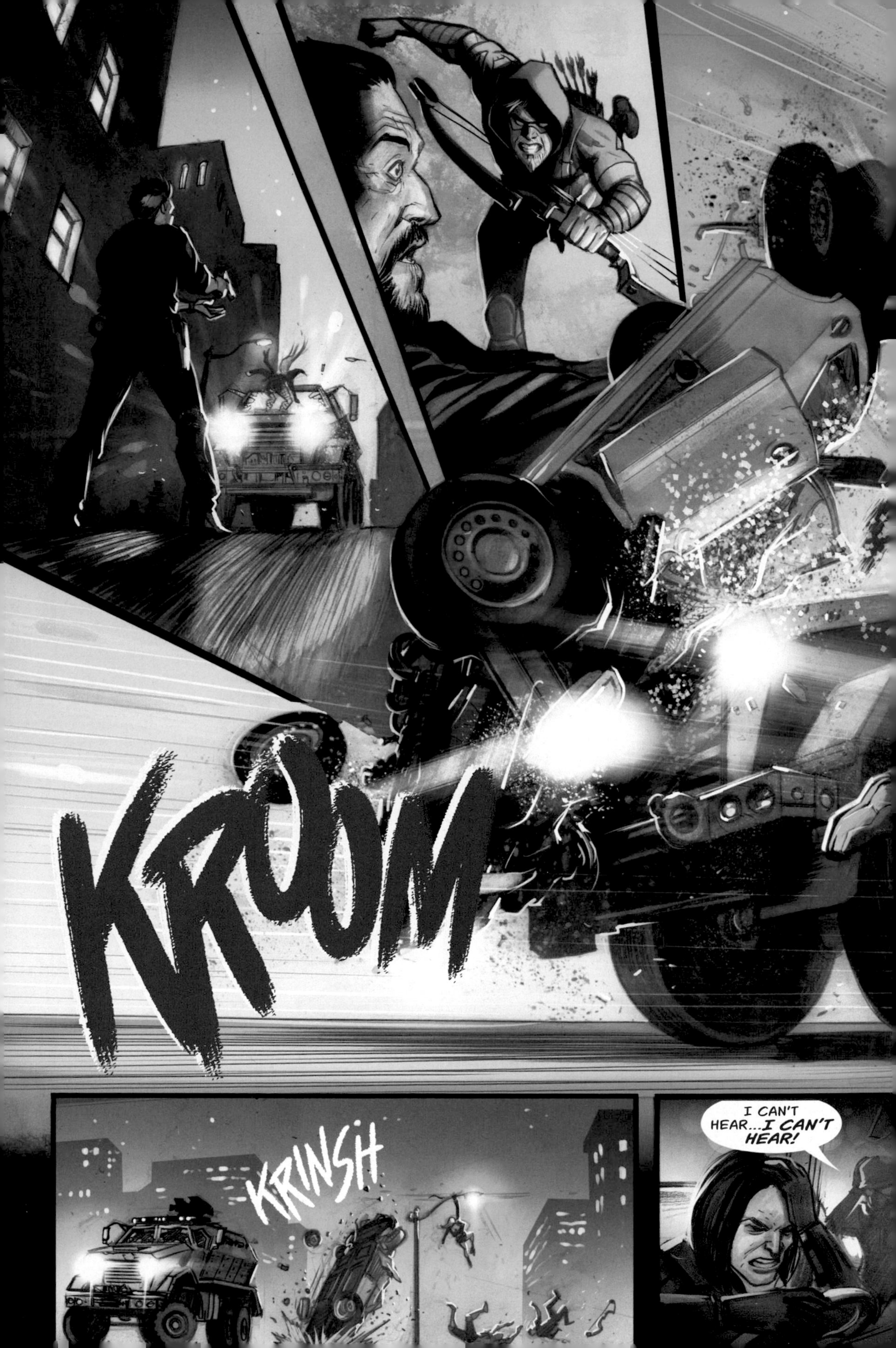
KROOM
KRINSH
I CAN'T HEAR...I CAN'T HEAR!

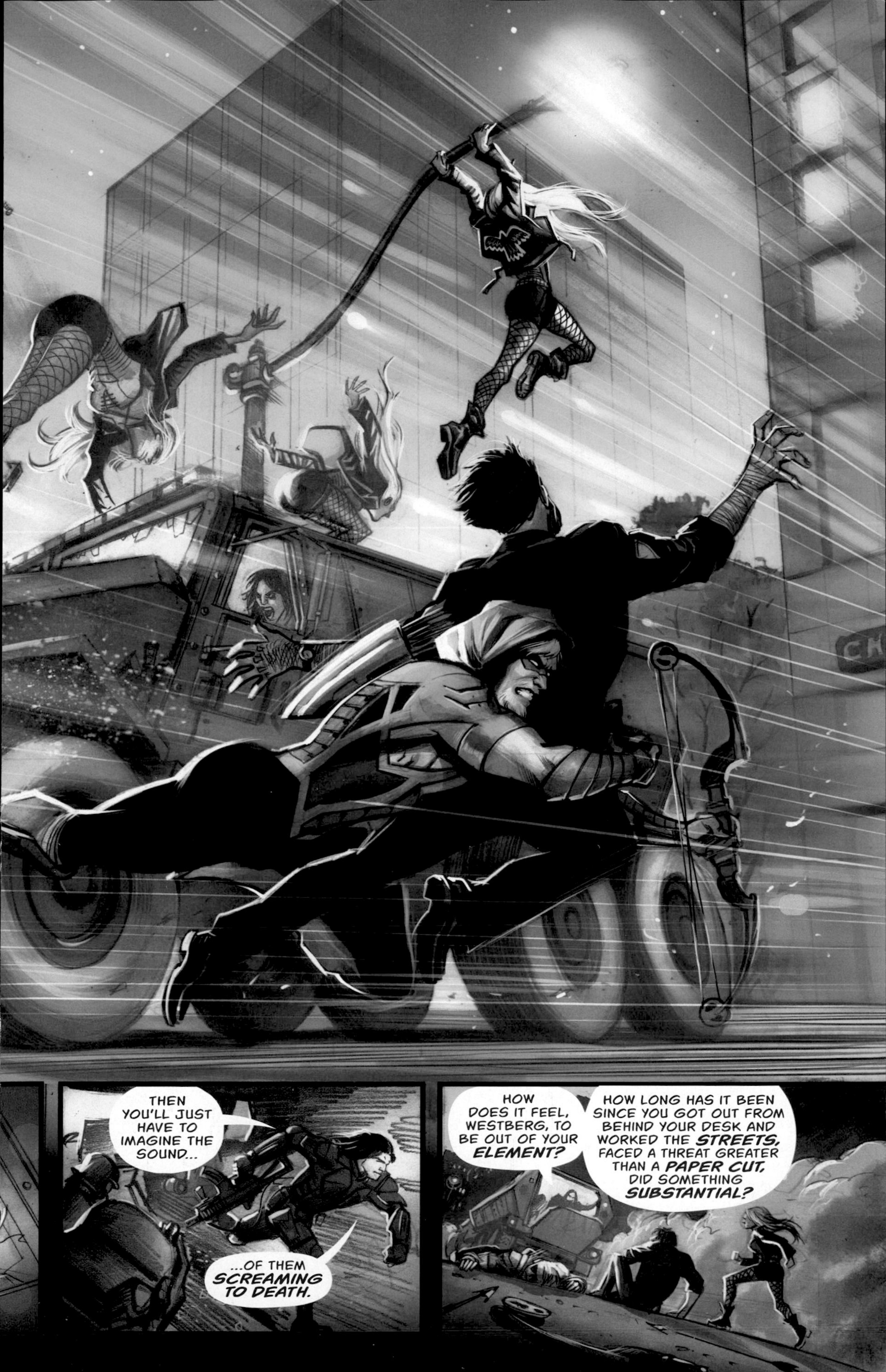
THEN YOU'LL JUST HAVE TO IMAGINE THE SOUND...
...OF THEM SCREAMING TO DEATH.
HOW DOES IT FEEL, WESTBERG, TO BE OUT OF YOUR ELEMENT?
HOW LONG HAS IT BEEN SINCE YOU GOT OUT FROM BEHIND YOUR DESK AND WORKED THE STREETS, FACED A THREAT GREATER THAN A PAPER CUT, DID SOMETHING SUBSTANTIAL?

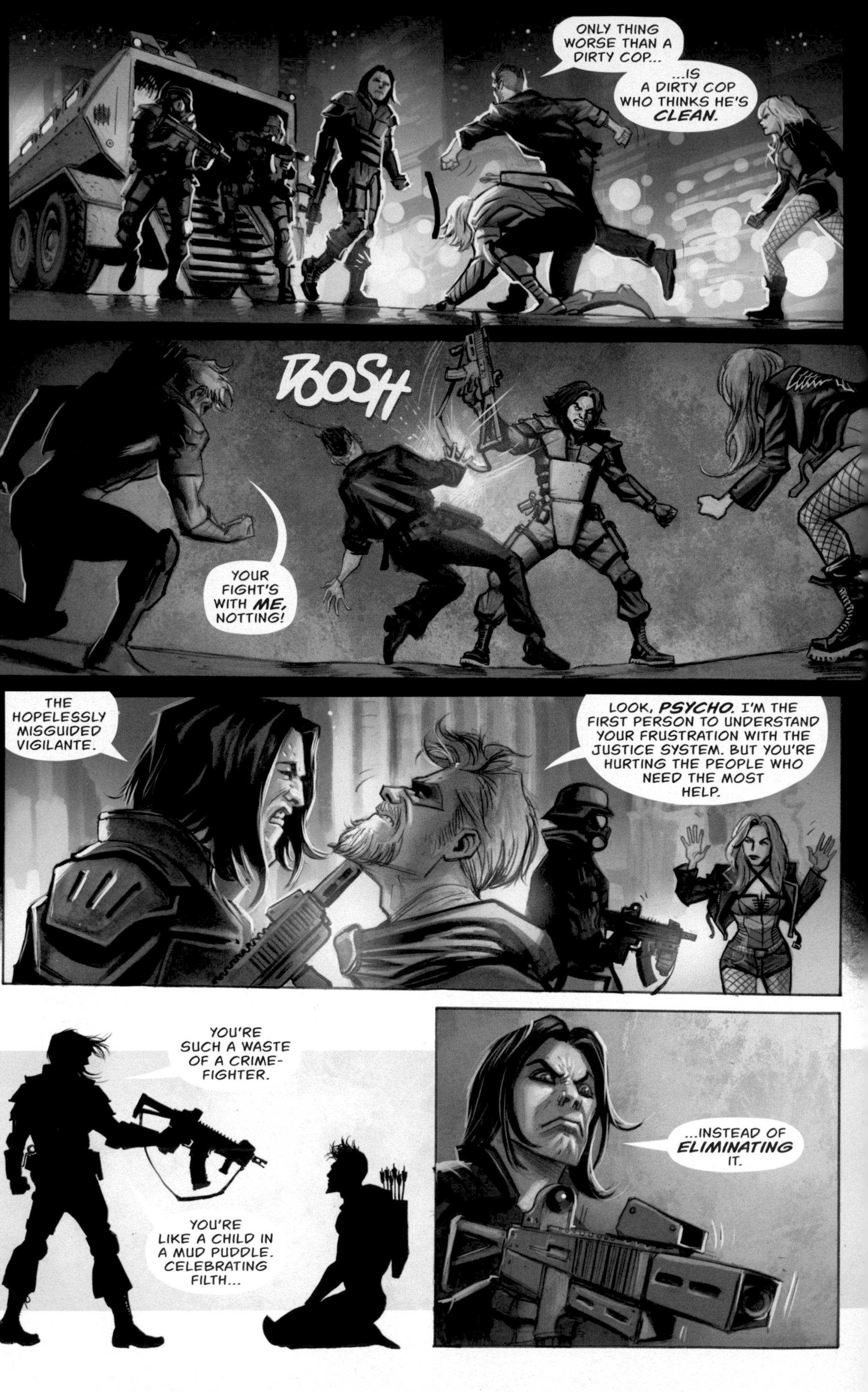
ONLY THING WORSE THAN A DIRTY COP...
...IS A DIRTY COP WHO THINKS HE'S CLEAN.
DOOSH
YOUR FIGHT'S WITH ME, NOTTING!
THE HOPELESSLY MISGUIDED VIGILANTE.
LOOK, PSYCHO. I'M THE FIRST PERSON TO UNDERSTAND YOUR FRUSTRATION WITH THE JUSTICE SYSTEM. BUT YOU'RE HURTING THE PEOPLE WHO NEED THE MOST HELP.
YOU'RE SUCH A WASTE OF A CRIME-FIGHTER.
YOU'RE LIKE A CHILD IN A MUD PUDDLE. CELEBRATING FILTH...
...INSTEAD OF ELIMINATING IT.

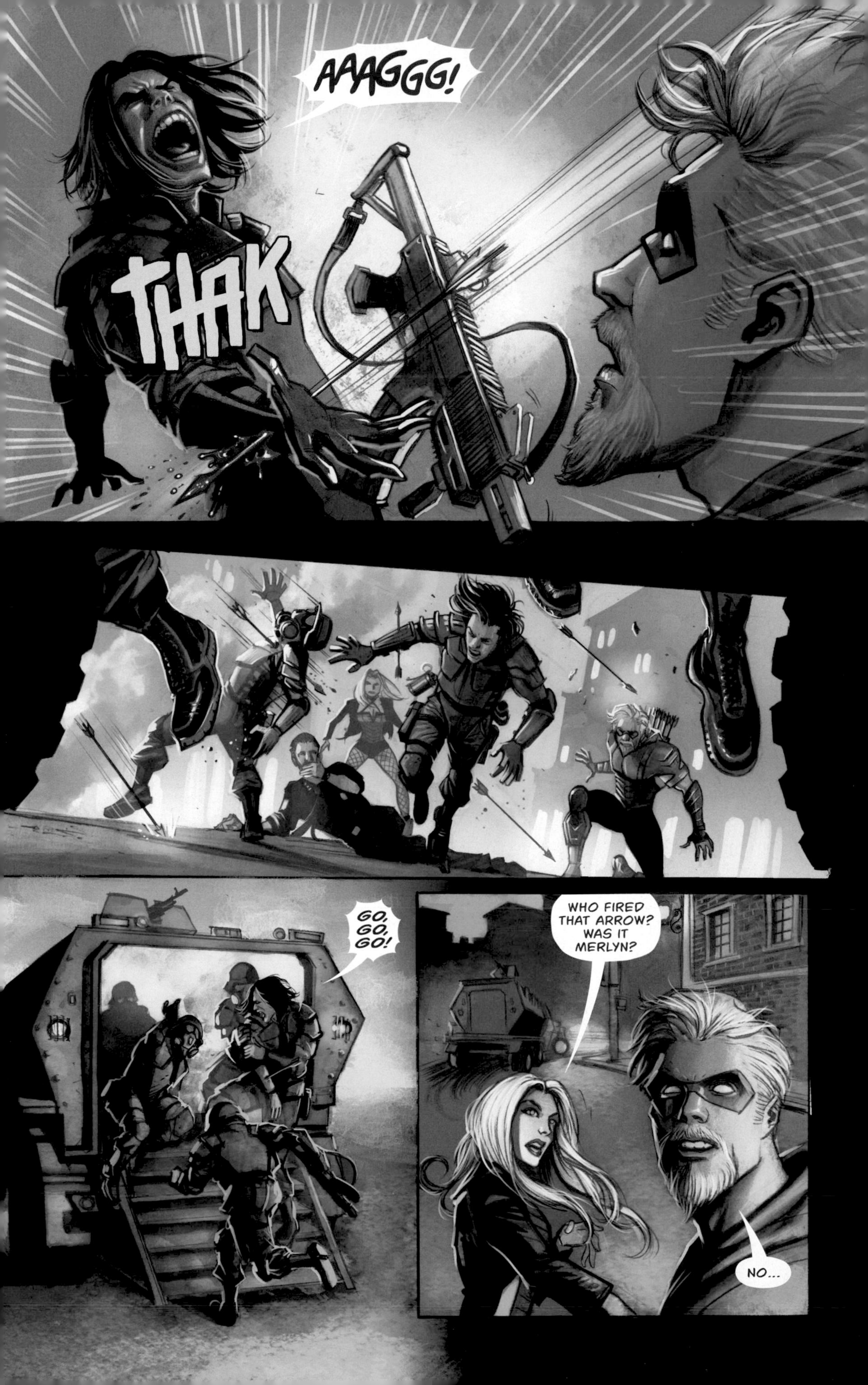
AAAGGG!
THAK
GO, GO, GO!
WHO FIRED THAT ARROW? WAS IT MERLYN?
NO...

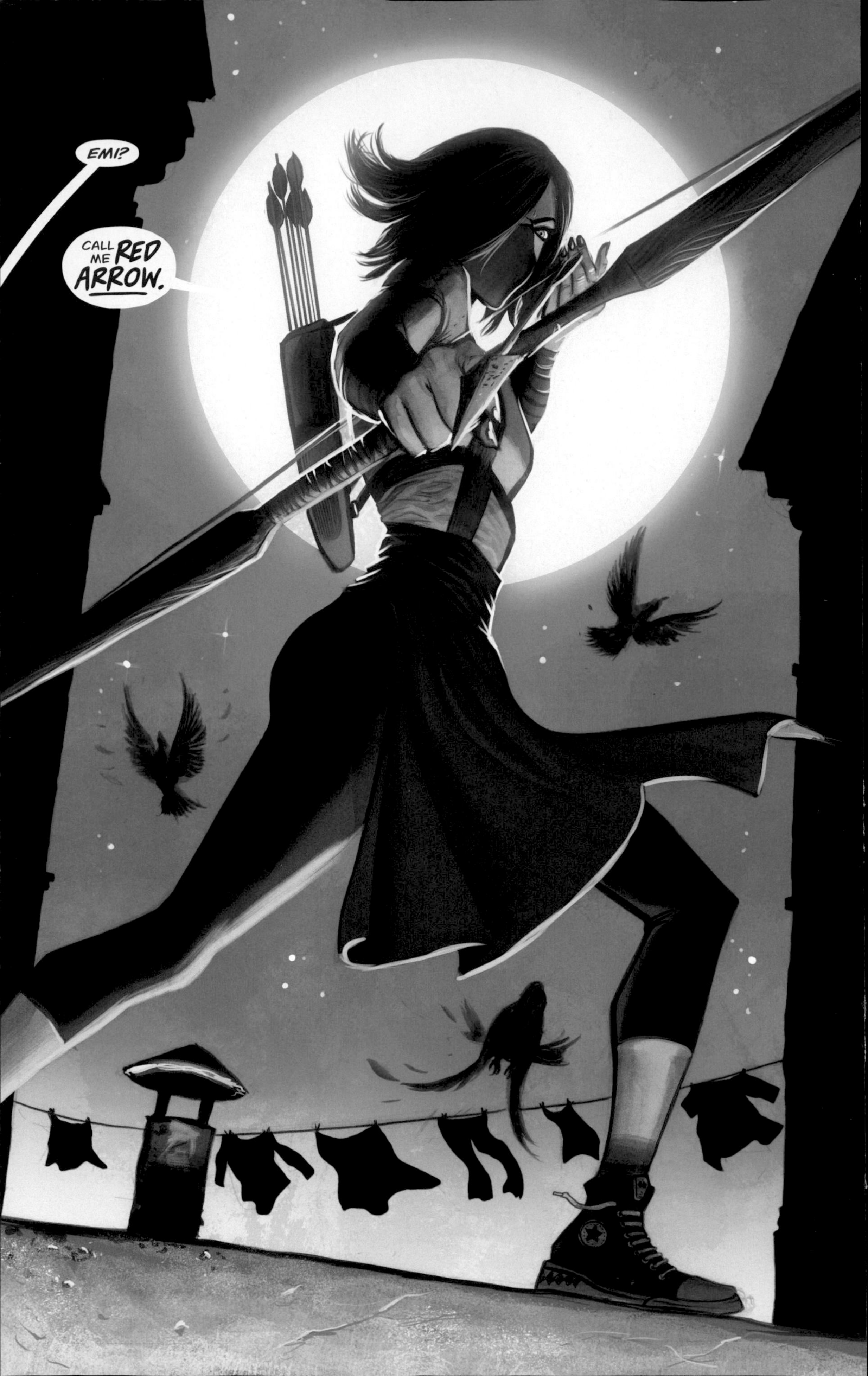
EMI?
CALL ME RED ARROW.

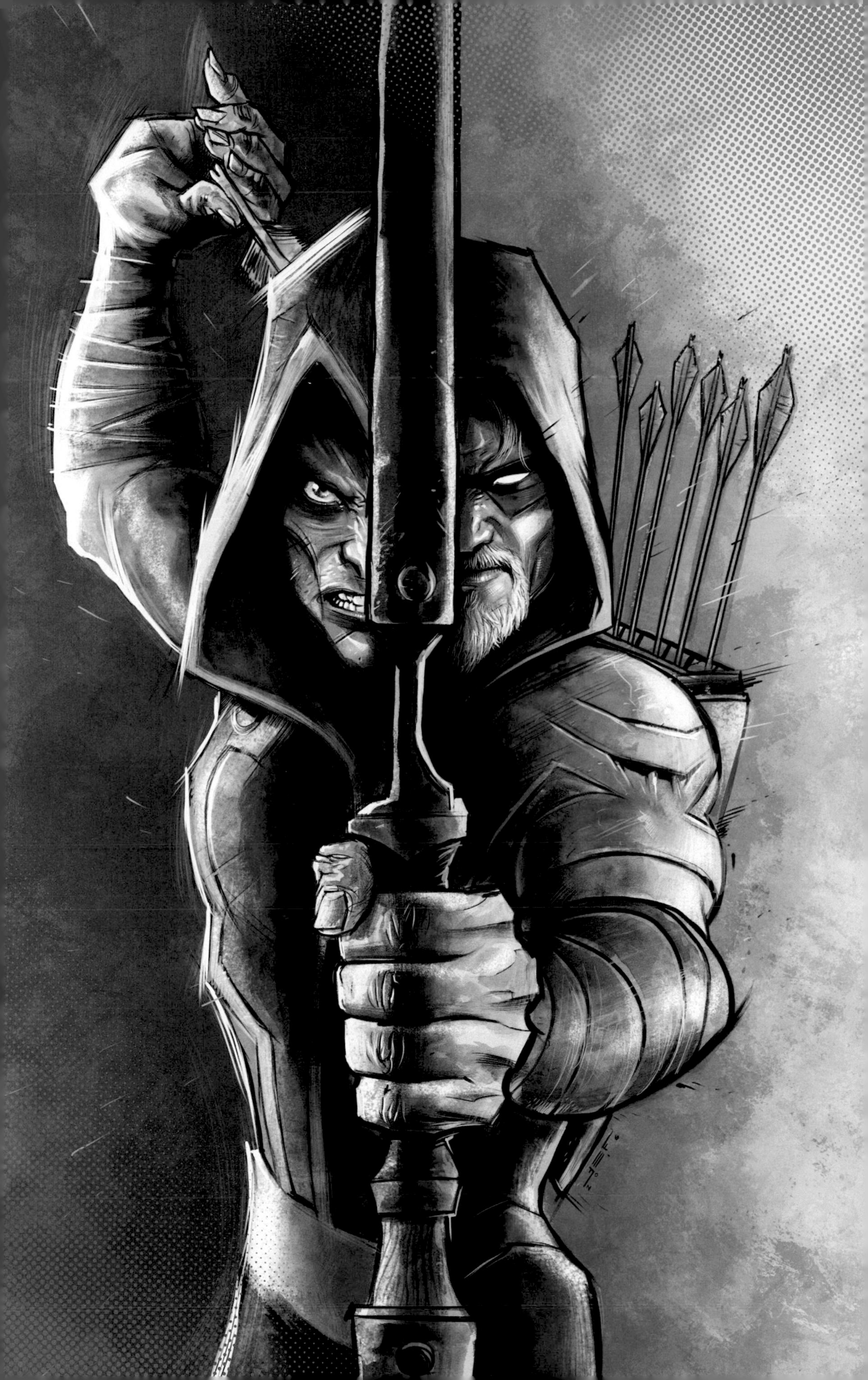

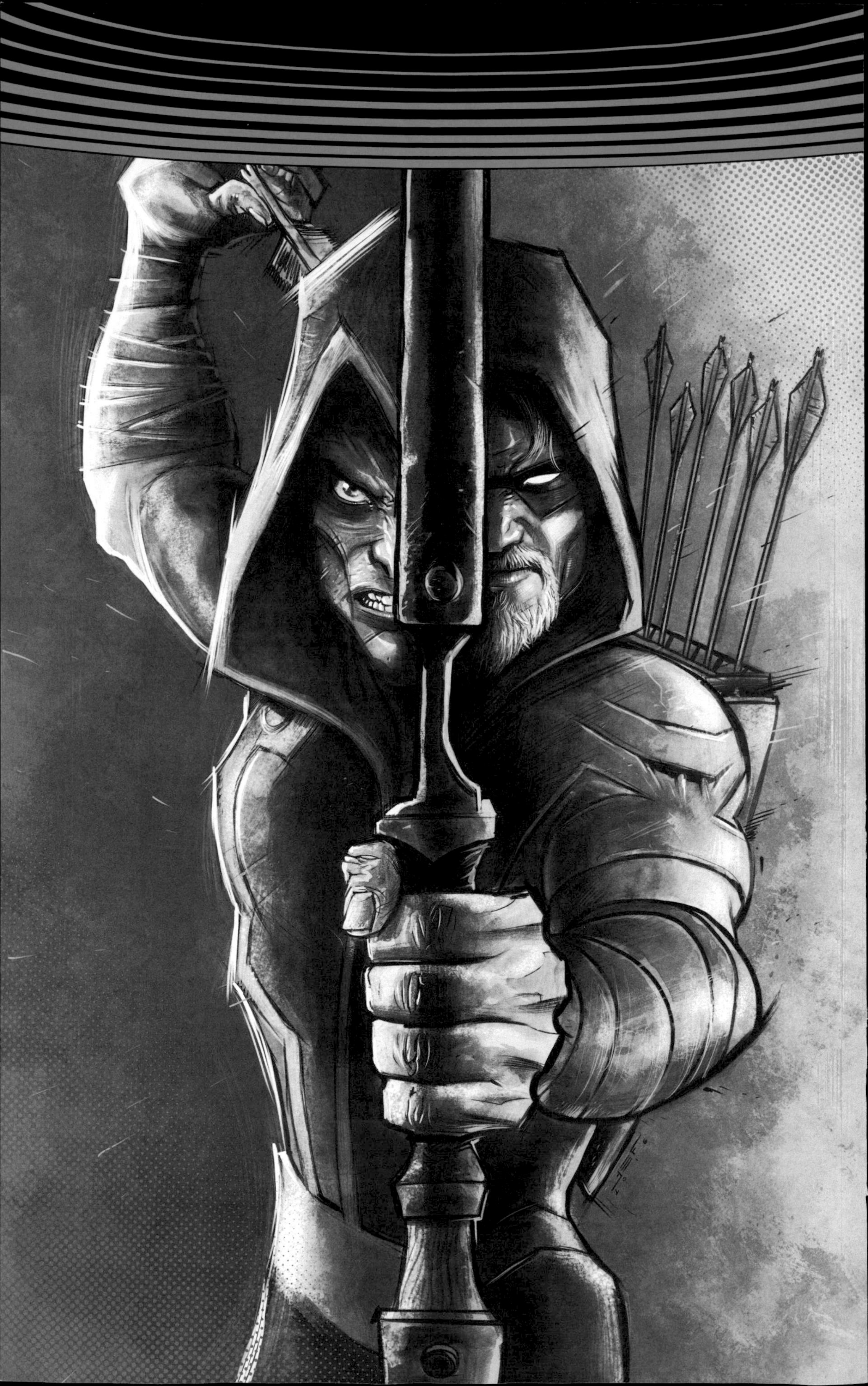

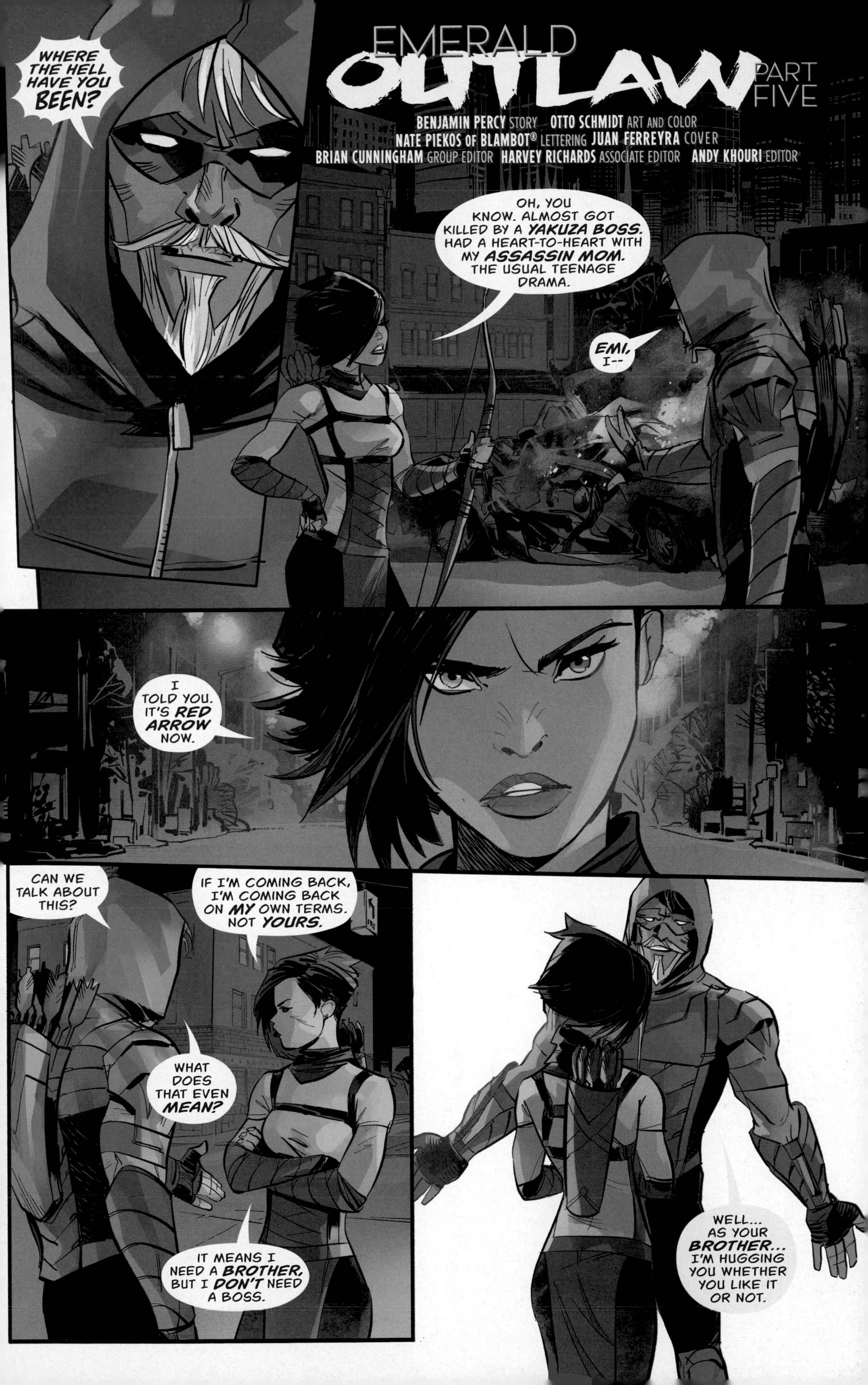
WHERE THE HELL HAVE YOU BEEN?
EMERALD OUTLAW PART FIVE
BENJAMIN PERCY STORY OTTO SCHMIDT ART AND COLOR
NATE PIEKOS OF BLAMBOT® LETTERING JUAN FERREYRA COVER
BRIAN CUNNINGHAM GROUP EDITOR HARVEY RICHARDS ASSOCIATE EDITOR ANDY KHOURI EDITOR
OH, YOU KNOW. ALMOST GOT KILLED BY A YAKUZA BOSS. HAD A HEART-TO-HEART WITH MY ASSASSIN MOM. THE USUAL TEENAGE DRAMA.
EMI, I--
I TOLD YOU. IT'S RED ARROW NOW.
CAN WE TALK ABOUT THIS?
IF I'M COMING BACK, I'M COMING BACK ON MY OWN TERMS. NOT YOURS.
WHAT DOES THAT EVEN MEAN?
IT MEANS I NEED A BROTHER, BUT I DON'T NEED A BOSS.
WELL... AS YOUR BROTHER... I'M HUGGING YOU WHETHER YOU LIKE IT OR NOT.

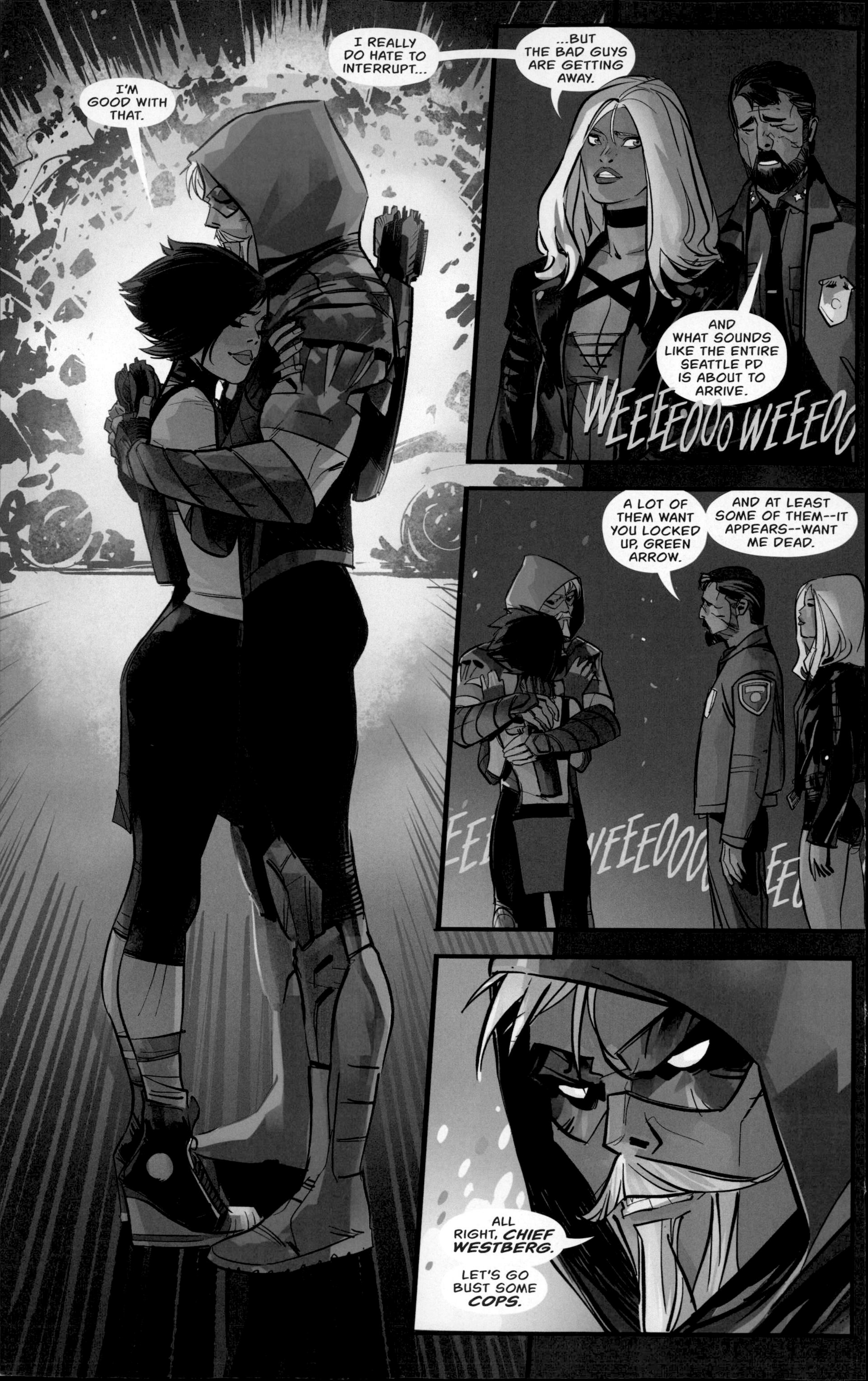

I'M GOOD WITH THAT.
I REALLY DO HATE TO INTERRUPT...
...BUT THE BAD GUYS ARE GETTING AWAY.
AND WHAT SOUNDS LIKE THE ENTIRE SEATTLE PD IS ABOUT TO ARRIVE.
WEEEOOO WEEEOO
A LOT OF THEM WANT YOU LOCKED UP, GREEN ARROW.
AND AT LEAST SOME OF THEM--IT APPEARS--WANT ME DEAD.
WEEEOOO
ALL RIGHT, CHIEF WESTBERG.
LET'S GO BUST SOME COPS.

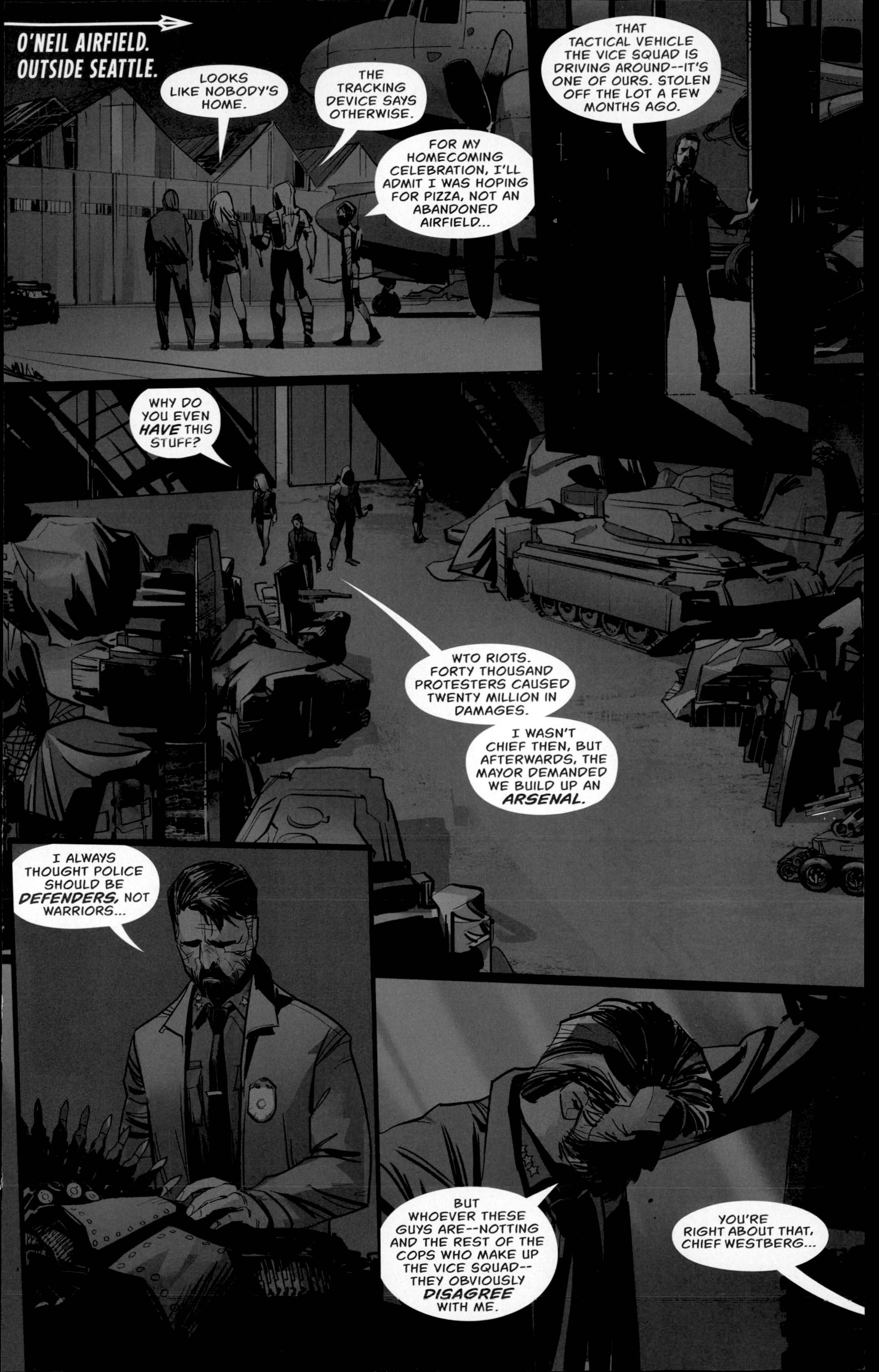
O'NEIL AIRFIELD. OUTSIDE SEATTLE.
LOOKS LIKE NOBODY'S HOME.
THE TRACKING DEVICE SAYS OTHERWISE.
FOR MY HOMECOMING CELEBRATION, I'LL ADMIT I WAS HOPING FOR PIZZA, NOT AN ABANDONED AIRFIELD...
THAT TACTICAL VEHICLE THE VICE SQUAD IS DRIVING AROUND--IT'S ONE OF OURS. STOLEN OFF THE LOT A FEW MONTHS AGO.
WHY DO YOU EVEN HAVE THIS STUFF?
WTO RIOTS. FORTY THOUSAND PROTESTERS CAUSED TWENTY MILLION IN DAMAGES.
I WASN'T CHIEF THEN, BUT AFTERWARDS, THE MAYOR DEMANDED WE BUILD UP AN ARSENAL.
I ALWAYS THOUGHT POLICE SHOULD BE DEFENDERS, NOT WARRIORS...
BUT WHOEVER THESE GUYS ARE--NOTTING AND THE REST OF THE COPS WHO MAKE UP THE VICE SQUAD--THEY OBVIOUSLY DISAGREE WITH ME.
YOU'RE RIGHT ABOUT THAT, CHIEF WESTBERG...

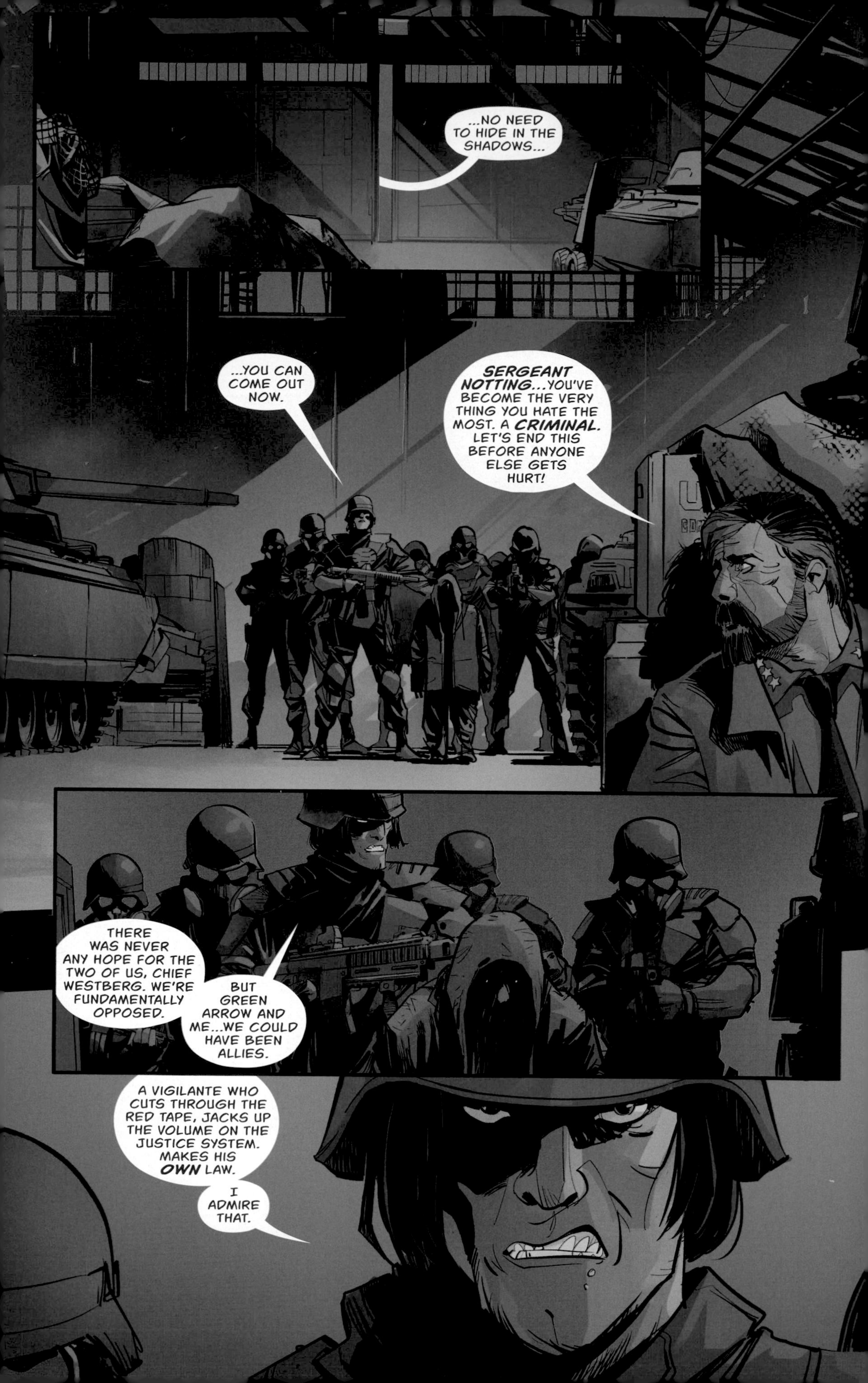
...NO NEED TO HIDE IN THE SHADOWS...
...YOU CAN COME OUT NOW.
SERGEANT NOTTING... YOU'VE BECOME THE VERY THING YOU HATE THE MOST. A CRIMINAL. LET'S END THIS BEFORE ANYONE ELSE GETS HURT!
THERE WAS NEVER ANY HOPE FOR THE TWO OF US, CHIEF WESTBERG. WE'RE FUNDAMENTALLY OPPOSED.
BUT GREEN ARROW AND ME...WE COULD HAVE BEEN ALLIES.
A VIGILANTE WHO CUTS THROUGH THE RED TAPE, JACKS UP THE VOLUME ON THE JUSTICE SYSTEM. MAKES HIS OWN LAW.
I ADMIRE THAT.

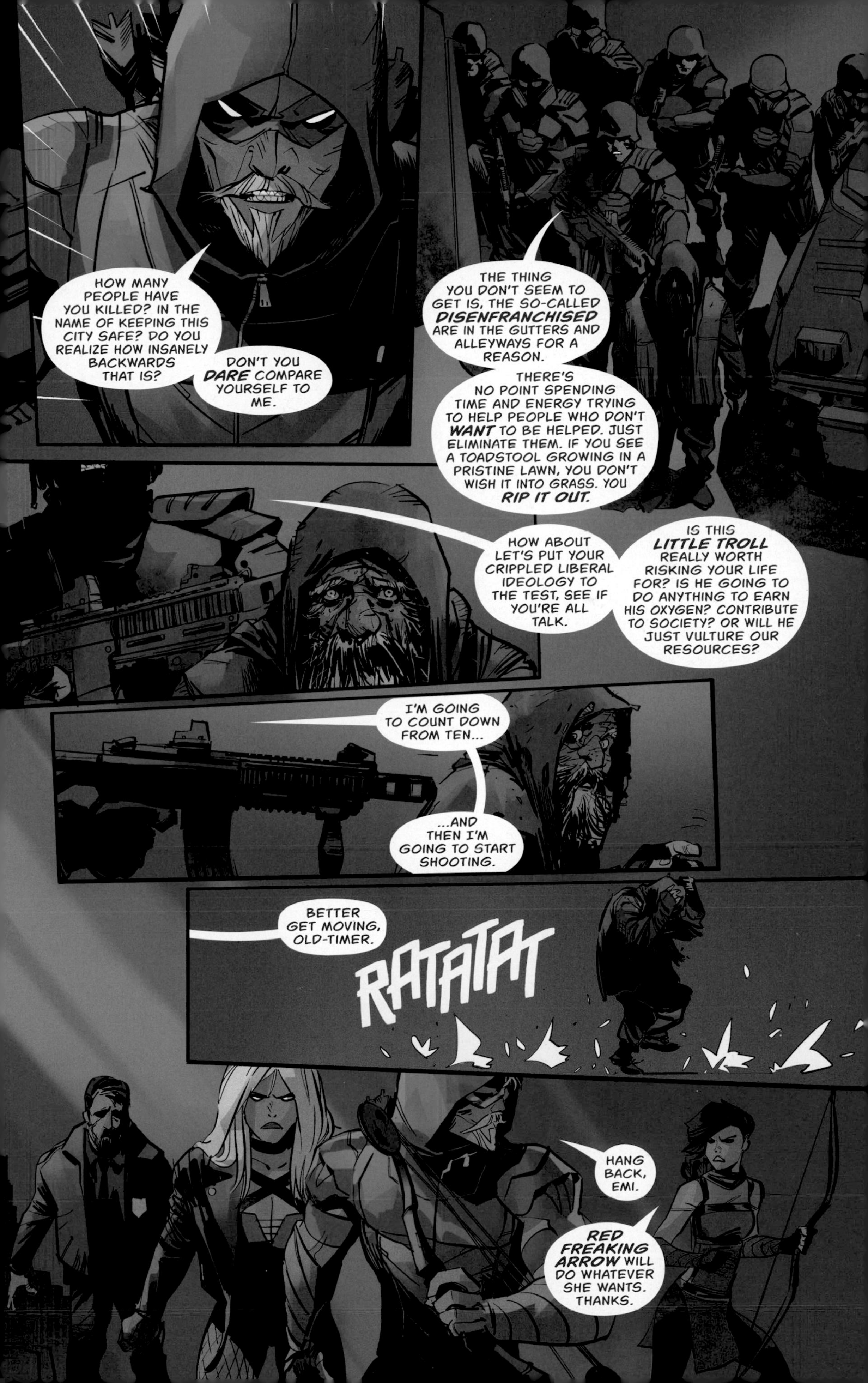
HOW MANY PEOPLE HAVE YOU KILLED? IN THE NAME OF KEEPING THIS CITY SAFE? DO YOU REALIZE HOW INSANELY BACKWARDS THAT IS?
DON'T YOU DARE COMPARE YOURSELF TO ME.
THE THING YOU DON'T SEEM TO GET IS, THE SO-CALLED DISENFRANCHISED ARE IN THE GUTTERS AND ALLEYWAYS FOR A REASON.
THERE'S NO POINT SPENDING TIME AND ENERGY TRYING TO HELP PEOPLE WHO DON'T WANT TO BE HELPED. JUST ELIMINATE THEM. IF YOU SEE A TOADSTOOL GROWING IN A PRISTINE LAWN, YOU DON'T WISH IT INTO GRASS. YOU RIP IT OUT.
IS THIS LITTLE TROLL REALLY WORTH RISKING YOUR LIFE FOR? IS HE GOING TO DO ANYTHING TO EARN HIS OXYGEN? CONTRIBUTE TO SOCIETY? OR WILL HE JUST VULTURE OUR RESOURCES?
HOW ABOUT LET'S PUT YOUR CRIPPLED LIBERAL IDEOLOGY TO THE TEST, SEE IF YOU'RE ALL TALK.
I'M GOING TO COUNT DOWN FROM TEN...
...AND THEN I'M GOING TO START SHOOTING.
BETTER GET MOVING, OLD-TIMER.
RATATAT
HANG BACK, EMI.
RED FREAKING ARROW WILL DO WHATEVER SHE WANTS. THANKS.

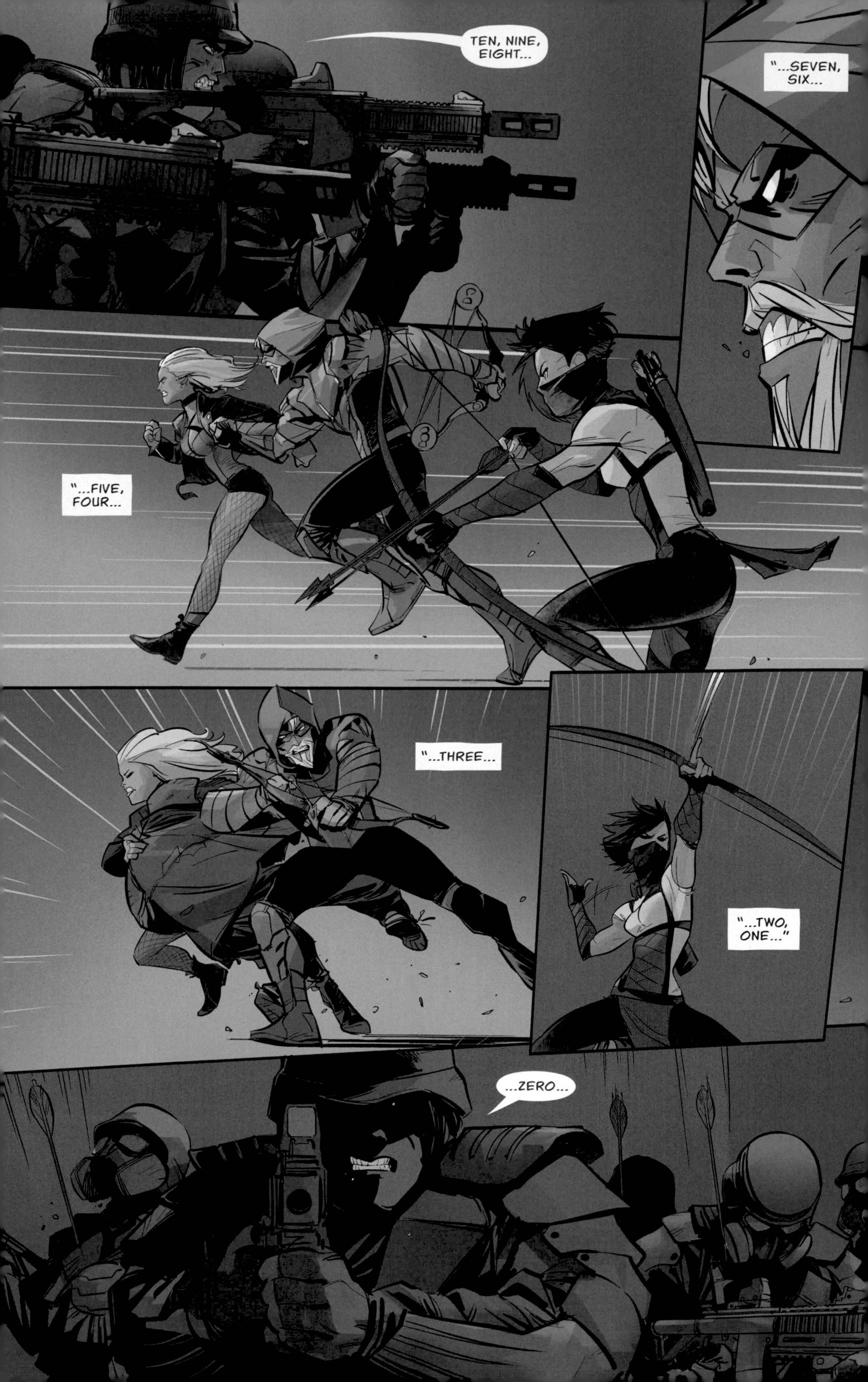
TEN, NINE, EIGHT...
"...SEVEN, SIX...
"...FIVE, FOUR...
"...THREE...
"...TWO, ONE..."
...ZERO...

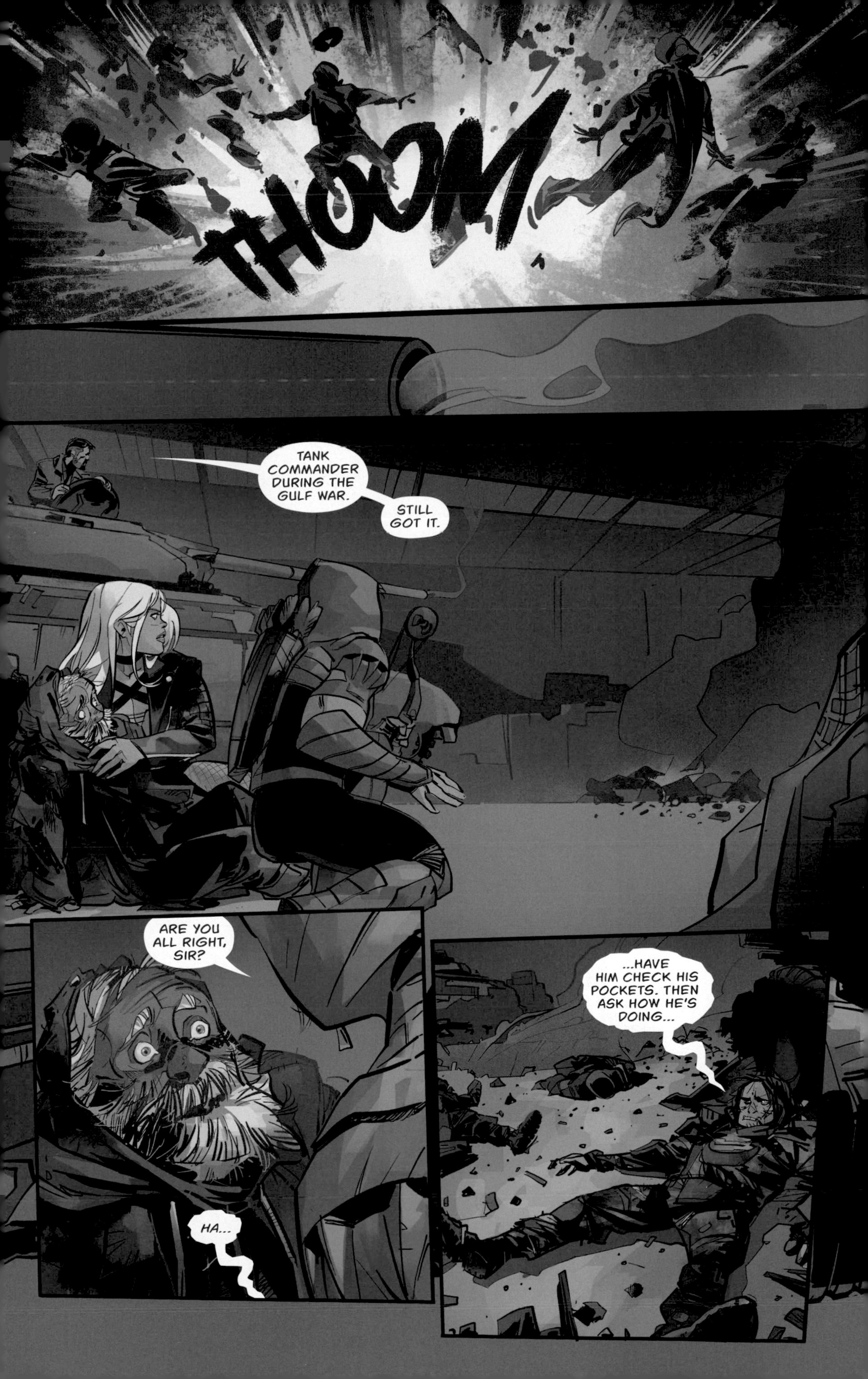
THOOM
TANK COMMANDER DURING THE GULF WAR.
STILL GOT IT.
ARE YOU ALL RIGHT, SIR?
HA...
...HAVE HIM CHECK HIS POCKETS. THEN ASK HOW HE'S DOING...

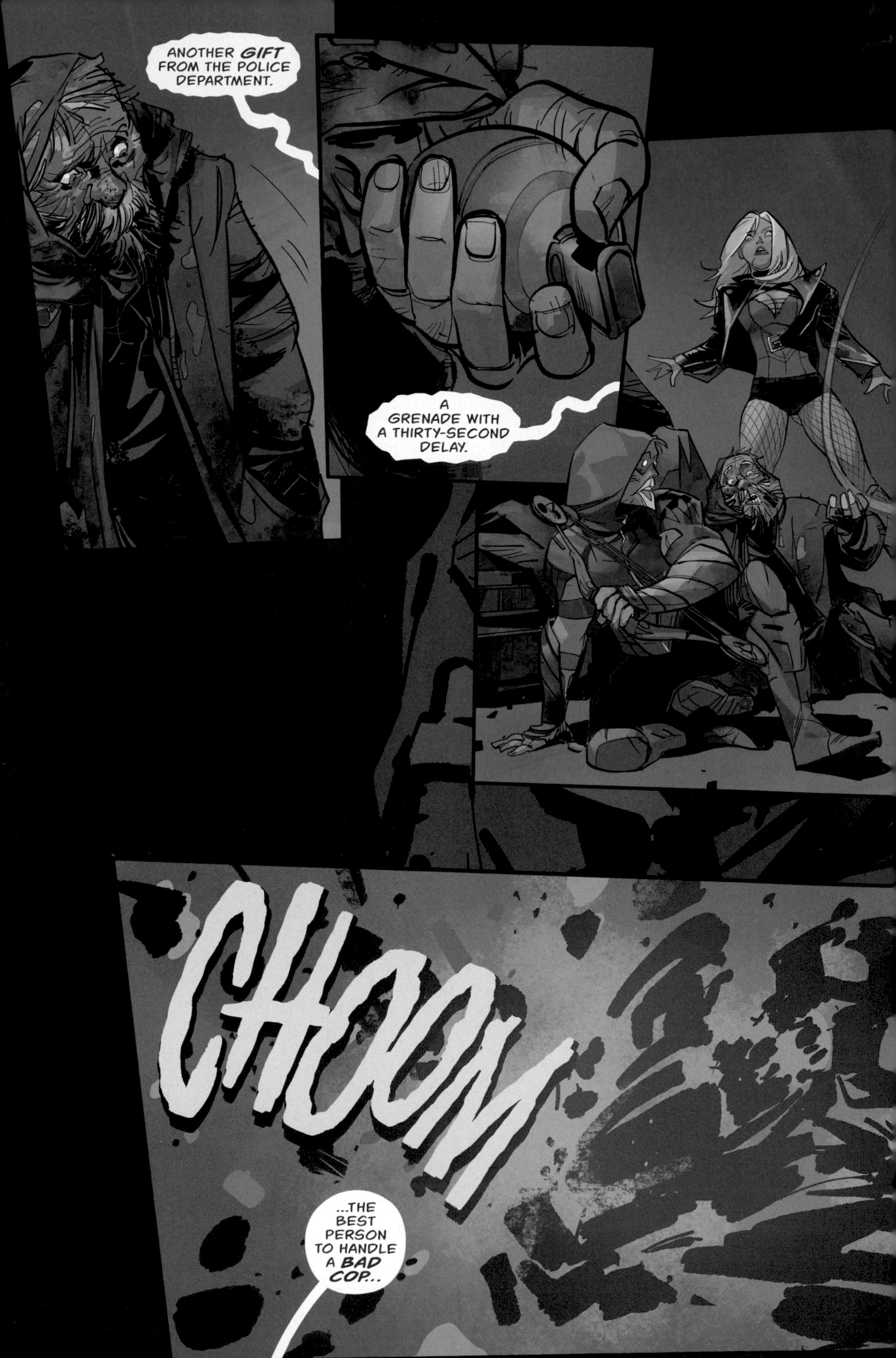
ANOTHER GIFT FROM THE POLICE DEPARTMENT.
A GRENADE WITH A THIRTY-SECOND DELAY.
CHOOM
...THE BEST PERSON TO HANDLE A BAD COP...

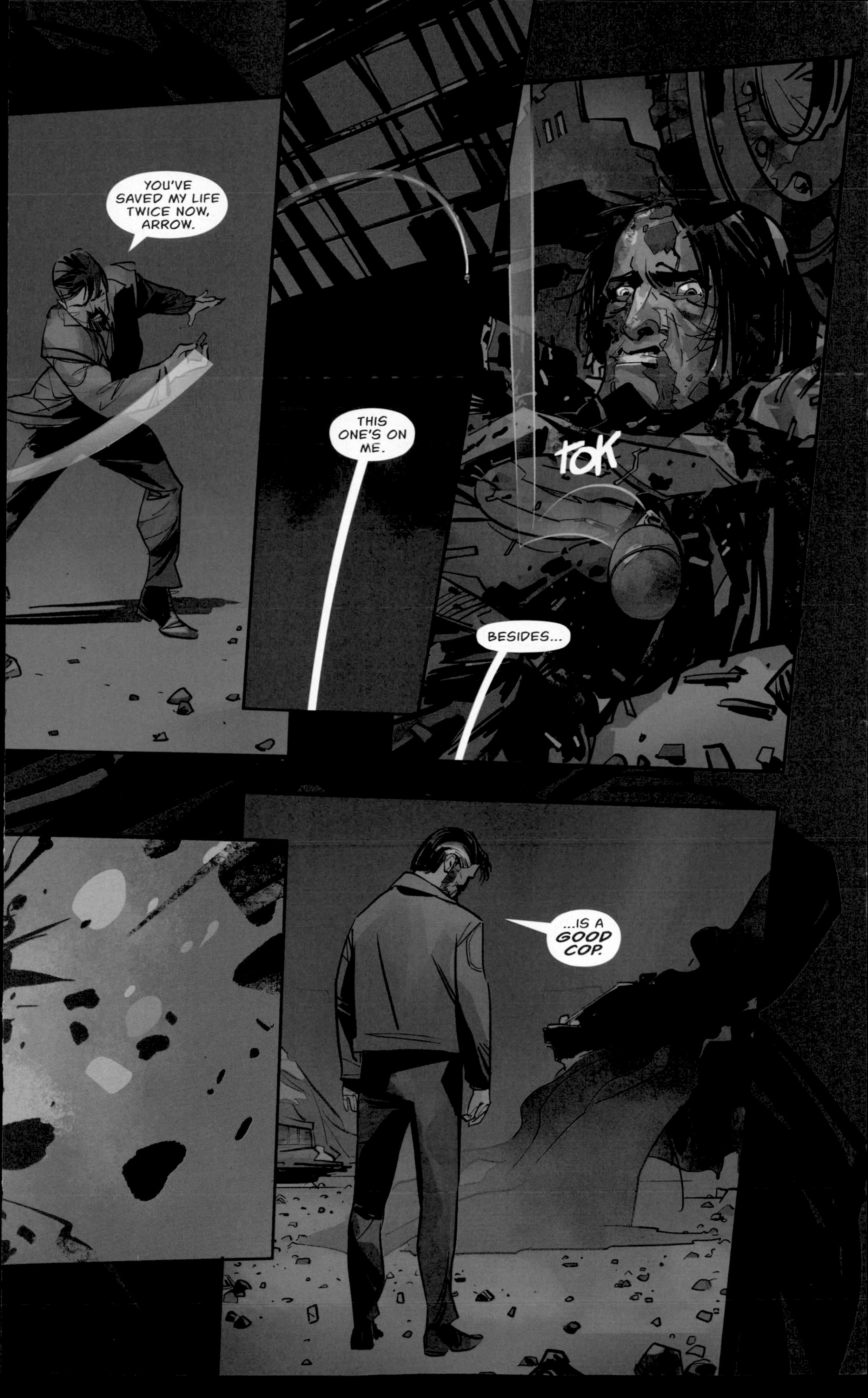
YOU'VE SAVED MY LIFE TWICE NOW, ARROW.
THIS ONE'S ON ME.
TOK
BESIDES...
...IS A GOOD COP.

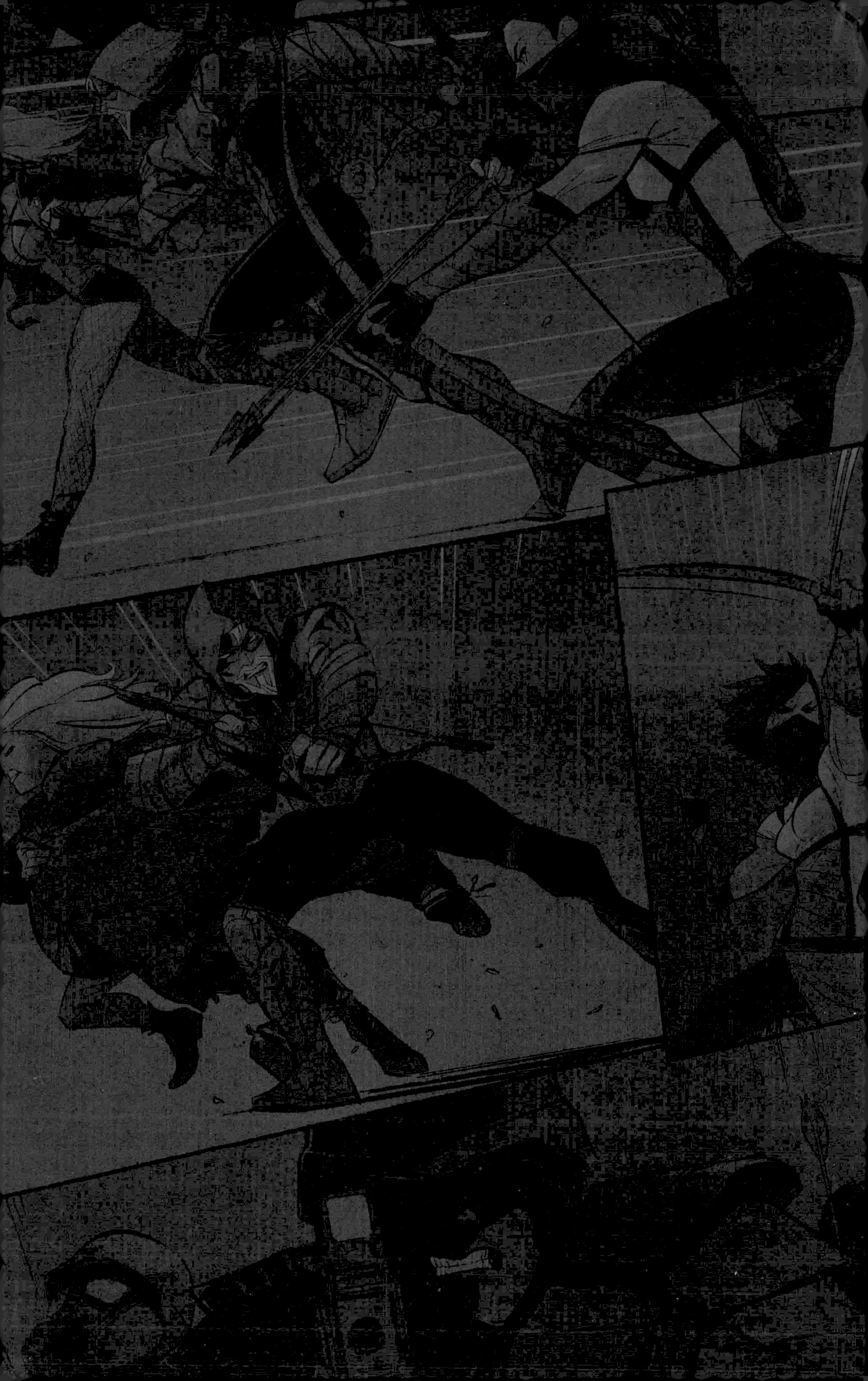

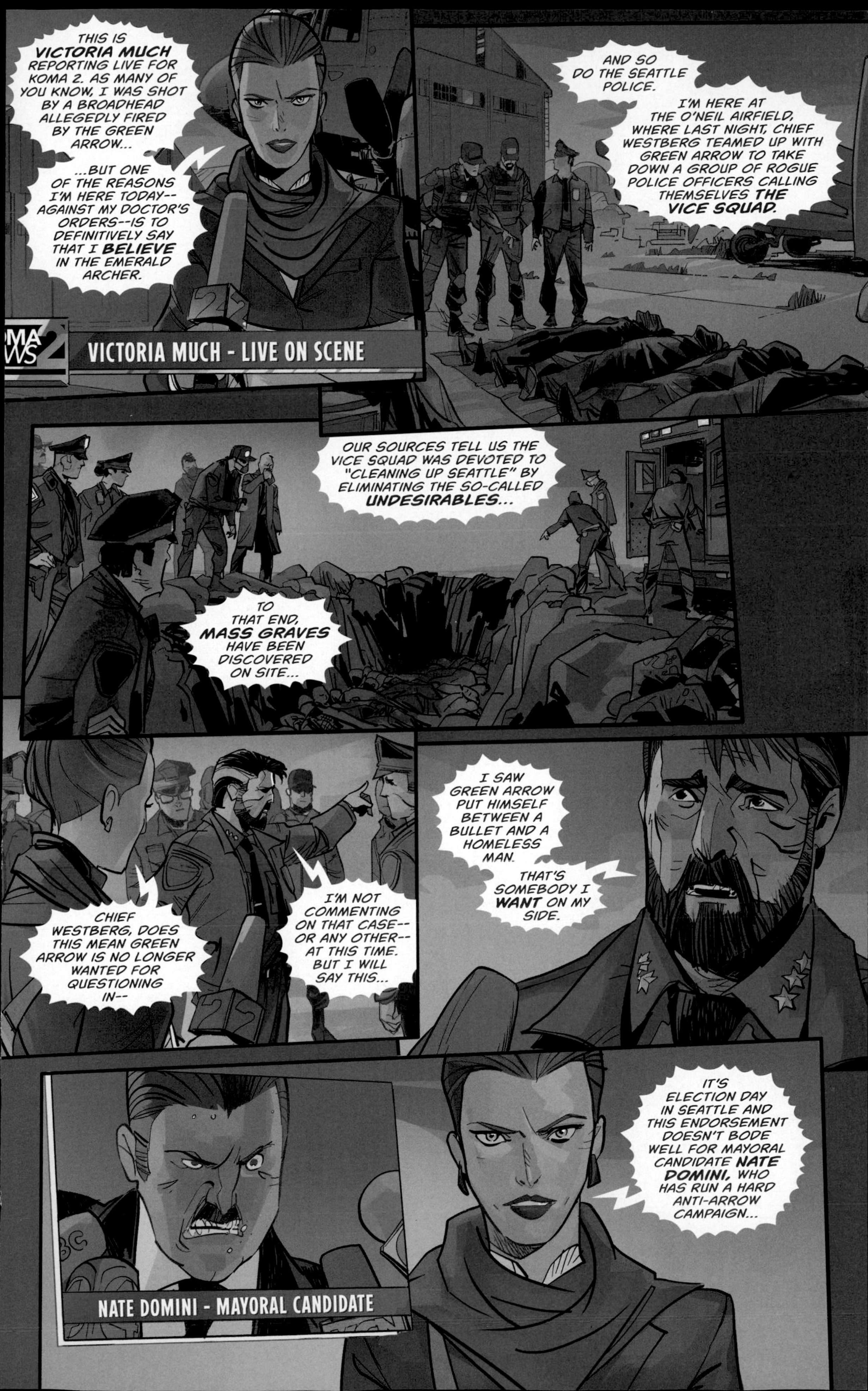
THIS IS VICTORIA MUCH REPORTING LIVE FOR KOMA 2. AS MANY OF YOU KNOW, I WAS SHOT BY A BROADHEAD ALLEGEDLY FIRED BY THE GREEN ARROW...
...BUT ONE OF THE REASONS I'M HERE TODAY--AGAINST MY DOCTOR'S ORDERS--IS TO DEFINITIVELY SAY THAT I BELIEVE IN THE EMERALD ARCHER.
VICTORIA MUCH - LIVE ON SCENE
AND SO DO THE SEATTLE POLICE.
I'M HERE AT THE O'NEIL AIRFIELD, WHERE LAST NIGHT, CHIEF WESTBERG TEAMED UP WITH GREEN ARROW TO TAKE DOWN A GROUP OF ROGUE POLICE OFFICERS CALLING THEMSELVES THE VICE SQUAD.
OUR SOURCES TELL US THE VICE SQUAD WAS DEVOTED TO "CLEANING UP SEATTLE" BY ELIMINATING THE SO-CALLED UNDESIRABLES...
TO THAT END, MASS GRAVES HAVE BEEN DISCOVERED ON SITE...
CHIEF WESTBERG, DOES THIS MEAN GREEN ARROW IS NO LONGER WANTED FOR QUESTIONING IN--
I'M NOT COMMENTING ON THAT CASE--OR ANY OTHER--AT THIS TIME. BUT I WILL SAY THIS...
I SAW GREEN ARROW PUT HIMSELF BETWEEN A BULLET AND A HOMELESS MAN.
THAT'S SOMEBODY I WANT ON MY SIDE.
NATE DOMINI - MAYORAL CANDIDATE
IT'S ELECTION DAY IN SEATTLE AND THIS ENDORSEMENT DOESN'T BODE WELL FOR MAYORAL CANDIDATE NATE DOMINI, WHO HAS RUN A HARD ANTI-ARROW CAMPAIGN...

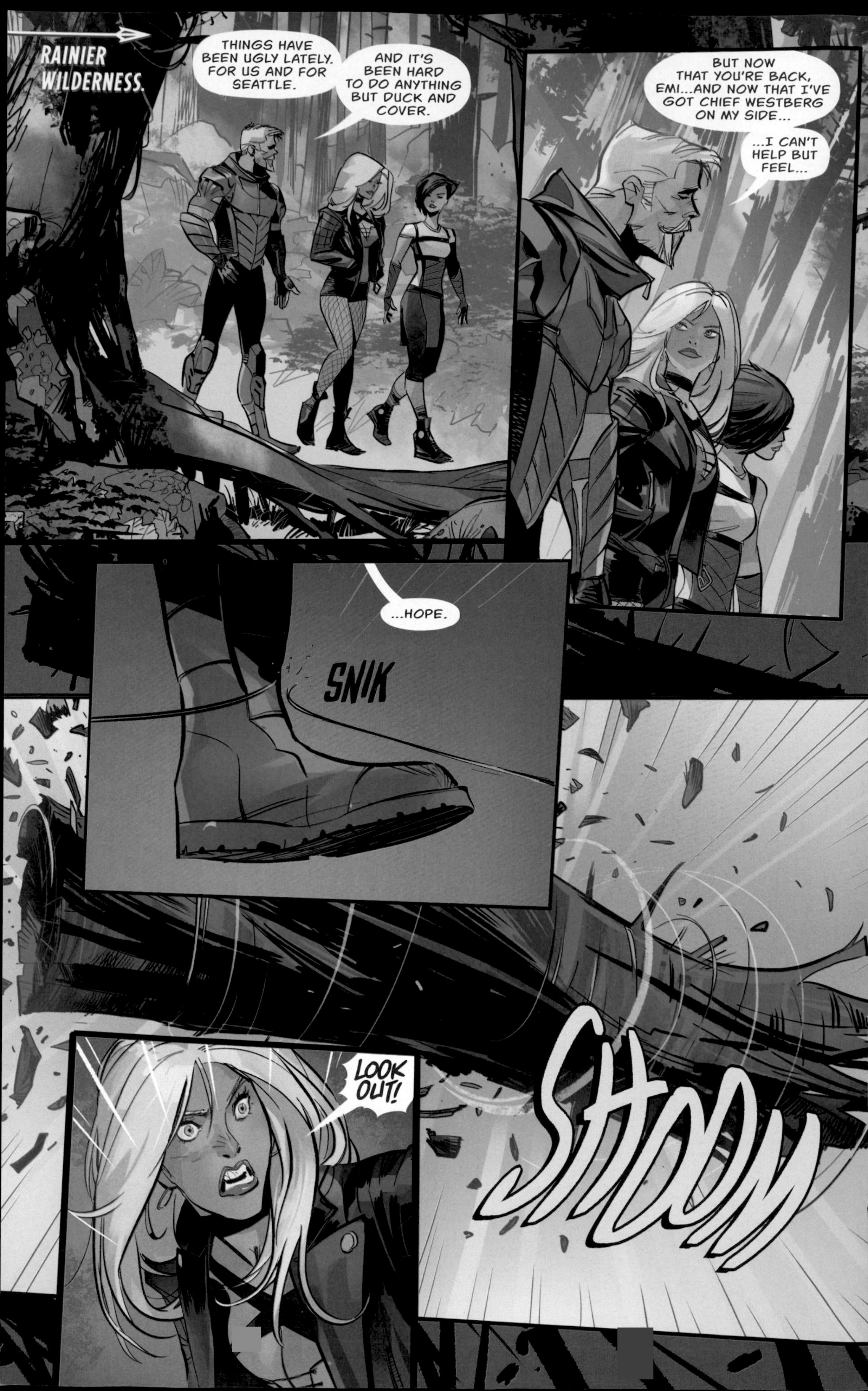
RAINIER WILDERNESS.
THINGS HAVE BEEN UGLY LATELY. FOR US AND FOR SEATTLE.
AND IT'S BEEN HARD TO DO ANYTHING BUT DUCK AND COVER.
BUT NOW THAT YOU'RE BACK, EMI...AND NOW THAT I'VE GOT CHIEF WESTBERG ON MY SIDE...
...I CAN'T HELP BUT FEEL...
...HOPE.
SNIK
LOOK OUT!

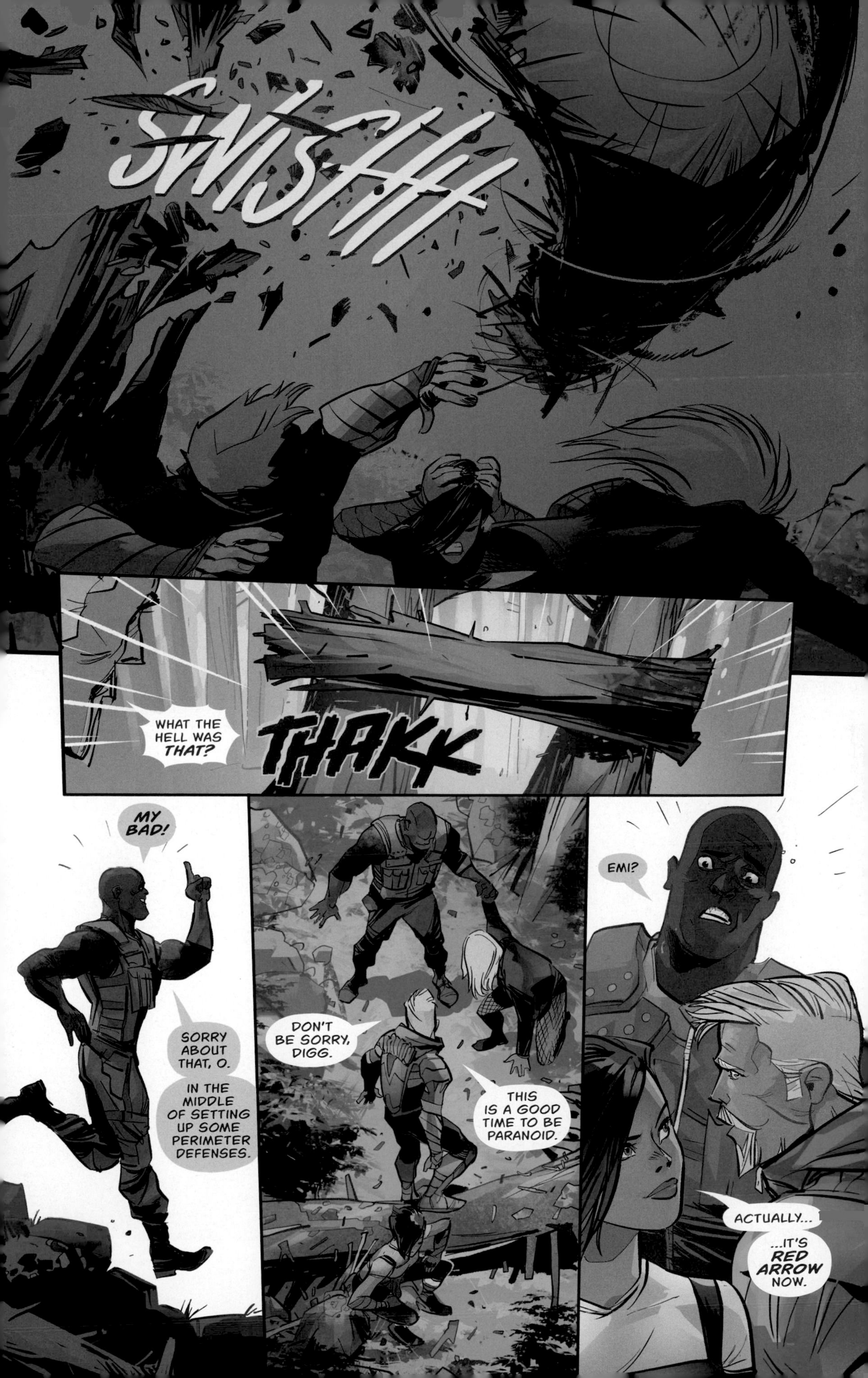
SHWSHHH
WHAT THE HELL WAS *THAT?*
THAKK
MY BAD!
SORRY ABOUT THAT, O.
IN THE MIDDLE OF SETTING UP SOME PERIMETER DEFENSES.
DON'T BE SORRY, DIGG.
THIS IS A GOOD TIME TO BE PARANOID.
EMI?
ACTUALLY...
...IT'S *RED ARROW* NOW.

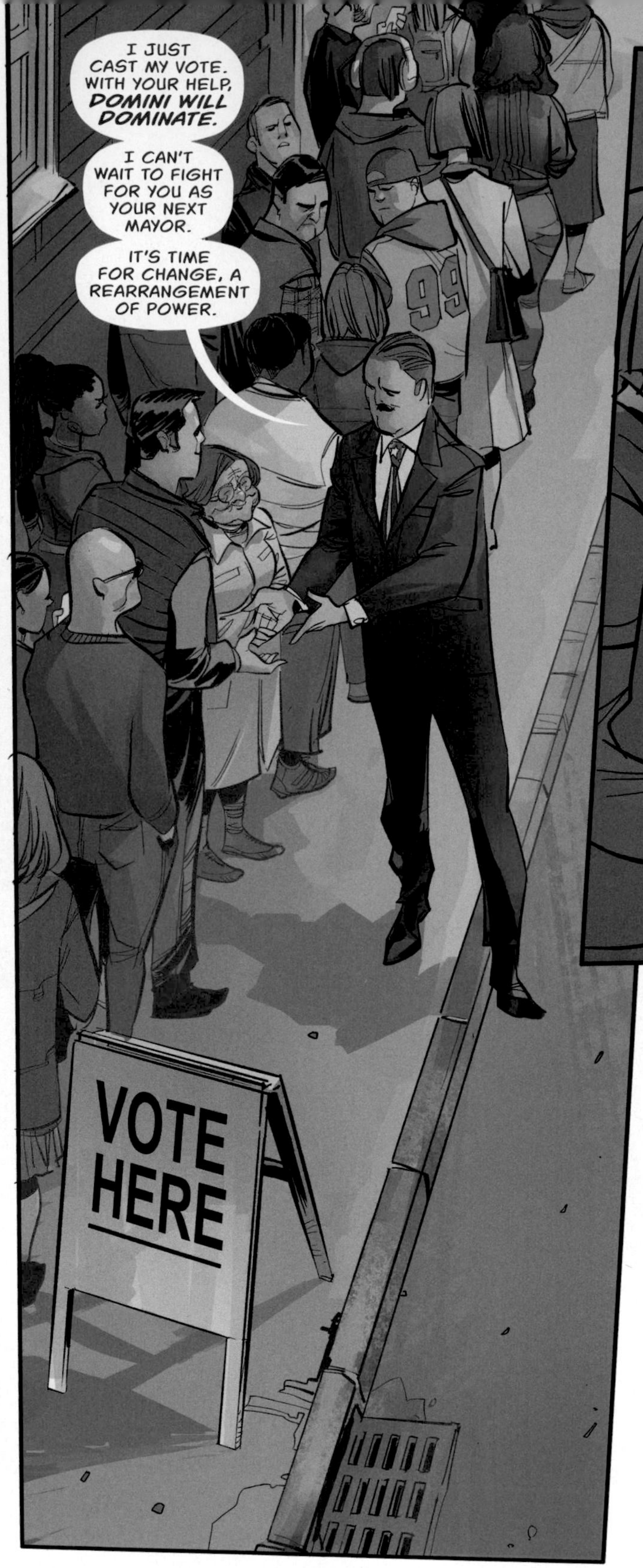
I JUST CAST MY VOTE. WITH YOUR HELP, DOMINI WILL DOMINATE.
I CAN'T WAIT TO FIGHT FOR YOU AS YOUR NEXT MAYOR.
IT'S TIME FOR CHANGE, A REARRANGEMENT OF POWER.
VOTE HERE

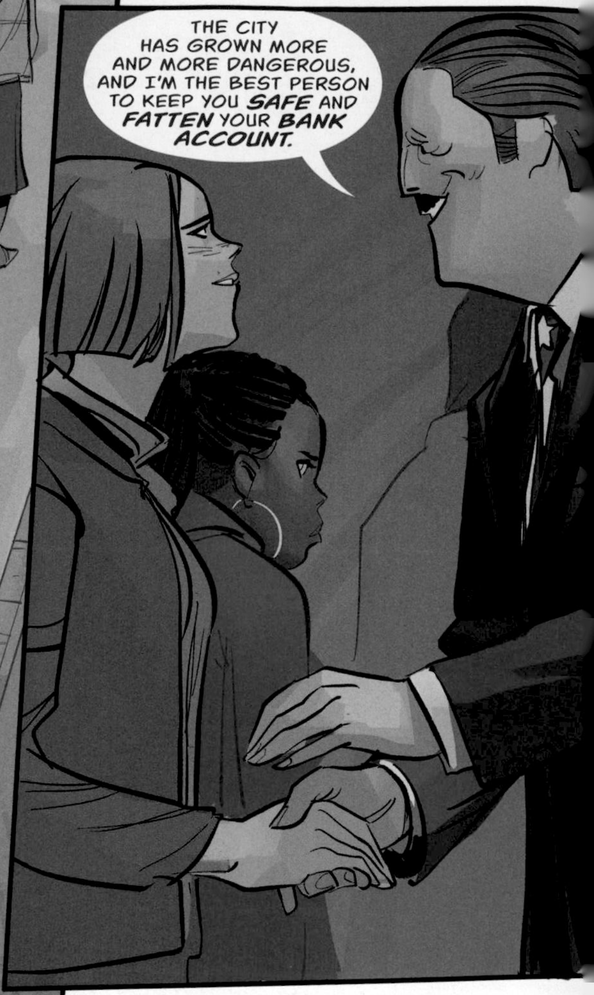
THE CITY HAS GROWN MORE AND MORE DANGEROUS, AND I'M THE BEST PERSON TO KEEP YOU SAFE AND FATTEN YOUR BANK ACCOUNT.

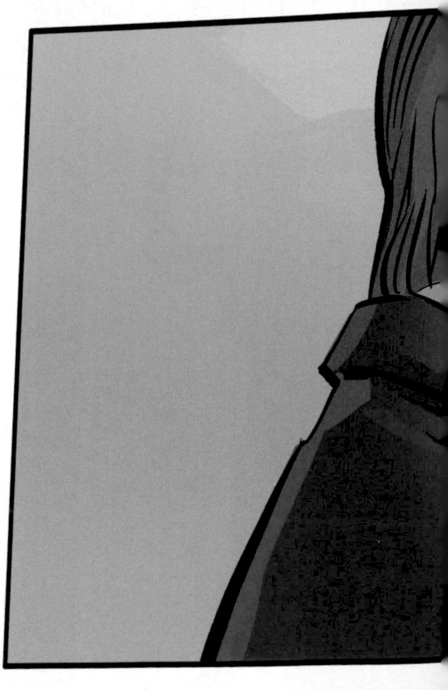

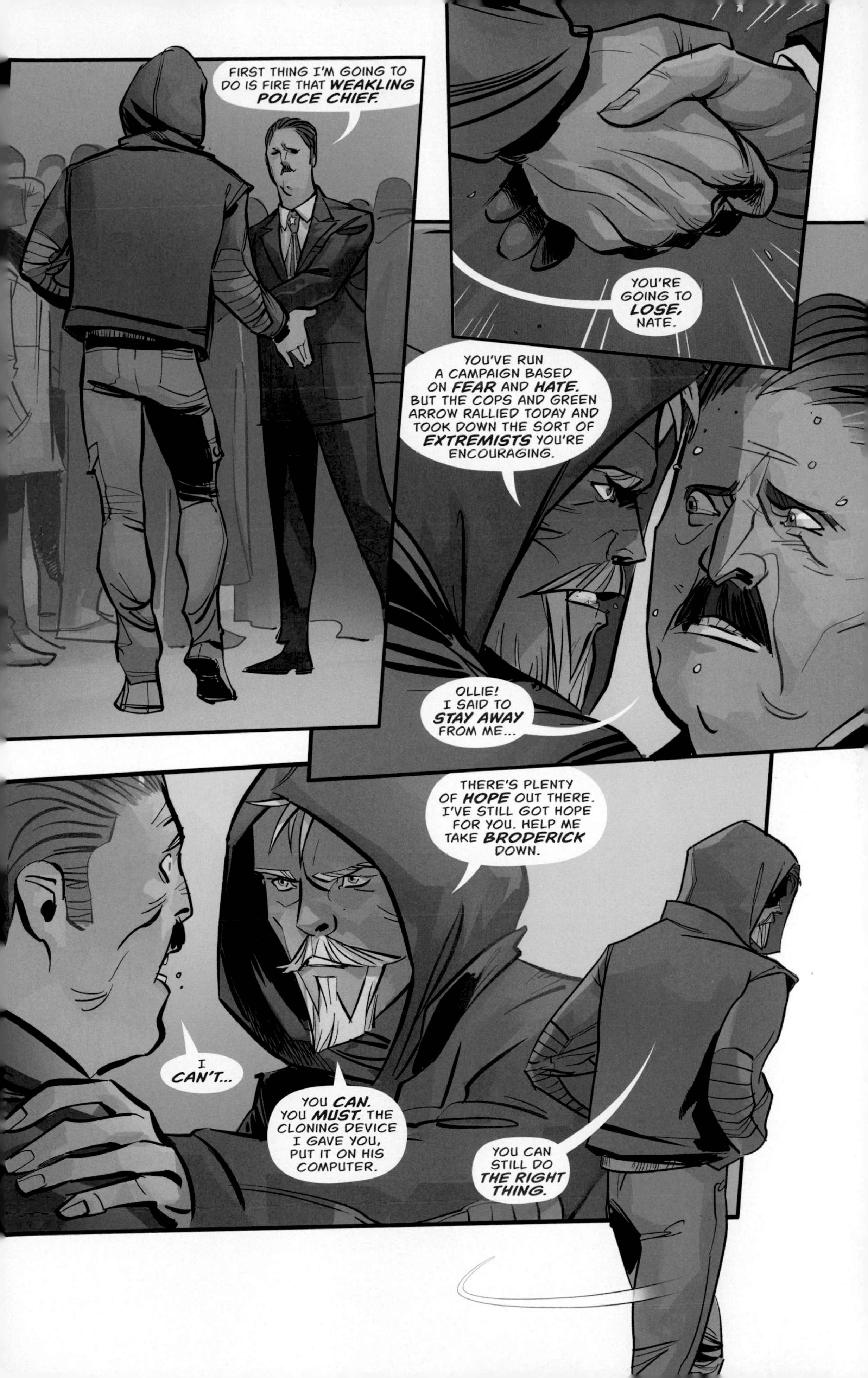
FIRST THING I'M GOING TO DO IS FIRE THAT WEAKLING POLICE CHIEF.
YOU'RE GOING TO LOSE, NATE.
YOU'VE RUN A CAMPAIGN BASED ON FEAR AND HATE. BUT THE COPS AND GREEN ARROW RALLIED TODAY AND TOOK DOWN THE SORT OF EXTREMISTS YOU'RE ENCOURAGING.
OLLIE! I SAID TO STAY AWAY FROM ME...
THERE'S PLENTY OF HOPE OUT THERE. I'VE STILL GOT HOPE FOR YOU. HELP ME TAKE BRODERICK DOWN.
I CAN'T...
YOU CAN. YOU MUST. THE CLONING DEVICE I GAVE YOU, PUT IT ON HIS COMPUTER.
YOU CAN STILL DO THE RIGHT THING.

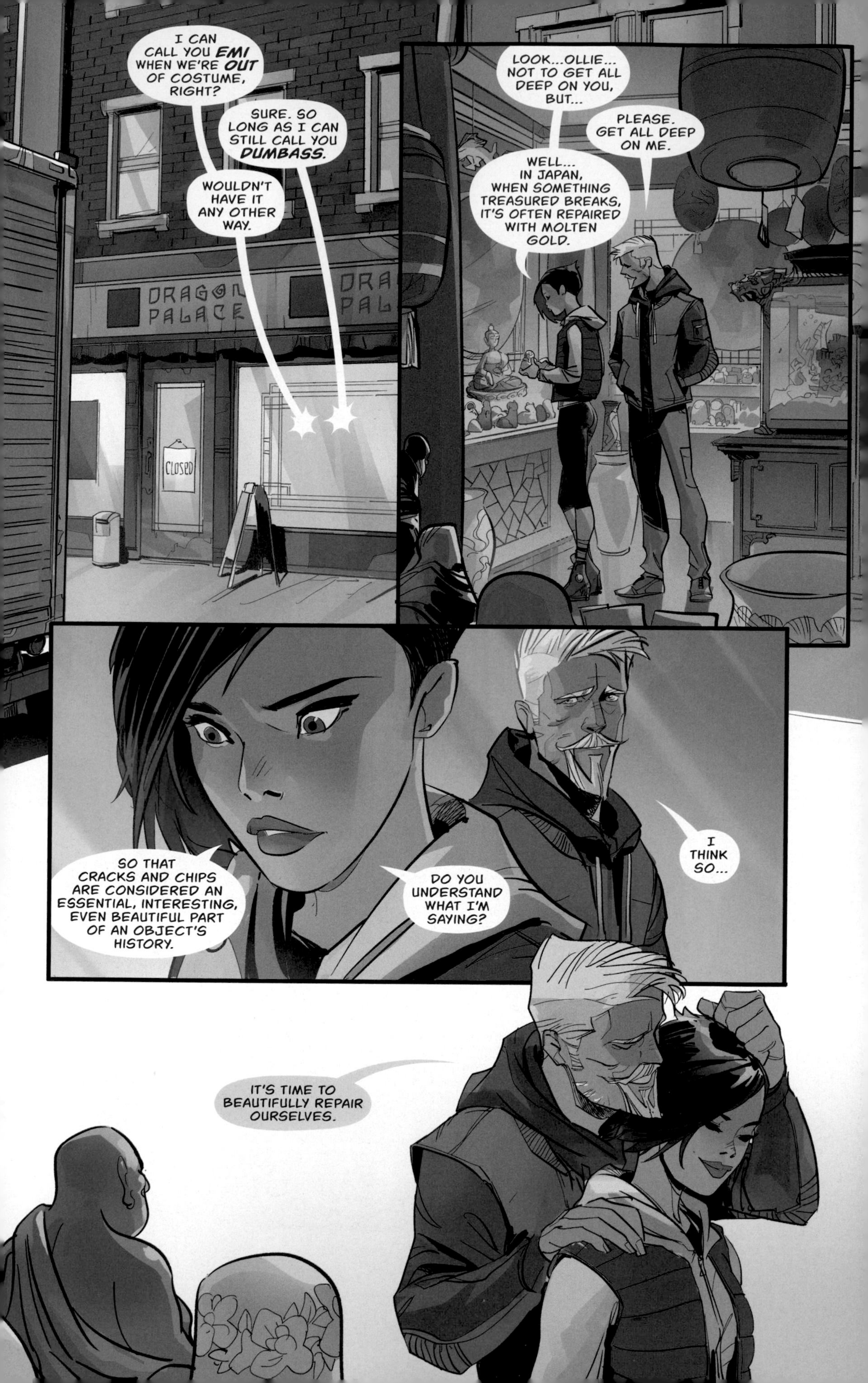

I CAN CALL YOU EMI WHEN WE'RE OUT OF COSTUME, RIGHT?
SURE. SO LONG AS I CAN STILL CALL YOU DUMBASS.
WOULDN'T HAVE IT ANY OTHER WAY.
DRAGON PALACE
CLOSED
LOOK...OLLIE... NOT TO GET ALL DEEP ON YOU, BUT...
PLEASE. GET ALL DEEP ON ME.
WELL... IN JAPAN, WHEN SOMETHING TREASURED BREAKS, IT'S OFTEN REPAIRED WITH MOLTEN GOLD.
SO THAT CRACKS AND CHIPS ARE CONSIDERED AN ESSENTIAL, INTERESTING, EVEN BEAUTIFUL PART OF AN OBJECT'S HISTORY.
DO YOU UNDERSTAND WHAT I'M SAYING?
I THINK SO...
IT'S TIME TO BEAUTIFULLY REPAIR OURSELVES.

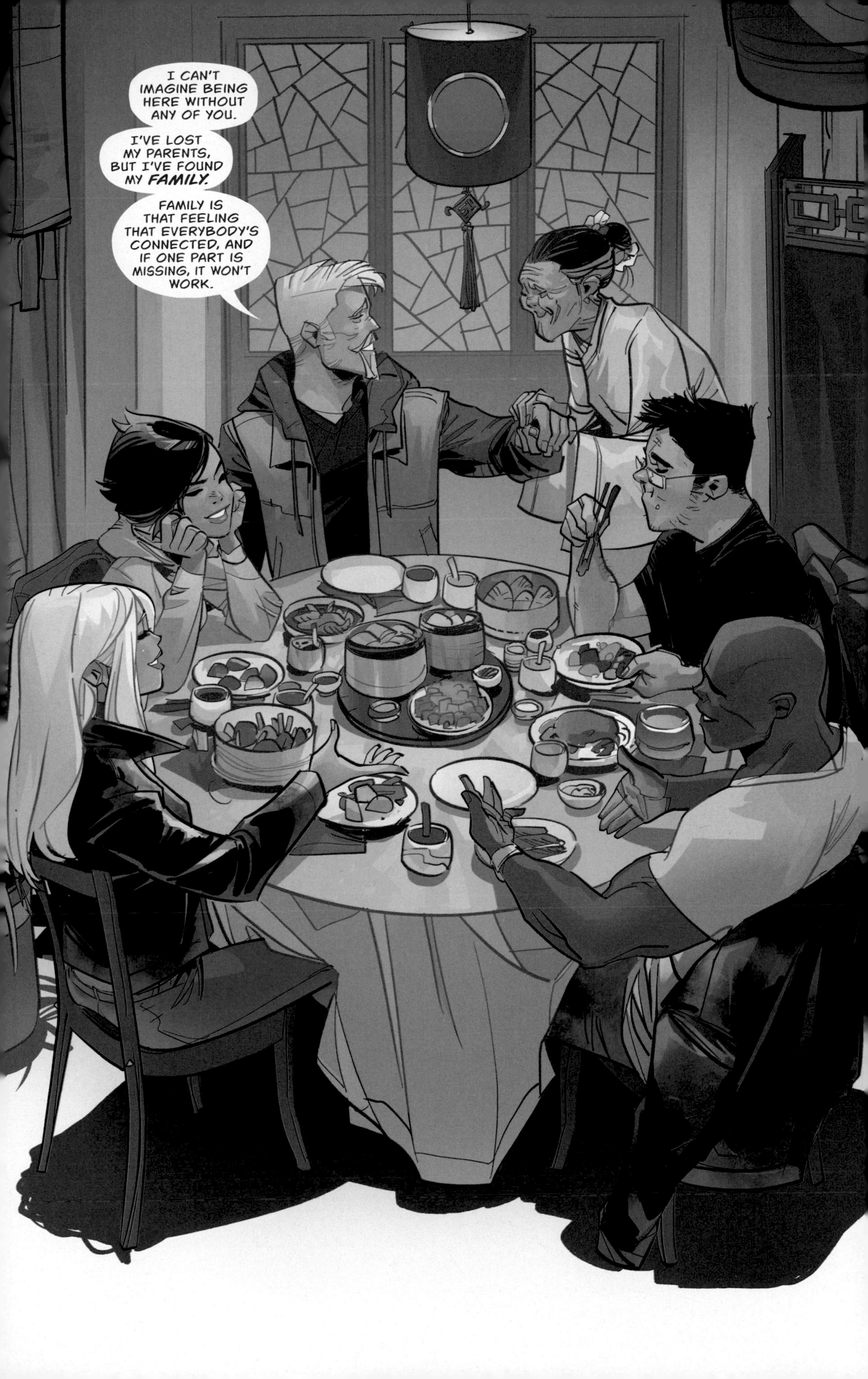
I CAN'T IMAGINE BEING HERE WITHOUT ANY OF YOU.
I'VE LOST MY PARENTS, BUT I'VE FOUND MY ***FAMILY.***
FAMILY IS THAT FEELING THAT EVERYBODY'S CONNECTED, AND IF ONE PART IS MISSING, IT WON'T WORK.

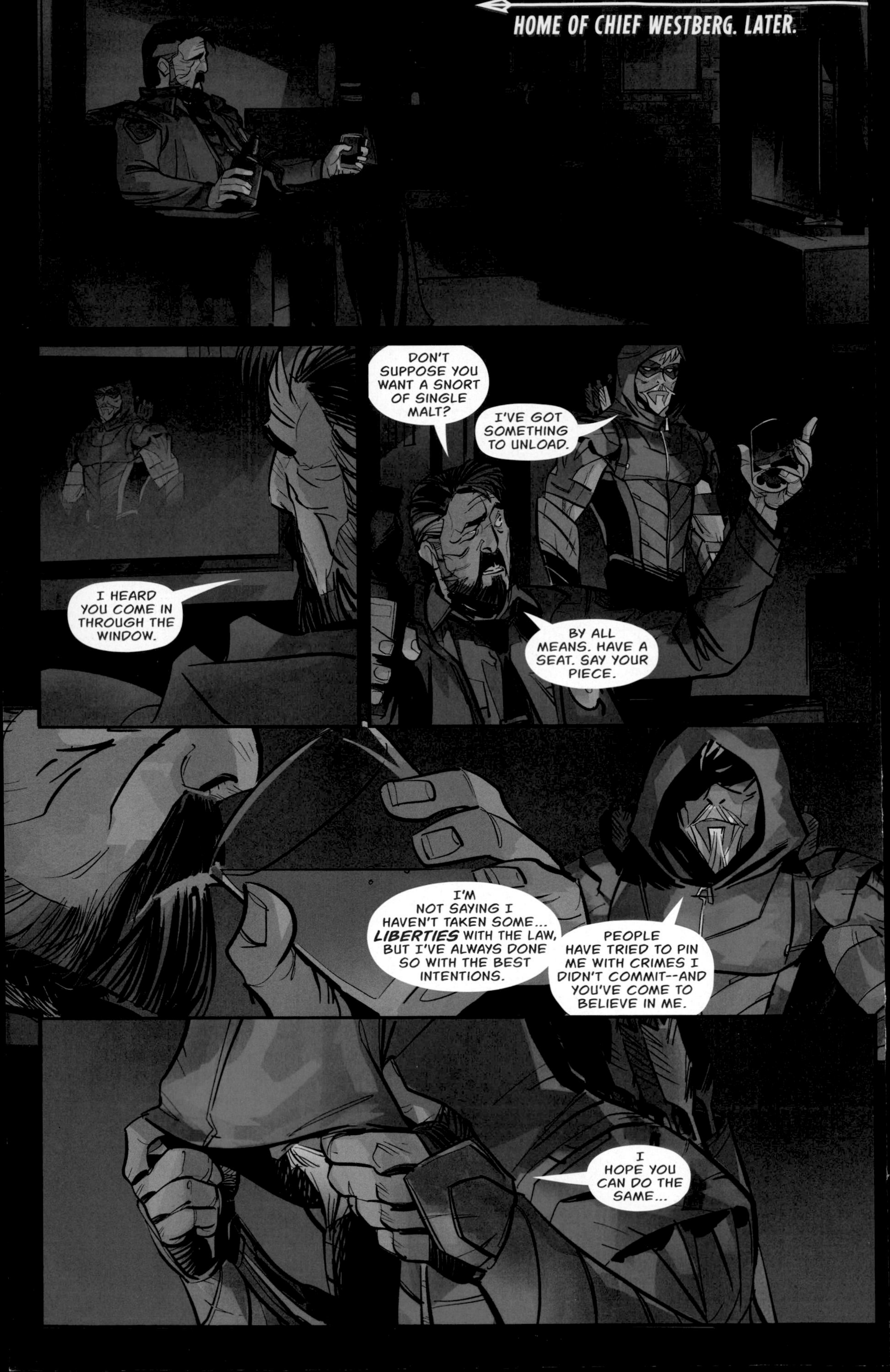
HOME OF CHIEF WESTBERG. LATER.
I HEARD YOU COME IN THROUGH THE WINDOW.
DON'T SUPPOSE YOU WANT A SNORT OF SINGLE MALT?
I'VE GOT SOMETHING TO UNLOAD.
BY ALL MEANS. HAVE A SEAT. SAY YOUR PIECE.
PEOPLE HAVE TRIED TO PIN ME WITH CRIMES I DIDN'T COMMIT--AND YOU'VE COME TO BELIEVE IN ME.
I'M NOT SAYING I HAVEN'T TAKEN SOME... LIBERTIES WITH THE LAW, BUT I'VE ALWAYS DONE SO WITH THE BEST INTENTIONS.
I HOPE YOU CAN DO THE SAME...

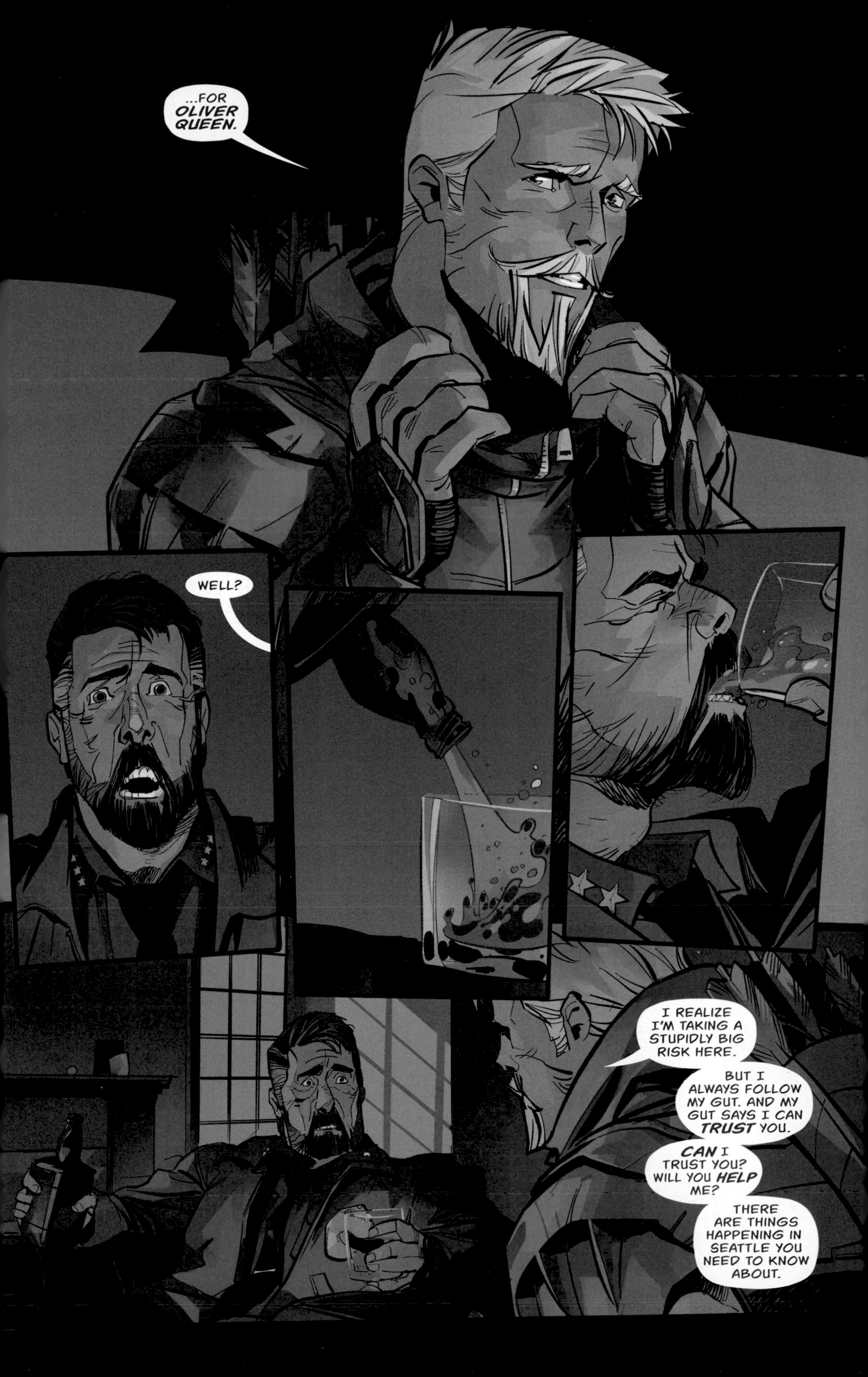
...FOR OLIVER QUEEN.
WELL?
I REALIZE I'M TAKING A STUPIDLY BIG RISK HERE.
BUT I ALWAYS FOLLOW MY GUT. AND MY GUT SAYS I CAN TRUST YOU.
CAN I TRUST YOU? WILL YOU HELP ME?
THERE ARE THINGS HAPPENING IN SEATTLE YOU NEED TO KNOW ABOUT.

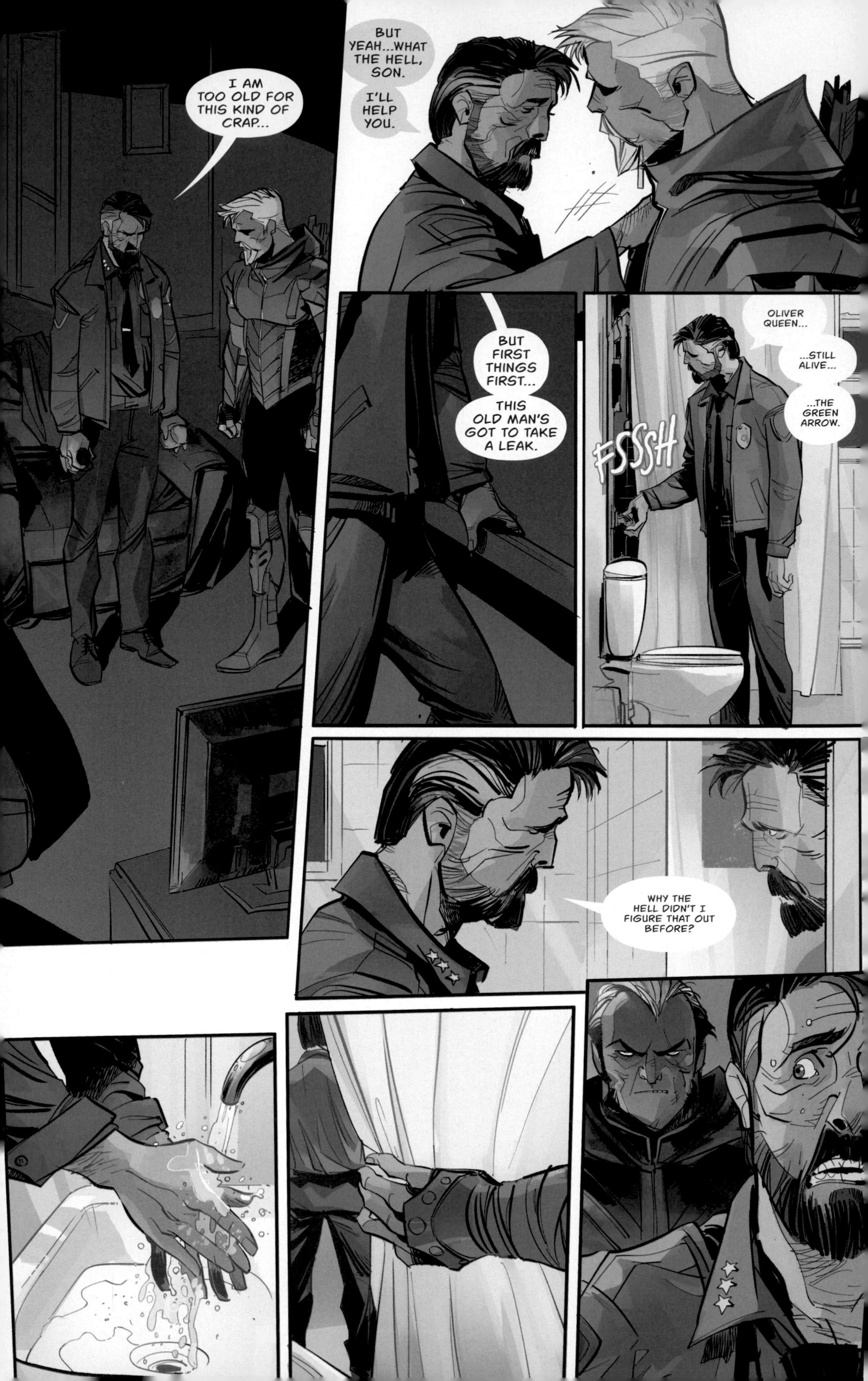
I AM TOO OLD FOR THIS KIND OF CRAP...
BUT YEAH...WHAT THE HELL, SON.
I'LL HELP YOU.
BUT FIRST THINGS FIRST...
THIS OLD MAN'S GOT TO TAKE A LEAK.
FSSSH
OLIVER QUEEN...
...STILL ALIVE...
...THE GREEN ARROW.
WHY THE HELL DIDN'T I FIGURE THAT OUT BEFORE?

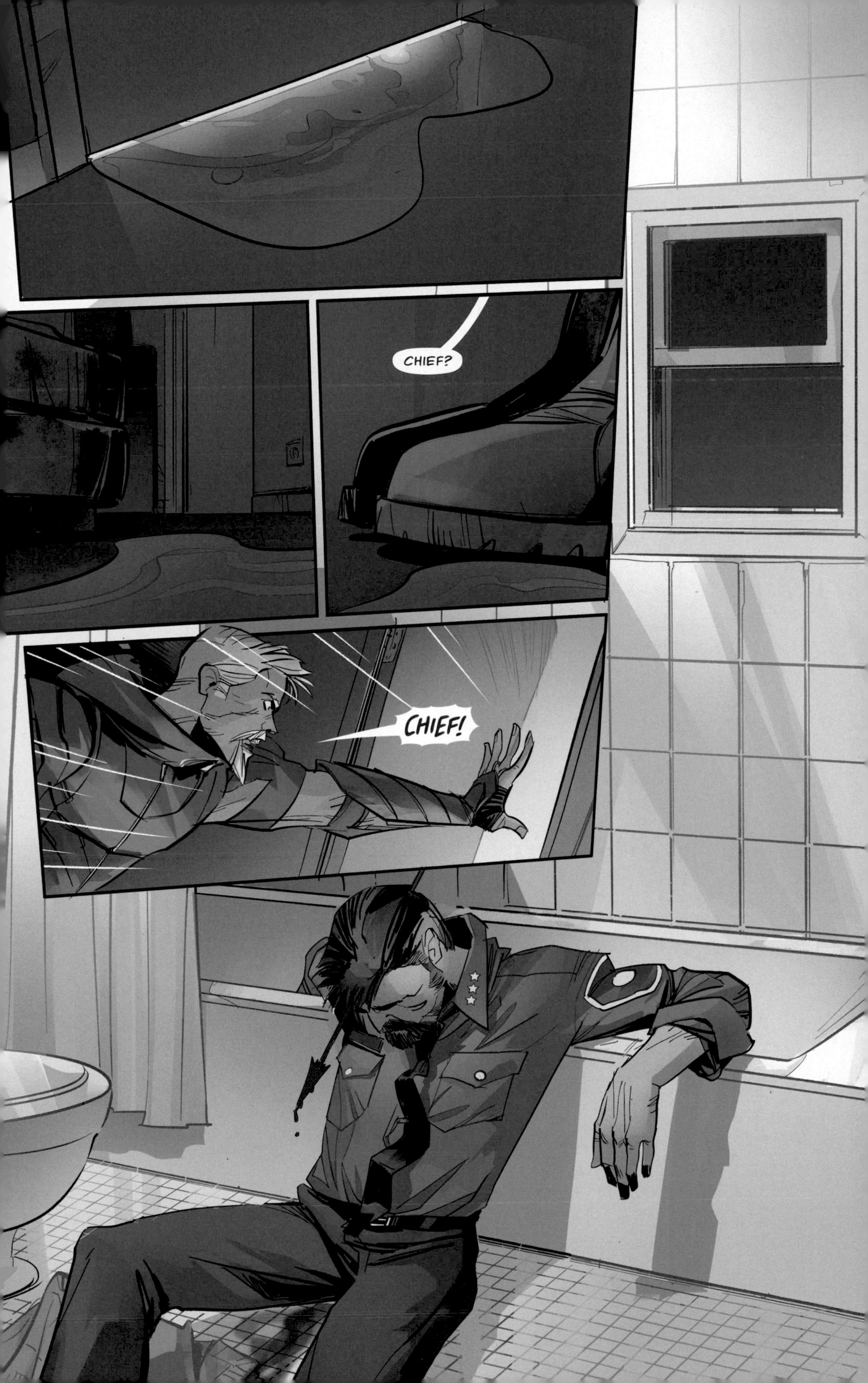
CHIEF?
CHIEF!

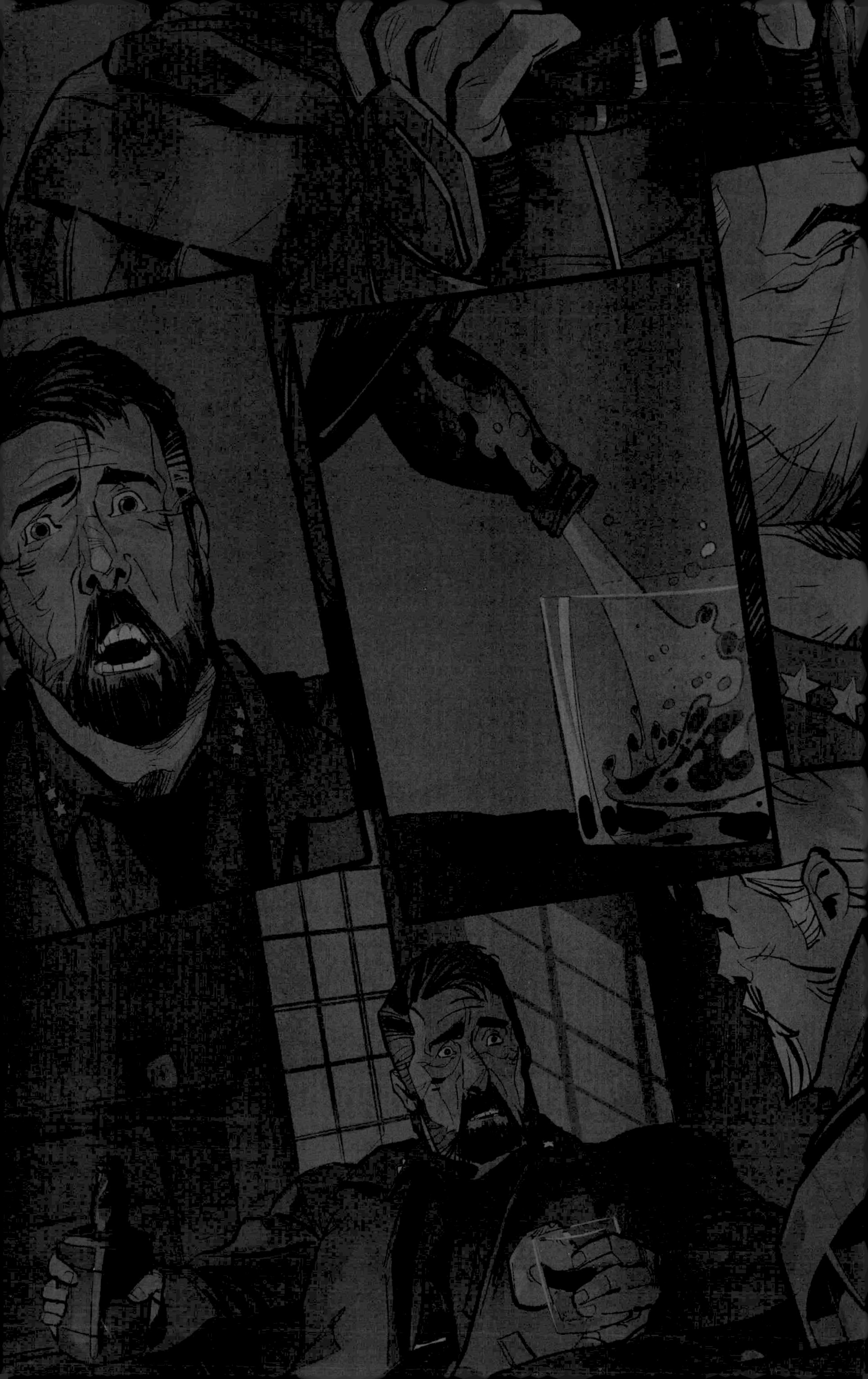

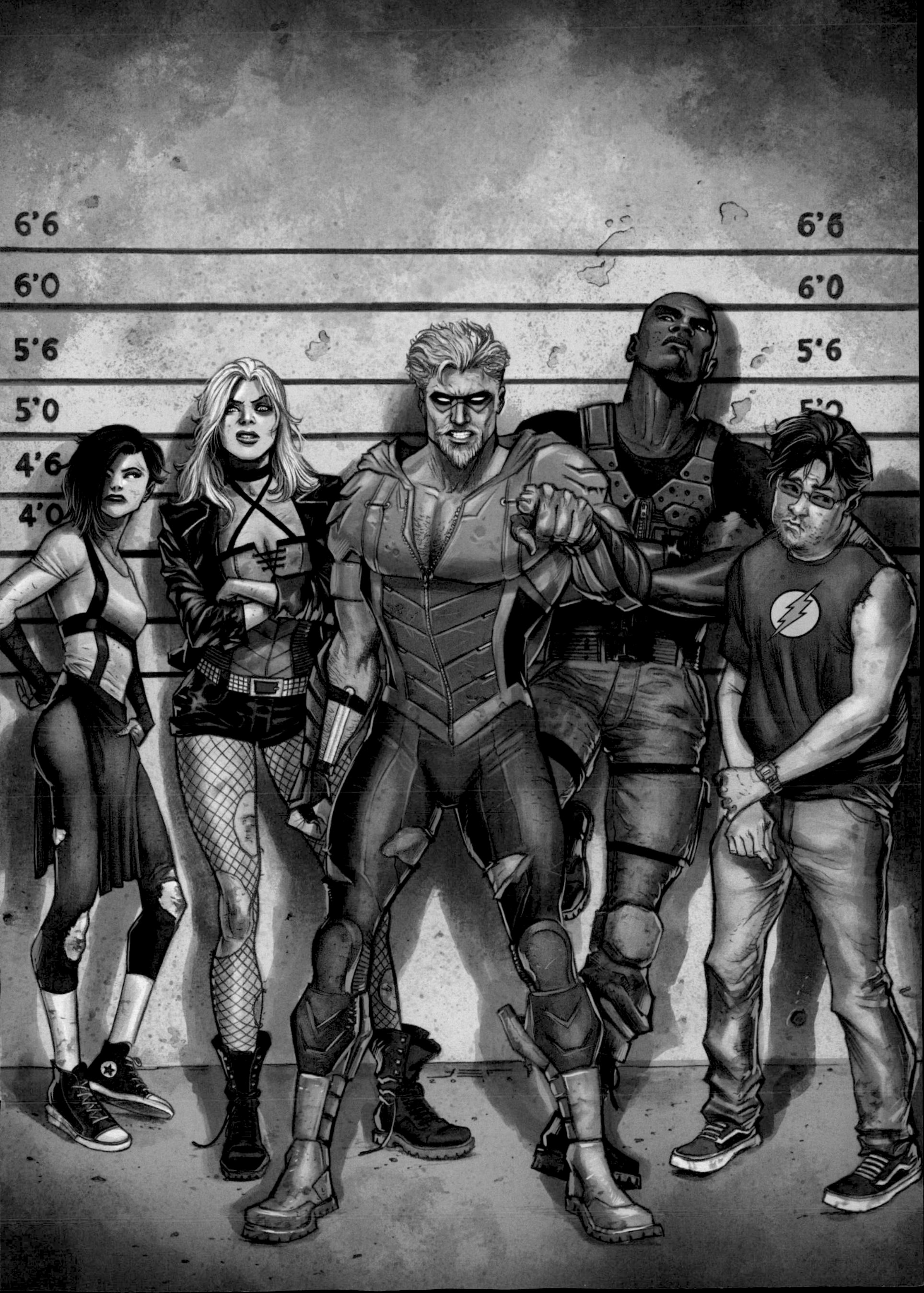
6'6
6'0
5'6
5'0
4'6
4'0
6'6
6'0
5'6

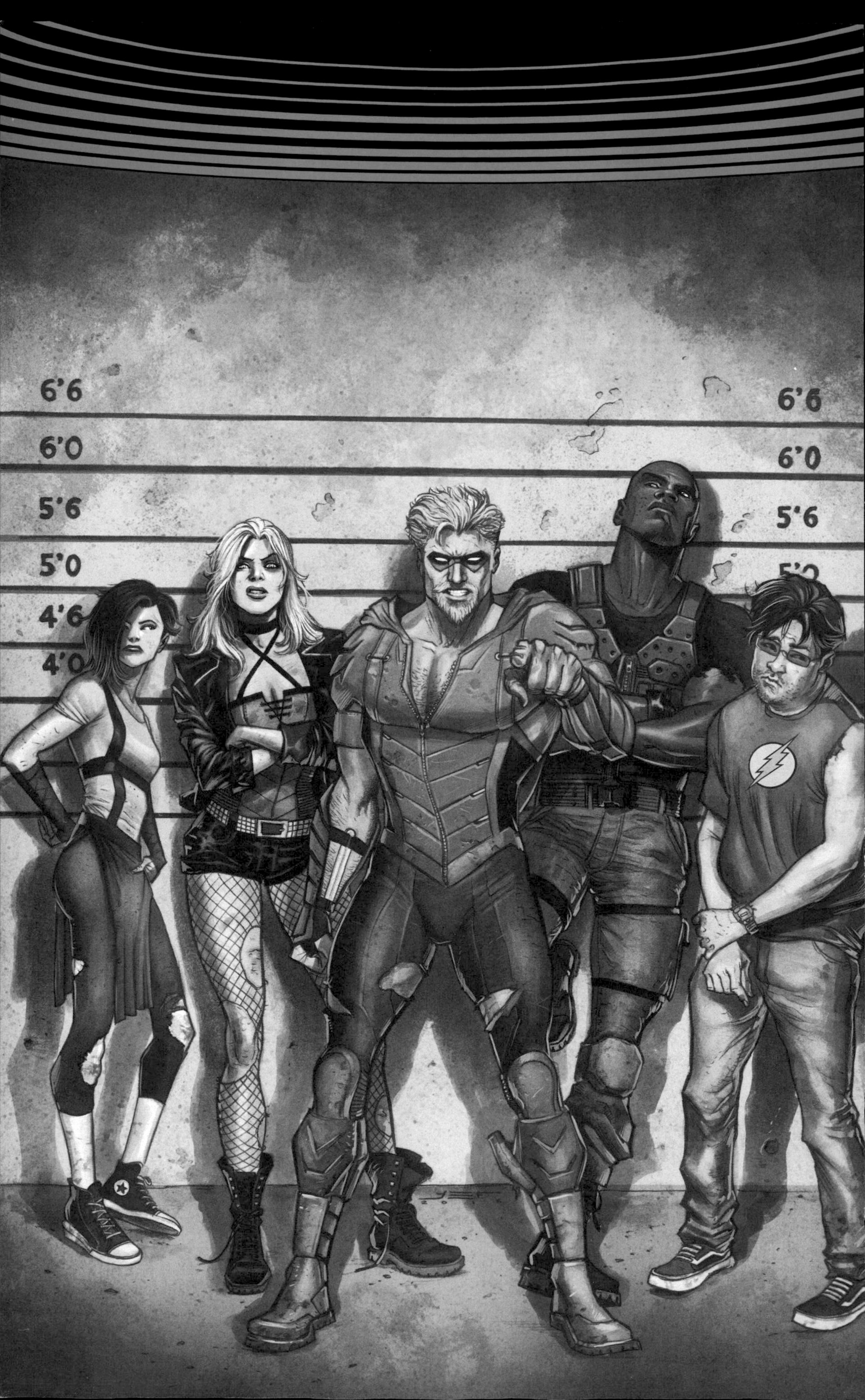
6'6
6'0
5'6
5'0
4'6
4'0
6'6
6'0
5'6

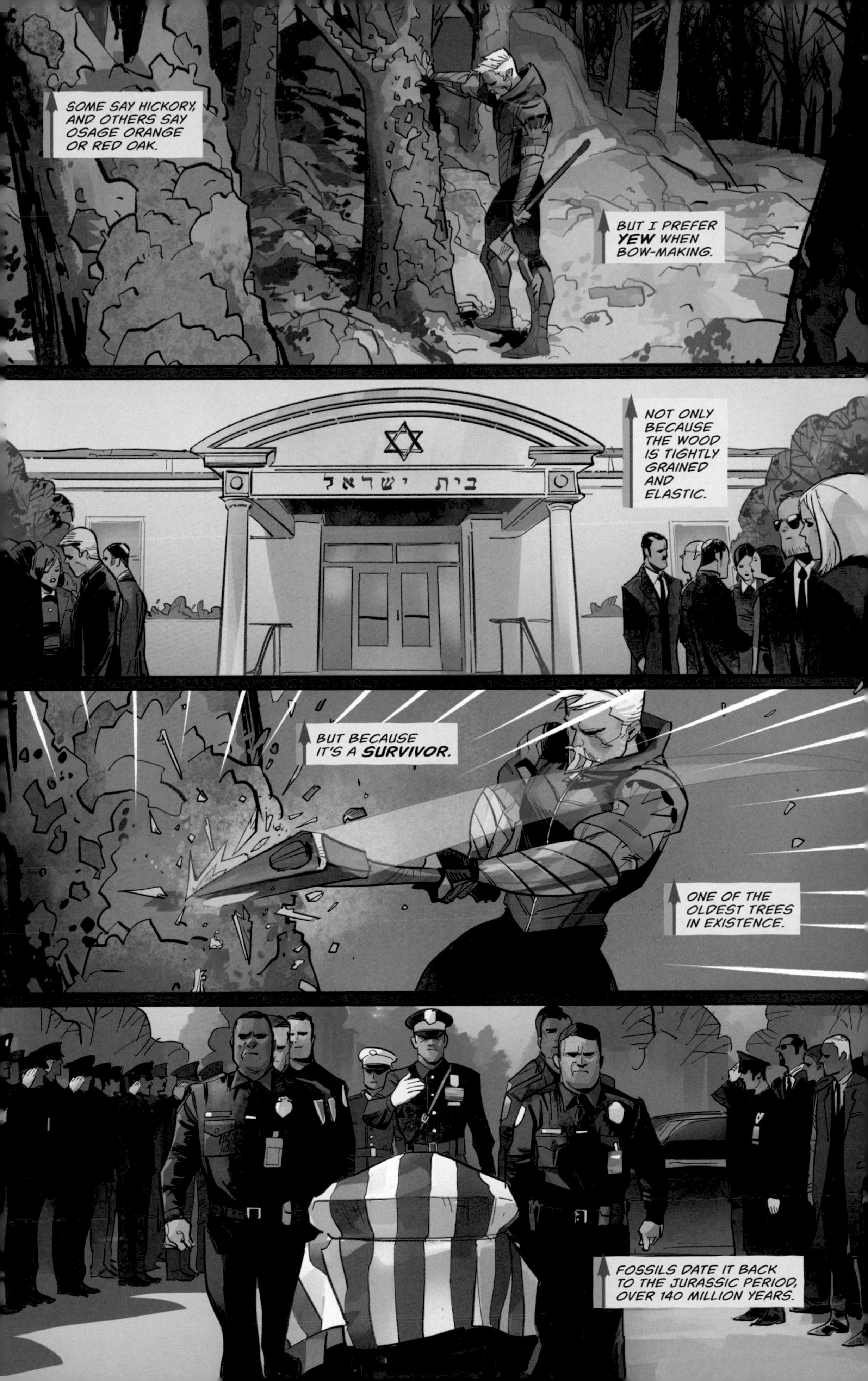
SOME SAY HICKORY, AND OTHERS SAY OSAGE ORANGE OR RED OAK.
BUT I PREFER **YEW** WHEN BOW-MAKING.
NOT ONLY BECAUSE THE WOOD IS TIGHTLY GRAINED AND ELASTIC.
בית ישראל
BUT BECAUSE IT'S A ***SURVIVOR***.
ONE OF THE OLDEST TREES IN EXISTENCE.
FOSSILS DATE IT BACK TO THE JURASSIC PERIOD, OVER 140 MILLION YEARS.

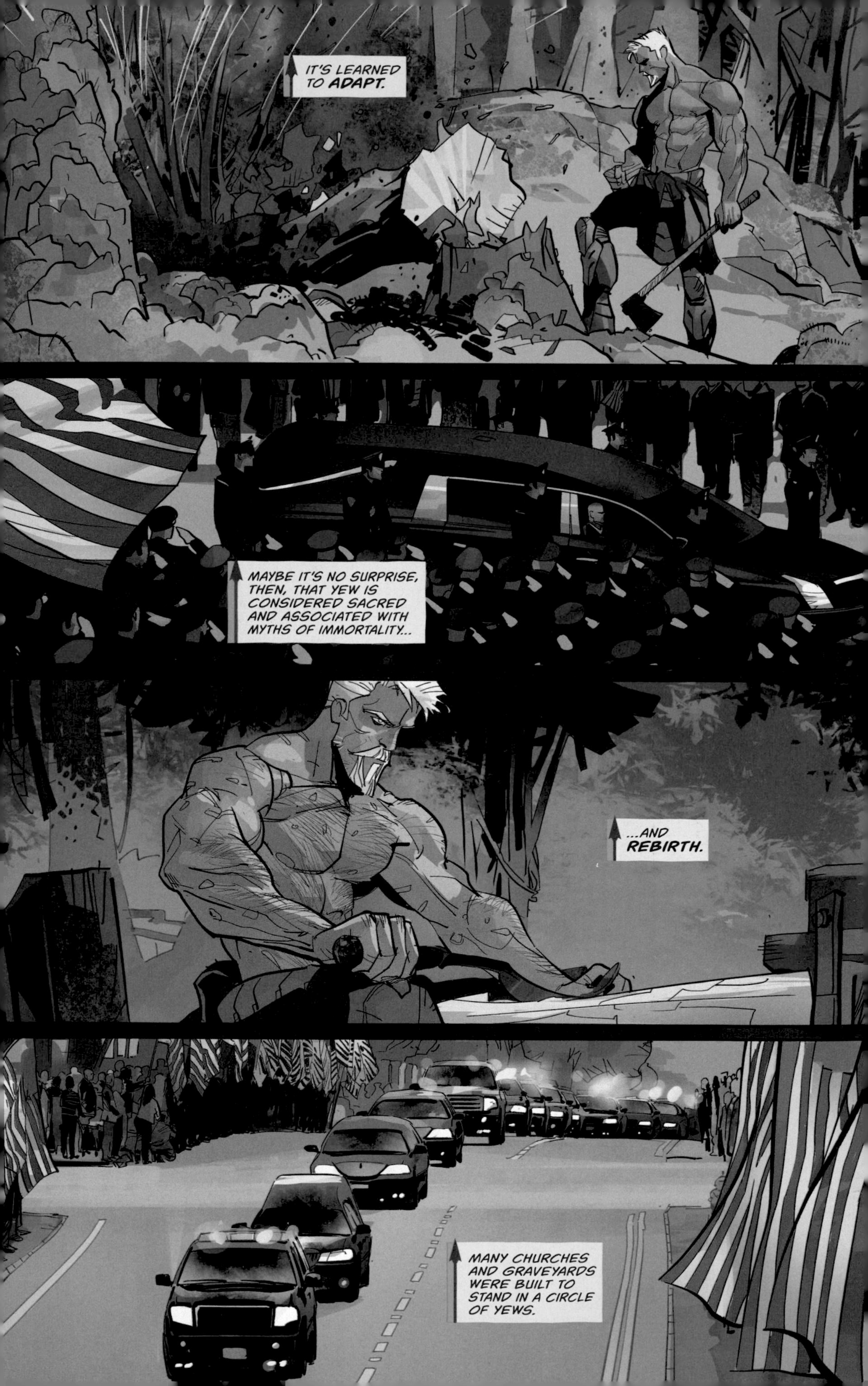
IT'S LEARNED TO ADAPT.
MAYBE IT'S NO SURPRISE, THEN, THAT YEW IS CONSIDERED SACRED AND ASSOCIATED WITH MYTHS OF IMMORTALITY...
...AND REBIRTH.
MANY CHURCHES AND GRAVEYARDS WERE BUILT TO STAND IN A CIRCLE OF YEWS.

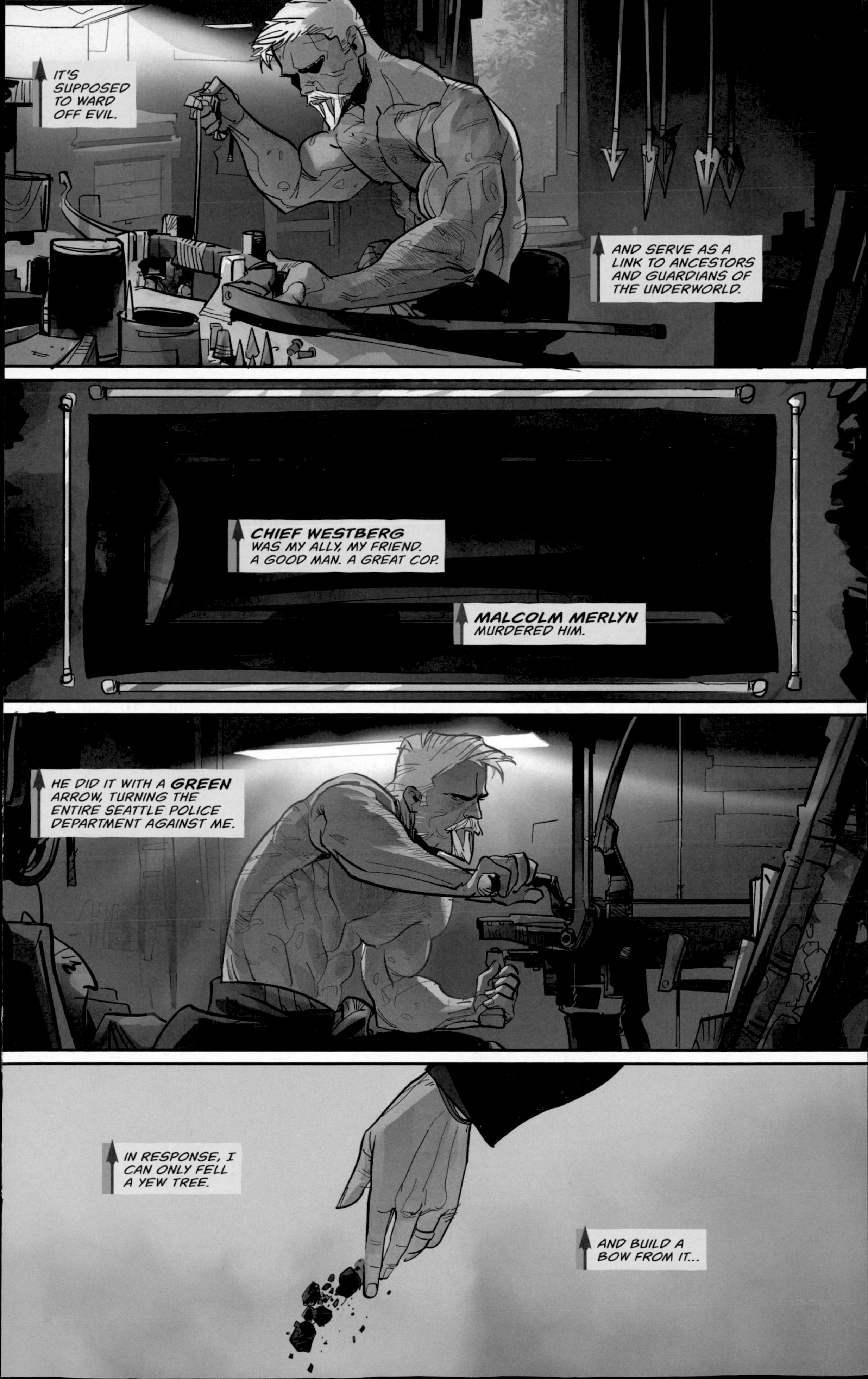
IT'S SUPPOSED TO WARD OFF EVIL.
AND SERVE AS A LINK TO ANCESTORS AND GUARDIANS OF THE UNDERWORLD.
CHIEF WESTBERG WAS MY ALLY, MY FRIEND. A GOOD MAN. A GREAT COP.
MALCOLM MERLYN MURDERED HIM.
HE DID IT WITH A GREEN ARROW, TURNING THE ENTIRE SEATTLE POLICE DEPARTMENT AGAINST ME.
IN RESPONSE, I CAN ONLY FELL A YEW TREE.
AND BUILD A BOW FROM IT...

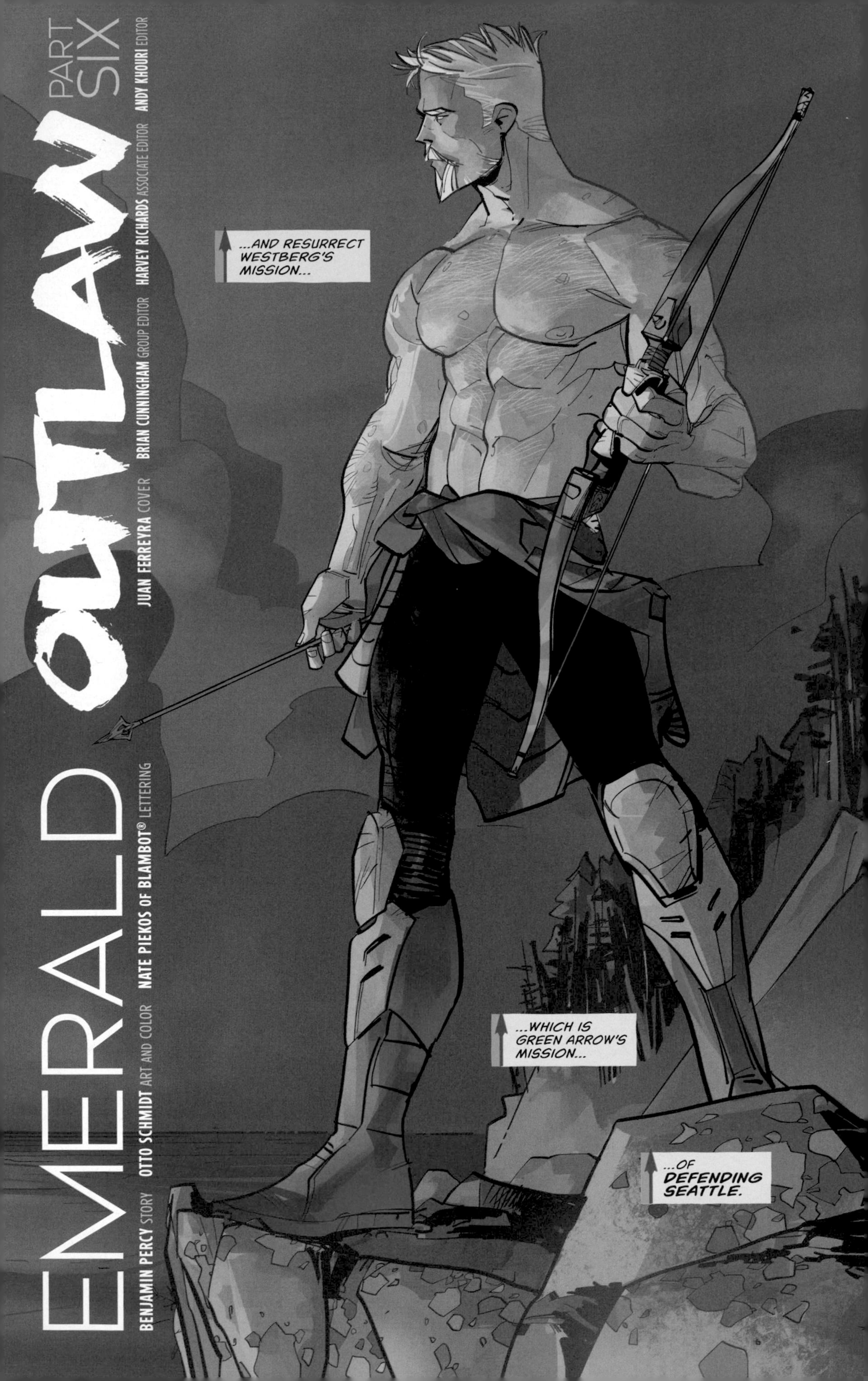
EMERALD OUTLAW PART SIX
BENJAMIN PERCY STORY OTTO SCHMIDT ART AND COLOR NATE PIEKOS OF BLAMBOT® LETTERING
JUAN FERREYRA COVER BRIAN CUNNINGHAM GROUP EDITOR HARVEY RICHARDS ASSOCIATE EDITOR ANDY KHOURI EDITOR
...AND RESURRECT WESTBERG'S MISSION...
...WHICH IS GREEN ARROW'S MISSION...
...OF DEFENDING SEATTLE.

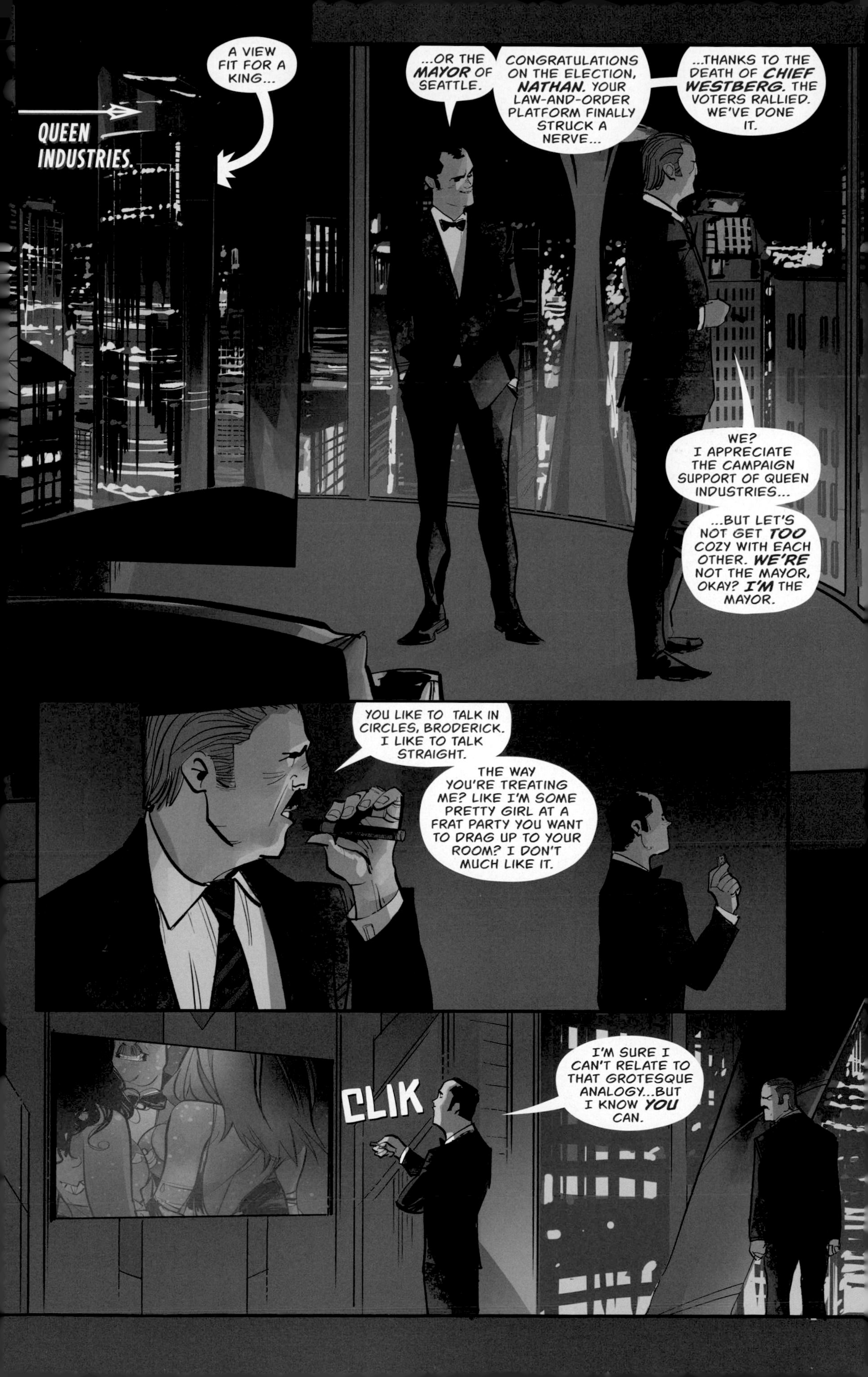
QUEEN INDUSTRIES.
A VIEW FIT FOR A KING...
...OR THE MAYOR OF SEATTLE.
CONGRATULATIONS ON THE ELECTION, NATHAN. YOUR LAW-AND-ORDER PLATFORM FINALLY STRUCK A NERVE...
...THANKS TO THE DEATH OF CHIEF WESTBERG. THE VOTERS RALLIED. WE'VE DONE IT.
WE? I APPRECIATE THE CAMPAIGN SUPPORT OF QUEEN INDUSTRIES...
...BUT LET'S NOT GET TOO COZY WITH EACH OTHER. WE'RE NOT THE MAYOR, OKAY? I'M THE MAYOR.
YOU LIKE TO TALK IN CIRCLES, BRODERICK. I LIKE TO TALK STRAIGHT.
THE WAY YOU'RE TREATING ME? LIKE I'M SOME PRETTY GIRL AT A FRAT PARTY YOU WANT TO DRAG UP TO YOUR ROOM? I DON'T MUCH LIKE IT.
CLIK
I'M SURE I CAN'T RELATE TO THAT GROTESQUE ANALOGY...BUT I KNOW YOU CAN.

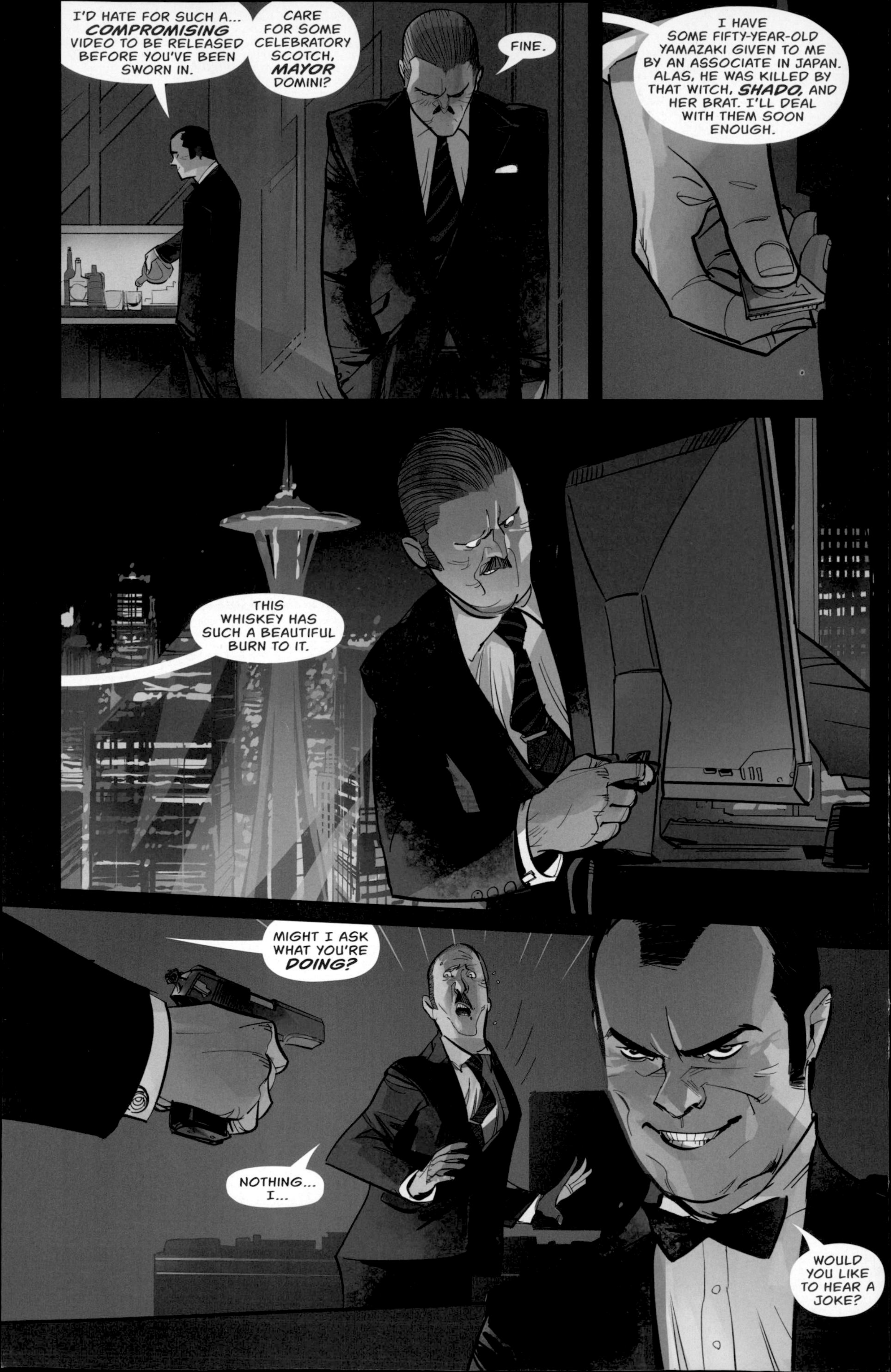
I'D HATE FOR SUCH A... COMPROMISING VIDEO TO BE RELEASED BEFORE YOU'VE BEEN SWORN IN.
CARE FOR SOME CELEBRATORY SCOTCH, MAYOR DOMINI?
FINE.
I HAVE SOME FIFTY-YEAR-OLD YAMAZAKI GIVEN TO ME BY AN ASSOCIATE IN JAPAN. ALAS, HE WAS KILLED BY THAT WITCH, SHADO, AND HER BRAT. I'LL DEAL WITH THEM SOON ENOUGH.
THIS WHISKEY HAS SUCH A BEAUTIFUL BURN TO IT.
MIGHT I ASK WHAT YOU'RE DOING?
NOTHING... I...
WOULD YOU LIKE TO HEAR A JOKE?

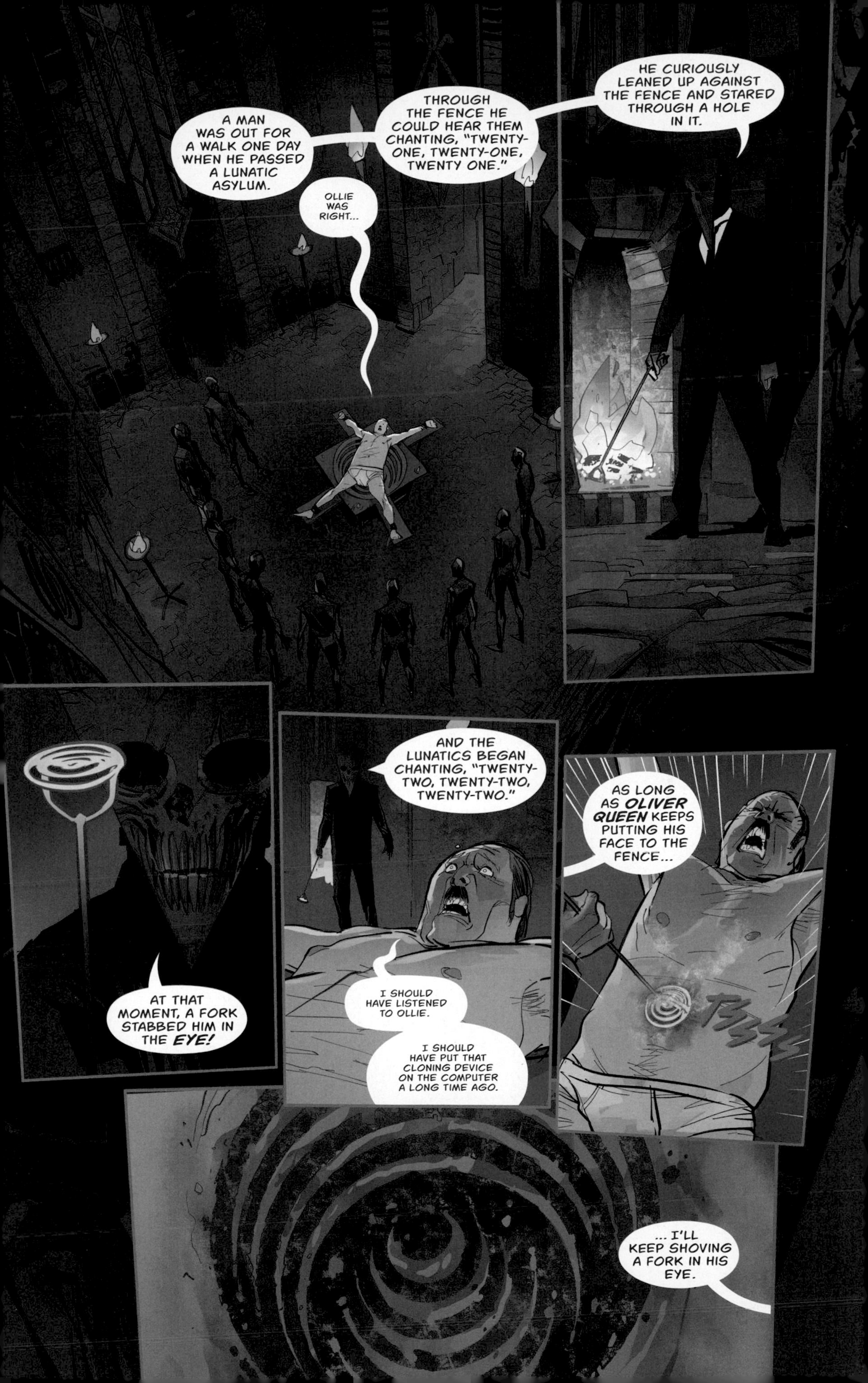
A MAN WAS OUT FOR A WALK ONE DAY WHEN HE PASSED A LUNATIC ASYLUM.
THROUGH THE FENCE HE COULD HEAR THEM CHANTING, "TWENTY-ONE, TWENTY-ONE, TWENTY ONE."
HE CURIOUSLY LEANED UP AGAINST THE FENCE AND STARED THROUGH A HOLE IN IT.
OLLIE WAS RIGHT...
AT THAT MOMENT, A FORK STABBED HIM IN THE EYE!
AND THE LUNATICS BEGAN CHANTING, "TWENTY-TWO, TWENTY-TWO, TWENTY-TWO."
I SHOULD HAVE LISTENED TO OLLIE.
I SHOULD HAVE PUT THAT CLONING DEVICE ON THE COMPUTER A LONG TIME AGO.
AS LONG AS OLIVER QUEEN KEEPS PUTTING HIS FACE TO THE FENCE...
TSSSS
... I'LL KEEP SHOVING A FORK IN HIS EYE.

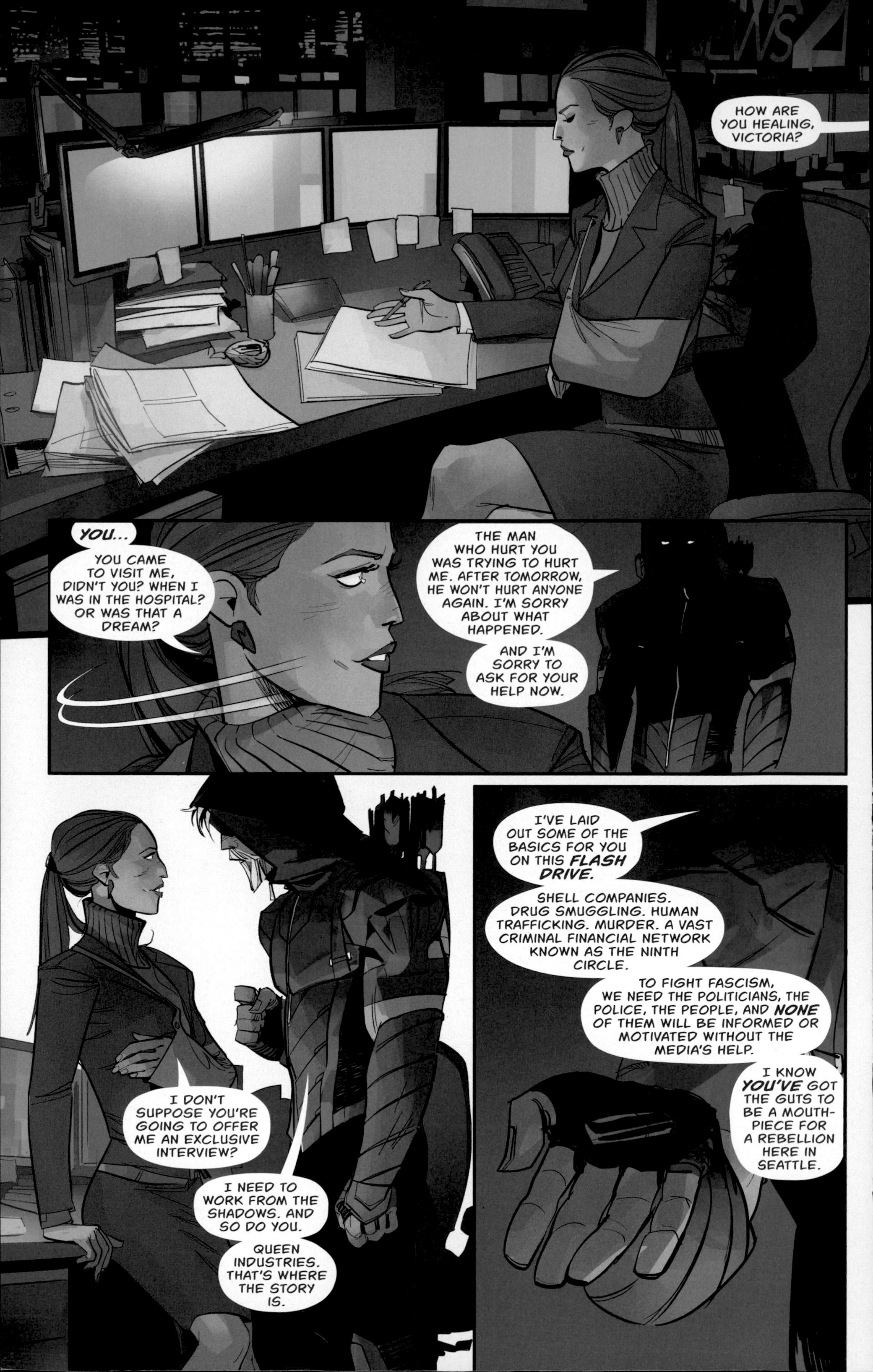
HOW ARE YOU HEALING, VICTORIA?
YOU...
YOU CAME TO VISIT ME, DIDN'T YOU? WHEN I WAS IN THE HOSPITAL? OR WAS THAT A DREAM?
THE MAN WHO HURT YOU WAS TRYING TO HURT ME. AFTER TOMORROW, HE WON'T HURT ANYONE AGAIN. I'M SORRY ABOUT WHAT HAPPENED.
AND I'M SORRY TO ASK FOR YOUR HELP NOW.
I DON'T SUPPOSE YOU'RE GOING TO OFFER ME AN EXCLUSIVE INTERVIEW?
I NEED TO WORK FROM THE SHADOWS. AND SO DO YOU.
QUEEN INDUSTRIES. THAT'S WHERE THE STORY IS.
I'VE LAID OUT SOME OF THE BASICS FOR YOU ON THIS FLASH DRIVE.
SHELL COMPANIES. DRUG SMUGGLING. HUMAN TRAFFICKING. MURDER. A VAST CRIMINAL FINANCIAL NETWORK KNOWN AS THE NINTH CIRCLE.
TO FIGHT FASCISM, WE NEED THE POLITICIANS, THE POLICE, THE PEOPLE, AND NONE OF THEM WILL BE INFORMED OR MOTIVATED WITHOUT THE MEDIA'S HELP.
I KNOW YOU'VE GOT THE GUTS TO BE A MOUTHPIECE FOR A REBELLION HERE IN SEATTLE.

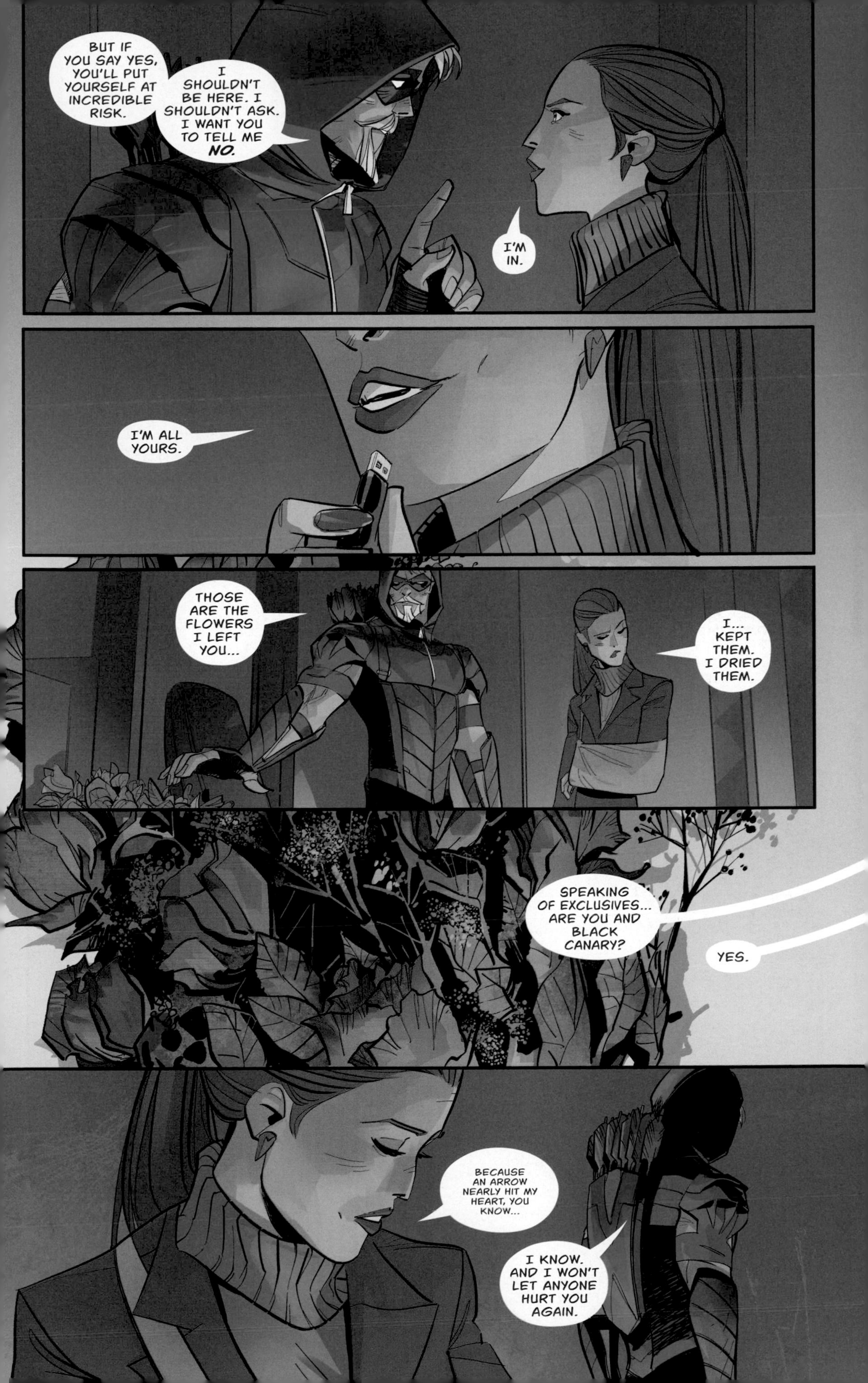
BUT IF YOU SAY YES, YOU'LL PUT YOURSELF AT INCREDIBLE RISK.
I SHOULDN'T BE HERE. I SHOULDN'T ASK. I WANT YOU TO TELL ME *NO.*
I'M IN.
I'M ALL YOURS.
THOSE ARE THE FLOWERS I LEFT YOU...
I... KEPT THEM. I DRIED THEM.
SPEAKING OF EXCLUSIVES... ARE YOU AND BLACK CANARY?
YES.
BECAUSE AN ARROW NEARLY HIT MY HEART, YOU KNOW...
I KNOW. AND I WON'T LET ANYONE HURT YOU AGAIN.

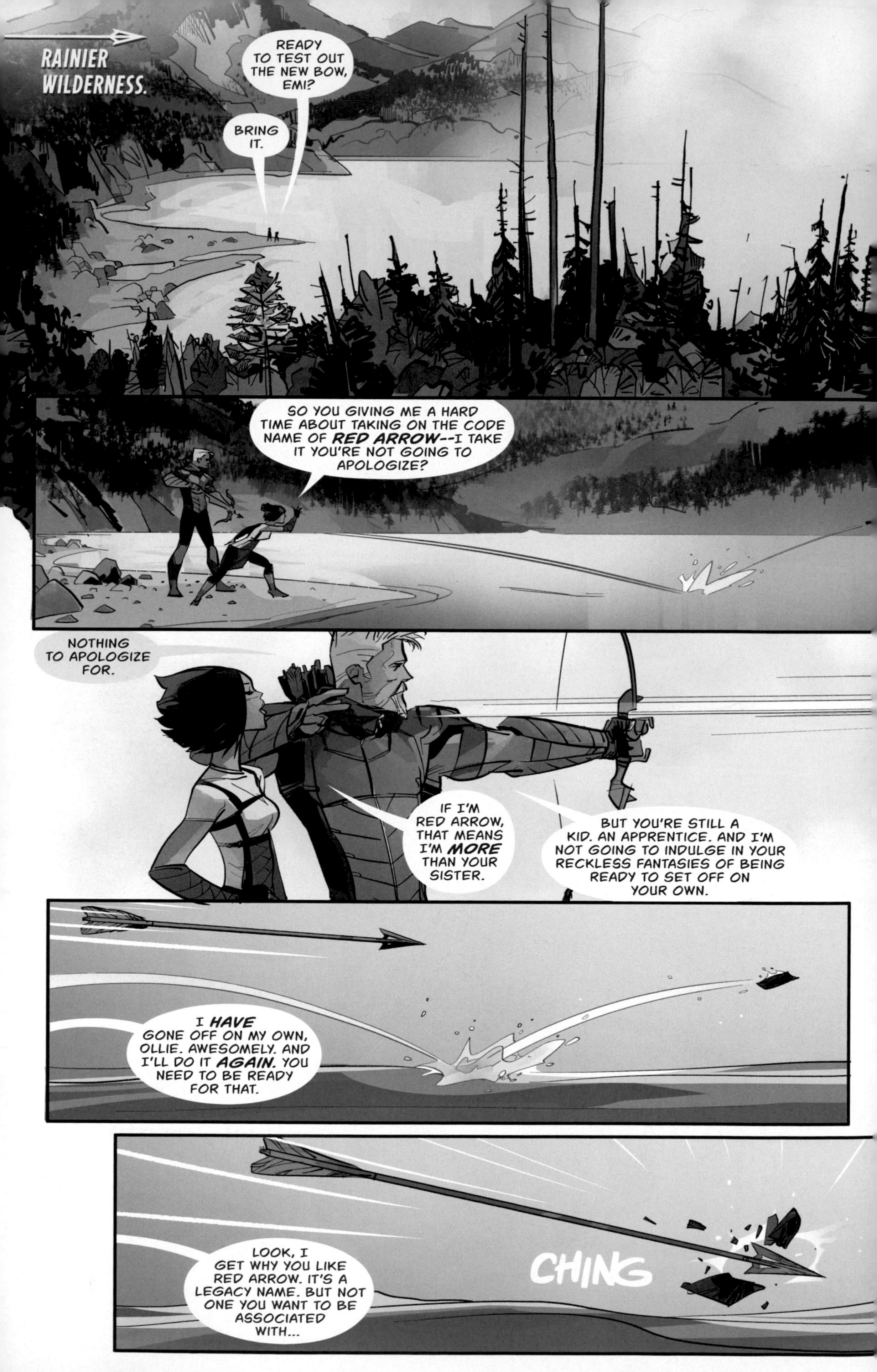
RAINIER WILDERNESS.
READY TO TEST OUT THE NEW BOW, EMI?
BRING IT.
SO YOU GIVING ME A HARD TIME ABOUT TAKING ON THE CODE NAME OF RED ARROW--I TAKE IT YOU'RE NOT GOING TO APOLOGIZE?
NOTHING TO APOLOGIZE FOR.
IF I'M RED ARROW, THAT MEANS I'M MORE THAN YOUR SISTER.
BUT YOU'RE STILL A KID. AN APPRENTICE. AND I'M NOT GOING TO INDULGE IN YOUR RECKLESS FANTASIES OF BEING READY TO SET OFF ON YOUR OWN.
I HAVE GONE OFF ON MY OWN, OLLIE. AWESOMELY. AND I'LL DO IT AGAIN. YOU NEED TO BE READY FOR THAT.
LOOK, I GET WHY YOU LIKE RED ARROW. IT'S A LEGACY NAME. BUT NOT ONE YOU WANT TO BE ASSOCIATED WITH...
CHING

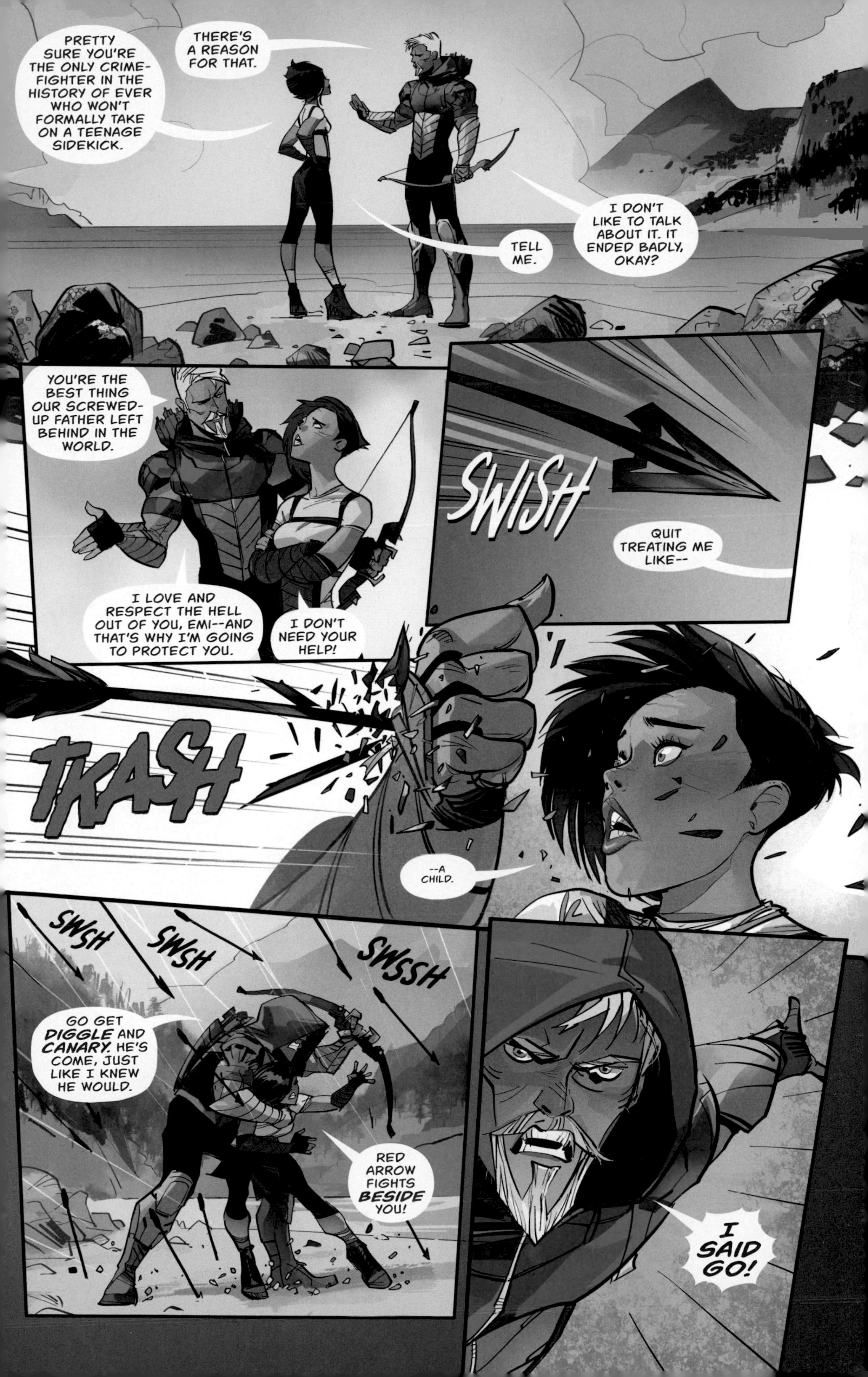
PRETTY SURE YOU'RE THE ONLY CRIME-FIGHTER IN THE HISTORY OF EVER WHO WON'T FORMALLY TAKE ON A TEENAGE SIDEKICK.
THERE'S A REASON FOR THAT.
TELL ME.
I DON'T LIKE TO TALK ABOUT IT. IT ENDED BADLY, OKAY?
YOU'RE THE BEST THING OUR SCREWED-UP FATHER LEFT BEHIND IN THE WORLD.
I LOVE AND RESPECT THE HELL OUT OF YOU, EMI--AND THAT'S WHY I'M GOING TO PROTECT YOU.
I DON'T NEED YOUR HELP!
SWISH
QUIT TREATING ME LIKE--
TKASH
--A CHILD.
SWSH
SWSH
SWSSH
GO GET DIGGLE AND CANARY. HE'S COME, JUST LIKE I KNEW HE WOULD.
RED ARROW FIGHTS BESIDE YOU!
I SAID GO!

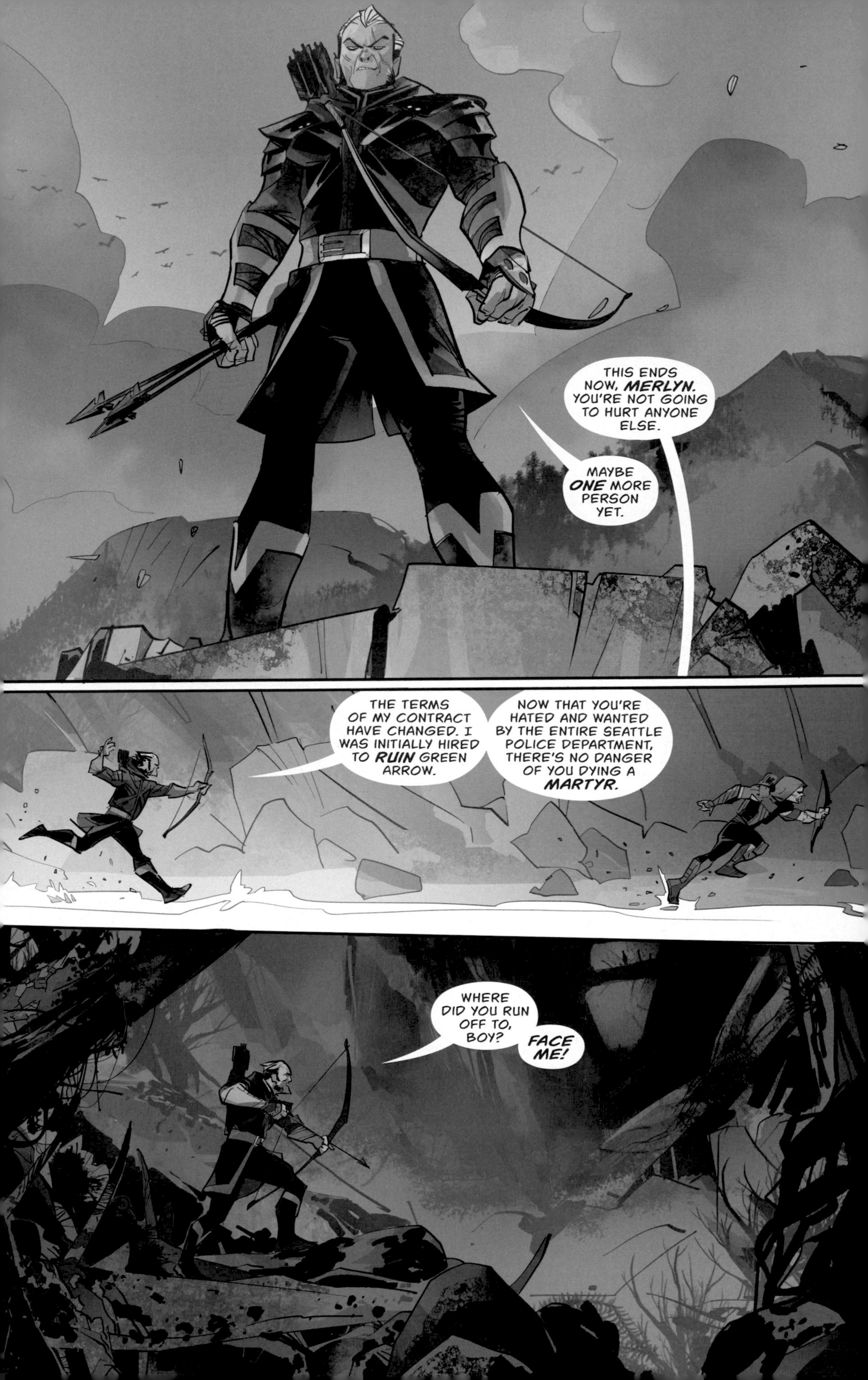
THIS ENDS NOW, MERLYN. YOU'RE NOT GOING TO HURT ANYONE ELSE.
MAYBE ONE MORE PERSON YET.
THE TERMS OF MY CONTRACT HAVE CHANGED. I WAS INITIALLY HIRED TO RUIN GREEN ARROW.
NOW THAT YOU'RE HATED AND WANTED BY THE ENTIRE SEATTLE POLICE DEPARTMENT, THERE'S NO DANGER OF YOU DYING A MARTYR.
WHERE DID YOU RUN OFF TO, BOY?
FACE ME!

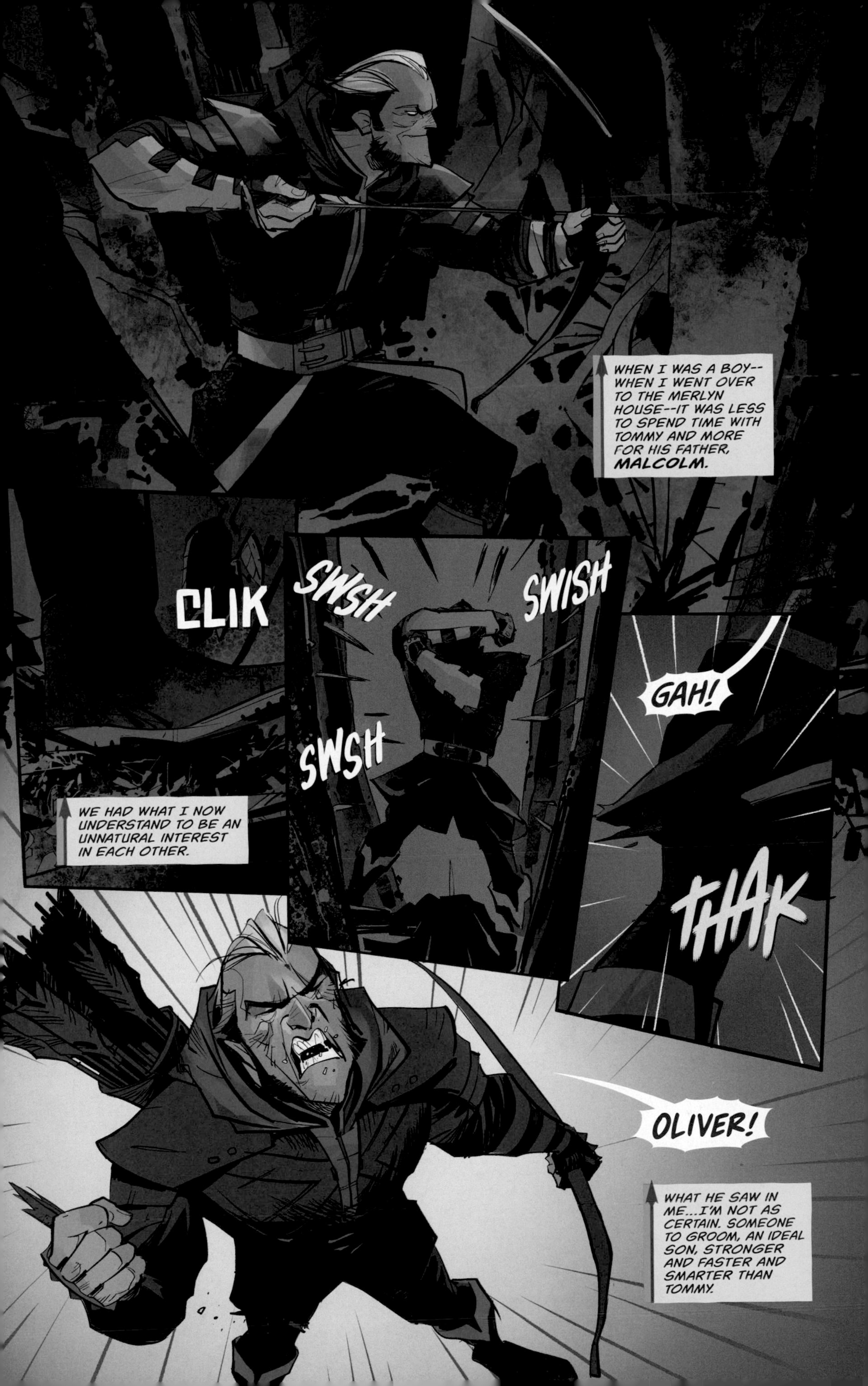
WHEN I WAS A BOY--WHEN I WENT OVER TO THE MERLYN HOUSE--IT WAS LESS TO SPEND TIME WITH TOMMY AND MORE FOR HIS FATHER, MALCOLM.
CLIK
WE HAD WHAT I NOW UNDERSTAND TO BE AN UNNATURAL INTEREST IN EACH OTHER.
SWSH
SWISH
SWSH
GAH!
THAK
OLIVER!
WHAT HE SAW IN ME...I'M NOT AS CERTAIN. SOMEONE TO GROOM, AN IDEAL SON, STRONGER AND FASTER AND SMARTER THAN TOMMY.

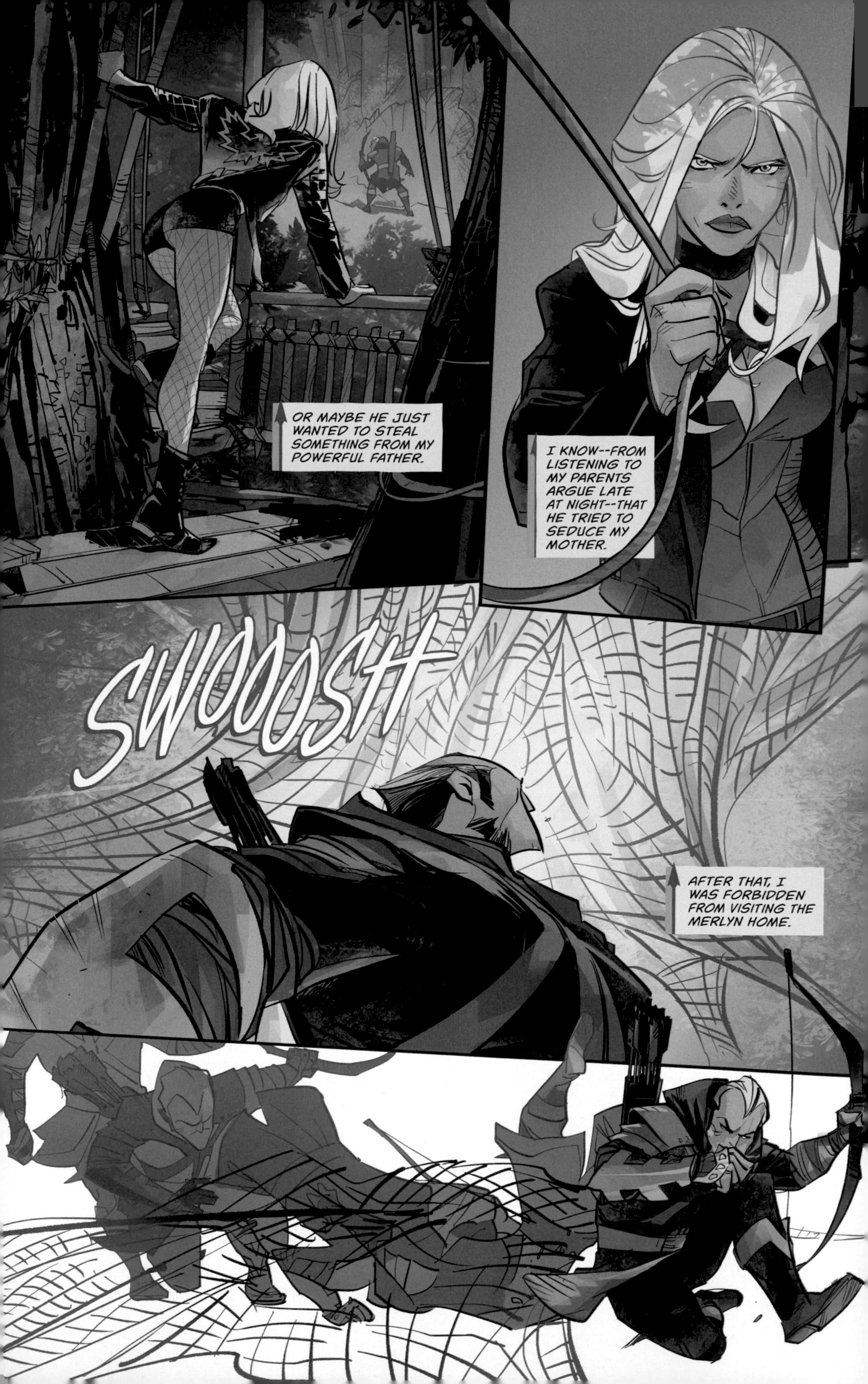
OR MAYBE HE JUST WANTED TO STEAL SOMETHING FROM MY POWERFUL FATHER.
I KNOW--FROM LISTENING TO MY PARENTS ARGUE LATE AT NIGHT--THAT HE TRIED TO SEDUCE MY MOTHER.
SWOOOSH
AFTER THAT, I WAS FORBIDDEN FROM VISITING THE MERLYN HOME.

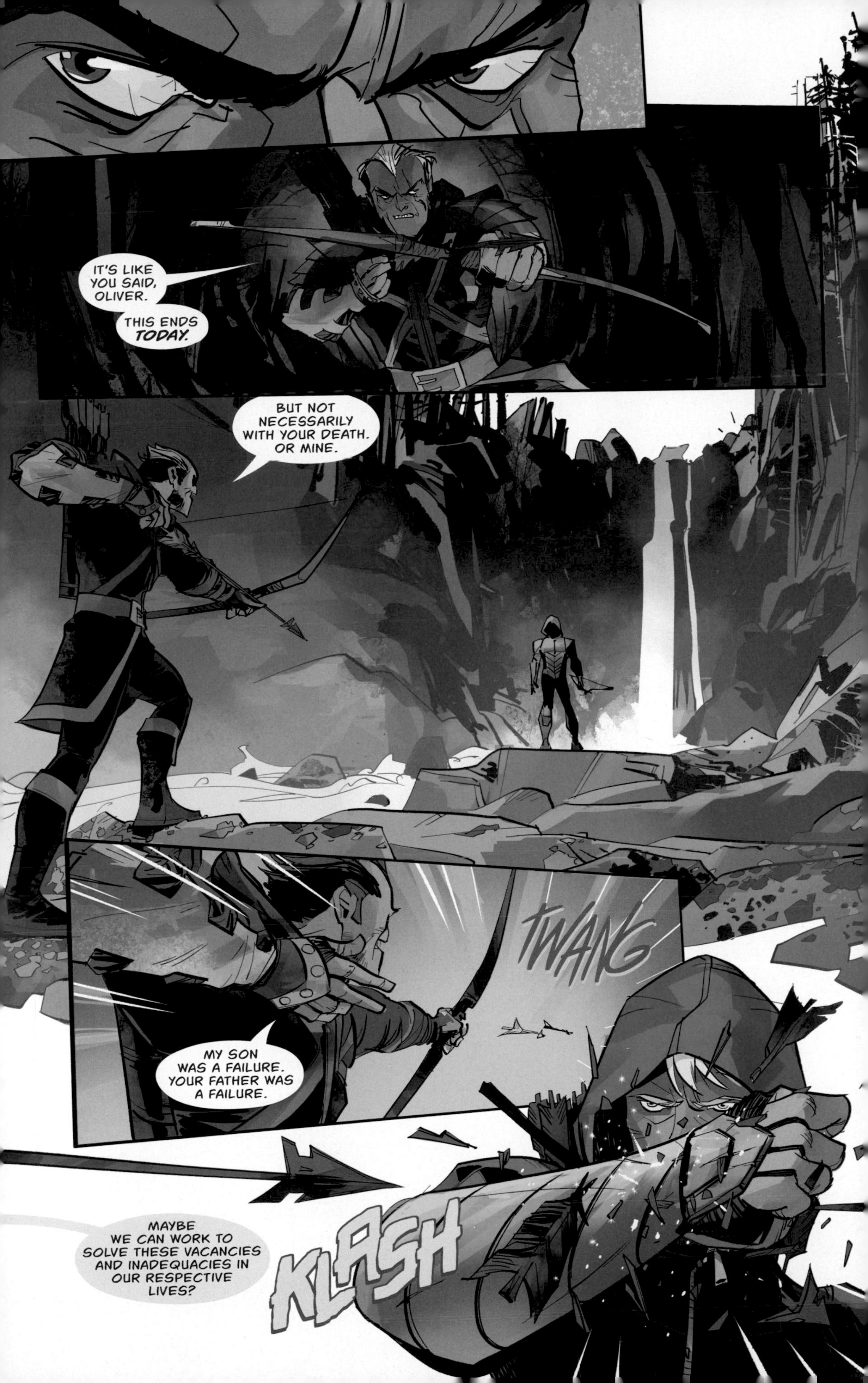
IT'S LIKE YOU SAID, OLIVER.
THIS ENDS *TODAY.*
BUT NOT NECESSARILY WITH YOUR DEATH. OR MINE.
TWANG
MY SON WAS A FAILURE. YOUR FATHER WAS A FAILURE.
MAYBE WE CAN WORK TO SOLVE THESE VACANCIES AND INADEQUACIES IN OUR RESPECTIVE LIVES?
KLASH

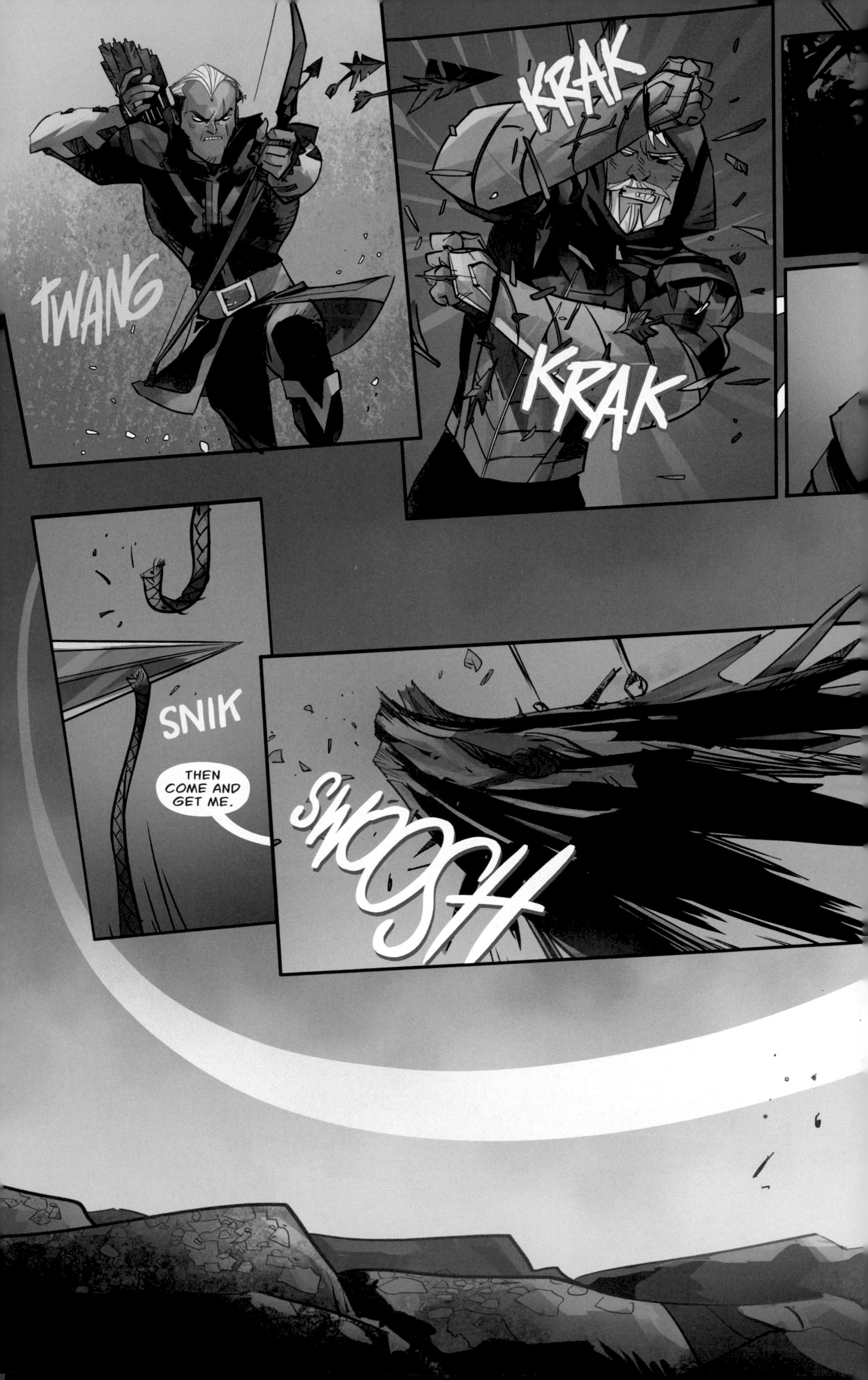
TWANG
KRAK
KRAK
SNIK
THEN COME AND GET ME.
SWOOSH

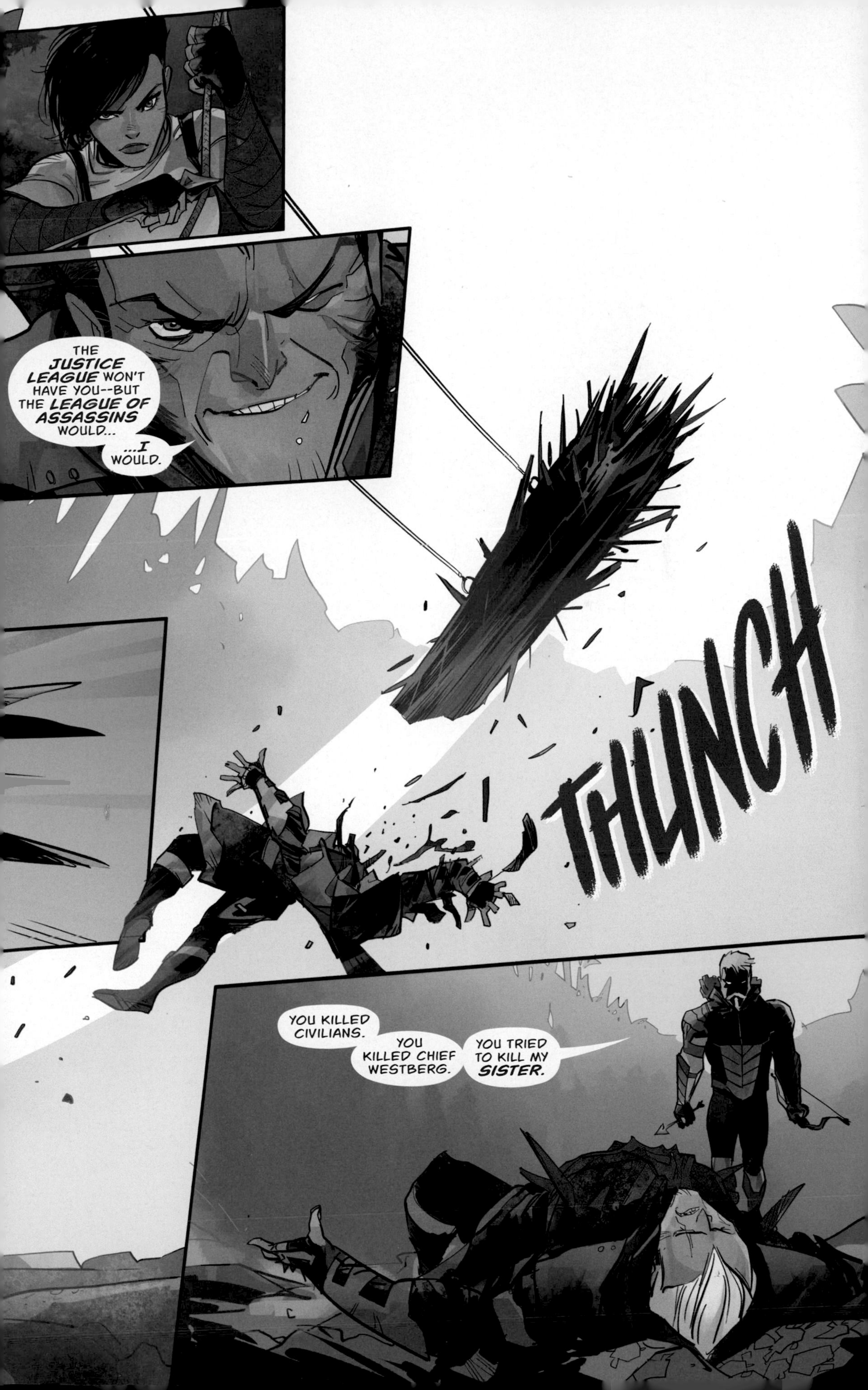
THE JUSTICE LEAGUE WON'T HAVE YOU--BUT THE LEAGUE OF ASSASSINS WOULD...
...I WOULD.
THUNCH
YOU KILLED CIVILIANS.
YOU KILLED CHIEF WESTBERG.
YOU TRIED TO KILL MY SISTER.

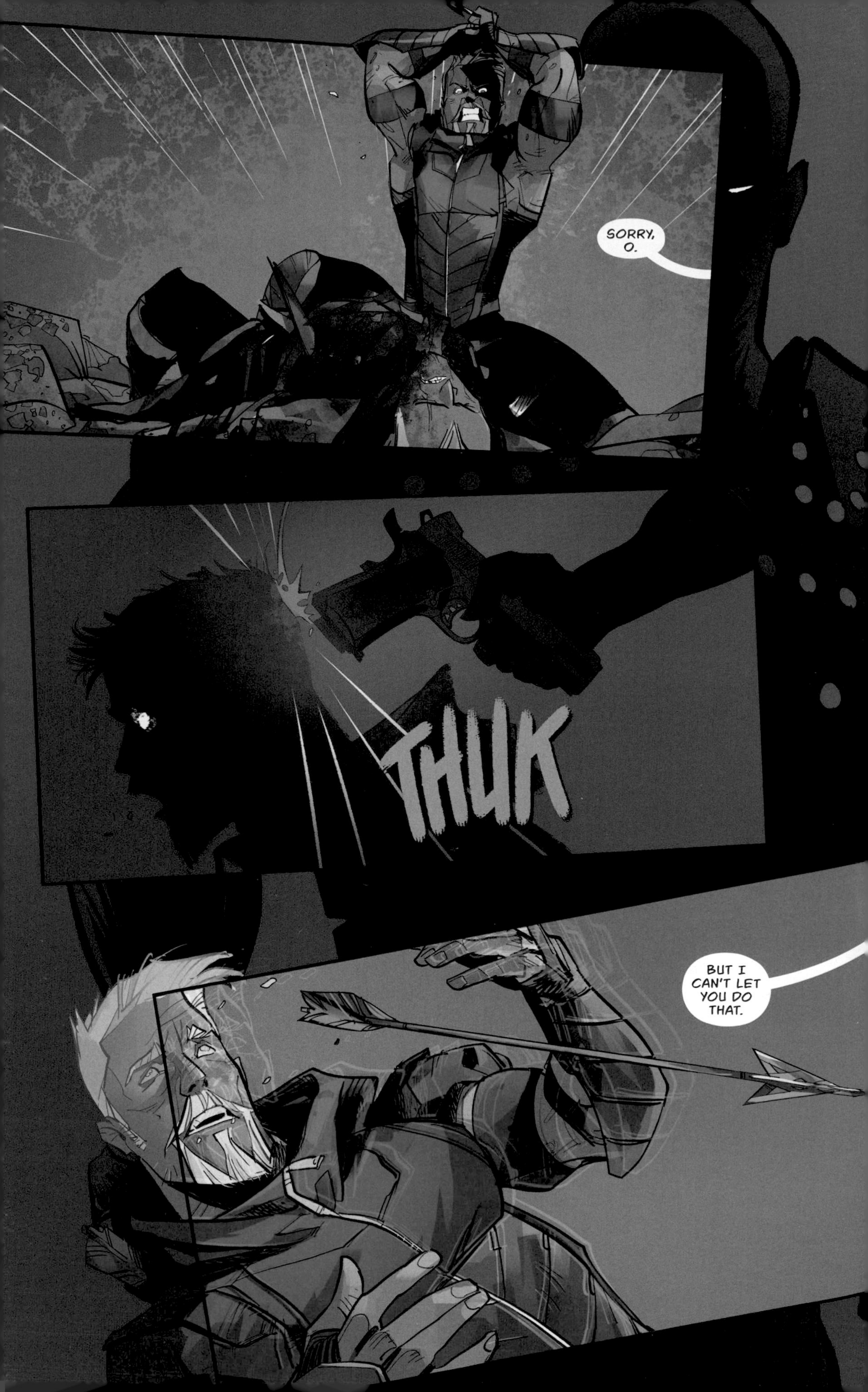
SORRY, O.
THUK
BUT I CAN'T LET YOU DO THAT.

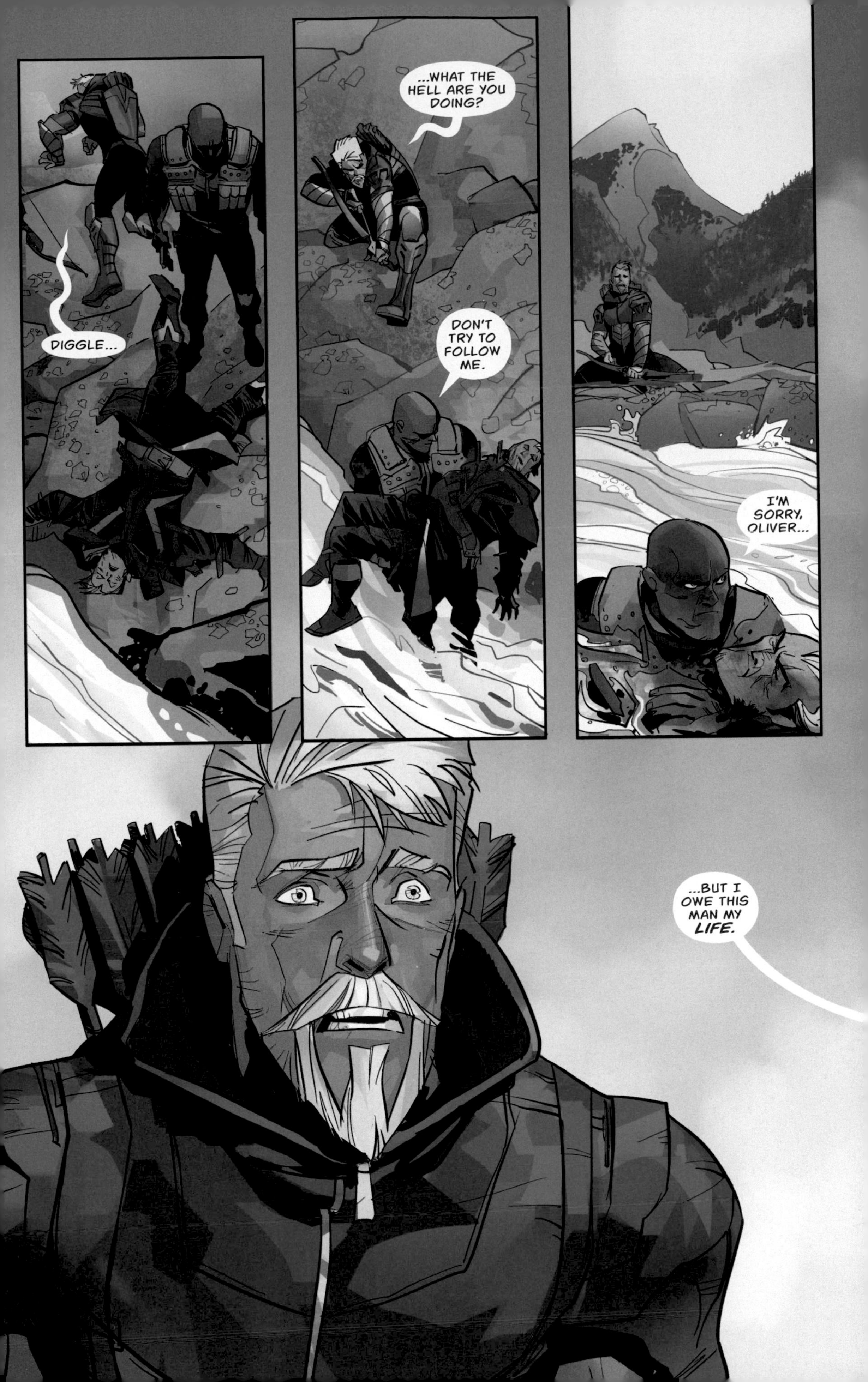
DIGGLE...
...WHAT THE HELL ARE YOU DOING?
DON'T TRY TO FOLLOW ME.
I'M SORRY, OLIVER...
...BUT I OWE THIS MAN MY *LIFE.*

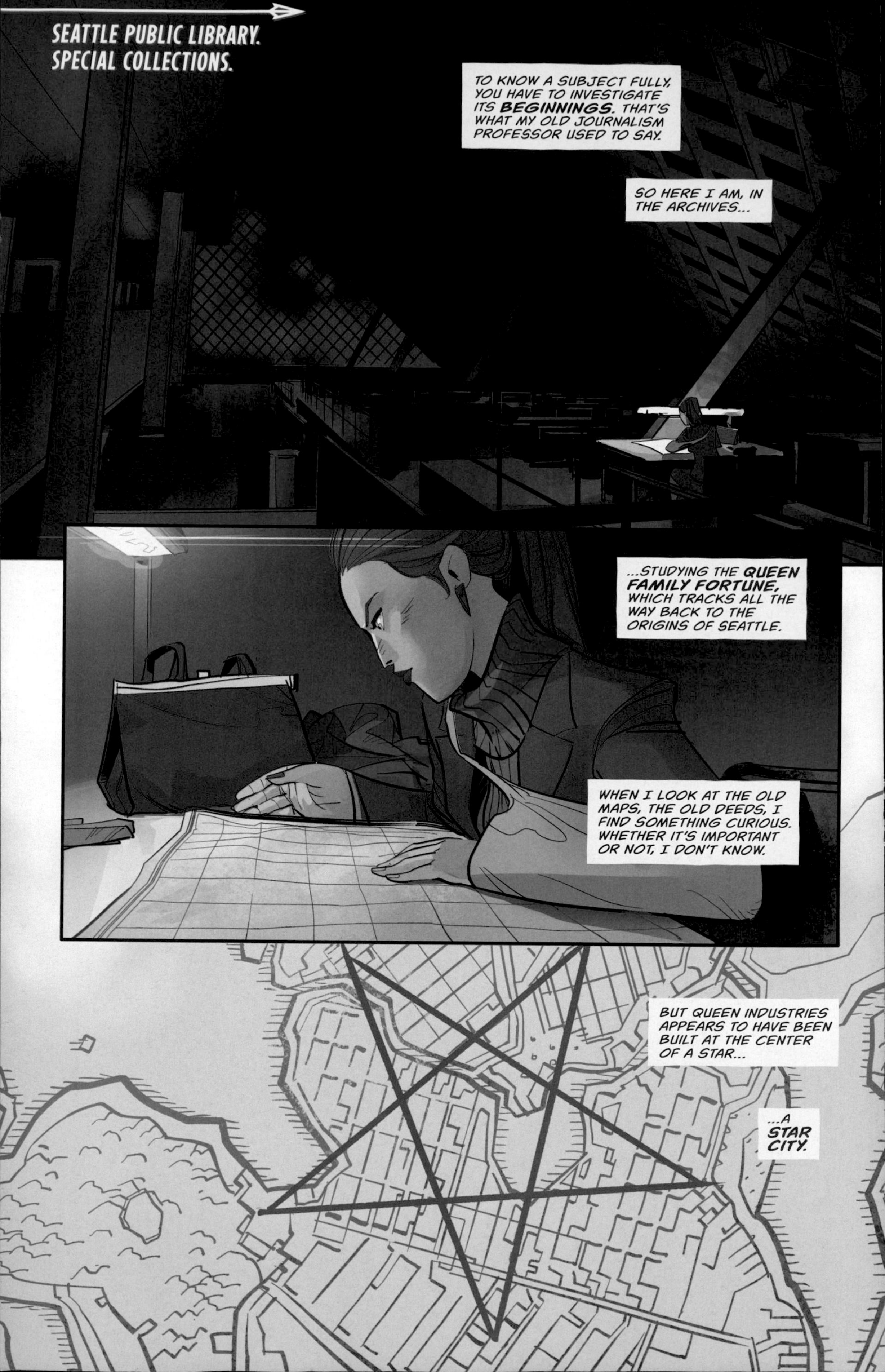
SEATTLE PUBLIC LIBRARY. SPECIAL COLLECTIONS.
TO KNOW A SUBJECT FULLY, YOU HAVE TO INVESTIGATE ITS BEGINNINGS. THAT'S WHAT MY OLD JOURNALISM PROFESSOR USED TO SAY.
SO HERE I AM, IN THE ARCHIVES...
...STUDYING THE QUEEN FAMILY FORTUNE, WHICH TRACKS ALL THE WAY BACK TO THE ORIGINS OF SEATTLE.
WHEN I LOOK AT THE OLD MAPS, THE OLD DEEDS, I FIND SOMETHING CURIOUS. WHETHER IT'S IMPORTANT OR NOT, I DON'T KNOW.
BUT QUEEN INDUSTRIES APPEARS TO HAVE BEEN BUILT AT THE CENTER OF A STAR...
...A STAR CITY.

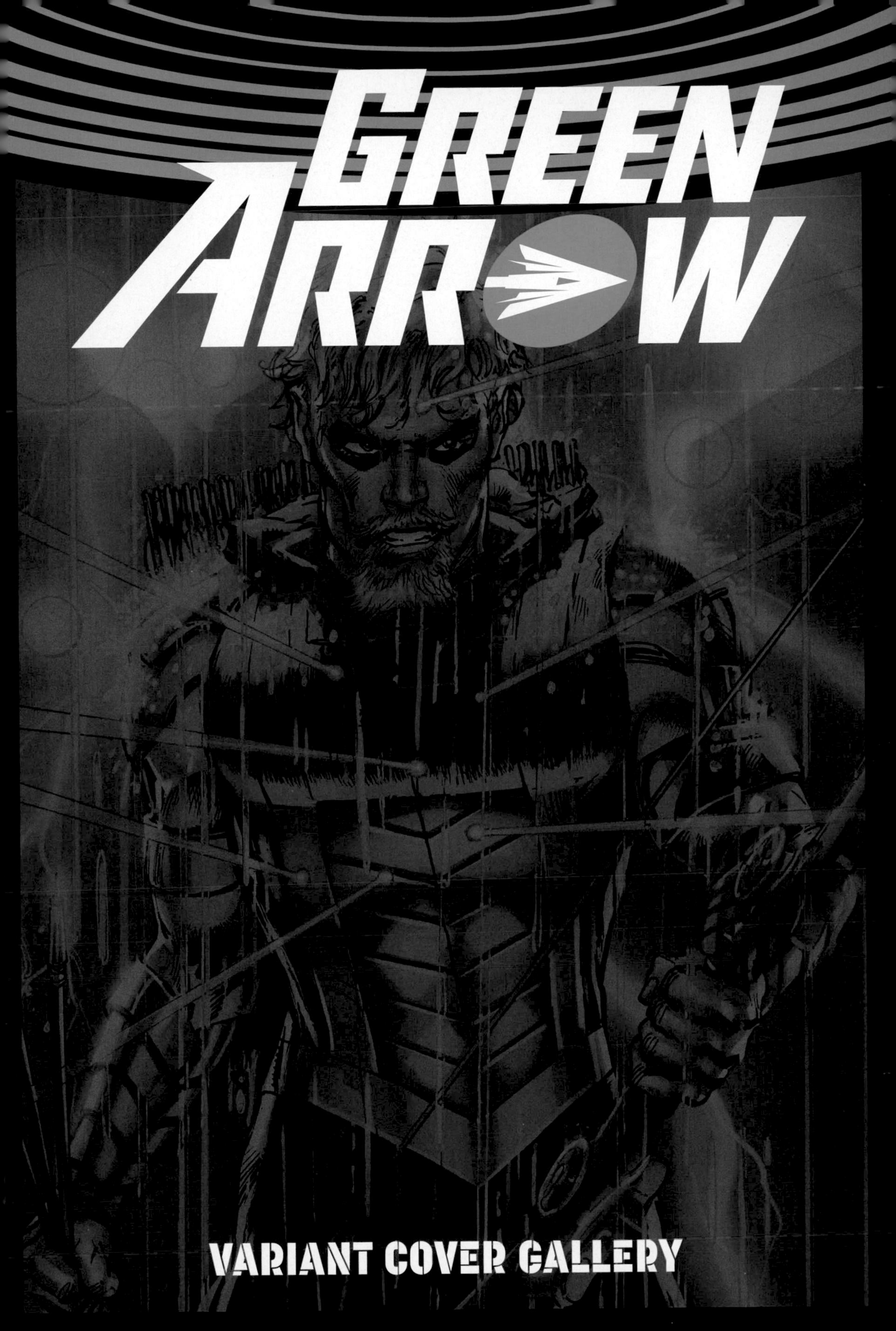
GREEN ARROW
VARIANT COVER GALLERY

GREEN ARROW #12 Variant Cover by NEAL ADAMS with JEROMY COX

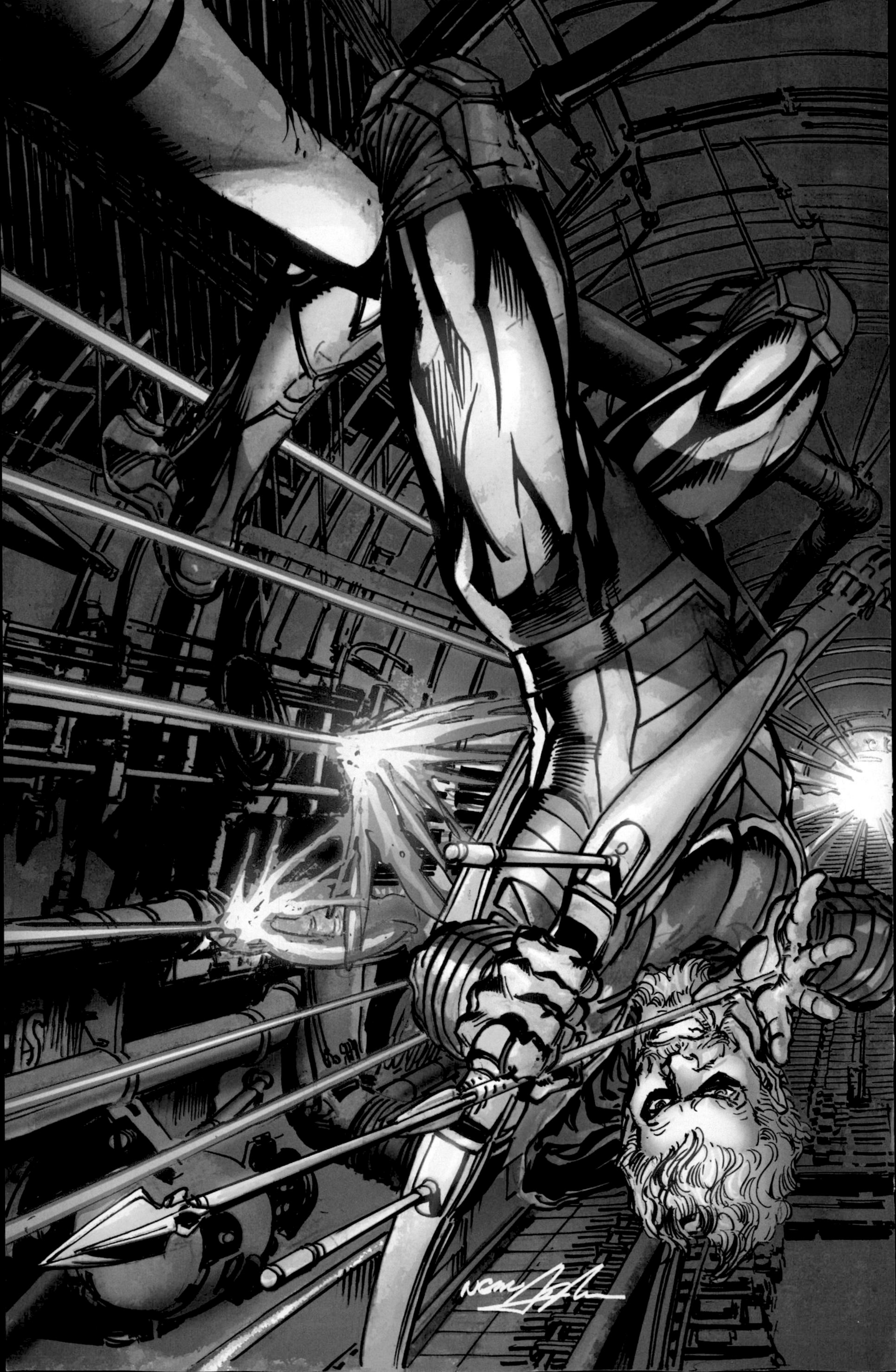

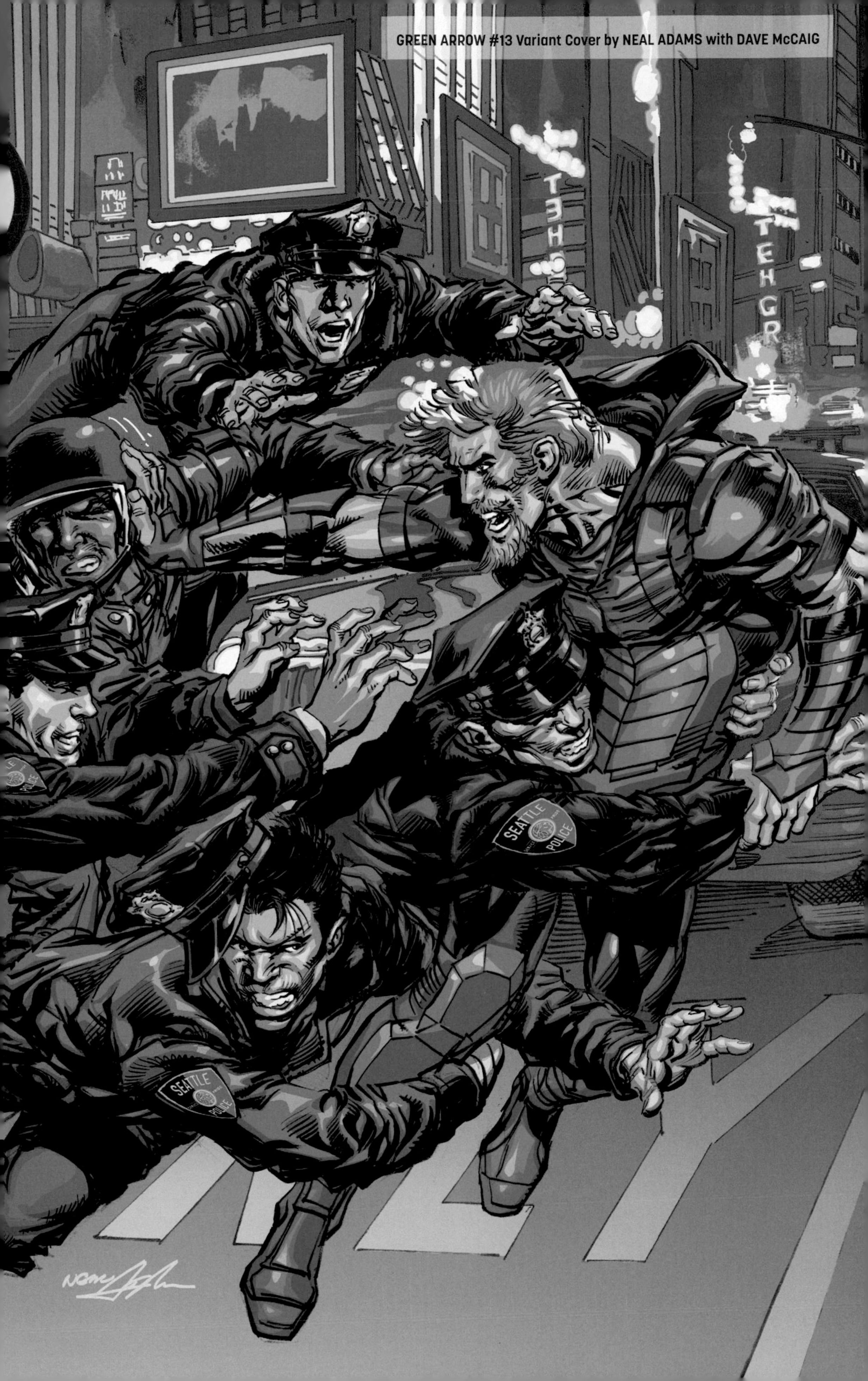
SEATTLE
POLICE
SEATTLE
POLICE
GREEN ARROW #13 Variant Cover by NEAL ADAMS with DAVE McCAIG

GREEN ARROW #14 Variant Cover by NEAL ADAMS with DAVE McCAIG

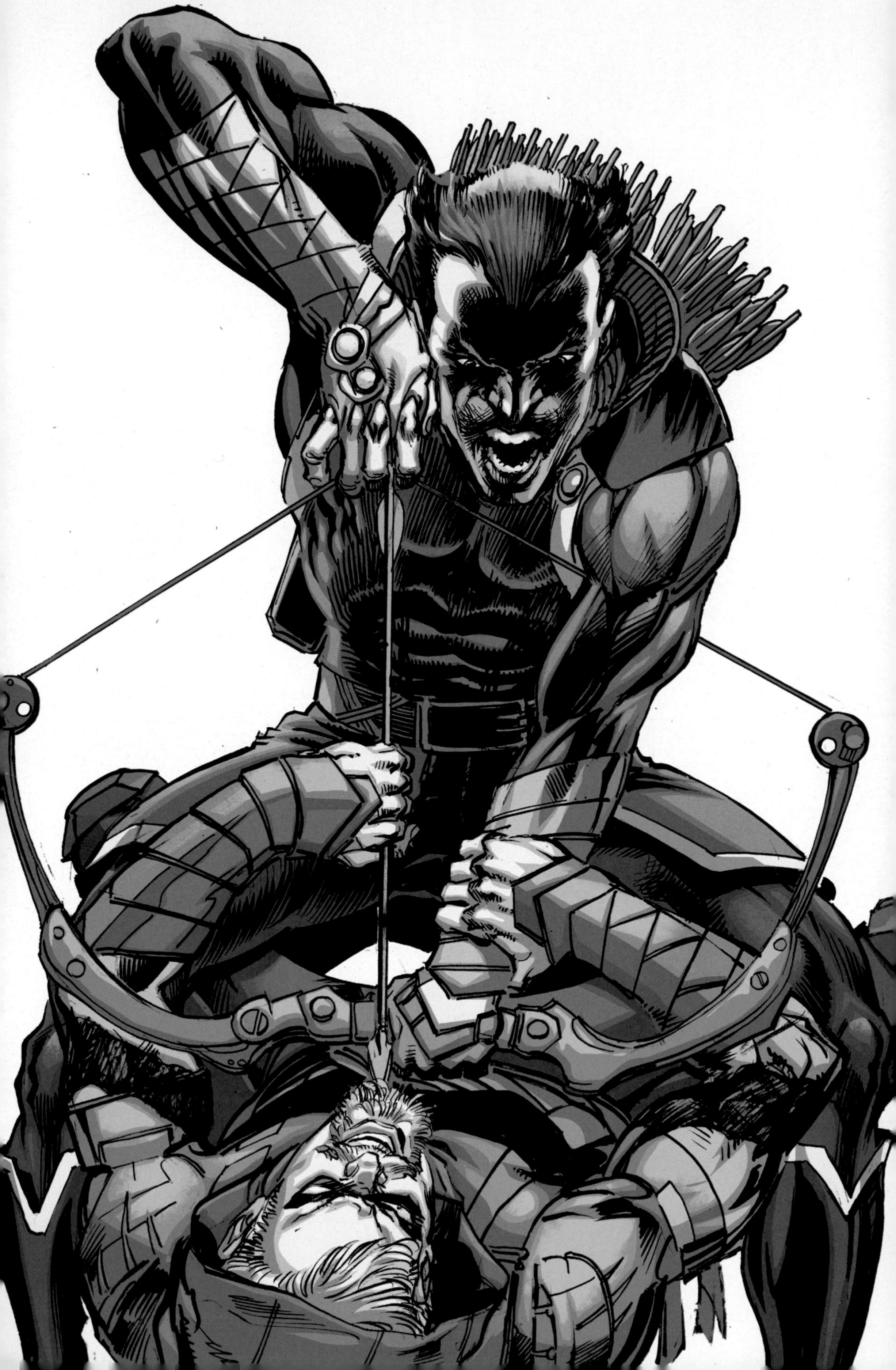

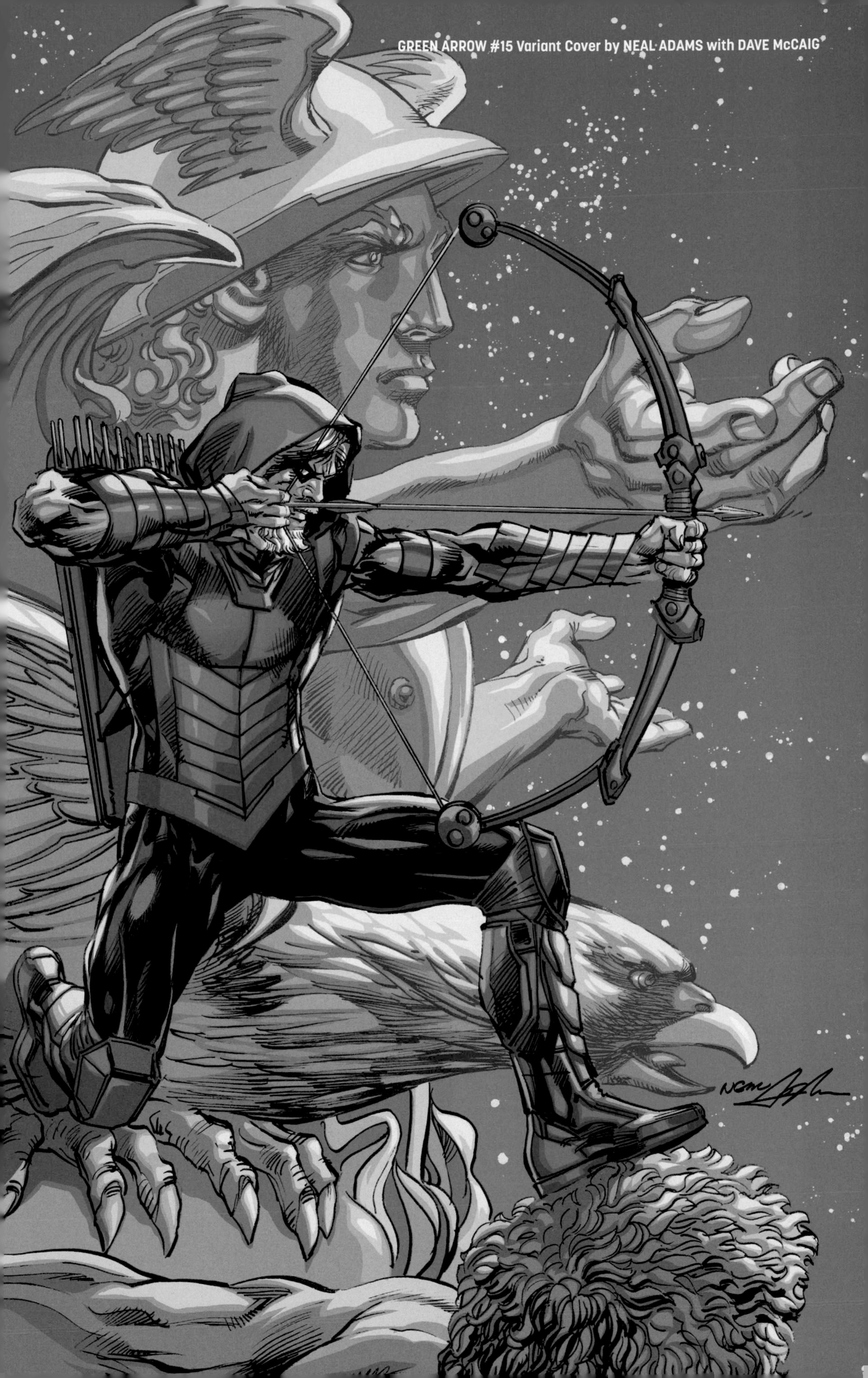

GREEN ARROW #15 Variant Cover by NEAL ADAMS with DAVE McCAIG

GREEN ARROW #16 Variant Cover by NEAL ADAMS with DAVE McCAIG

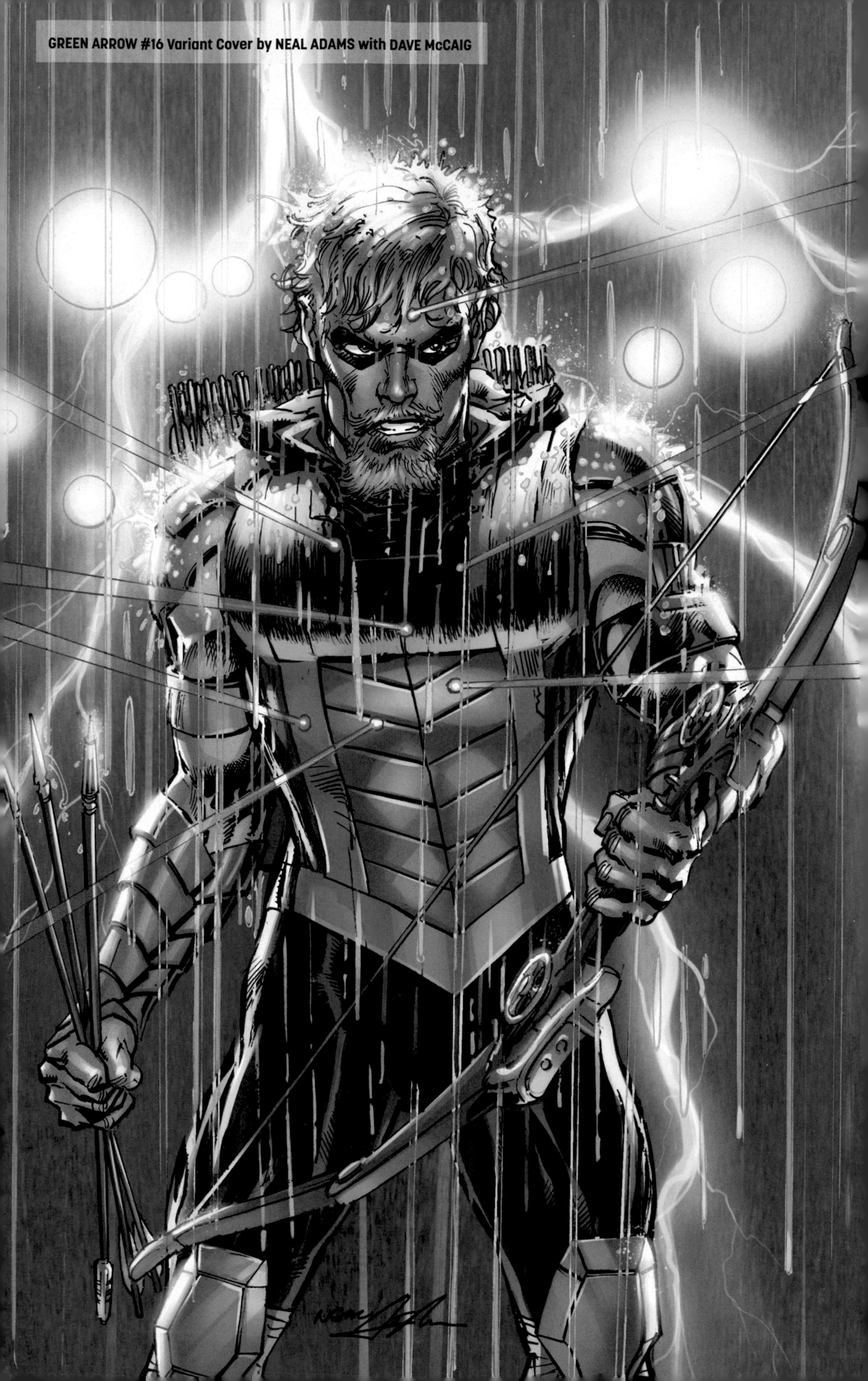

GREEN ARROW #17 Variant Cover by NEAL ADAMS with ALEX SINCLAIR

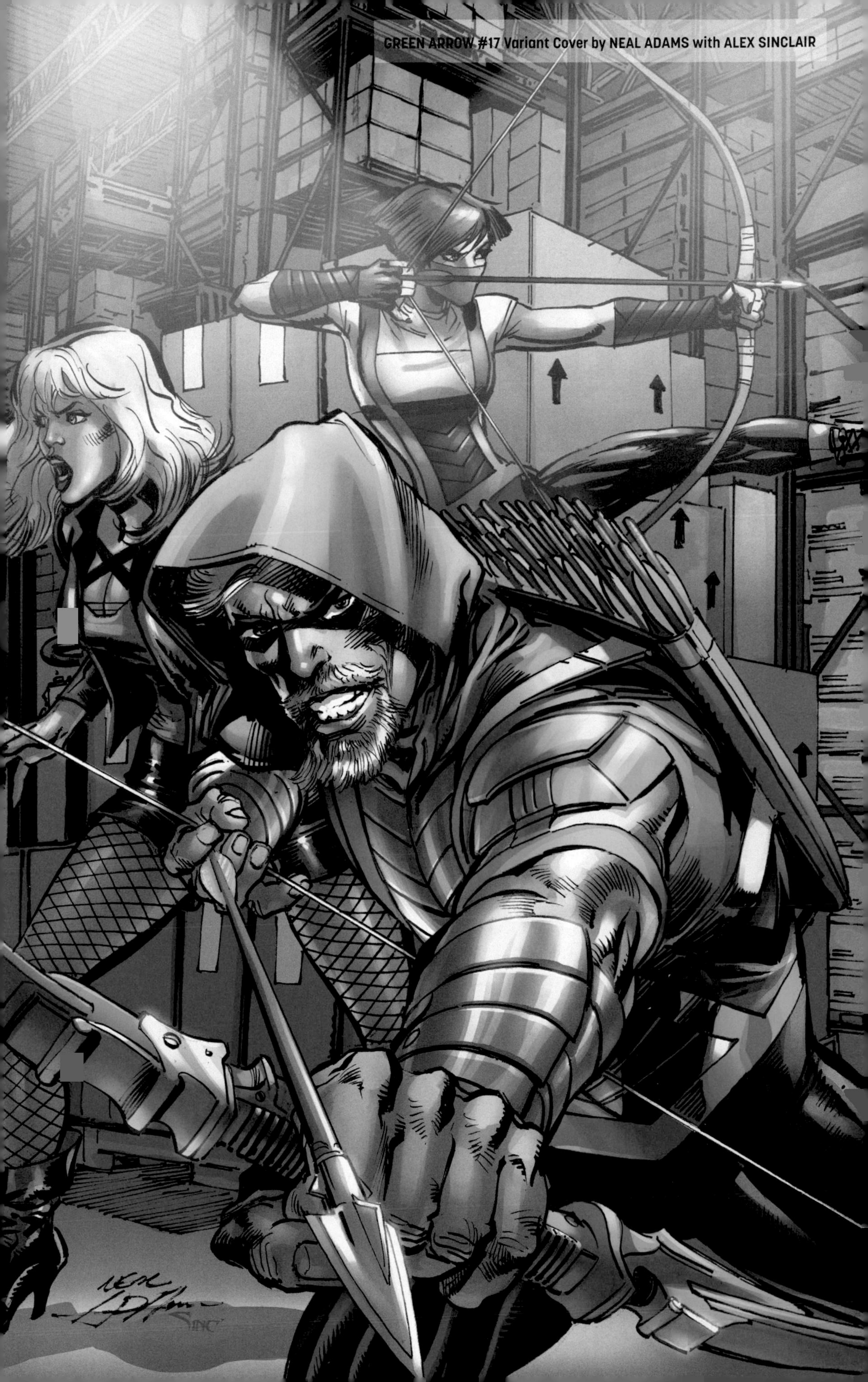

GREEN ARROW #15 COVER SKETCHES
By JUAN FERREYRA

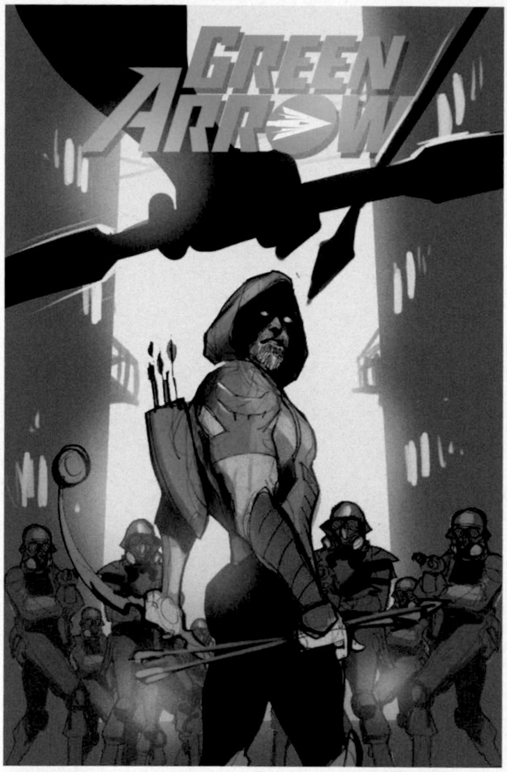
GREEN
ARROW

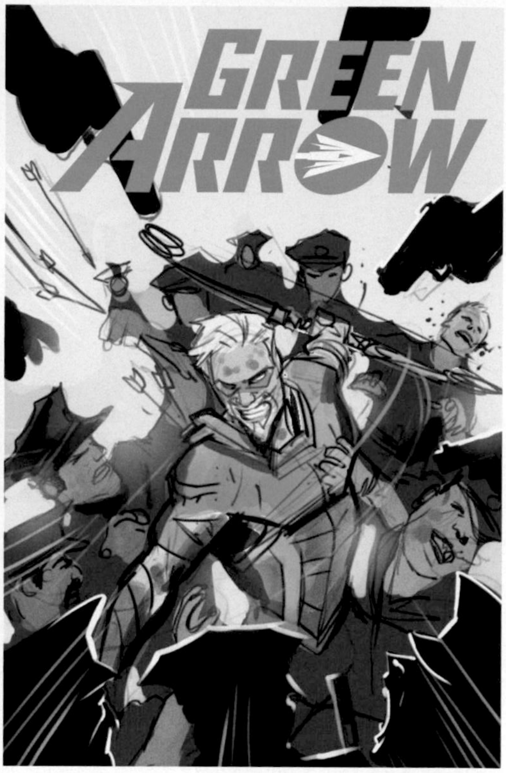
GREEN
ARROW

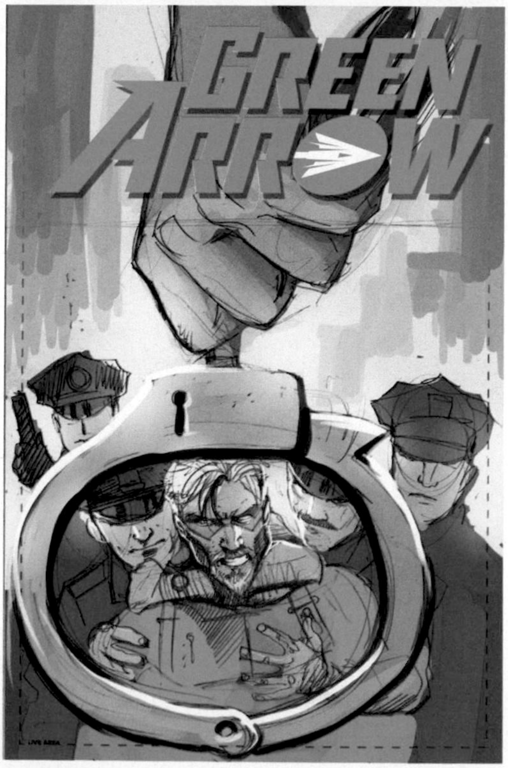
GREEN
ARROW

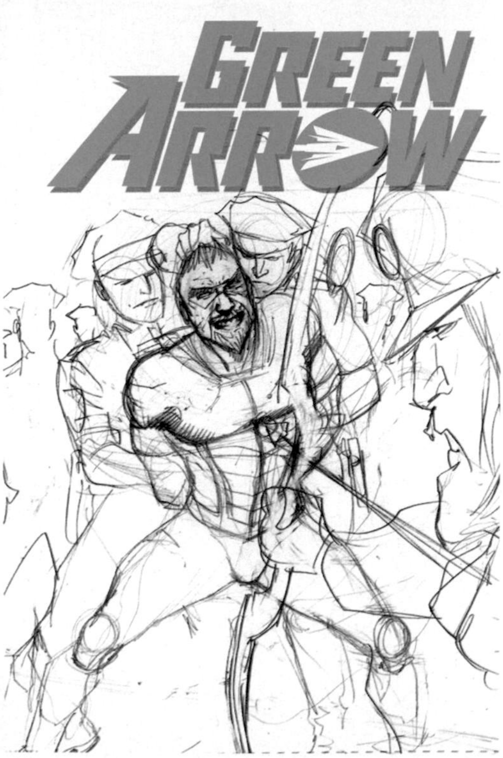
GREEN
ARROW

GREEN ARROW #16 COVER SKETCHES
By JUAN FERREYRA

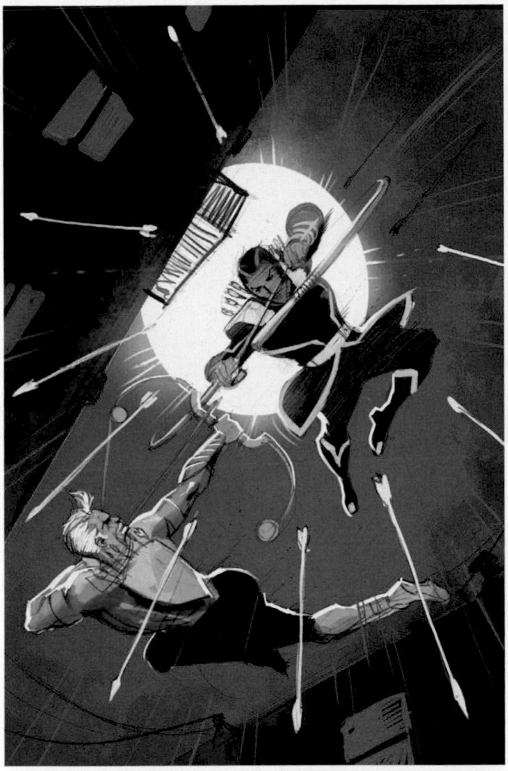

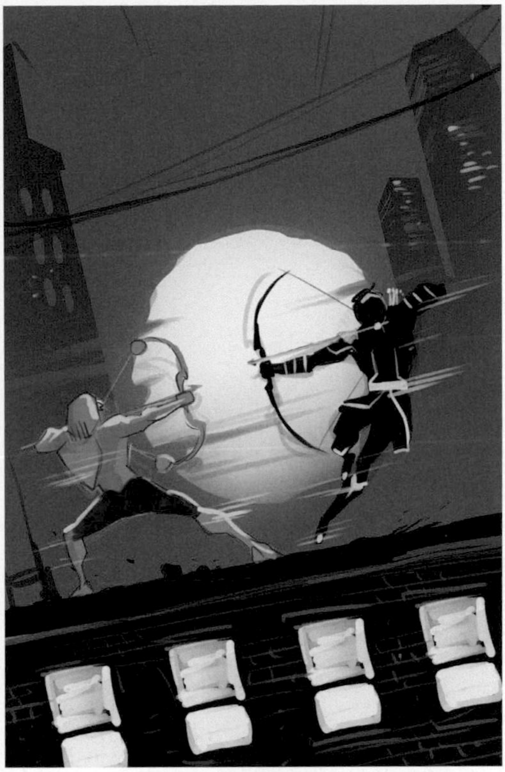

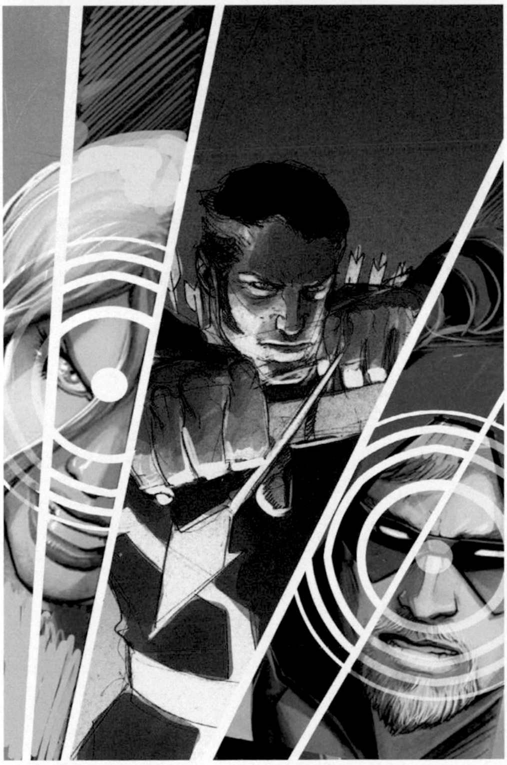

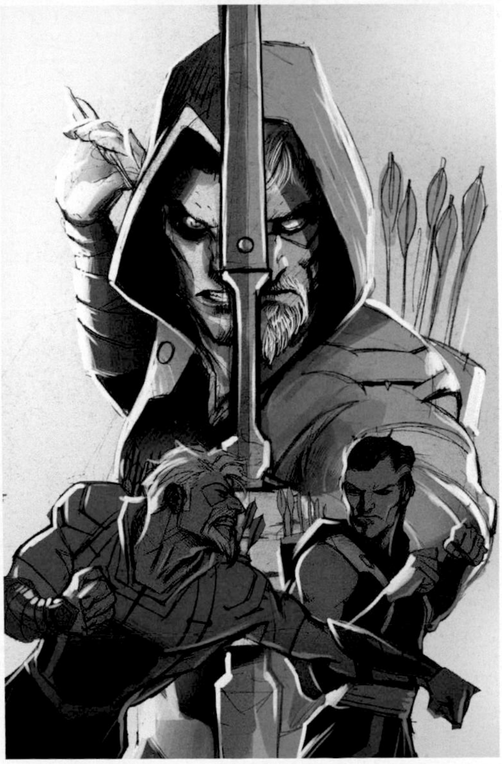

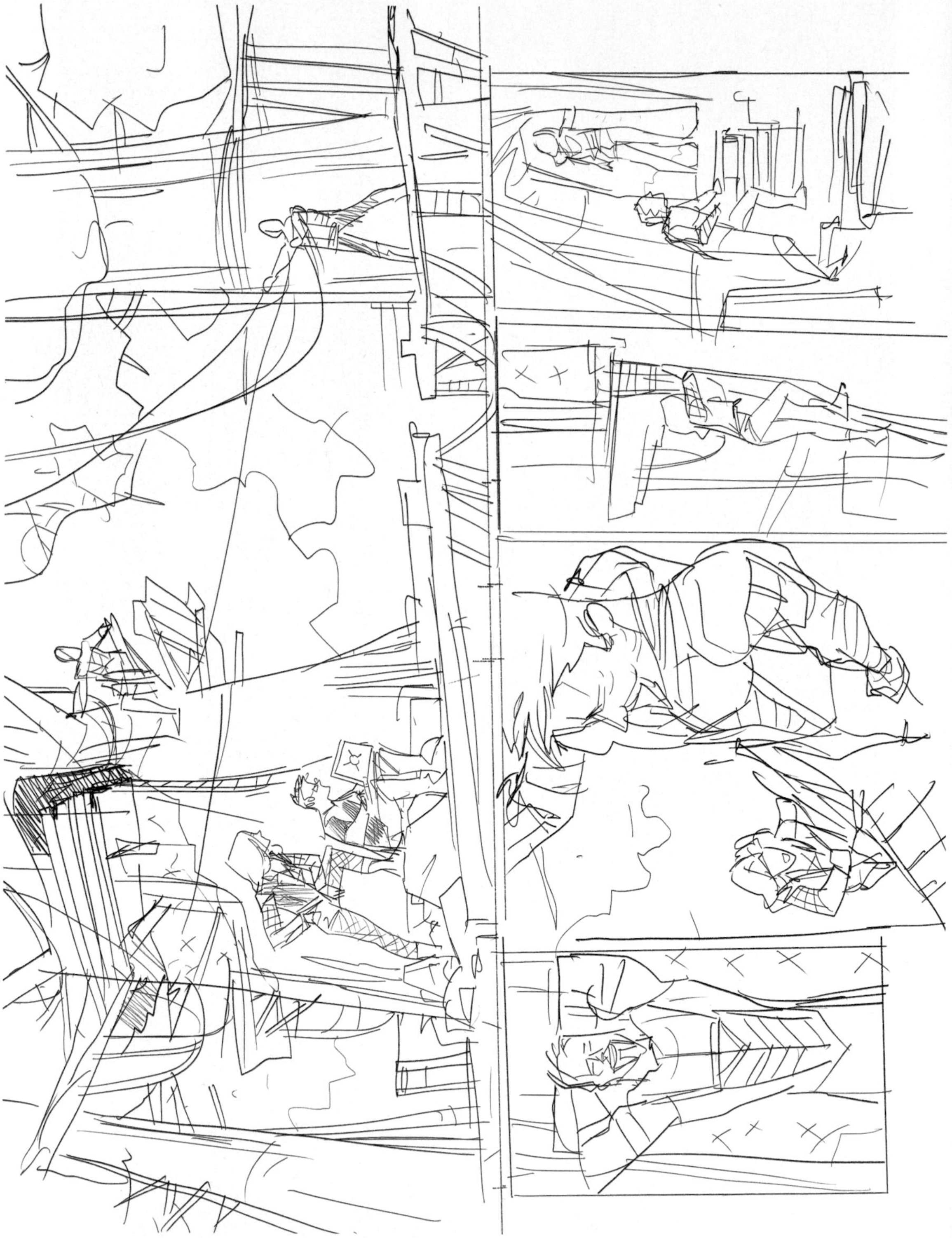

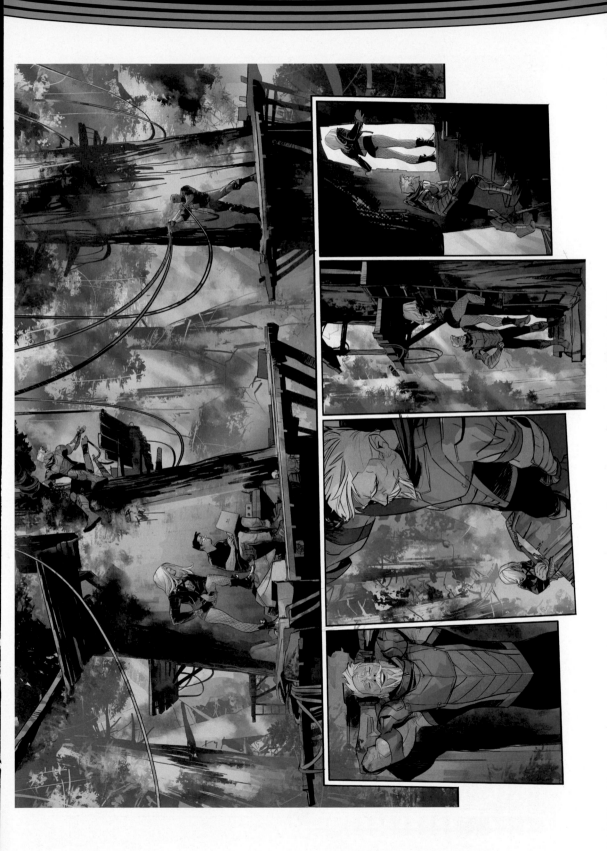

GREEN ARROW #15, PAGES 4-5 FROM SKETCH TO COLOR

By JUAN FERREYRA

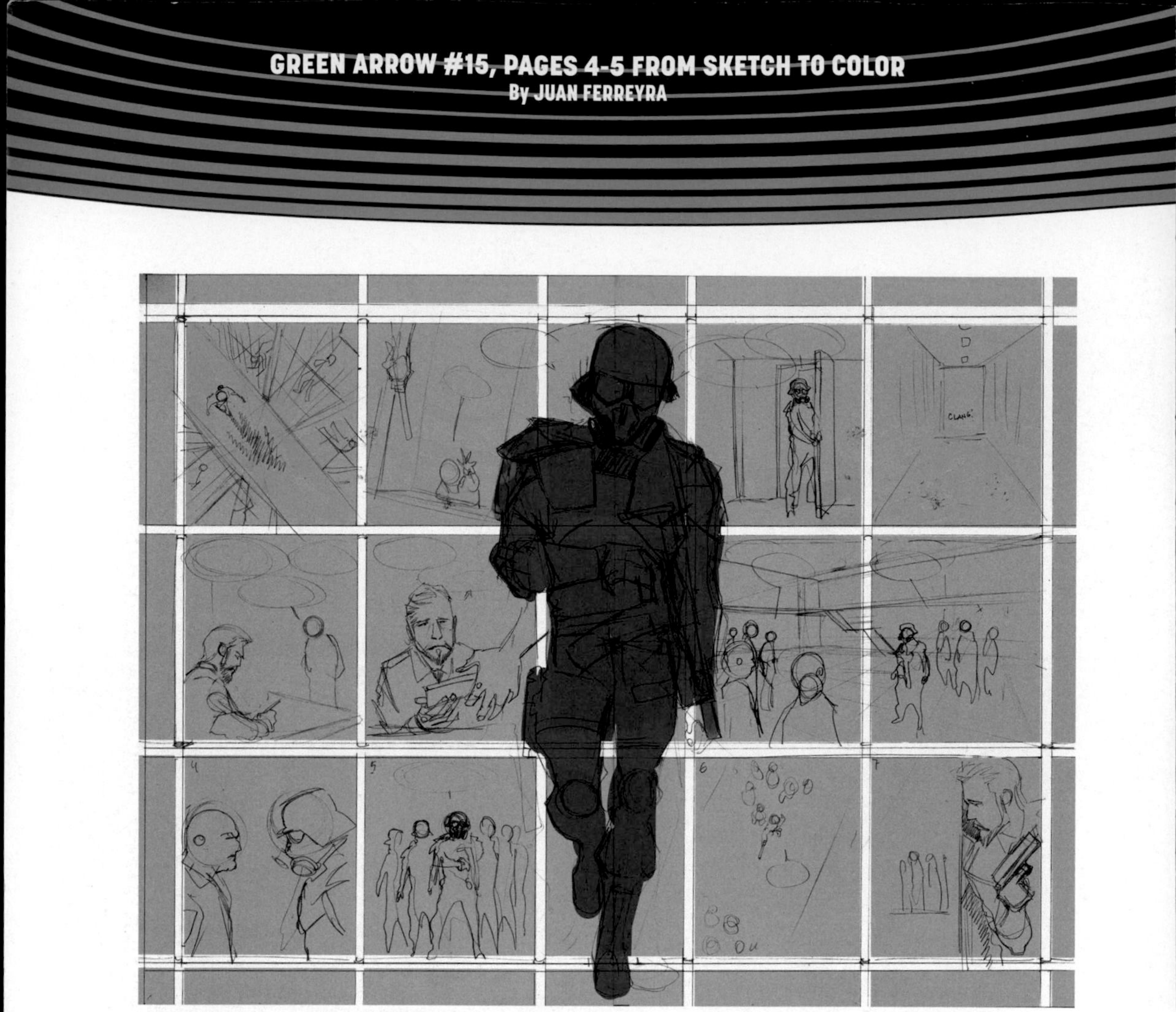
CLANG!

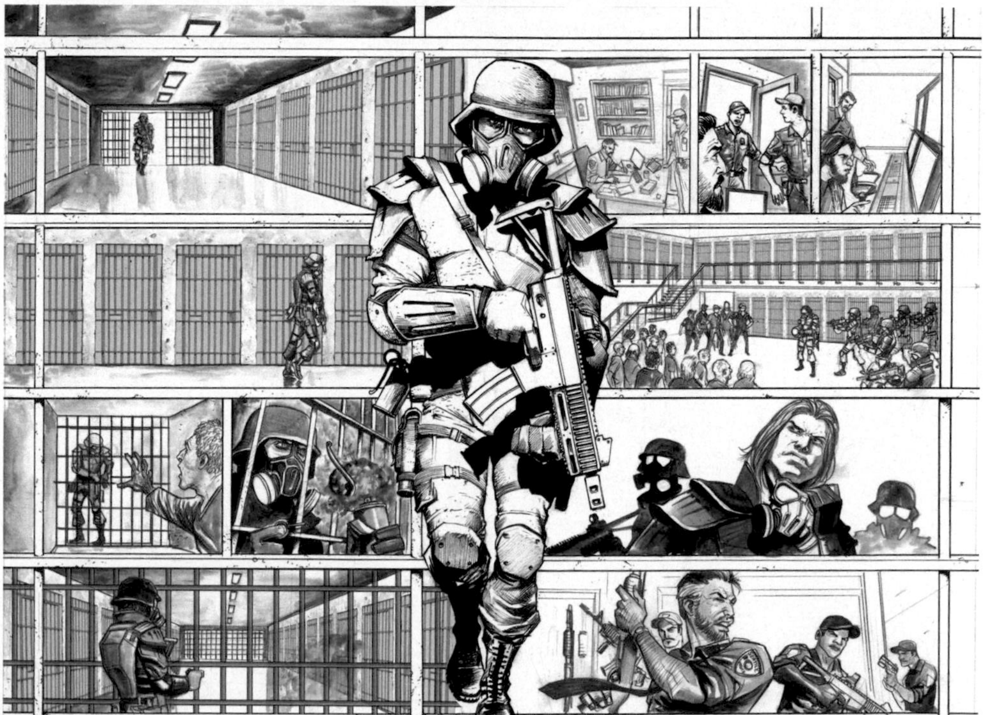

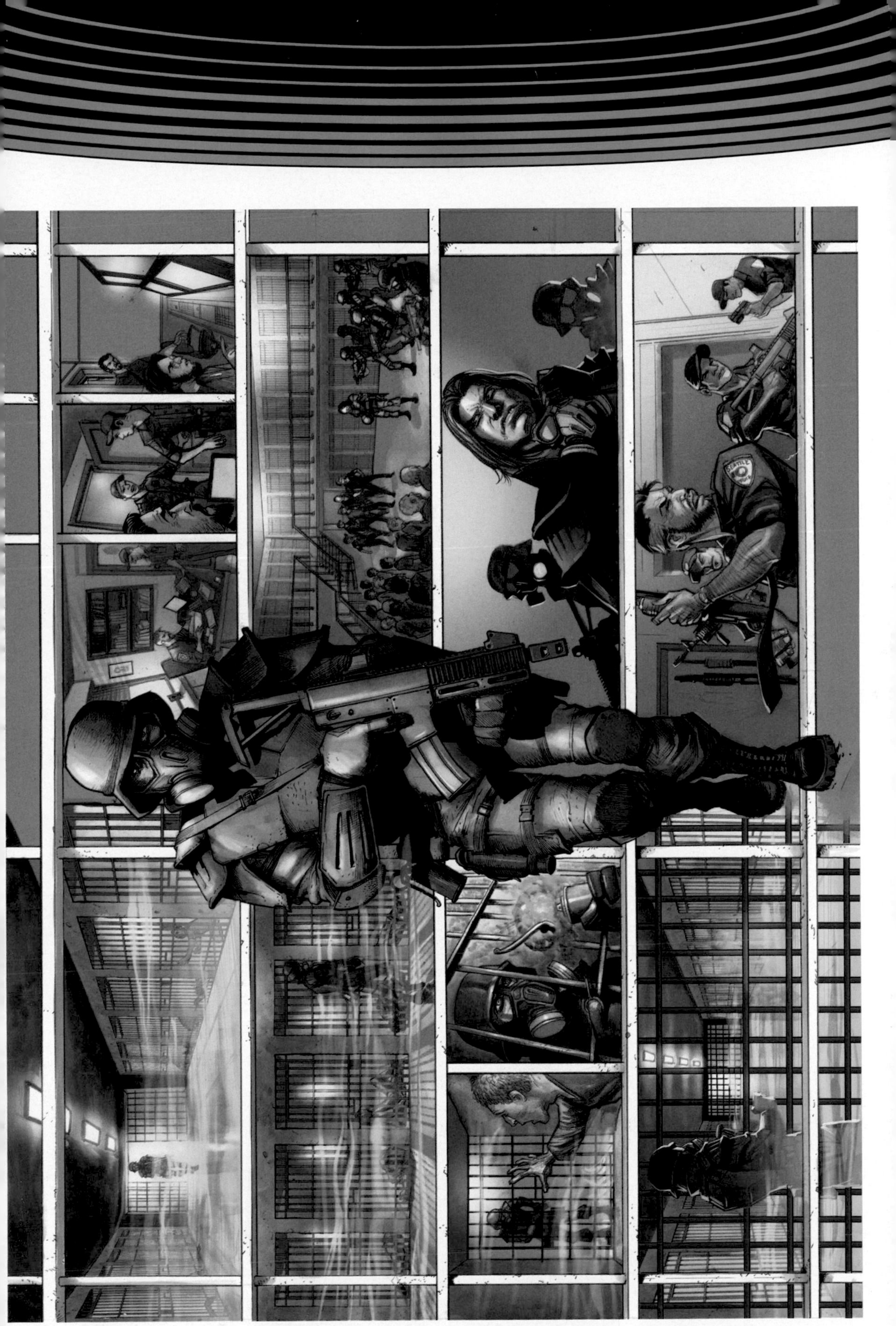

GREEN ARROW #17, PAGE 4 FROM SKETCH TO COLOR
By OTTO SCHMIDT

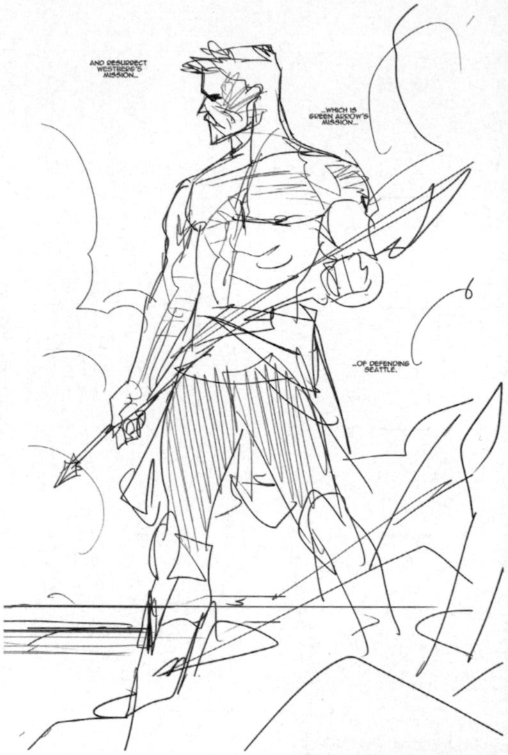
AND RESURRECT WESTBERG'S MISSION...
...WHICH IS GREEN ARROW'S MISSION...
...OF DEFENDING SEATTLE.

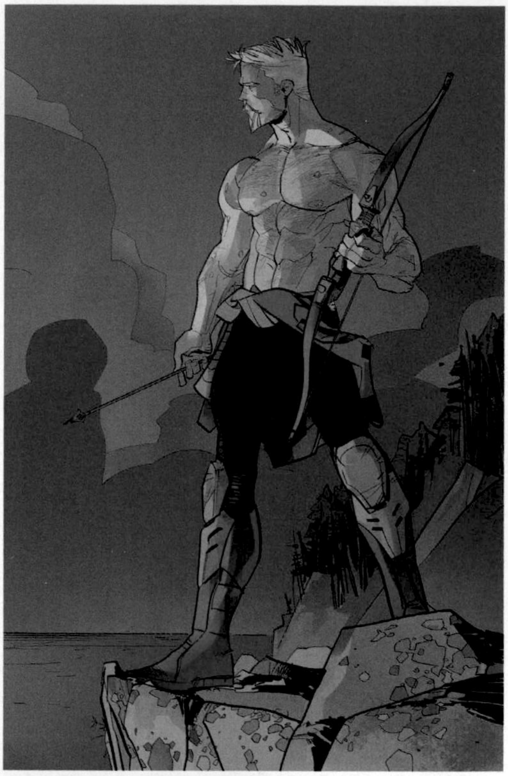

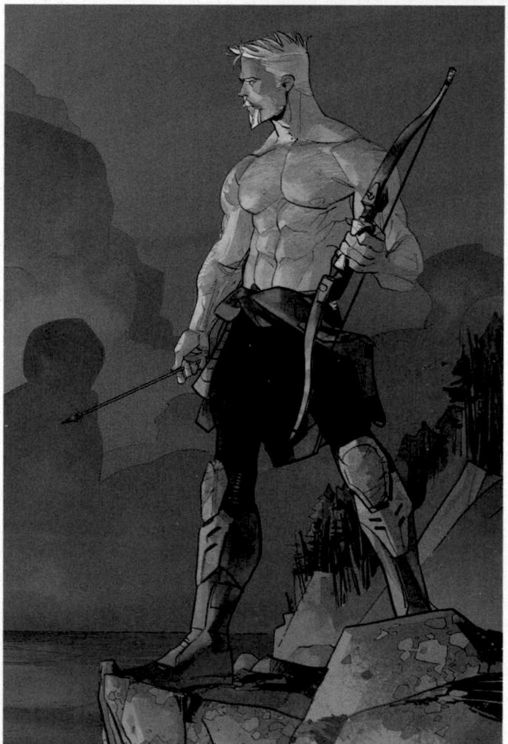